Human Values and Ethics for Engineers and Professionals

Kameshwar Singh Verma

Copyright © 2018 by Axiom Nutrifit, all rights reserved.

No part of this publication may be reproduced, distributed or transmitted in any form or by any means, including photocopying, recording, or other electronic or mechanical methods, without the prior written permission of the publisher, except in the case of brief quotations embodied in critical reviews and certain other noncommercial uses permitted by copyright law. For permission requests, write to the publisher:

Yogesh Verma
630 Palomino Dr., Pleasanton, CA 94566
yogeshv@hotmail.com, Phone: 510 364-5177

Managing Editor Kamalakar Pallela
Copy Editor Yogesh Verma
Formatted by Kamalakar Pallela
Cover Design by Kamalakar Pallela
Author Photograph by Rajesh Verma

ISBN: 978-0-9973794-2-6

Testimonials

Modern Humanism is concerned about ill effects of modernization, and impact of scientific developments on human being and society. Engineering ethics is a result of this pursuit of Modern Humanism.

National Design & Research Forum (NDRF), the R&D wing of Institution of Engineers (India), has been engaged in development and promotion of safe and risk-free technologies as well as publishing books and monographs in various fields of engineering.

This book on Human Values and Ethics is an excellent effort to educate and sensitize scientists, technologists, and engineers, on the moral and ethical issues of professional and social concern. The book has been reviewed by the NDRF Editorial Committee and I am sure it will be very useful to scientific community in understanding their professional role and responsibilities towards end users, society, nation, and humanity at large.

It more importantly meets the curriculum requirements of both undergraduate and post-graduate engineering programs of many Engineering Institutions and Universities with which I am associated. It is an appropriate resource material for engineering teachers to handle this important topic of importance to personality development training, which is one of the major focal points of bodies such as the All India Council for Technical Education.

Dr. K. Ramachandra
Director, National Design & Research Forum (NDRF) and Former Director-GTRE, India

Science, technology and engineering are the fields which are important for economic development, for improving the day to day life of the citizens as well as ensuring their safety and security during the times of strife and wars. The concept of good and bad, right and wrong do not belong to the sphere of science. While human actions and happiness are mostly centered on these concepts, wisdom lies in balancing outlook on science with equal stress on safeguarding interest of humanity.

Mr. Verma, in this book is trying to impress engineering students and professionals, about their balancing role towards society and humanity, in application of technology and talents. He has brought out very succinctly basic issues of human concern on social and moral development and ethical consideration of society; balancing of self-interest and happiness in professionalism, responsibility for ensuring public safety and minimizing risks factors; protection of natural resources and environment in developing and application of technology.

In education today, there is very little emphasis on the moral and ethical values. Our society is exploiting the natural resources in such a manner that instead of leaving a rich legacy for future generations, we are borrowing from them.

I believe that the book will be a very valuable guide to engineers and professionals to understand and balance personal goals of career and growth, with expectation of society for dynamic growth with social stability.

Mr. Pramod P. Kale
Former Director Space Applications Center (SAC), Indian Space Research Organization (ISRO), India.

The efforts of the author to write a book on "Human Values and Ethics for Engineers and Professionals" need to be appreciated as a sincere attempt to lay strong foundations on values and ethics in the minds of engineers and professionals in their formative period. The society looks at the engineers and professionals as nation builders and hence there exists an inherent responsibility on such set of people. The book emphasizes the inherent responsibility of engineers and professionals to preserve human values and follow ethical code of conduct.

This book has vivid description on the fact that, while science is engaged in discovering truth after truth about the natural forces and processes; the applications of this large body of knowledge in technological and engineering advancements is not always controlled, and carries certain degree of uncertainties, risks, and safety issues for humanity at large. In this sense, many of the engineering products and projects is of the nature of social experimentation; where along with plenty of success stories, there have been major disasters also due to human errors or failure of engineering design.

An attempt is made to sensitize engineers and professionals about their roles and responsibilities towards safety, and welfare of end users of their products or projects. The book has enough reading material to acquaint the engineering students about many agencies, organizations, national and international bodies engaged into making their recommendations, treaties and code of ethics for the profession as well as engineering ethics about human and environmental safety. This book also provides enough teaching material for the R & D organizations to acquaint scientist and engineers engaged in research and development, on relevant guidelines and work ethics of their jobs. Over all focus of the book is on scientists and engineers, who should take wider care of ethical responsibilities in design of their equipment, systems, as well as their applications, and technologies in compliance with the international conventions and treaties relevant to their work.

Professor V. Vasudeva Rao
Mechanical and Industrial Engineering, Chairman School of Engineering Research Committee, University of South Africa (UNISA), Republic of South Africa

Scientific-education without value-education produces the professionals who are ill equipped, sometimes unconcerned, and insensitive to impact of their scientific development on the humanity. The relation of sciences to the humanities can be thought as the relation of means to ends. This book has nicely elaborated on the need for engineering and scientific professionals to have the comprehensive understanding of human values, ethics, code of conduct, and psycho-social dimension of the human; which is the focus of modern humanism. They must try to synthesize the scientific progress with the human values for the noble cause while strengthening the means i.e. scientific development, they should not overlook the ends i.e. impacts on the humanity.

Professor Ram Mohan Reddy Guddeti
Head, Dept. of Information Technology, NITK Surathkal, India

Dedication

To the venerable Rishis, Munis, Saints, Sad Gurus and Holy Persons of all faiths, who gave, eternal guiding principles as universal aphorism, to evolve Human Values, Moral and Ethical Values of life, for peaceful coexistence and prosperity of all. Some of leading dictums are:

|| सबका मालिक एक ||
(SAB KA MALIK EK)
(One Owner-God of all mankind)

||अहिंसा परमो धर्मः||
(AHIMSA PARAMO DHARMA)
(Non-violence is the ultimate dharma)

|| ओम्, सर्वे भवन्तु सुखिनः सर्वे सन्तु निरामयाः ||
(OM, SARVE BHAVANTU SUKHINAH)
(Om, may all be Prosperous and Happy)

|| वसुधैव कुटुम्बकम ||
(VASUDHAIVA KUTUMBAKAM)
(The world is one Family)

|| सत्यमेव जयते ||
(SATYAMEV JAYATE)
(Truth alone triumphs)

|| तमसो मा ज्योतिर् गमय ||
(TAMASO MA JYOTIR GAMAYA)
(Lead us from darkness to light)

|| Do unto others as you would have them do unto you ||

Such dictums are having universal character and applicability. They are at foundation or core essence of Human Values, and Moral and Ethical considerations, in all spheres of human activity, be it physical, relating to mind, or spiritual in nature.

Preamble

Broadly, Scientists are devoted to explore the field of natural forces, processes, structures, and phenomena.

Technologists are focused on developing technologies and processes to realize useable materials, methods, and applications through the use of available scientific knowledge.

Engineers are primarily concerned with fabricating, constructing or manufacturing useful products, systems, networks, and infrastructures based on current proven technologies.

Through engineering supports and efforts only, scientists and technologists are able to make apparatus or setup facilities for their technical and research work.

Thus, Engineers have directly contributed to modernization of human living conditions throughout the globe, primarily by exploiting and synthesizing various technologies to design, manufacture and operate various infrastructures of modern life, like electrification, automobiles, airplanes, telephony, radio and television, mobile and satellite communication, computers, internet, imaging technologies, health technologies, petrochemical technologies, nuclear technologies etc.etc.

In this book the word engineer or professional is used to refer collectively all technical people such as scientists, technologists, and engineers. The main focus of the book is on value education for engineers and professionals on human values, morals and ethics, so that they better understand needs of society and their professional services improve overall living conditions and environment for human beings throughout the globe.

Professional means, people whose professional activities are governed by, legally established procedures, and professional bodies; which are frames to regulate the professional practices by prescribing proper code of conduct or code of ethics for the profession.

Acknowledgement

I had natural impulse of moral and ethical life from childhood which was nurtured by my parents, uncle and aunty. They brought me up and gave joint family environment which was very conducive to learn blending of family values with values of the social and the community life. I venerate and acknowledge their contribution for giving me good *samskara*, to honor and value the human relations while growing in professional area. My professional field of work has been *Satellite and Wireless Communication Engineering*. My exposure to cultural values and advanced engineering fields prompted to share my experience with younger generation of engineers and professionals via this book. I hope the book will provide adequate clarity on complex web of *value system* prevailing in daily life, be it family or job or profession or society at large, and finally globalization of values and issues.

After 30 years of service in industry, I took retirement and joined Sreenidhi Institute of Science and Technology (SNIST), Hyderabad, as Professor and Dean Curriculum Development. When SNIST became autonomous, I proposed introduction of a subject on Human Values, Moral and Ethics for all engineering branches of SNIST.I acknowledge with thanks, **Dr. P. Narasimha Reddy**, Executive Director, SNIST, who readily agreed for introduction of this subject. At that time basic work for preparation of a book on **Human Values, Morals and Ethics** was undertaken through collective effort of many faculty members and I acknowledge their contribution towards collecting the basic material. Along with technical subjects of my engineering field, I also taught this subject to engineering graduates, and it was a rewarding experience in this area, again prompting me to write the book on this subject.

I acknowledge the encouragement and moral support given by **Prof. Bhujanga Rao Sanapala**, Director, School of Electronics and HOD, Electronics and Computer Engineering, for writing this book. My special thanks to both Prof. Bhujanga RaoSanapala and **Dr. Siva Sai Krovvidi** (Prof. of Dept. of Bio-Tech) for perusing basic draft of the Book. **Dr. Siva Sai** also provided basic material on Intellectual Property Rights (IPR).

I want to specially acknowledge the contribution of my senior colleague **Mr. Pramod P. Kale**, Former Director Space Applications Center, Indian Space Research Organization for taking pains to go through all the chapters of the book and provided valuable suggestions for improvements.

I want to thank **Prof. Ram Mohan Reddy Guddeti**, Dean Dept. of Information Technology, NITK, Surathkal, for his valuable suggestions and support to enhance the quality of book and sharing valuable information to make this book more dynamic for all kinds of professionals.

I admire and acknowledge the efforts of Editorial Board of NDRF headed by (Late) **Dr. Baldev Raj**, Chairman of NDRF and Director of NIAS along with **Dr. K. Ramachandra**, Director-NDRF and Former Director-GTRE, for reviewing the manuscript and giving positive suggestions and comments to improve the book.

I want to thank and acknowledge contribution of my Managing Editor **Mr. Kamalakar Pallela**, for his support and overall structuring of the book. His back up support has been a great assistance to me.

Finally, I acknowledge the great contribution of my wife **Mrs. Chandrakala Verma** who has taken care of all family activities and spared me to pursue my goal of book writing. My thanks to my sons **Yogesh, Rajesh** and **Abhishek** who themselves are Professional Engineers working in USA and their families for providing forum for discussion and experimentation on the subject of Human Values.

Finally, I heartily acknowledge contribution of my grandchildren **Shashwat** and **Raina**, for taking up the task of proof reading from student point of view.

Key Takeaways from this Book

- Culture helps in understanding and shaping of vision of life and how to realize it.
- The agencies of social control are both informal and formal and include culture, customs, folkways, mores, public opinion, education, law, religion, morals, etc.
- Families are the basic building block of a society. Family environment shapes the personality and character of any person to a large extent. Family is primarily characterized by relationships and not necessarily by living under one roof or home.
- The members of family share goals and values and have common long-term commitments to one another.
- Social responsibility implies need for balancing relationship of *Self* with *family* and *society* i.e. understanding of *harmonizing life with nature and physical facilities.*
- Violating the *responsibility* for *truthfulness* undermines trust. Commitment is like a *pledge, a promise,* and an *obligation* to adhere to certain *activity, value, responsibility* or *duty.*
- The *conscientious engineer* must by definition be, *truthful, factual, alert* and *accurate* - all key elements of any definition of *ethical behavior.*
- *Accountability* of a person to an organization or institution means that he/she is required to account for *being answerable, responsible* and *justifiable in his/her actions* or *decisions*
- Engineer's responsibility for safety and risks is multi-dimensional and multi-directional. Safety and risk management in *air and train travel, nuclear plants, power plants, transport vehicles, multi-story buildings* etc., directly fall on engineer's responsibility for safety and risk.
- In engineering, "... the one choice engineers, designers and their employers no longer have is whether or not to pursue safety goals. To ignore or pay only lip service to safety can jeopardize corporate survival"
- Engineers must learn to keep their *individual conscience* separate from *corporate actions.*
- Developing best practices for corporate conduct is a slow process and takes time to mature.

- Cultivate the heart; *heart is the source of all humanistic feelings and impulses such as love, service, compassion, etc.*
- *Spirituality develops feelings of oneness of the universe, universal belonging, love for humanity and openness to all.*
- *Leading is different from managing. A leader requires vision.*
- Aristotle, a great philosopher truly pointed that *"... moral virtue in humans does not emanate from nature and need to be imbibed by habit"*.
- Records show that *prosperous nations* have achieved greatness through high level of *work discipline, honesty, sincerity and moral integrity* prevailing among their citizens.
- Philosopher Bertrand Russell amongst others, sought to respond to the resulting dilemma: *Without civic morality, communities perish; without personal morality their survival is of no value.*
- There is a need to distinguish between the *Authority of Custom* and the *Authority of Law*.
- Corporate business environment includes corporate goals, profit motive of the company, corporate policies on ethics, employees, customer service, etc.
- Global issues are connected with cross-cultural matters, environmental ethics, computer ethics, codes of ethics, ethical problems in research, Intellectual Property Rights, etc.

Preface

In this book the word ***Engineer*** is used to refer collectively all technical people such as ***scientist, technologist and engineers***. Similarly, word ***Professional*** implies people whose professional activities are governed by legally established procedures, or ***Professional Institutions***, which are established to regulate the professional activities, and prescribe proper ***code of conduct*** *or code of ethics* for the profession. Further, to elaborate the point of discussion, many times examples of / from Indian scenarios have been adopted. But this in no way limits the validity of the point in general or global context.

Purpose of *education system* is to transform human being from unskilled raw state to a skilled-intellectual with some specialization. Today we have scientists, technologists, engineers and professionals with great specialization in their field of activity, but still society is not at peace, even after having all sorts of facilities for human comfort.

Value clashes and operational disharmony at Individual and Social level: Among educated masses, at individual level there is lack of cohesiveness and clarity about goal of life. There is widespread sense of insecurity, stressful relationships, misunderstandings, distrust, etc. At social level, problems of urbanization, imbalance in demographic settlement, poor quality of services, corruption, unethical professional practices, religious polarization, caste and creed considerations, exploitation, lack of gender equality etc. are factors of great concern disturbing social equilibrium. Scientific developments have also given rise to new problems, like depletion of natural resources, environmental pollution, cyber-crimes, etc. at national and global level

Problem Identification: The root cause, to above referred disharmony, discord, strife as well as poor work culture, indiscipline etc., is identified by the educationists, as lack of ***value education*** in the education system. So far, the focus of Education System has been on development of academic excellence among students in various fields of knowledge; without any worthwhile exposure to moral and ethical character-building principles; which are essential ingredient for peaceful coexistence with good behavioral traits in public life.

After realizing the need for Value Education, course on **Human Values and Professional Ethics** are introduced in many Technical Universities globally. In USA, ABET (Accreditation Board for Engineering and Technology, Inc.), the recognized U.S. accreditor of college and university programs in applied science, computing, engineering, and technology, has also recommended introduction of

education *Program Objectives* with emphasis to include component of Value Education like
1. An understanding of professional and ethical-responsibility.
2. The broad education necessary to understand the impact of engineering solutions in a global, economic, environmental, and societal context.

in the curriculum design as part of accreditation criteria to evaluate *Students Outcomes.*

This book is an effort to provide teaching material; for courses in Value Education of various institutions and universities; to prepare upcoming engineers and professionals to understand need for balance between professional responsibilities and moral and ethical conduct; as well as short term and long-term impact of their work on consumers, end users and public at large.

The book provides comprehensive material content to most of the course on *human values and ethics* prescribed by technical institutions and universities. Attempt has been made to synthesize and expose student on *historical-background* of developments of *social-structures* with their distinct *Culture* and *Value System*; which provides milieu for contemporary thoughts on **moral values and ethics**.

Brief history of development of societies and cultures: Human society has seen tremendous growth over past many centuries. Various civilizations with different cultures developed independently at different parts of the globe. These civilizations also evolved different *lifestyles, social-organizations* and *moral, ethical value-system* for their survival as distinct *cultural-units* of the society.

In due course of time, cultural interaction started between these societies through growth of trade and commerce among them. *Continental-trade* is only recent phenomena of past few centuries whereas globalization of human beings is hardly two to three hundred years old.

Cultural exchanges and trade and commerce between societies within any nation and among nations gave impetus to formation of strong national identities with distinct economic, political, education, social-lifestyle and value-system to mention few.

In this background of geographical variations in *human development*; secular and global character of *science and technology* provided common grounds for integration, perpetual growth and survival of *human societies.* It also promoted global perception on human-values and professional-ethics.

Education system of science and technology ignored holistic personality development
Science is not a regional construct but has a *universal-character* in its findings which are valid throughout the universe. Science as a human enterprise satisfies, human curiosity, provides understanding and fundamental insights into material world, including physical Human-Body. However, *scientific thinking process* has to a large extent shaped human perception about overall nature i.e. world surrounding human-being (inanimate part of nature). Science is also trying to understand inner-self i.e. human psyche; consisting of emotional-being, mind, and intellect, through studies on brain functioning.

Science, as discipline of investigative studies, is primarily concerned with decoding discernible reality of inanimate-nature (i.e. the physical materialistic world/universe). In this pursuit of exploring *knowledge about the nature, science and technology* has branched out in different fields of studies. In the process, technical-education-system ignored study of *human nature and values*. It limited its' investigations, broadly to inanimate part of nature.

Study of *Human personality* reflected through his, personal and social *behavior, attitudes, mindset, goal of life, motivations, value-system*, etc. are ignored in education of science and technology including engineering education.

Science and technology provided material and physical comfort to humanity, but it has also injected vital irreversible changes in our collective consciousness and disturbed to a larger extent *human-cultural-equilibrium*.

Understanding human values and psycho-social dimension of man is focus of modern Humanism, which tries to synthesize the scientific progress with the human values.

Desired role of engineering education: Engineering is application of technology and tries to integrate scientific knowledge in providing solutions to the external problems of humanity. Engineers are required to address these problems of humanity and find out best and economical solutions. Therefore, they must not only be trained to be proficient in technical knowledge, but also be trained for understanding *work-ethics, cultural framework* of their *working environment, societal norms and values, professional code of conduct* governing their professional services, *customer-care*, etc. They must develop *aptitude* to distinguish and prioritize their responsibilities towards family, employer, customers, profession, society, and the nation as well as have global-concern towards humanity. This training must be an essential component of engineering education because scientists, technologists and engineers, are primarily responsible to modernize society, keep on developing and creating solutions through application of technology, and work for sustainable and comfortable life of human beings on the earth.

Quality of products, services and solutions are highly dependent on awareness of engineers about the fields of applications and requirements of ultimate users. They are responsible for building reliability in the products and processes. They must build safety and hazard prevention measure in their products and services. Sensitivity towards deleterious impact of application of technology on short term and long-term effect on environment should be analyzed by engineers.

Teamwork and professional role of engineers: An engineer, while working on a product, system or project, is consumer of knowledge developed by science and technology. As the engineering field has branched out in so many specialized domains, it is impossible for any-one engineer to have proficiency and understanding in all fields connected with the product or process. In this era of specialization, teamwork becomes very important factor for any engineer to become a successful professional. They have to broaden their outlook towards associated technologies, holistic understanding of the technical problems, as well as issues of interpersonal relationship and group dynamics of working as the team; for smooth integration of multiple engineering and allied technologies involved in any product or process.

Any engineering product or solution is result of chain of, technical activities at various stages and, associated processes like development, manufacturing, production, evaluation, marketing, field maintenance etc. An engineer is expected to involves and interact, with the members of the technical-team, supporting staff and other managerial teams associated with the production process (consisting of different stages of manufacturing, sales, marketing etc.). In actual jobs an engineer may be employed for any part of technical or non-technical business activity. Thus, engineers must be prepared to deal with different technical and non-technical persons during their professional roles.

Quite often in professional life, interactions with *human beings* have a concern of *moral and ethical* nature. It is vital for engineers have good understanding of the moral and ethical considerations in their profession. They must also be aware of their social responsibilities. They must be aware of their rights, duties and obligations also.

Engineers as agents of social change: All educated persons in general and scientists, technologist and engineers in particular are agent of change

in society. They have an important social role to modernize the traditions, social customs, biases, norms and practices including the prevailing superstitions, unscientific beliefs etc. Thus, they must have clear understanding of:
1. Distinction between good man, good citizen and good professional-from the point of view of human, moral and ethical values.
2. Word *society* commonly used to refer to different type of social human groupings like locality, mohalla, community, business group, groupings based on caste, language, region, religion, etc. Further, how they are structured individually, accommodated collectively, and integrated socially, economically, politically, and legally.
3. Clarity in *professional ethics*, *code of conduct* and *moral values*.
4. Different roles played in life and profession by an individual and prioritization of values in each role.

Why value education?
Any student may feel that he/she knows about moral and ethical values like truth, honesty, compassion, respect, obedience, sincerity, integrity etc. But he/she finds it difficult to apply them in his day to day dealings and operations. Practical situations or issues in life are quite complex in nature. Quite often they involve balancing between diverse emphasis of moral and ethical values of individual, and family; employment related compulsions; values invoked from culture, religion, community, society, professional codes of conduct, modern thinking and, global trends etc.

When students enter into their corporate life, they face many situations which involve moral and ethical issues, where choice of any action is not straight forward. In reality, multiple conflicting considerations like different perceptions and expectations of self, boss, employer, customer, professional code of ethics etc. need to be accommodated to arrive at a clear decision or line of action. The *value conflicts* of professional life may get further complicated when there is conflict with family, social and religious values. These values do not lead to unique solution but create a web of conflicting environment of values, where one has to carefully analyze his role and prioritize spectrum of values to choose best option. The book provides clarity on above referred factors influencing moral ethical decisions making.

Value education prepares Engineers with right frame of social and professional ethics with better understanding of *human relation* considerations. It finally makes them, better adjusted to their working environment and, more effective and productive in their profession. It expands their vision to wider horizon of thinking about human relations, human dynamics and social equilibrium through better understanding of contemporary philosophy on sociology of moral and ethical consideration. It develops their capability to analyze the situation more objectively than depend on customary solutions of the past.

Why this book?
The purpose of this book is, to provide prospective scientists, technologists, engineers and professionals, a logical understanding of **Human Values and Professional Ethics**, for effective and efficient operations in their professional work, family and social environment. It facilitates logical and reasoned thinking for arriving at an optimum solution out of multitude of arguments and reasoning on any conflicting situation.

The book provides guidance and education to prospective Engineers and Professional on moral ethical and professional *value system* through developing understanding of:
1. Their own *self, identity* and *personality*
2. Their *family* and *family value system*
3. Sociological understanding of society, community, culture, religion etc.
4. National and global imperatives on trade, laws, moral and ethical considerations, Patent laws and Copyrights, etc.
5. Moral responsibility, authority, rights, autonomy and moral dilemmas of engineers and professionals.
6. Global-ethical issues arising from industrialization, impact of science and technology, Internet, cyberspace, environment, pollution, etc.

Each one of the above areas of consideration is loaded with a set of *values*. However, on any practical situations all values are not equally important and applicable. In practical situations, only certain *set of values* have their relevance which are used to establish *standards of norms or values*. These values are used to evolve *model code of conduct* as guidance for desirable transactional behavior of individual engineers and professionals.

Organization of content of book:
The book is organized into six sections with each section dealing with a specific subject matter. The content of each section is distributed into four chapters with each chapter addressing specific group of topics. Thus, whole book contains 24 chapters. Scope and content of each section is briefly described below:

Section 1: Role of Engineering Education in Imparting Basic Human Values and Transforming Society

Deals with need for *value education* in engineering, goals of *higher education* and, *professional role* of engineers in industry, understanding *social factors*, *system*, *structure* and source of *generic values*, engineers as *agent of social change*, detailed study of specific *moral and ethical values* like integrity and confidentiality, work ethics, civic virtues, etc. social control of values and norms in society, human values necessary for professional responsibility like ethics of caring, honesty, character, etc.

Section 2: Engineering ethics and factors of success, growth and personality development

Deals with the history of ethics, ethical principles, ethical theories, use of ethical theories, purpose for engineering ethics, professional and professionalism, professional role of an engineer, moral autonomy of engineers, professional ethics, global business, factors of success, human personality, our identity and understanding self, goals of personal life, impact of family, happiness and self-interest , professional ethics, engineering and ethics, Kohlberg's theory- Gilligan's argument and Heinz's dilemma, positive thinking, custom and religion, understanding national and cultural ethos.

Section 3: Engineering as social experimentation and engineer's roles and responsibilities

Elaborates on social responsibility of engineers for *products* developed and *projects* executed by them, *engineering as social experimentation* having uncertainties in technology and design works, knowledge gained for future works, *social impact* of industrialization, industrial pollution, engineer role as manager or leader or consultant. This section also explains about engineer *personality trait*, *big five personality models*, self-governance virtues, conscientiousness, moral responsibility and autonomy to engineers, etc. Issue of accountability, roles of professional codes and experimental nature of engineering are discussed in sufficient details.

Section 4: Engineer's responsibility for design with safety features, risk control, quality and reliability

The section is devoted to sensitize engineers towards their responsibility for *safety and risk*, concept of risk, type of risks, voluntary *vs.* involuntary risk, short term *vs.* long term consequences, threshold levels for risk, delayed *vs.* immediate risk etc. Further, basic responsibility of engineers to design for safety is explained in detail. For example, safety and reliability, workplace safety, product safety and liability, and design for reliability are issues to be of concern for engineers. For industry *software reliability*, *fault tolerance* and *reliability versus quality* are of great concern for survival in marketplace. These issues are explained in this section.

Section 5: Corporate Culture, Professionalism, Professional Conflicts, Responsibilities, and Rights

In this section responsibilities and rights of engineers as an individual are discussed in detail. Engineer must understand collegiality and techniques for achieving collegiality, loyalty in all its shades like two senses of loyalty, obligations of loyalty, misguided loyalty, professionalism, loyalty, professional authority, rights and responsibilities. Matter of confidentiality, secrecy, self-interest and conflicts of interest, moral obligation to avoid conflicts of interest etc. are discussed. Ethical issues in the prevailing working environment like customs and religion, collective bargaining, bribery, kickbacks and gifts, occupational crimes, industrial espionage etc. are discussed. A full chapter is devoted to whistle blowing, types of whistleblower, when it should be attempted and *preventing whistle blowing*, etc.

Section 6: Globalization of technology, engineering and, consequential ethical issues

Science is promoting global culture. Ethical issues arising due to globalization in the form of cross-cultural issues, environmental issues, technology transfer to host countries, global networking and Internet ethics, ethical use of computers, unethical behavior and acts in use of computers as the instrument or autonomous computers, computer codes of ethics, global arms trade, weapons development and ethical problems of defense and military operations, ethical issues in R&D, technology spin offs and diffusion of *dual-use* technologies, Intellectual Property Rights, trademarks, Patents etc. are discussed in this section.

Topics of course material are covered in sufficient detail and depth to sensitize the reader on their relevance to moral and ethics concern in decision making. Further, the text content in the book is in accordance with prescribed syllabus of many technical universities/institutions. The book can also be used for teaching human values and professional ethics in professional, business and social science courses.

Need for exposure to engineers on sociological perspective of Culture and Society: An engineer must understand historical evolution of various societies to trace the reasons and causes of typical responses and behavior pattern of individuals or group of people. What distinguishes human beings from all other forms of life- is their *reflexivity*. The most salient manifestation of human reflexivity is found in culture. The culture manifests itself in the human ability to constantly create and innovate. Accordingly, human beings have been constantly reshaping their social milieu too. Evolution of society from primitive communism to tribal kingdoms to city-states and finally empires to nation-estate- the range has indeed been wide and variant. This knowledge of social awareness will make engineers more effective and efficient in their profession when dealing with matters of human concern and behavior.

Religion becoming source of Values in human conduct: The belief that the world is originated from an unknown source called God was the central idea behind origin of religion which means to trace and relate the individual life's principle back to its source. The shortest path to reach the source is for one to observe the basic tenets of one's own religion.

Basic tenets of any religion for purposeful life are right conduct, truthfulness, love, nonviolence and peace. In a healthy body lives a healthy mind, a healthy mind does not have place for wickedness, anger, greediness, jealousy, arrogance and such negative qualities.

Imbibing qualities such as truthfulness, humility, tolerance, nonviolence, obedience, honesty, righteousness, punctuality, confidence, courage, compassion, patience, kindness, courtesy, integrity and such possible qualities into one's own character leads to a moral and ethical life.

K. S. Verma

ks.verma.snist@gmail.com
Pleasanton, California
Guru Purnima, July 2018

Foreword

Many developing countries are progressing at a fast pace in science and technology and modernizing overall infrastructure for better living conditions of general public. However, in spite of having excellent educational institutions and system as well as large number of trained scientists, technologists, engineers, professionals, and administrators etc. the social life, in general, is not peaceful as it was a few decades ago.

The cause of poor discipline and, moral and ethical behavior in public life has been traced to fault in Education policies, with no emphasis in curriculums on moral and ethical development of students, based on culture and values. The current education policies in many universities recognized this deficiency in curriculum design and started including Human Values and Ethics courses in their technical education programs.

This book is an effort to train prospective Engineers and Professionals to become excellent professional not only in their fields of specialization but also equally proficient in human values and moral and ethical considerations in their professional practices, as well as family and social life. In this way, upcoming professionals will be able to help in promoting balanced behavior and outlook towards society at large.

The book has excellent coverage of topics to guide students on human values, moral and ethical issues, professional ethics and codes of conduct etc. Broadly the students are exposed to understand their own self, identity, personality, family, development of family value system, meaning of happiness and success. In order to integrate the students outlook with the society, adequate material is included on sociological understanding of society, community, culture, religion etc. Preparatory to his future career, a student must also understand moral responsibilities, authority, rights, autonomy and dilemmas of engineers and professionals

Today all types of economic activities; business, trade etc. are becoming globalized. This integration of transactions at global level throws up many global issues having bearing on human values with Ethical dimensions. A student must be exposed to global ethical issues arising from industrialization, continuous improvements in science and technology, Internet, cyberspace, environment, pollution etc. He/ She must also know regulatory mechanism on issues like national and global imperatives on trade, laws, Patent laws, copyrights, etc.

The book contains wealth of knowledge about ethical theories, how the ethical values are developed and acquired from childhood; how it should be practiced in design, production, management, business, etc.; how to maintain equilibrium between self-interest and interest of consumer, public at large and how they relate with global environmental issues.

The book is written in clear and concise manner for ease of understanding the clarity of thoughts and perception on subject matter. It will be an excellent text book on **Human Values and Ethics** subject, which is the need of the hour for Engineering Education.

Dr. P. Narasimha Reddy

Executive Director
Sreenidhi Institute of Science & Technology
Hyderabad, Telangana.

Table of Content

1　VALUE EDUCATION IN ENGINEERING　1

  1.1　Problems associated with Advanced Technology and Modern Humanism　2
  1.2　What is valuable to us?　3
  1.3　Students preference for Engineering Profession　4
      1.3.1　Attraction of Engineering Career for personal happiness　4
      1.3.2　Thrill of scientific knowledge, activity and improvement of human society　4
      1.3.3　Choice of Engineering Profession for the pleasure of Self-Worth　5
      1.3.4　Broad Spectrum of Engineering Disciplines and scope of employment opportunities　5
  1.4　Multiple Roles and Responsibilities of engineers in future　6
  1.5　Need for Value Education in Engineering Curriculum　7
  1.6　Role of Engineers in Industry　8
  1.7　Value Education for holistic personality development　9
  1.8　Global Trends for Value Education in Engineering Curriculum　10
      1.8.1　Goals of Higher Education in India　10
      1.8.2　Goals of Higher Education in USA　11
  1.9　Value Education for building National Character　11
  1.10　Value Education must blend with core Cultural Values　12
  1.11　Value Education for balancing between inner nature with external nature　13
  1.12　Summary　14

2　SOCIAL VALUES AND SYSTEMS, EDUCATION FOR TRANSFORMING THE SOCIETY　17

  2.1　Introduction　17
  2.2　Engineers role as an Agent of Social Change　18
  2.3　Ethical Values Expected from Members of any Society　18
      2.3.1　Becoming Ethical Person requires　20
  2.4　Role of Family on Personality and Character Development　20
      2.4.1　Child Socialization　21
      2.4.2　Adult Socialization　21
  2.5　Conflicts during Social Change　22
  2.6　Socialization Agencies, Process, Pattern and Character Formation　22
      2.6.1　Family as socialization unit　23
      2.6.2　Socialization with Peer Group　23
      2.6.3　Socialization in Schools and Academic Institutions　23
  2.7　Various terms used to indicate Values and Character　23
      2.7.1　Value education for development of integrated view of national, global and nature's universal order　24

2.8	TYPE OF SOCIETAL GROUPINGS OF PEOPLE WHICH AFFECT VALUES, ETHICS AND BEHAVIOR OF PERSON	25
2.9	SOCIAL CONTROL OF VALUES AND NORMS IN SOCIETY	26
	2.9.1 Status of Civic and Personal Morality in India	26
2.10	EDUCATION AS A PRIMARY INSTRUMENT OF MODERNIZATION OF SOCIETY	27
	2.10.1 Social factors and process of social changes	28
2.11	IMPACT OF EDUCATION SYSTEM, INDUSTRIALIZATION AND GLOBALIZATION ON SOCIAL AND CULTURAL VALUES	29
2.12	WHAT IS MODERNIZATION OF SOCIETY?	30
2.13	NEED FOR INDIAN SOCIETY TO MODERNIZE BUT NOT WESTERNIZE	31
2.14	SHIFT FROM TRADITIONAL VALUES, NORMS AND SOCIETAL STANDARDS IN MODERN INDIA	31
2.15	BASIC DIFFERENCE OF EASTERN AND WESTERN APPROACH TO DEAL WITH HUMAN WEAKNESSES	32
	2.15.1 Negative impact of Western Culture on Eastern Life	32
	2.15.2 Positive Impact of Western Culture	32
2.16	SUMMARY	33
3	**UNDERSTANDING VALUES, MORALS, ETHICS AND RELEVANCE TO WORK ETHICS AND BEHAVIOR**	**37**
3.1	GENESIS AND MEANING OF VALUES, MORALS AND ETHICS	37
	3.1.1 Genesis of Morals and Values	37
	3.1.2 What are the Values?	38
	3.1.3 Morals or Moral Values?	38
	3.1.4 What is Ethics?	39
	3.1.5 Morality	40
3.2	SCOPE AND FIELD OF MORAL THEORIES	41
	3.2.1 Descriptive Ethics	41
	3.2.2 Normative Ethics	42
	3.2.3 Morality as synonymous with Ethics	42
	3.2.4 Moral realism	42
	3.2.5 Moral relativism	42
	3.2.6 Moral universalism	43
3.3	MORALS VS. VALUES	43
3.4	INTEGRITY AND CONFIDENTIALITY	43
	3.4.1 How to maintain integrity?	44
3.5	WORK ETHICS	44
3.6	WORKING WITH ETHICS	45
3.7	ETHICAL AND UNETHICAL BEHAVIOR	46
	3.7.1 Ethical behavior in the Society	46
	3.7.2 Ethical behavior within the Workplace	46
	3.7.3 Employee's Unethical behavior	46
	3.7.4 Employers Unethical behavior	47
	3.7.5 Ethical behavior in Academic Institutions	47

	3.8	SERVICE LEARNING	47
		3.8.1 Principles of Universalizability in conflicts on moral and ethical issues	48
	3.9	SUMMARY	48
4	**ETHICAL VALUES, VIRTUES AND CHARACTER FOR PEACEFUL HAPPY LIVING**		**51**
	4.1	ART OF LIVING PEACEFULLY	51
		4.1.1 Tips for reduction of worries for peaceful living	52
		4.1.2 Tips for right Attitude and Mindset for living peacefully	53
	4.2	MOTIVATING EMPLOYEES TO ADOPT ORGANIZATIONAL WORK CULTURE	55
	4.3	ETHICS OF CARING	57
		4.3.1 Theory of Care giving as relationship	57
		4.3.2 Applied Care Ethics	58
	4.4	GLOBAL COMMONS AND SHARING ETHICS	58
		4.4.1 Preservation of Global Common Resources	59
		4.4.2 Sharing of National Common Resources	59
		4.4.3 Sharing of Open Source Software	59
		4.4.4 Sharing of Internet Resources	60
		4.4.5 Sharing of Data resources	60
	4.5	HONESTY AS BASIC MORAL AND ETHICAL VALUE	61
		4.5.1 For students need to practice Honesty and Academic Integrity	61
		4.5.2 You can't find Truth without Honesty	62
		4.5.3 Honesty sacrificed due to wrong emphasis on Group Identity	62
		4.5.4 Poor Code of Conduct in public domain policies	62
		4.5.5 How to maintain Honesty	63
		4.5.6 Honesty in Engineering Profession	63
	4.6	COURAGE IN PROFESSIONS	64
	4.7	VALUE OF TIME	65
	4.8	ETHICS OF COOPERATION	66
	4.9	ETHICS OF COMMITMENT	67
		4.9.1 Status of commitment of people to Moral and Ethical values	67
	4.10	EMPATHY ETHICS	68
		4.10.1 Empathy vs. Sympathy	68
	4.11	VIRTUES	69
		4.11.1 Virtues in Public Service	69
		4.11.2 Virtue Ethics	70
		4.11.3 Empathy vs. Caring	71
		4.11.4 Why to practice Empathy?	72
	4.12	SELF-CONFIDENCE	72
	4.13	SPIRITUALITY	74
		4.13.1 Why Spirituality to Engineers and Professionals	75
		4.13.2 Yoga for balance of mind	76

		4.13.3 Meditation for Inner Awakening	76
		4.13.4 Understanding Spirituality	77
		4.13.5 Differentiating Spirituality from Religion	77
		4.13.6 Spirituality and Engineering Education	78
	4.14	RESPECT FOR OTHERS	79
	4.15	VIRTUE OF CHARACTER	80
		4.15.1 Professional Character	80
	4.16	SUMMARY	81

5 HISTORICAL DEVELOPMENT OF ETHICS, ETHICAL THEORIES AND KOHLBERG'S THEORY ON MORAL DEVELOPMENT — 87

	5.1	HISTORICAL DEVELOPMENT OF ETHICS	88
		5.1.1 History of Ethics in India	88
		5.1.2 History of Ethics in Western World	92
		5.1.3 Ancient Ethics and Modern Morality	94
	5.2	ETHICAL PRINCIPLES	95
		5.2.1 Beneficence	95
		5.2.2 Least Harm	96
		5.2.3 Autonomy	96
		5.2.4 Justice	96
	5.3	ETHICAL THEORIES	96
		5.3.1 Kantianism or Deontological Ethics or Duty ethics	97
		5.3.2 Utilitarianism	98
		5.3.3 Ethical Theories having direct applications to Professionalism	98
		5.3.4 Self-Realization	100
	5.4	TYPES OF INQUIRY	100
		5.4.1 Normative Inquiries	101
		5.4.2 Conceptual Inquiries	101
		5.4.3 Factual / Descriptive Inquiries	102
	5.5	TOOLS OF ETHICAL ANALYSIS	102
	5.6	USE OF ETHICAL THEORIES	103
	5.7	KOHLBERG'S THEORY- GILLIGAN'S ARGUMENT-HEINZ'S DILEMMA	104
		5.7.1 Theories on Moral Development	104
		5.7.2 Piaget's Theory of Moral Development	104
		5.7.3 Kohlberg's Theory on Moral Development	105
		5.7.4 Gilligan's Theory of Moral Development	107
		5.7.5 Heinz's Dilemma	108
	5.8	SUMMARY	110

6 ROLE OF ENGINEERING AND PROFESSIONAL ETHICS IN INDUSTRY AND BUSINESS OPERATIONS — 115

	6.1	PURPOSE OF ENGINEERING ETHICS	115
		6.1.1 Moral Dilemmas	117

6.2	ENGINEERING AND ETHICS		118
6.3	ENGINEERING ETHICS		119
	6.3.1	Moral Rights in Engineering Profession	119
	6.3.2	Ethics of Proficiency Virtue	120
6.4	MORAL AUTONOMY OF ENGINEERS		120
6.5	PROFESSIONAL ETHICS		121
	6.5.1	Characteristic features of Professional Ethics	122
	6.5.2	Ethical Assumption of Professional Organizations	123
	6.5.3	Professional Ethics vs. Personal Morality	123
6.6	PROFESSIONAL ATTITUDE IN ENGINEERING WORKS AND TRADE OFF WITH ROLE OF OTHER FUNCTIONARIES		124
	6.6.1	Consequences of Responsibility without Ethical Concern	125
	6.6.2	Engineer's roles of non-technical nature	125
	6.6.3	Technical and Professional Competence	126
	6.6.4	Conflict in role of Engineering Professionals and Management	127
	6.6.5	Managers Trade-Off with conflicting situation	128
	6.6.6	Models of Professional Roles	129
6.7	CONSENSUS AND CONTROVERSIES ON WORK SITUATIONS/ BUSINESS OPERATIONS		130
6.8	ETHICS IN BUSINESS		132
6.9	GLOBAL BUSINESS		133
6.10	SUMMARY		135
7	**UNDERSTANDING OUR PERSONALITY, POTENTIAL, MOTIVATIONS AND GOALS OF LIFE**		**139**
7.1	EXPLORE YOUR POTENTIAL AND VALUE SYSTEM		139
	7.1.1	Tips for harnessing Potential of Growth and fulfilling goals of life	140
	7.1.2	Understanding Internal Values System	141
7.2	BASIC HUMAN NEEDS		141
7.3	UNDERSTANDING PERSONALITY AND IMPORTANT BEHAVIORAL VALUES		142
	7.3.1	Understanding Personal Values	143
	7.3.2	Trustworthiness	143
	7.3.3	Virtue of Contentment	144
	7.3.4	Motivational factors as we grow	145
	7.3.5	Self-Management	146
7.4	UNDERSTANDING OUR INDIVIDUAL IDENTITY		146
	7.4.1	Shocks of Identity loss	147
7.5	FORMATION IDEA OF SELF OR SENSE OF "I" IN AN INDIVIDUAL AND ITS FUNCTIONAL REALITY		148
	7.5.1	Understanding Spiritual SELF identified as "I", the faculty of reason, rationality and emotional balance(also addressed as Third Eye of man)	149

		7.5.2	Few quotes to stimulate thinking about SELF	151
	7.6	\multicolumn{2}{l	}{WHAT IS POSITIVE THINKING?}	151

- 7.5.2 Few quotes to stimulate thinking about SELF — 151
- 7.6 WHAT IS POSITIVE THINKING? — 151
    - 7.6.1 Positive Thinking is a way of life — 153
    - 7.6.2 Words inculcating Positive Thoughts — 153
    - 7.6.3 Benefits of Positive Thinking — 154
    - 7.6.4 Strategies to cultivate Positive Thinking — 154
    - 7.6.5 Overcome Negative Thoughts — 156
    - 7.6.6 Avoid Negative Self-Talk — 156
    - 7.6.7 Tips for maintaining Positive Attitude and overcome Negative Traits — 157
- 7.7 HAPPINESS — 158
    - 7.7.1 Understanding happiness through balloon analogy — 159
    - 7.7.2 Reasons of Unhappiness — 160
    - 7.7.3 Holistic Happiness — 160
- 7.8 SELF-INTEREST — 162
    - 7.8.1 Diversity of Self-Interest in different ages and Professional Groups — 162
    - 7.8.2 Self-Interest at the core of happiness in life — 163
    - 7.8.3 Money centered Self-Interest to ensure financial well being — 164
    - 7.8.4 Self-Interest in economic context — 164
    - 7.8.5 Self-Interest in personal context — 165
    - 7.8.6 Self-Interest and Ambitions — 166
    - 7.8.7 Self-Interest and Morality — 166
    - 7.8.8 Self-Interest in Business — 167
- 7.9 SUMMARY — 167

8 UNDERSTANDING BEHAVIOR, MORAL AND ETHICAL VALUES, TO MATCH WITH THE EXTERNAL ENVIRONMENT — 171

- 8.1 TIPS FOR SUCCESS IN THE PROFESSIONAL CAREER — 171
- 8.2 CUSTOMS — 172
    - 8.2.1 Culture and Customs — 173
    - 8.2.2 India and its Cardinal Values — 174
- 8.3 RELIGION — 175
    - 8.3.1 Religious Pluralism — 176
- 8.4 HOLISTIC VIEW OF HUMANITY — 176
    - 8.4.1 Contemporary meaning and scope of Human Values — 177
- 8.5 TECHNOLOGY FORCING FAST CHANGES IN CORPORATE CULTURE — 178
- 8.6 ROLE OF ATTITUDE AND ENVIRONMENTAL FACTORS ON ETHICAL BEHAVIOR — 179
    - 8.6.1 Social learning from life around us — 180
- 8.7 INSTITUTION OF FAMILY AND INFLUENCE OF URBANIZATION AND GLOBALIZATION — 181
    - 8.7.1 Marriage and the Family — 181
    - 8.7.2 Shrinking of family units and impact on values and relationships — 182

		8.7.3 Impact of Urbanization on family and relationship	183
		8.7.4 Life with family and friends	183
	8.8	RESPONSIBILITIES AS GOOD CITIZEN	184
	8.9	DIRECTION OF INDIAN STATE	184
	8.10	SUMMARY	185
9	**ENGINEERING AS SOCIAL EXPERIMENTATION**		**191**
	9.1	SOCIAL RESPONSIBILITY OF ENGINEERS	191
	9.2	EXPERIMENTATION DURING ENGINEERING PRODUCT-DESIGN PROCESS	192
	9.3	EXAMPLE OF ENGINEERING AS SOCIAL EXPERIMENTATION	194
		9.3.1 Engineers Responsibilities with regard to Technology	194
	9.4	PROCESS OF ENGINEERING DEVELOPMENT OF PRODUCTS OR PROJECTS	195
		9.4.1 Knowledge-Gaps in Engineering of new Products/Projects or improving the existing one to compete in the market, requires experimentation	195
		9.4.2 Experiential Learning	197
	9.5	COMPLEXITY OF MEGAPROJECTS FROM THE POINT OF SOCIAL ENGINEERING	197
	9.6	IMPACT OF INDUSTRIALIZATION AND INDUSTRIAL POLLUTION	198
	9.7	INFORMED CONSENT	199
	9.8	KNOWLEDGE GAINED	200
	9.9	SUMMARY	201
10	**ENGINEER AS MANAGER, CONSULTANT, LEADER AND RESPONSIBLE SOCIAL EXPERIMENTER**		**205**
	10.1	TYPICAL GROWTH PROFILE OF A FRESH ENGINEER IN INDUSTRY	205
	10.2	ORGANIZATIONAL ROLES AND AUTHORITY OF ENGINEERS AND MANAGERS	206
		10.2.1 Functional Roles of Engineers and Managers	206
		10.2.2 Role of Engineers	206
		10.2.3 Functionality of decision making by Managers and Engineers	207
	10.3	ENGINEER AS A CONSULTANT	208
		10.3.1 Responsibilities of Consultants in promotion of business	209
	10.4	ENGINEER AS A LEADER	209
		10.4.1 Role of Leaders	210
		10.4.2 Leaders vs. Managers	210
	10.5	ENGINEERS AS RESPONSIBLE SOCIAL EXPERIMENTER	211
	10.6	SUMMARY	212
11	**ENGINEERS PERSONALITY TRAIT, BIG FIVE PERSONALITY MODEL, CONSCIENTIOUSNESS**		**215**
	11.1	UNDERSTANDING PERSONALITY TRAITS OF EMPLOYEES	215
	11.2	PERSONALITY TRAITS REQUIRED IN ENGINEERING PROFESSION	216
	11.3	UNDERSTANDING PERSONALITY TRAITS	216
		11.3.1 Big Five-Factors Personality Model	217

	11.4 SELF-GOVERNANCE VIRTUES	218
	11.5 CONSCIENTIOUSNESS	218
	11.5.1 Characteristics of Conscientious Individuals	219
	11.5.2 Conscientiousness in academic and workplace performance	219
	11.5.3 Characteristics of conscientious engineers	220
	11.6 MORAL RESPONSIBILITY OF ENGINEERS	220
	11.6.1 Engineers must take comprehensive perspective of their works	221
	11.7 COMPLEXITY OF MORAL AND ETHICS ISSUES FOR ENGINEERING PROFESSIONALS	222
	11.8 SUMMARY	222
12	**ACCOUNTABILITY, ROLES OF CODES AND EXPERIMENTAL NATURE OF ENGINEERING**	**227**
	12.1 ACCOUNTABILITY IN ENGINEERING PROFESSION	227
	12.1.1 Creating culture of Accountability	228
	12.1.2 Problems of Accountability fixation for engineers in Big Projects	229
	12.2 ROLE OF CODES	230
	12.2.1 Examples to illustrate the Gravity of Engineer's Responsibility for Safety and Risk	231
	12.2.2 Understanding scope of Codes of Ethics, Conduct, Practice and Moral Codes	234
	12.3 SPECTRUM OF CODES	235
	12.3.1 NSPE Code of Ethics for engineers- general principles	235
	12.3.2 Engineering Codes, Standards and Responsibilities for Engineers	236
	12.3.3 Responsibility for compliance to Codes of Practice	237
	12.3.4 Purpose of Codes of Ethics	238
	12.4 ENGINEERS DILEMMAS ON DUTY ETHICS OF ENGINEERING PRACTICE	238
	12.4.1 General Ethical Issues	239
	12.5 LIMITATIONS OF CODES	239
	12.6 INDUSTRIAL PRODUCT, PROCESS AND INTERFACE STANDARDS	240
	12.7 SUMMARY	241
13	**ENGINEERS RESPONSIBILITY FOR SAFETY AND RISK**	**245**
	13.1 RISKS FACTORS IN ENGINEERING PROFESSION AND ACTIVITIES	245
	13.2 ENGINEERS RESPONSIBILITY FOR SAFETY AND RISK	246
	13.2.1 Engineering necessarily and inherently involves risk	247
	13.3 SAFETY AND RISK	248
	13.3.1 The Concept of Risk	248
	13.3.2 The Concept of Safety	249
	13.3.3 Magnitude and Proximity	250
	13.4 TYPE OF RISKS	251
	13.5 VOLUNTARY VS. INVOLUNTARY RISK	252

	13.6 SHORT TERM *vs.* LONG TERM CONSEQUENCES	254
	13.7 SUMMARY	255
14	**RISK PERCEPTIONS AND RISK ASSESSMENT ANALYSIS**	**259**
	14.1 RISK PERCEPTION AND PROBABILITY OF RISK	259
	14.1.1 Delayed vs. Immediate Risk	*260*
	14.2 UNDERSTANDING RISK, HAZARD, HARM AND UNCERTAINTY	261
	14.2.1 Definitions of Risk	*261*
	14.3 RISK THRESHOLD AND RISK APPETITE	262
	14.3.1 Relationship between Risk Appetite and Risk Threshold	*263*
	14.4 RISK MANAGEMENT AND SOURCES OF RISK	263
	14.5 QUANTIFYING THE RISK ASSESSMENT	263
	14.6 RISK ASSESSMENT IN VARIOUS FIELDS OF ACTIVITY	265
	14.6.1 Methodology	*265*
	14.6.2 Risks in terms of financial losses	*265*
	14.6.3 Risks in project management	*266*
	14.6.4 Risks in High Reliability Organizations	*266*
	14.6.5 Enterprise Risk Management	*266*
	14.6.6 Risk Assessment in public health	*267*
	14.6.7 Risks in IT field	*267*
	14.7 SUMMARY	268
15	**ENGINEERING DESIGN FOR SAFETY AND RELIABILITY**	**271**
	15.1 SAFETY ISSUE IN ENGINEERING DESIGNS	271
	15.1.1 Engineers Duty for Safe Designs	*272*
	15.1.2 OSHA and Workplace Safety	*273*
	15.2 SAFETY AND RELIABILITY	273
	15.3 RESPONSIBILITY AND LIABILITY OF UNSAFE DESIGNS	274
	15.4 PRODUCT SAFETY AND LIABILITY FOR CONSUMERS	275
	15.4.1 Problems of launching New Products	*276*
	15.5 ENGINEERING GUIDELINES FOR SAFE DESIGNS	277
	15.5.1 Safety Engineering	*278*
	15.5.2 Design for Reliability	*279*
	15.5.3 Techniques of Reliability Assessment	*280*
	15.6 RELIABILITY ENGINEERING	280
	15.6.1 Parameters of System Reliability	*281*
	15.6.2 Accelerated Testing	*282*
	15.6.3 Software Reliability	*282*
	15.6.4 Reliability Engineering vs. Safety Engineering	*283*
	15.7 RELIABILITY *vs.* QUALITY	284
	15.8 SUMMARY	285
16	**RISK BENEFIT ANALYSIS AND ACCIDENTS**	**289**
	16.1 RISK-BENEFIT ANALYSIS	289

	16.2 Technology Evaluation and Risk-Benefit Analysis for New Venture or Product	290
	16.3 Risk-Benefit Analyses of Large Engineering Projects	290
	16.3.1 Complexity of Risk-Benefit analysis	291
	16.3.2 Engineers to look beyond Risk-Benefit complex	291
	16.3.3 Personal and Public Risks	292
	16.4 Examples of Major Disasters to showcase importance of Risk and Safety concern to Engineers	293
	16.4.1 Accidents in Escalator	293
	16.4.2 Chernobyl Nuclear Plant accident (Ukraine-1986)	293
	16.4.3 Fukushima Nuclear Disaster (Japan-March 11, 2011)	294
	16.5 Provision for Safe Exits	295
	16.5.1 Examples of Safe Exit provisions	295
	16.6 Examples of improved Safety in products of daily use	296
	16.7 Summary	297
17	**CORPORATE WORK CULTURE, PROFESSION, LOYALTY AND COLLEGIALITY**	**303**
	17.1 Need for Culture of Teamwork among Different Departments in Industry	303
	17.1.1 Example of execution of a Defense Supply Order	303
	17.1.2 Failure of Design Samples	304
	17.1.3 Design Failure Analysis	304
	17.1.4 Deficiencies of Organizational Work Culture	305
	17.2 Defining Features of an Organization	306
	17.3 Profession vs. Job and Occupation	307
	17.3.1 Job	307
	17.3.2 Occupation	307
	17.4 Defining Profession	308
	17.4.1 Defining Features of Profession	308
	17.4.2 Engineering Qualifying as Profession	309
	17.5 Collegiality	310
	17.5.1 Main features of Collegiality	311
	17.5.2 Techniques for achieving Collegiality	311
	17.6 Engineer's Trustworthiness	312
	17.7 Loyalty	313
	17.7.1 Two senses of Loyalty	313
	17.7.2 Obligations to Loyalty	314
	17.7.3 Misguided Loyalty	314
	17.8 Summary	315
18	**PROFESSIONAL RIGHTS, RESPONSIBILITIES AND OTHER QUALITIES OF PROFESSIONALISM**	**319**
	18.1 Professionalism	319

18.2	Professional Responsibilities	320
	18.2.1 Responsibilities of Professional Engineers are broadly	320
18.3	Professionalism vs. Loyalty	321
18.4	Engineers career as Employees	321
	18.4.1 Employees' Rights at Workplace	321
18.5	Engineers Rights as Employee	322
	18.5.1 Definitions of terms used in connection to employment	322
	18.5.2 Rights affecting the employment relationship	323
18.6	Engineer Rights as a Professional	323
18.7	Complexion of Authority Structure	325
	18.7.1 Area of Engineers and Managers Authority	325
18.8	Confidentiality and Secrecy	326
	18.8.1 Defining Confidential and Proprietary Information	327
	18.8.2 Professional responsibility for maintaining confidentiality while changing jobs	328
	18.8.3 Obligation to Confidentiality vis-à-vis Personal Interest of employees and employers Rights	328
	18.8.4 Confidentiality and Secrecy for both Employees and the Employer	329
	18.8.5 Misuse of Confidentiality clauses	330
18.9	Conflicts due to Indirect Interests in other Companies	330
	18.9.1 Moral Obligation to avoid Conflicts of Interest	330
	18.9.2 Solving Conflict of Interest problem	331
18.10	Summary	331
19	**Ethical Operational Issues Encountered in Business and Engineering Profession**	**335**
19.1	Self-Realization Ethics	335
19.2	Ethical Corporations	336
19.3	Attempts to evolve a Global Ethical Framework	337
19.4	Corruption and acceptance of Gifts	338
	19.4.1 Varieties of corruption in Global Business	338
19.5	Impact of Gifts and Bribery on Business	339
	19.5.1 Difference between Gift and Bribe	340
	19.5.2 Bribe given as Kickbacks	340
	19.5.3 How Kickbacks work?	341
19.6	Status of Anti-Graft Laws	341
19.7	Action for prevention of Fraud and Corruption Problem	341
	19.7.1 Actions at Employees level	341
	19.7.2 Actions at Organizational level	342
	19.7.3 Actions required in execution of International Contracts	343
	19.7.4 Global Principles for Zero Tolerance Corruption	343
19.8	Collective Bargaining	343
19.9	Occupational Crime	344

19.10	INDUSTRIAL ESPIONAGE	345
	19.10.1 Forms of Economic and Industrial Espionage	345
19.11	PRICE FIXING	346
	19.11.1 Methods of price manipulations	346
	19.11.2 US Federal Antitrust Enforcement	346
19.12	ENDANGERING LIVES	347
	19.12.1 Socially harmful corporate activity	348
19.13	SUMMARY	348

20 WHISTLEBLOWING   353

20.1	INTRODUCTION	353
20.2	WHAT IS WHISTLEBLOWING?	354
20.3	HISTORICAL BACKGROUND OF WHISTLEBLOWING	354
20.4	WHISTLEBLOWERS PROTECTION ACT 2011 OF INDIA	355
20.5	TYPES OF WHISTLEBLOWING	356
20.6	WHEN WHISTLEBLOWING SHOULD BE ATTEMPTED?	357
	20.6.1 Internal whistleblowing	357
	20.6.2 External whistle blowing	358
20.7	PUBLIC INTEREST WHISTLEBLOWING	358
20.8	LEGAL PROTECTION TO WHISTLEBLOWING ACTIVITY	358
20.9	PREVENTING WHISTLEBLOWING	359
20.10	SUMMARY	360

21 GLOBALIZATION, CROSS-CULTURAL OPERATIONS AND RESEARCH   365

21.1	SCIENCE PROMOTING GLOBAL CULTURE	365
	21.1.1 Role of MNCs in Cross-Cultural Environment	366
	21.1.2 Issues related to Technology Transfer to host countries	367
21.2	DEFENSE OPERATIONS AND WEAPON DEVELOPMENT	367
	21.2.1 Ethical problems of Defense Industry and Military Operations	368
	21.2.2 Globally, Defense Budgets are big compulsive burden on economy	368
	21.2.3 Technology Spin-Offs and diffusion of Dual-Use Technologies	369
	21.2.4 Scientists and engineers role in the development of dual-use products and applications	369
	21.2.5 Environmental problems due to modern industrial and military developments	370
	21.2.6 Examples of Military Technologies Transferred to Civilian Sector	371
21.3	RESEARCH AND DEVELOPMENT	371
	21.3.1 Definition of Research	371
	21.3.2 Characteristics of Research	372
	21.3.3 Nature of Research	373

	21.3.4 Types of Research	373
	21.3.5 Ethics and Research	374
	21.3.6 Guidelines and Codes for Ethical problems in Research	375
21.4	SUMMARY	376

22 ENVIRONMENTAL ETHICS — 381

22.1	ENVIRONMENTAL ETHICS AND HUMAN VALUES	381
22.2	MORAL BASIS OF ENVIRONMENTAL ETHICS	382
22.3	JUSTICE AND SUSTAINABILITY	383
22.4	SUFFICIENCY AND COMPASSION	383
22.5	SOLIDARITY AND PARTICIPATION	384
22.6	MODES OF ETHICAL REASONING ABOUT THE ENVIRONMENT	384
22.7	IMPACT OF ENVIRONMENTAL DEGRADATION CREATING HUMAN PROBLEMS	385
22.8	THE SPECIAL RELATIONSHIP OF ECOLOGY AND ENVIRONMENTAL ETHICS	386
22.9	ENGINEERS RESPONSIBILITY TOWARDS ENVIRONMENTAL ETHICS	387
22.10	CONCERN ABOUT ENVIRONMENT INCLUDED IN ENGINEERING CODES	387
22.11	SUMMARY	388

23 ETHICAL ISSUES ON COMPUTER, INTERNET AND DATA PROCESSING — 391

23.1	GLOBAL NETWORKING AND ISSUES OF INTERNET ETHICS	391
23.2	NEED FOR GLOBAL LAWS ON INTERNET AND CYBERSPACE	392
	23.2.1 Global Cyber-Business	392
	23.2.2 Global Online information via Internet	393
	23.2.3 Disbursal of information among rich and poor	393
23.3	IMPACT OF COMPUTING POWER AND INTERNET ON POWER STRUCTURE AMONG PEOPLE AND ORGANIZATIONS	393
23.4	COMPUTERS AND INVASION OF PRIVACY	394
23.5	FIELD OF COMPUTER ETHICS	396
23.6	THE TEN COMMANDMENTS OF COMPUTER ETHICS	397
23.7	COMPUTERS AS THE INSTRUMENT OF UNETHICAL BEHAVIOR	399
	23.7.1 Why people resort to use computers as instrument of unethical behavior?	400
23.8	COMPUTER CRIME	400
23.9	COMPUTER SECURITY	401
23.10	COMPUTER AS THE OBJECT OF UNETHICAL ACTS	401
23.11	AUTONOMOUS COMPUTERS AND INTERNET	403
23.12	SUMMARY	404

24 INTELLECTUAL PROPERTY RIGHTS — 409

24.1	WHAT IS INTELLECTUAL PROPERTY?	409
24.2	SCOPE OF INTELLECTUAL PROPERTY LAW	410
24.3	INDIA'S INTELLECTUAL PROPERTY REGIME	411
24.4	TRADEMARKS	411
24.5	COPYRIGHTS AND RELATED RIGHTS	412

	24.5.1 Type of rights under Copyrights	413
	24.5.2 Transfer of economic rights	414
	24.5.3 Extent of use of someone else's work without permission	414
	24.6 PATENTS	414
	24.7 TRADE SECRETS AND OTHER FORMS OF INTELLECTUAL PROPERTY	415
	24.7.1 Unfair Competition	416
	24.7.2 Protection of Trade Secrets	416
	24.8 INDUSTRIAL DESIGNS	416
	24.9 SUMMARY	418
25	**BIBLIOGRAPHY**	**421**
26	**APPENDIX**	**425**

Section 1: Role of Engineering Education in Imparting Basic Human Values and Transforming Society

1 Value Education in Engineering

Learning objectives

In this chapter you will learn about

- Importance of engineering profession in creating modern facilities for human living
- Engineering disasters leading to growth of modern Humanism
- Motivations for engineering career, opportunities and professional expectations
- Need for *value education* in *engineering curriculum*
- Need for building national character among professionals with global outlook
- Education Policy and global trends towards moral education in engineering discipline

In this book the word *engineer* or *professional* is used to refer collectively all *technical* people such as *scientist, technologist and engineers*. The main focus of the book is on *value education* to engineers and professionals on human values, moral and ethics. Professional means, people whose professional activities are governed by legally established procedures, or professional bodies, which are established to regulate the professional activities, and prescribe proper *code of conduct* or *code of ethics* for the profession.

In the society, a person plays three roles, at any time during his *active life*. In the first role as an individual, a person has his own personal values and desires about *the life*. Each person has his own views on the *values* about what is good or bad and what is right or wrong. Similarly, at the same time each individual is also a *social being* governed by a set of moral values, of each of the societal groupings, like religious, business, political etc., with which he/she is connected in the second role. Finally, in the third role as a professional, he/she is supposed to follow professional ethics and *code of conduct* of his profession.

1.1 Problems associated with Advanced Technology and Modern Humanism

Most of the people are aware of advantages from various top *engineering technologies*, which are evolved in last six to seven decades. All modernization of human living conditions is primarily due to various technologies like electrification, automobiles, aero planes, telephony, radio and television, mobile and satellite communication, computers, Internet, imaging technologies, health technologies, petrochemical technologies, nuclear technologies etc.

Along with success stories of technological advances, there also have been major disasters due to human errors or failure of engineering designs. For example, accidents like Bhopal gas tragedy, collapses of freshly built bridges, roads, buildings, flyovers etc. automobile fire and railway accidents are due to serious design failures, poor implementation, operation, training and maintenance. Similarly, failure of Challenger Space Shuttle after launch, accidents at the nuclear plant at Chernobyl and Three Mile Island at Pennsylvania, etc., at international level, can be treated as failures of the *engineering design* or *plant construction* or *operations*.

Above disasters are cases of negligence at various levels of *engineering design and safety principles*, non-adherence to standard work practices, lack of *professional conduct*, inadequate supervision, suppression of known defects for the fear of financial loss and loss of image, etc. Engineering disasters and similar catastrophes in the *Product/ Process and Projects* in various sectors of industry are examples of *professional delinquency* on the part of some individuals or group of technical or managerial personals.

Most of the times the responsible people, such as enlightened educated personalities, employers, employees, entrepreneurs, citizens, etc. do not focus on the safety and risks element possible over operational life of product or project. This attitude of unconcern results into disastrous situations or consequences; which are preventable if people are alert, fearless and consciously concerned about welfare of fellow being. Sometimes, it is also ignorance of technical personnel about the hidden deficiencies in a *working system*, which leads to disasters or of enormous losses and unpleasant consequences.

Scientific-education without *value-education* produces professionals who are, unconcerned and insensitive to impact of their scientific activity on the humanity. Understanding human values and psycho-social dimension of man is focus of *modern Humanism*, which tries to synthesize the *scientific progress with the human values*.

Development of Modern Humanism: The scientific revolutions have largely shaped the modern world and impacted modern thinking of human beings about the world order. On the other hand, the same *development* and *drive of modernization* gave birth to so many problems that are linked to health and peace of human society by disturbing the natural balance of nature. This concern of bad impact of scientific development on humanity is called Modern Humanism. Engineering ethics is a result of this pursuit of Modern Humanism. While science is engaged in discovering truth after truth about the natural forces and processes; the applications of the scientific knowledge culminating into technological and engineering advancement, is being simultaneously evaluated for their long-term impact on human being and society.

Modern Humanism shaped modern civilization: This development of modern Humanism is not a local issue but has travelled to far flung areas of the Globe. Any incidence in any part of the world raises voices of concern throughout the world. Thus, science through discoveries, inventions and industrial revolution created Modern civilization and at the same time globalized concern about long term impacts and influences on mankind. Thanks to Internet which converted globe into a village where global awareness has grown and separation between people has dissolved.

1.2 What is valuable to us?

Many times, people call their desires (about lifestyle, career, profession, etc.) as their values in life. But under *value education*, we study those values which come from within and, mostly they are part of our *belief-system* also. Further, under value education we consider those values also that are prescribed by profession and the society.

Everybody has a list of *hierarchy of desires*, which they nurture and attach the value to them. They would like to fulfill these desires some time or the other. For students of engineering, the desire of getting a good job, decent career and happy life are of paramount importance. This desire can be fulfilled by acquiring proper qualification and a job matching with their qualification. Meaning of *decent life* implies possession of resources to fulfill desires, like good personality, happy family, enough security, plenty of wealth, good job, status and power etc.

Human desires and their priorities keep on changing with time as one passes through various phases of life. Time is a valuable resource. How much one values time in student life and where they spend it, determines their future career and growth? For example, students may choose to spend more time on education and studies or in personal improvements. Alternatively, they may spend more time on all other activities like watching TV, going for gym or jogging, spend time with family, sleeping longer, etc. Their talent will enrich in the type of activities in which they spent most of their time, which will also shape their future.

In today's environment students give more value to success, their measure of success is all about having better grade point average (GPA), or being stronger physically and, in job good earning and accumulating wealth to enjoy life. But success is much more than those like sense of fulfillment, higher status, reputation, good image, achieving objectives whatever is valuable to them, clarity on goal of life and satisfactory achievement etc.

1.3 Students preference for Engineering Profession

Among students of science background, aspiration to become an engineer is highest. This choice is clear, if one looks at the strength of students appearing for competitive entrance exams, compared to number of students appearing in other entrance exams, like medical profession or competitive entrance exams of other professions. Their goal is to become a successful *engineering professional* to fulfill their goals and dreams of better future making best use of their talent. Various motivational factors, working behind the decision of opting for an engineering profession, are given below:

1.3.1 Attraction of Engineering Career for personal happiness

A student of engineering, while choosing careers normally considers prospects of job offers, advancement, security, salary, prestige, life style, personal challenge and personal satisfaction. These factors indicate motivation in seeking personal happiness than anything related to morality. Indirectly, it reflects their first moral duty to achieve their own happiness and welfare of their people (i.e. family) and then only think of moral duty towards others.

1.3.2 Thrill of scientific knowledge, activity and improvement of human society

Function of Engineers in society can be explained/ defined as "... a person providing solutions for the existing problems with available resources". Engineering as a profession is loaded with full of challenging and complex problems, which triggers the creative impulse of young engineers to face and solve them. Engineering has wider impact to shape the life style of common man. For example, the skill of other professionals like a medical doctor or surgeon affects one patient at a time, whereas the judgment of a *design-engineer* can influence hundreds of lives at a time. People use the medicine when they feel sick but engineering products are used /useful for every moment. Everyday utility items like clothes, food items, house, car, mobile phone, computers, TV, Internet etc. are made available through production and delivery systems established by engineering technologies. Engineering is the core discipline which transforms knowledge gained from science and technology into useful products and builds infrastructure to design, develop, produce, and make available ultimate consumers / users through a distribution network.

1.3.3 Choice of Engineering Profession for the pleasure of Self-Worth

Self-realization is a motive force working behind student's preference for choosing engineering profession is discussed below:
- Self-realization comes through the application of one's highest talents, interests, skills and virtues. Within limits, the greater the complexity and challenge to one's talent, the greater one's happiness tends to be.
- Undergraduate curriculum for engineering is acknowledged to be more rigorous and difficult than majority of other academic disciplines. One might guess that students are attracted to engineering, at least in part because of the challenge it offers to intelligent people.
- Students are motivated to enter engineering primarily by a desire to do some interesting and challenging works. For them making some technological products is very appealing and challenging work, where they can contribute their talent and prove the Self-Worth.
- Self-Worth means deep rooted feeling of one's own potential (Ego System), which searches avenues for its demonstration. In Engineering, a student gets an opportunity to apply his/her knowledge to fulfillment of human needs and desires. This desire is related to the finest aspirations and deepest impulses of human beings.
- In contrast with the scientist's whose main interest is in discovering new knowledge, the engineer's greatest enjoyment drives from creativity in solving practical problems.

1.3.4 Broad Spectrum of Engineering Disciplines and scope of employment opportunities

There is a wide range of disciplines open in engineering field like Electronics and Communication, Electrical, Mechanical, Civil, Aeronautics, Computer Science and Information Technology (IT) etc.; and many more specialization streams including Research and Development in each field. The job opportunities are spread over application fields in various sectors of industry like Communication, Transportation, Power, IT, Defense, aero-space, Chemical, etc. Engineers are also absorbed in non-technical fields like *Finance and Banking, Administrative Services* etc. or become an Entrepreneur.

Engineering and professional decisions are very critical in industry, during product or project management process; important from the applications point of view and safety and security of general public as well as from health and environmental considerations, etc. Thus, it is essential to train the students of engineering disciplines on *value education* to broaden their understanding of different roles to be played by them in their professional career.

1.4 Multiple Roles and Responsibilities of engineers in future

An engineering student is a prospective professional of tomorrow. The industry looks upon them as future employee and family looks upon them for future support to parents and family members. Similarly, society looks upon them as role model and an important member to guide the younger generations. They are considered to be important citizens who will contribute to the well-being of the public and the nation. With so many roles expected from them, students must be prepared, during their education period, to play these roles effectively. Purpose of *value education* is to prepare and sensitize them for these roles and responsibilities, as holistic personalities, so that they play all roles effectively and efficiently.

Engineering Student's role as Mature Adult: All citizens after attaining age of 18 years are legally considered to be an adult. Thus, almost all engineering students are adults. They are future strength of the nation. As an adult, engineering students are expected to acquire certain degree of emotional and social maturity.

Some personal characteristics, defining an emotionally and socially mature adult are given below:
1. Maturity is an ongoing process, and requires lot of introspection within, as well as during interactions with external world to understand: who am I? How society is structured? What are social conditions, constraints, problems, and possible solutions? They must grow in maturity through *self-Introspection* and *understanding* of their moral and ethical perceptions about all *social issues*
2. An engineer should be able to manage personal weaknesses like fear, anger jealousy and feelings of envy.

Chapter 1: Why Value Education in Engineering ?

3. Mature requires a cool temperament to listen and evaluate the viewpoints of others rationally and unbiasedly. It also requires practicing and maintaining patience and flexibility under all circumstances. Having patience is a measure of inner strength.
4. Student must understand that always they can't be winners and need to learn from mistakes. They need to keep moving forward rather than keep on grumbling about the unfavorable outcomes.
5. One should not focus too much on negative side of the picture or situation; but look for and search the positive points in the subject being analyzed.
6. Engineer should be able to judge between rational decisions makings and differentiate from emotional impulsive decisions.
7. Engineer should be capable of managing his temper and anger. Many intellectuals fail in their tasks due to poor interrelationship with boss, peers and subordinates due to their bad temperament and anger.
8. On personal values one should be able to distinguish between *need* and *greed*. Need can be fulfilled but greed is bottomless well which never fills but many times allures to do wrong and immoral things.
9. For success confidence is a must. Confidence releases a psychic energy of a person to face the challenge and handle pressure with self-composure.
10. Normally in any situation, there are various shades of grey between the extremes of black and white picture. An Engineer should be able to distinguish between these shades in every situation.
11. Maturity demands to recognize that open communication is the key element to build trust, which is essential for success. Transparency, honesty, integrity and sincerity are the virtues communicated along with the subject matter, through openness in communication.

Above all, Engineers have to understand their roles and responsibilities very clearly and perform them as a professionally and socially mature adult.

1.5 Need for Value Education in Engineering Curriculum

Even though engineering education attracts best brains and they have desire to solve problems of society, most of them are not exposed to the social dynamics and prevailing factors which shape the society. In order to familiarize engineering students about the salient features of *sociological models* of study of society, a short note is appended as Appendix-A.

To many students, the subject of *Human Values, Moral and Ethics* (i.e. Value Education) may look very simple as compared to their Engineering subjects. They may feel that, they know what is right and wrong, what are good and bad values, etc. For example, truth, compassion, honesty, sincerity, integrity etc. are good values whereas telling lies, stealing, cheating, deceiving etc. are bad values. This shallow unstructured knowledge of values at personal level will make their behavioral responses and professional dealings very short sighted and ad-hoc. Without understanding real import, meaning and interrelationship among these values, it is difficult to have smooth sailing in the career. Further, students are not aware of relevance of human values and ethical considerations in the job-environment and business climate. They do not have knowledge of many issues related to *engineering ethics* and *professional code of conduct*. This level of limited understanding of Human Values does not integrate *Professional Behavior* with *Harmonious living conditions* in the society.

From moral and ethics point of view, there are many behavioral deficiencies among educated people, professionals and general public as well, which in turn become the sources of various problems in the society. Some of the behavioral deficiencies are listed below:

- Ignorance of professional ethics
- Lack of honesty, integrity and sincerity
- Lack of accountability, confidentiality, secrecy, etc.
- Disrespect, indifference and lack of concern
- Lack of creative aptitude and unhealthy competition
- Lack of quality on all activities
- Adulteration in material supplies

Education planners have realized these behavioral deficiencies among educated masses and general public. Accordingly, they introduced educational training on *value education* in engineering courses. Many universities in their engineering curriculum introduced a subject on Human Values, Moral Ethical Values and Professional Ethics.

1.6 Role of Engineers in Industry

The moment students enter the corporate life, they face situations involving conflict between their own conscience and judgment on moral and ethical values vis-à-vis multiple demands/ requirements of boss, employer, customers, professional code of ethics, etc. Value education enables them to apply their learning of human values and ethics to resolve priority among conflicting and competing values *vs.* their responsibilities.

Many engineers after some experience become team leaders or project managers. Their role in an industry will demand sometime to lead team of junior engineers, and also discharge some non-technical administrative

functions also. Therefore, they should have an aptitude and understanding of human behavior and motivational techniques. For example, they should:
1. Be able to judge people and their character from the point of moral ethical considerations.
2. Need to understand *value system* of any person, based on his family *back ground* and *social conditions of upbringing*. Impact of society, locality, family business, social environment, etc. play a key role on molding the basic values and behavior.
3. An engineer should have clear understanding of relative priorities of moral and ethical values, logical demarcation of their applicability and validity.
4. A professional must be strong in character while playing different roles in life. These roles demand different set of values for each role and different emphasis on hierarchy of values.

Thus, it is necessary to educate, sensitize and broaden understanding of engineers and professionals, on different roles to be played by them in future.

1.7 Value Education for holistic personality development

Everybody is borne as complete man or women with full potential of life. They already possess many of the core values with them from birth. Initial traits of love, hate, fear, anger, jealously, greed, honesty, possessive nature, etc. are visible in the children's behavior, which he/she displays time to time instinctively. The family, community, and society give additional exposure and knowledge about how to behave with others. This external knowledge of behavior makes them to regulate and moderate their innate natural behaviors based on situations. This little knowledge is ok for dealing within family and within small community level.

As child enters the school and college for education, he/she gets exposure to an entirely different social environment with children of different backgrounds and cultures. The people in general have similar initial traits by birth, but their level of sensitivity and intensity to learn values from others will be different. These traits are modulated by their family and nature of upbringing. This is the time, when some clash of values starts surfacing in behavioral responses. Further, by virtue of higher education (qualification), when the professional life of person starts and their field of operations and interactions enlarge; If not trained properly, they find themselves poorly equipped to deal with people of different disciplines, backgrounds and cultures.

In the student life, engineers are focused to excel in their academic and technical performance. But in the job situation, being part of a team, their performance is judged along with the team performance. Here technical knowledge alone is not sufficient. They have to learn to deal with many people of different traits, moral and ethical values, background and temperament. Therefore, there is an urgent need to train the engineers on *Human values* and *professional ethics* during their student life. Value education is also required to prepare students, mentally and emotionally for global work culture, where people of different cultures and faiths work together.

1.8 Global Trends for Value Education in Engineering Curriculum

1.8.1 Goals of Higher Education in India

In India, university grant commission (UGC) primarily sets the *goals of education*. The national assessment and accreditation council (NAAC) an autonomous institution established by the UGC of India is responsible to assess and accredit institutions of higher education in the country. NAAC has stipulated *five core values* for higher education institutions (HEI) in India, where *Human Value Development* has been clearly identified as an important component of core values. Core values of higher education (engineering education) are given below:

a. **Contributing to national development:** That implies HEIs have a significant role in human resource development and capacity building of individuals to cater to the needs of the economy, society and the country as a whole, thereby contributing to the development of the Nation.

b. **Fostering global competencies among students:** It implies HEIs role in skill development of students, on par with their counterparts elsewhere i.e., meeting the demand for internationally acceptable standards in higher education.

c. **Inculcating a value system among students:** It implies that technical skill development is crucial to the success of students in the job market, but these skills are of less value in the absence of appropriate *Human Value Systems*. HEIs, through proper curriculum redesign, have to inculcate desirable value systems amongst the students.

In a country like India, with cultural pluralities and diversities, it is essential that students imbibe appropriate values commensurate with social, cultural, economic and environmental realities, of the local, national and universal levels.

d. **Quest for excellence:** Thus, role of technical education system implies generation of technical man power with appropriate human values and creative skills.

1.8.2 Goals of Higher Education in USA

ABET (Accreditation Board for Engineering and Technology, Inc.), is the recognized United States of America (USA) accreditor of college and university programs in applied science, computing, engineering, and technology. ABET wants these institutions to have clearly stated *Program Educational objectives* where *Students Outcomes* stipulate what students are expected to know and be able to do by the time of graduation. These are related to the skills, knowledge, and behavior that students acquire as they progress through the program.

Some of the *student outcomes* are very relevant for engineer's education which students must acquire during their education along with their *technical excellence* in the field chosen. These are:

a. An ability to design a system, component, or process to meet desired needs within realistic constraints such as economic, environmental, social, political, ethical, health and safety, manufacturability, and sustainability.
b. An ability to function on multidisciplinary teams.
c. An understanding of professional and ethical responsibility.
d. The broad education necessary to understand the impact of engineering solutions in a global, economic, environmental, and societal context.

It is clear from the above that a student must develop good understanding of human behavior; realistic constraints in their projects and jobs; understanding of ethical, health and safety requirements; impact of economic, environmental, social and political considerations on manufacturability, and sustainability. These objectives require study of human values and ethics applicable to various work situations, societies and organizations throughout the Globe.

1.9 Value Education for building National Character

Science and engineering are having *global character*. They are same throughout the globe. A world, in spite of overdose of cultural-conflicts appears inescapably driven to become a single global entity from the technology point of view. The role played by the science and engineering in developing a common global culture is attributed to the fact that, the fundamental scientific knowledge does not depend on the ethnic, political or religious backgrounds. Rather, scientific thinking is a process through which curiosity liberates us from the chain of various myths and prejudices prevailing in the society. It has shown the ability to transcend historical limitations. Knowledge leads to awareness, which in turn leads to reasonable actions.

However, Science and Engineering could not foster the same global character to human, moral and ethical values throughout the world. Even though there is global trend of modernization in all sections of life, there is perceptible gap in development of national character in many developing countries among professionals, general public and political system. One reason for this state of affairs is normally quoted as cultural diversity, multiple languages, religions, castes, etc. which are responsible for nurturing dominance to regional character among people. This regional emphasis in character, most of the time leads to various types of conflicts in public life and retarding the progressive policies of federal government. Poor national character among most of the educated people points towards defective education policy, which so far has focused on technical development, but ignoring character building among students through proper value education.

The main cause of this national malady has been traced to education system, and recently 'Education of Human Values and Ethics' has been introduced in many technical universities as part of their education policy. The Curriculum of Engineering Education is being modified accordingly to accommodate subject on Human values, Moral and Ethics.

1.10 Value Education must blend with core Cultural Values

In ancient times, sense of values in personal, family and social life, was very profound which made great cultures throughout the world. For example, since ancient times, Indian culture judged the greatness of a *state* by the degree of righteousness and justice practiced in its public administration; private lives of its citizens and not by the size of its empire or the wealth. The timeless teaching of Indian sages and masters was that true progress of any man should be judged by moral and spiritual standards of the society as per dharma, and not by material or physical standards. The social status of citizens was according to their character, virtues and the level of learning and not according to their power or wealth.

So far, the focus of technical education has been on developing students with excellence in different fields of studies without any exposure on Human Values and Ethics. Now it has been recognized that moral and ethical development of students, including cultural understanding can galvanize the national character among them, which can arrest degradation in moral and ethical values in public life.

It is now acknowledged all over the world that value-based education is the only instrument for transmuting national talent into national progress. Educational training only can correct existing deficiencies of professional behavior and commitment of educated people towards society as responsible citizens.

Therefore, students must introspect and understand themselves, their goals of life, inner nature, their strengths and weakness, etc. in the light of core cultural values. Culture helps in understanding and shaping of vision of life and how to realize it. Vision largely depends on personal belief and value system; utilization of available resource of time and talent; personal efficiencies, effectiveness, interrelationship, soft skills etc.

Attitudes of a person decide the altitude of success in life. And culture plays an important role in shaping the choices in life. Right attitude facilitates choice of realizable goals; rationalizes the internal system of desires, values, motives, temperament, behavior etc. and also establishes balance with the values, norms and expectations of the society; where they live, work and interact as professionals.

Whether the emphasis is on INDIVIDUAL or SOCIETY, one has to develop understanding of cultural impact on behavior pattern and character vis-à-vis control mechanism for bringing proper alignment of the value system for social equilibrium.

1.11 Value Education for balancing between inner nature with external nature

Education is a process to develop inner talent and potential of a student i.e., manifestation of his divine potential and perfection within him. Education should necessarily include training on physical, mental, emotional, spiritual and social development of the student. The problems faced by the society, in various fields of activity like social, political, economic, ecological, etc. are traceable to the lack of concern of the key people managing those functions and services; because of their lower standards of dedication, character values, moral, ethical values, etc.

Value education must inculcate harmony, in functioning of internal nature of man and external nature of mother earth, to bring balance between the two planes of human existence throughout the globe. Value Education must develop following understanding among students:
- National character
- Exposure to cultural heritage, history and ethos of the country
- Understanding of social structure, its pluralism and diversity of the country
- Understanding and maturity in dealing with emotional issues
- Sensitivity and concern about the problems of society
- Service attitude towards all, irrespective of caste, creed, language, region, religion and background of upbringing, in his professional and social work
- Display high level of moral and ethical values and character in his life style

Value education is not restricted to the classroom. The process of analyzing, self- verification and thinking over the issues/questions continues even after the class as well. Moral and ethical values must promote universality and rationality in student's thinking process. This will establish harmony in student's internal and external nature with global concern.

1.12 Summary

A person lives in three modes of life simultaneously at any time. These modes of life are personal life, social life and professional life. In these modes of life, values, beliefs and desires of an individual keep on changing with time, status and stage of life. All their actions and reactions are driven by their own concept of lifestyle, belief system and hierarchy of desires in that stage or phase of life.

During college life the students dream for a decent career and life after education. A decent life for them may mean fulfillment of desires like good health, good personality, good family life, job security, wealth, good friendship, status, freedom, power etc. For realizing all above, proper utilization of time is essential during college life.

Among students of science and mathematics background, aspiration to become an engineer is highest. A student of engineering, while choosing career normally considers prospects of job offers, advancement, security, salary, prestige, life style, personal challenge, and personal satisfaction.

On the other hand, society expects from students to bring growth, peace and social equilibrium in the society, through their future roles as a professional, an adult, a citizen, a leader, a business man, a bureaucrat, an administrator, etc. Thus, engineers have to understand very clearly their roles and responsibilities and perform them as professionally and socially mature adults.

Technology, Engineering and Modern Humanism: Modern technology and engineering are prime factors for building modern society and its supporting infrastructure. Along with success stories of technological advances, there have been some major disasters also due to human errors or failure of engineering design or some unknown causes/ factors or due to professional delinquency on the part of some individual or group of technical personals.

Many professionals are not able to visualize and relate their professional responsibility towards the society and general public at large. There are many deficiencies among professionals as well as general public, which are source of the moral and ethical problems present in the society. Some of these are like ignorance of professional ethics, lack of honesty, integrity and sincerity, lack of accountability, lack of maintenance of confidentiality and secrecy, lack of quality on all activities, adulteration in material supplies, etc.

The scientific education, without value education so far, produced professionals who were ill equipped or unconcerned and insensitive to impact of scientific development on humanity. Understanding human values and psycho-social dimension of man is focus of modern Humanism, which tries to synthesize scientific progress with human values. Engineering ethics is a result of the pursuit of modern Humanism.

Global Character of Corporate World: In student life, one has to work hard to show his excellence and academic performance. But in the Job, it is always teamwork. Value education trains students on dynamics of corporate culture and teamwork, which improves personal efficiency and effectiveness. Science and engineering have global character. They are same throughout the globe and free from any local considerations of culture, religion, faith, belief system, etc. Value education along with engineering education promotes building national character with global thinking.

Value education attempts develop student's mental frame of thinking about national character; exposure on cultural heritage and ethos of the country; understanding of social structure, its pluralism and diversity; develops sensitivity and concern about the problems of society; display high level of moral and ethical values in the student life.

Global Trend in Value Education: There are global trends for inclusion of value education in engineering curriculum. In India, UGC primarily sets the *goals of education*. NAAC has stipulated five core values for HEIs in India which clearly identify human values development as an important component of core values.

Similarly, in USA goals of Higher Education are evolved by ABET, which is the recognized U.S. accreditor of college and university programs in applied science, computing, engineering, and technology. ABET stipulated students to be trained on skills, knowledge, and behaviors like a) an ability to system designs within realistic constraints such as economic, environmental, social, political, ethical, health, safety, manufacturability, and sustainability; b) an ability to function on multidisciplinary teams; c) an understanding of professional and ethical responsibility; d) understand the impact of engineering solutions in a global, economic, environmental, and societal context.

Review questions

1. Throw light on technological revolutions and how it contributed to growth of modern Humanism?

2. What are the motivations for students to choose engineering profession?
3. What do you feel should be role of students as an engineer and adult in the society?
4. Why there is need for value education to engineers. What is their professional role in industry?
5. Justify the statement that "Science and Engineering are having Global Character".
6. Explain why there was need for fresh look on education policy. What are goals of higher education?
7. What are Goals of Human Values in Higher Education in USA?
8. Comment on that "Value Education helps to promotes Global Outlook" among engineers?

2 Social Values and Systems, Education for transforming the Society

Learning objectives

In this chapter you will learn about

- Impact of urbanization and modernization on society and its value system
- Role of engineers as agent of social change and expectations of ethical values by society
- Process of socialization, value formation and, character development of an individual
- Agencies of socialization and character formation, conflicts of social changes
- Social associations/ groups which influence value, ethics and behavior of a person
- Role of education in modernization of society and their social and cultural values

2.1 Introduction

This chapter is focused on ground realities of *societal structure* of societies in India including the prevailing *values* and *functions* vis-à-vis task of modernization of the society in line with national values and priorities. Further, salient features of process of socialization, value formation and character development of an individual are also explained. Education is the process through which existing *value-system* of the societies can be modernized and students can be trained in proper *value education* who later on becomes an *agent of social change*. The *value education* should necessarily include training on physical, mental, emotional, spiritual and social awareness of the student (Ramdass, 2010).

In order to explain clearly impact of social factors, social system and generic values, we take example of India for the purpose of elaboration of points of discussion, as it is a country with rich cultural and social diversity.

Education is specific and limited to few years but has high impact on moral and ethical values through modernization and westernization of mindset of students. Technical and professional education imparts modern scientific outlook along with professional skills whereas value education encourages cultivation of self or individuality. It leads to the enrichment of one's life or to the awakening of one's inherent potentialities. For full realization of own potential with proper balance between self and society, it is essential to understand social structure, values, ethos as well as constraints and conflicts in society.

Lifestyles of urban centers influence the process of change in rural areas. Many persons living in rural area commute to urban centers for jobs and these commuters act as *carrier of urban life styles and values* to rural areas.

Spread of liberal and democratic values made education a common quest in the modernization of societies. In the new epoch, education became an instrument of material progress also. The schools became a great socializer and diluter-if not breaker-of social barriers.

2.2   Engineers role as an Agent of Social Change

All Educated persons in general and scientists, technologist and engineers in particular are agent of social change. They have an important social role to modernize the traditions, social customs, remove biases, rationalize the norms and practices, work against superstitions and unscientific beliefs, etc. For this purpose, they must have a clear understanding of:
1. Distinction between good man, good citizen and good professional, from moral and ethical value point of view.
2. Contextual use of the term Society, which may refer to commonly used words like locality, community, business group, groupings based on caste, language, region, religion, etc.
3. Clarity in *professional ethics*, *code of conduct* and *moral values*.
4. Different roles played in life and profession by an individual and prioritization among cluster of value in each role.

2.3   Ethical Values Expected from Members of any Society

Following are expectations of society from its members, be it an individual or an organization, whenever they are engaged in any form of activity related to the society.

1. Giving of one's best service to society

The first and foremost distinguishing feature of an ethical member of the society is the spirit of service itself. It basically stipulates demonstration of seven traits:

- **Pursuit of Excellence:** For any organization excellence in its all-round operations and performance, is an important goal. Organizational goals demand that its staff members should operate ethically and work with the zeal of pursuit of excellence individually as well as collectively. Pursuit of excellence should be an essential trait of their ethical member.
- **Being Sensitive:** Sensitivity is an essential feature of ethical personality. Any member in a society or organization must be sensitive enough for the feelings, emotions and reactions of others during any transaction or dealings with them.
- **Having Integrity**: Integrity is part of ethical character of members of Society. It indicates about trustworthiness in their words and actions. Integrity demands a holistic consistency of principles and practice of ethical members towards their actions, values, methods and measures adopted by them.
- **Being Responsive:** Responsiveness is the character of positive and open-minded nature of a person towards new or other's ideas, feedbacks, suggestions, criticism and requests for help and cooperation.
- **Full of Vigor:** Any ethical person should be full of vigor and enthusiasm towards his responsibilities and duties. He/She should demonstrate energy and dynamism in his actions and operations.
- **Being Committed**: Commitment is part of positive attitude of any member for his duties and assignments and passion to complete the tasks within the time and resources available or allotted for the task.
- **Having Empathy:** The term empathy is used to describe a wide range of emotional experiences of concern about others in problem. An ethical member must have empathy to understand other's emotions, feelings and demonstrate the spirit of concern and sharing.

All the above ingredients define the expectations of society and the type of personality traits of its members. The members should maintain the highest standards of conduct and behavior.

2. Loyalty to Team Members

The second most important characteristic is loyalty towards the team members associated in the task and their self-esteem, capabilities and competence. Everyone should aim to be an inspiration and an example to others. The achievement of a team depends on harmony, discipline and involvement of all team members.

3. **Loyalty to Customers**
In marketing or delivery of services or products to society members, the third important characteristic is loyalty towards customers. It demands maximum effort to ensure that the customers are satisfied. Sensitivity towards customer's needs makes loyal customers, who help to enlarge the market share by attracting new customers, by their endorsement of the quality of the product or service received from the organization.

4. **Social Responsibility**
The last and final characteristic is social responsibility which is generally ignored by many members in the society. Various important considerations such as tangibly and social responsibility will make sense towards a successful pathway for maintaining good public relations and acceptance.

2.3.1 Becoming Ethical Person requires

- Right understanding of own *psychic nature*, *attitudes*, *motivations*, etc. i.e. their own psychological makeup or *own-self*.
- Understanding the need for balancing relationships with the own family and the society.
- Understanding the need for harmonizing life with nature and physical facilities.
- Understanding implications of the *life* and the values that are influenced by relationships with the *self, family, society* and the *nature*.

These domains of life influence the formation of value system of any person. Hence a person must be careful in terms of selecting, involving and practicing different roles in real life.

2.4 Role of Family on Personality and Character Development

Next to an individual's, families are the basic building block of a society. Family is the fundamental unit in the entire social structure throughout the globe. It is a social group typically consisting of parents and their children. Affinity, blood kinship and cohabitation are the three primary aspects of a family. A common ancestor, adoption and marriage are the basic features of a family. From children point of view, the prime functions of a family are acculturating, value orientation and development of socializing skills. However, family is primarily characterized by *relationships* and not necessarily by living under one roof or home. The members of family share goals and values and have common long-term commitments to one another.

Thus, family environment shapes the personality and character of any person to a large extent. It is the place, where one learns how family relationships work by a keen observation on every individual. This includes the relationships between parents and kids, grandparents and kids and as a whole family toward the society. The behavior, outlook, values about life, career, profession, etc. of a person directly or indirectly have the influence of family backgrounds. These parameters carry very deep imprint of a family life and childhood upbringing. Whatever one learns from the family, it becomes the value system and forms the basis for his perceptions and actions when they grow in social life. It is the family that gives *identity* to an individual. For an individual, the importance of family is incalculable.

Many psychologists reported and believe that the influence of family, their behavior and how they treat a child will have a serious impact on the personality of a person for throughout the lifetime. Usually children are physically and emotionally closer to their parents and their siblings as compared to any other outside person. Parents behavior and nature of treatment and relationship with their kids is actually most important deciding factor of what those kids will be like as human beings when they grow up. Apart from that, role of siblings, cousins and different relatives also shape kids outlook on the value and context of relationships within the family.

2.4.1 Child Socialization

Children use the language and distinguish between themselves and others; they embark upon a process of self-evaluation. The youngster patterns himself on the *generalized other* that is his perception of the collective self. But they do not merely imitate others and their own sense of *Self*, which develops in due course of time and attains own *Individuality*. Often the individual's aspirations do not coincide with the social ethos. This sometimes leads to mental conflicts and can become the cause of social deviance.

2.4.2 Adult Socialization

Gradually when children grow up to adulthood, they go to jobs, make family, find good friends, and colleagues to exchange and learn from each other's life and experiences. Although with time there is bound to be change in complexion of these relationships and experiences but the impact and importance of family remains deeply ingrained there. The children who have a sound family background and strong family ties are almost always happier. Their values about life and society are stable and possess strong character.

An adult plays various roles in different social groups or situations:

a. Adult socialization involves the learning from different role to be played by them and performances expected in these new roles.
   b. Adult socialization does not begin from scratch and it involves the unlearning of existing ways of behaviors and learning of new behaviors; and
   c. Adult socialization tends to take place in an impersonal atmosphere.

Factories, offices, trade unions, voluntary associations, etc. are among the many agencies which impart adult socialization.

2.5 Conflicts during Social Change

Conflicts may arise because of the possibility of clash between the emotional orientation of a family and the rational orientation at the factory/ organization or place of work.

Conflict and Process: Conflict is one of the most important sources of social change.

- **Individual *vs.* Group conflicts**

This refers to incompatibilities between personalities and social institutions. Frequently conflicts are seen between the doctors and patients, teachers and students, bureaucrats and citizens, etc.

- **Conflicts without social change**

Conflict is inherent in all societies, but this may not eventually lead to change. For instance, both the European Feudal system and the Indian caste system contained strong elements of conflict within them and yet the system continued intact for centuries as they also contained mechanism for systemic absorption, resolution and/ or suppression of conflicts.

2.6 Socialization Agencies, Process, Pattern and Character Formation

The term *socialization* means the process of social interactions and networking, whereby the individuals internalize the prevailing values, norms, traditions of the society and tailor their own behavior as per the social expectations of others. Socialization is a lifelong process. The child who grows up within the family or neighborhood continues to socialize himself during adolescence or adulthood. Socialization is both informal and formal. We should not assume that socialization is always successful. There are divergent patterns which occur in the course of socialization. Some variation is always accepted by society, but if the departure of the individual is too marked it may be called *deviance* against which society metes out sanctions.

2.6.1 Family as socialization unit

Family is the basic unit of primary socialization of kids. In most human societies, the family assumes the responsibility for the care and training of the young ones. They are guided in moral conduct, and socially needed skills. They are exposed to sentimental content and impulses of human behavior. For children growing up within the family, socialization is not devoid of variations. In Asian societies boys are trained differently from girls. Family provides exposure to both, authoritarian (parent-child) and equalitarian (siblings) types of socialization. In extended family (joint-family), other than parents close relatives also contribute to the child's socialization. By contrast, in a nuclear or unitary family, it is mostly the parents who are responsible for it.

2.6.2 Socialization with Peer Group

Peer group consists of an individual's equals in terms of age and status. In peer groups, there are no hierarchical considerations and, all are treated equal. In those societies, where normally both the parents are employees and work outside the home, the peer groups provide substitute for warm and personal relationships for proper development of the adolescent.

2.6.3 Socialization in Schools and Academic Institutions

In modern society, most of the children spend some years in schools, colleges, hostels, camps, etc. The pattern of socialization in a school is more rationalistic. Schools and colleges train youngsters in humanities, sciences, technical education, etc. so that they can take up responsible positions in society.

2.7 Various terms used to indicate Values and Character

Values: The values in general come into the category of higher order norms, which preserve the different methods to be followed by an individual to fulfill the goals. Various courses of actions will get approved or rejected to provide a standard method to make a choice or alternatives. Based on these standard defined values, different actions will be judged. They deal with what is or what ought to be more appropriate in reaching the goals by defining the imperatives. They differ and diversify based on societies which leads to contradictions or conflicts.
Norms: Social behavior is governed by social norms, which are based on values. Values and norms are closely interconnected. Norms regulate the behavior of individuals and groups in various ways. The normative structure includes the *Folkways, Mores, Laws, Etiquette, Fads*, etc.

Customs: It is a broad term for Folkways and Mores. It connotes long established usage and refers to practices that have been followed for generations' altogether. Customs refer to the totality of behavioral patterns and are embedded in the collective psyche of people. Customs are the basis of rights and duties, as envisaged in Law and are also the *foundation of ethics* in society. However, customs do undergo change with time and generations.

Mores: The term mores has been coined to designate those norms which are of great significance and are considered crucial for the well-being of society. Their violation leads to strong social disapproval, while conformity to them brings social approval. Their observance is morally right and their violation is morally wrong.

Mores and law: When mores are institutionalized by a legal agency, they take the shape of law. But not all mores are transformed into laws. In earlier days, small scale societies, folkways and mores were sufficient to regulate the conduct of members. With the growth of large scale and complex societies there arose the need for the formal apparatus, which would regulate the conduct of people in accordance with mores.

In India, the legal text known as *dharma shastra* is written by law-givers. Traditionally, the laws have been based on customs, folkways and mores to a smaller or greater extent. But the modern law is more conscious, more rational and it is backed up by courts, police and other enforcement agencies. It may be stated here that the laws which are not supported by "folkways and mores" do not have much chance of enforcement generally.

Etiquettes: This term means *good manners and* it serves as a symbol of one's status in society. Etiquette informs the numerous ways in which an individual interacts with others. Of course, etiquette of one era looks outdated in another era.

Fashion: The term fashion refers to the novelty of dress, appearance or acquisition of goods (bikes, cars, etc.). Fashion is unstable and undergoes rapid changes with generations and cultures. Usually fashion starts in cultured or refined society and tickles down to others.

Fads: Fads are styles or preferences cultivated by small groups of teenagers or friends. The fads may range from preferences for music to eccentric food styles. Fads may also express the protest of some groups of people, especially youngsters, who dislike social conventions.

2.7.1 Value education for development of integrated view of national, global and nature's universal order

Evolution of universe is having an inherent built in order and cyclic nature of operation i.e. its evolution; sustenance and devolution are dynamic and stable. Value education blends scientific progress on material plane with modern Humanism on spiritual plane and brings balance between the two

planes of human existence. When translated in concrete actions, value education prepares students to:
- Invoke nationalistic feelings among the students
- Understand national and cultural ethos of the country
- Develop global understanding of pluralism and diversity
- Induce emotional balance and positive attitude
- Create awareness and concern about the problems around
- Develop attitude of selfless service, high moral ethical character and leadership qualities
- Develop human concern and imbibe high level of honesty, integrity and sincerity in the *professional conduct.*

2.8 Type of societal groupings of people which affect values, ethics and behavior of person

To understand spectrum of *values and ethics* prevailing among human beings, first it is essential to understand how the web of human beings are organized or structured as working social units or groupings. Background information on evolution of society and development of various types of social units/ groupings in India is furnished in Appendix B. Expectations on adherence to values and ethics of social units or groupings from its members will differ in content, depth and texture from each other. Further an individual may be a member of many social units simultaneously which sometimes may create conflicts of values and ethics between his roles in these units.

Social evolution can explain some of the major differences between societies. Each society inherits some of its cultural traditions and values and adds some new elements based on contemporary needs. Evolution of societies starts from *horticultural societies*. At present human grouping are organized in following type of societies:

1. **Agrarian society**: These societies are characterized by their settlement in agricultural fields and in these societies the dynastic rule is predominant.
2. **Industrial society**: When man started harnessing inanimate energy, the transition took place from agriculture to industrial production. Industrial societies are characterized by the democratic or socialist pattern of polity. India is in the path of industrialization and counted as a developed nation.
3. **Society *vs.* nation-state and its value orientation**: As societies become more complex in the social organization, a more distinct political structure emerges and the evolution of more complex forms like political institutionalization takes place. Nation-state of Egypt, Babylonia, India, Greece and Rome left their imprint on human history as distinct political entities.

4. **Community:** The term community can be defined as a body of people inhabiting usually the same locality and having identity of character, some joint ownership of property, some degree of political organization (e.g. among the tribes), and a sense of fellowship. Community has a more limited self-sufficiency than society. In an ethnic sense, communities emerge through the biological basis of reproduction and social basis of kinship, clan, etc.
5. **Institutions and associations as groups:** A group is different from society. Groups are collections of human beings existing within society, whereas society is a system of social relationship. Institutions and associations are groupings of people with more concrete structure, rules, regulations, code of conduct and membership criteria.
6. **Formal organizations and bureaucracy:** The term refers to the social unit which makes optimum use of men and materials to attain its goal. It often goes under the name bureaucracy. It has entered into all aspects of modern life. The military, police, administration, medical care, education, etc. are all organized. Organizations are based upon rational-legal principles.

2.9 Social control of values and norms in society

Social control refers to the arrangements by which the values and norms are communicated and instilled among society members. The agencies of social control are both informal and formal and include customs, folkways, mores, public opinion, education, law, religion, morals, etc.

The objective of social control is to realize the social equilibrium which is vital for the continuation of social structure. In preliterate societies the customs, taboos, etc., used to control divergence. In larger societies social control seeks to ensure conformity of individuals and groups with society by adopting explicit and objective methods.

In complex societies religion and morals, notion of *guilt* or *sin* have been powerful instruments of conformity. In the East, on a broad level, notion of conformity to the *cosmic order*, etc. have all guided the behavior of individuals and groups.

2.9.1 Status of Civic and Personal Morality in India

In India, the Legal and *Administrative Steps* taken so far to improve ethical norms in the *Executive*, the *Legislature* and the *Judiciary* are felt to be inadequate. It is very important to improve the ethical norms as the nation needs to face international society in an effective manner. Hence it demands a purposeful and result oriented approach. Aristotle, a great philosopher truly pointed that "... *moral virtue in humans does not emanate from nature and need to be imbibed by habit*". It is felt necessary to cultivate good habits of moral and ethical behavior among general public, individually and collectively, which are being neglected at every stage, i.e., at home, schools, college, public domains, etc. The urgency of change, in public behavior towards conformance to national ethos and values is expressed by many social activists.

Value education is not a matter of cultural options or selective virtue; and the records show that prosperous nations have achieved greatness through high level of work discipline, honesty, sincerity and moral integrity prevailing among their citizens.

In the context of Morality in public life, philosopher Bertrand Russell amongst others, sought to respond to the resulting dilemma: *Without civic morality*, he said, *communities perish, without personal morality their survival is of no value.* Therefore, civic and personal moralities are equally necessary to a good world. There is a need to distinguish between the *Authority of Custom* and the *Authority of Law*.

2.10 Education as a primary instrument of modernization of society

Education is often viewed as an important source of social change. In all human societies education is the cornerstone, which along with socialization marks the emergence of the young people into adulthood. Education is as much an instrument of *system stability* as it is an *agent of change*. Education to a large extent is a continuation of the socialization process started in the family, geared to the formation of conformist adult through inculcation of the primary set of *values and norms*. Socialization imparts values and beliefs. It develops inherited skills of the young people and prepares them gradually to assume adult responsibilities. Education thus becomes the transmission belt of traditions, to maintain the status quo; at the same time, the process of education contains in itself seeds of social change on two counts, viz.:

1. It emphasized certain values such as rationality, scientific spirit, questioning mentality, etc. Even though these values are effectively indoctrinated, but the new generation tends to question the existing values, pattern and the prevalent arrangements and institutions, thus creating tensions and conflicts eventually leading to change.
2. As the spread of education increases and it reaches to a large proportion of population, it becomes a major source of social mobility and consequently of change. However, the changes that are visualized or possible through education are usually the change in the *system* and not *of the system*.

The current system of education in India is lacking on emphasis on value education. Education without a course component of human values and professional ethics produces professionals and intellectuals who are not equipped with mental frame to fight with all the negative factors enumerated above. Value education can bring an improvement in behavior of professionals and general public.

2.10.1 Social factors and process of social changes

All societies adapt changes over a period of time. However, the rate of adaptation differs from society to society and within same society at two different points of time.

Social change refers to the changes in the social factors like structure and functioning of institutions such as family, property and education level in the society. It also refers to the changes in the *role relationship* between persons, persons and groups and between groups. Human conduct is regulated by institutions which allocate roles and resources; therefore, social changes also include the principles of resource allocations. The leading factors causing social change are

- Education, industrialization and urbanization of societies and their institutions.
- Cultural interaction, planning, legislation and, synergy among population, communities and institutions.
- Methods of resolution of conflict and protest by persons, public and institutions.

Cultural interaction: With globalization, Indian society and its culture got influenced by capitalist democratic countries as well as socialist countries. The impact of westernization, modernization, secularization and life styles of western countries or societies has taken deep roots in urban population of India.

Further, India being a socio-culturally plural society; having multiplicity of religions, languages, caste systems, regional, tribal groups, etc. having their own sub-cultures; required cultural interactions among them for desired social change. Brief details of major religions of India are furnished in Appendix C.

Planning: After Independence *planning process* initiated by Govt. of India, was one of the most important sources of social change. Objectives of planning process were building infrastructures and institutions for modernization of India as a developed nation. However, the planning process has not given some of the desired social changes. For example, in India benefits of planning have not reached to the weaker sections of society. Thus, the goal of socialistic pattern of society is not achieved due to defects in *distributive justice*. Planning has gone in favor of the vested interests and helped to perpetuate the status quo. The concentration of economic power has increased in the corporate sector, the assets of bigger companies have increased substantially and the disparity between urban and rural sectors has increased to further disadvantage of the rural population.

Legislation: Legislative power is an important instrument of change for the *state* or the *nation*.

2.11 Impact of Education System, Industrialization and Globalization on social and cultural values

Foundation of modern education system in India was laid during the British colonial rule; which introduced western education with sole objective to prepare local administrators, engineers, clerks, etc. to help them govern India. British system of education was devoid of promotion of studies on the subjects where India had rich heritage and reservoir of knowledge. Focus on moral education was missing altogether and this lapse continued even after the independence. After independence industrialization of India was national priority and education system was oriented towards that end.

Industrial-urbanization has brought substantial social changes in the contemporary world. The focus was shifted to high level technology, mass communication systems and means-end relationship that characterized contemporary world in the west. India pursued the path of Industrialization adopted by developed nations and introduction of modern technology has substantially altered the texture of Indian society. A change in one aspect of society spreads and influences other functional aspects too. However, changes in material dimension are faster than cultural values and life. There is time lag in shift of *cultural-value system*.

Establishment of modern industrial centers in India created employment opportunities, which led to large scale migration of people to these centers. Thus, persons and groups with a variety of socio-cultural background migrated to towns and cities. This migration led to separation between parents and children, siblings, even spouses; thereby affecting the nature of family relations. These changes impacted cultural values, classified as *traits, complexes*, and *patterns*. Students must be familiarized with many ways of propagation of cultural values through interaction between individuals and groups. With this purpose a brief note on theoretical background of *Social Process of Cultural Interactions* is furnished as Appendix D

Industrialization and socialization are an ongoing process. Important agencies or sources of socialization are educational institutions, job market, professional networks, communication media and facilities like smart phones, Internet, social networks, TV, radio, movies, mass media, etc.

These agents of socialization themselves sometimes sow seeds of conflicts in the minds of people, eventually preparing the ground for change.

Modern education emphasizes on value of rationality, critical ability and the questioning mentality among students. This gives rise to conflicts of values between the generations, which is a worldwide phenomenon. Thus, we come across inter-generational conflict between the students, youths and the elders. Such conflicts are seen in the educational system also i.e. between student and teacher or parents and management.

Further, the decline of religion in industrial societies brought up secular view of life. Western culture has deeply impacted on Indian life style, social values and the culture. A common and genuine fear of cultural degradation of moral and ethical values is visible due to the rampant westernization amongst Indians. Western culture, lifestyle and thoughts are slowly taking roots across the urban population in India, for example western goods, dresses, foods, etc. are becoming popular among Indian youths.

At the same time, Indian traditional dresses, cultural festivals, art, music, dance and Indian cuisine food, spices, etc. are also gradually spreading their wings in western world. Indians in other countries throughout the world are culturing Indian traditions. Indian foods, dresses, some of Indian festivals and traditional arts, etc. are becoming popular in the west.

2.12 What is Modernization of society?

Modernization symbolizes adaptation of scientific approach to solve problems of life, logical and rational thinking and cultured and civilized behavior. Modernization assumes that any society, while preserving its core cultural values, tries to innovate and utilize new knowledge, patterns, techniques and resources for betterment of civic life. Modernization also assumes betterment of many aspects of civic life, such as standards of living style, working culture, behavioral ethics (values, morals and principles), application of technology, methods of education system, nature of inter and intra relationships and so on. Modernization does not mean westernization. Each culture has its own merits and requires refining and redefining its human and social values and practices to weed out obsolescence in society.

A society is called modernized when modernization enters into all aspects societal life of people i.e. living style, thinking pattern, behavioral attitudes and relationships with society, social infrastructure and its amenities/ institutions. Modernization leads to better utilization of the manpower, resources and techniques. Technology with global reach and networking has penetrated in all facets of civic life, industry, education, transport, communication, personal comforts, life styles, etc.

Modernization has refined attitudes and thinking of people. It provided new outlook for values, cultural diversity and working principles to raise the standards of life. Modernization also implies society to adapt global character in its cultural and human values so that its members can integrate and develop healthy relationships with other societies and countries.

2.13 Need for Indian society to Modernize but not Westernize

Westernization means adoption of the western life styles, cultural ways, thinking pattern, working, organizing, and approach in handling various live situations including the behavioral pattern. Westernization is amounting to aping west at the cost and disregard of our own culture. In urban India there is craze for western life style and value system. Therefore, majority of families, individuals and youth are showing a keen interest in western life styles (dressing, outings, partying, housing, etc.) and attitudes (professionalism and individualism).

Any society must give full respect to its own culture and civilization first. Indian society needs to become more modern in terms of its own values, resources and opportunities. It is logical to make the society modern and then move towards any new adoption.

2.14 Shift from Traditional Values, Norms and Societal Standards in modern India

New norms and societal standards keep on evolving with changes in social thinking. Modern values in society emphasize the equality of sexes. This requires men to appropriately redefine their values because few women will show subservience to their spouses. For example, compared to earlier times, presently the concept of premarital chastity is obsolete for women today, as they are more educated, share the family burden and wait at least for a decade to get married after attaining puberty. Now they also enjoy greater freedom and autonomy in decision making. The men need to redefine his house hold values otherwise this may lead to tension and conflicts, more estranged spouses, broken homes and inadequately socialized and mentally ill children.

Further, democracy as a way of life has injected the desire for participation in the decision-making process, is yet another consequence of social change. Today all sections of the community want their participation in decision making on matters that is affecting them. For example, today the students demand participation in the governance of universities and also want to be a part of evaluation of their own performances. This was glimpse of changes in values and perception of society which gives rise to a number of social problems created by the very process of change.

2.15 Basic difference of Eastern and Western approach to deal with Human weaknesses

Human being throughout the world, whether in western or eastern countries has many common weaknesses at personal and social level. Violence, drugs, prostitution, gambling, smoking, smuggling, excessive drinking of liquors, gun culture, rapes, cheating, poor quality products and services etc. are examples of common problems to all societies. These weaknesses prevail in the society due to poor character and aberration on moral and ethical front of some people.

There is not much difference between East and West on their lookout on contemporary values of human life. Strengths and weaknesses of human beings in both cultures are also mostly same. They differ on the approach and mindset to deal with these weaknesses. Western Culture is mostly very tolerant to human weaknesses and tries to accept it at social level. There is lot of scope for study on human weaknesses and trend is to find solutions for them, rather than curb them out right through punitive measures. Such approach many times gives rise to profitable business opportunities also when the solutions in terms of products and services are commercialized. But these solutions try to cure the symptoms of problem on surface level without attempting to cure the root causes.

Eastern culture shows intolerance to basic human weakness and adopts the method of social condemnation with little tolerance to deviation from established norms or practices. It does not focus to find solutions to weaknesses and does not support sympathetic approach to them. It rather tries to curb it at the first stance and works to remove it from the root.

Western approach is infectious to society as the empire of human weaknesses slowly grows beyond control. West is suffering from human weaknesses and East is tempted to see meaning of life in those weaknesses under the garb of freedom.

2.15.1 Negative impact of Western Culture on Eastern Life

- Pollution of social and personal values
- Changing habits, food, attire and living style
- Breaking joint family system
- Promoting individualization
- Inducing liquor and drug habits
- Promoting pubs and club culture

2.15.2 Positive Impact of Western Culture

- Western culture is breaking inhibitions in eastern society
- It is helping in promoting communication skills

- Bringing openness, people are becoming frank
- Inducting scientific outlook
- Promoting health and hygiene
- Modernizing infrastructure, Industry, Governance
- Changing work culture
- Focus on human resource development
- Inducting higher education, technology like automation, ICT, etc.

2.16 Summary

With urbanization, modernization and westernization of society, wants and demands of people; particularly students and younger generation, have increased by leaps and bounds. The wants and demands also multiply in overall urban and rural areas, and urban centers push the thrust of change in rural areas.

Socialization and Social Responsibility: All educated persons in general and scientists, technologist and engineers in particular, have an important social role to modernize the traditions, social customs, remove biases, rationalize norms and practices and work against superstitions, unscientific beliefs etc. Society also expects certain *ethical behavior and moral values* to be practiced by them in their professional roles. Social responsibility implies need for balancing relationship of Self with family and society i.e. understanding of harmonizing life with nature and physical facilities. Socialization is a lifelong process.

Family environment shapes, to a large extent, personality and character of any person. The term *socialization* means the process whereby the individual internalizes the values, norms, traditions of society and shapes his own behavior in accordance with the social expectations of others. It takes place at various levels like family as socialization unit, socialization with peer group and socialization in schools and academic institutions.

Adult's socialization is the process where adults play various roles in different social groupings or situation like factories, offices, trade unions, voluntary associations, etc. Conflict may arise in socialization process because of the possibility of clash between the emotional orientation of a family and the rational orientation at the factory/organization or place of work.

There are various terms used to indicate the *values of personal, community or society*. The terms like values, norms, customs, mores, law, etiquettes, fashion, fads, etc. indicate some defined feature, practice or value. Each of these terms have different connotation with regard to ethics, values and character.

Forms of Social Units and Social Control: Term society implies organization of human grouping based on certain common characteristics. We use the terms like agrarian society, industrial society, community, institutions, associations, formal organizations, nation or state, etc. to indicate organization of human beings as a typical society. Bureaucracy is another term to address many professional groupings or organizations, like military, police, administration, medical care, education which are all organized, based upon rational-legal-principles, and are collectively called bureaucracy.

Social control refers to the arrangements by which the values and norms are communicated and instilled among society members. The agencies of social control are both informal and formal and include customs, folkways, mores, public opinion, education, law, religion, morals, etc.

Education is an important instrument of system stability and as an agent of change and prepares students gradually to assume adult responsibilities. Technical and professional education imparts modern scientific outlook along with professional skills, whereas *value education* encourages cultivation of self or individuality along with development of integrated view of national, global and nature's universal order.

Process of Social Change: India, being a socio-culturally plural society having multiplicity of religions, languages, caste systems, regional, tribal groups etc., having their own sub-cultures, requires cultural interactions among them for desired social change. Other factors to facilitate social change are planning process at government level and legislative measures. Further, Process of social changes includes interactions between India with other capitalist democratic and socialist societies or countries, which infuses values of westernization, modernization, secularization etc. in India.

Modernization assumes betterment of many aspects of civic life such as living standards, working styles, behavioral pattern (values, morals and principles) technology, education, inter and intra relationships, cultural patterns and so on.

Western culture has some adverse impact on eastern life and value system. It is polluting social and personal value system of east; Changing habits, food, attire and living style; breaking joint family system and promoting individualization; promoting pubs and club culture etc.

Western culture also has some positive impact on eastern culture. Western culture is breaking inhibitions in eastern society; it is helping in promoting communication skills; bringing openness and people are becoming frank; inducting scientific outlook; promoting health and hygiene; modernizing infrastructure, industry and governance; changing work culture; promoting human resource development; inducting automation, ICT, higher education and research culture, etc.

Review questions

1. Comment on "Engineers are Agent of Social Change".
2. What are Social Expectations from a Value based Ethical Person?
3. What are characteristic features of a Value based Ethical Person?
4. Explain role of family on basic personality and character development. Throw light on process of "Child" and "adult" Socialization.
5. What are agencies involved in socialization process and how?
6. In social context, explain different terminologies used to indicate "Values" and "Character".
7. What are types of societies or professional groupings of people which shape their Values, Ethics and Behavior?
8. What are agencies of informal and formal social control Values and Norms in society?
9. In your assessment what is status of civic and personal morality in India.
10. Education is Primary Instrument of Modernization of Society. Comment!
11. Justify that Value Education Develops 'Modern Outlook' and helps in bringing 'Social Balance'.
12. Justify that Value Education is essential to develop integrated thinking on National, Global, and Nature's universal order of life.
13. What do you understand by Modernization of Society? Distinguish it from Westernization of society.
14. Elaborate on basic characteristics of Eastern and Western Cultures and positive and negative Impact on Indian Culture.

3 Understanding Values, Morals, Ethics and Relevance to work Ethics and Behavior

Learning objectives

In this chapter you will learn about

- Understand meaning and the genesis of *values, morals, ethics* and *morality*
- Understanding scope of moral education and types of morals and ethics
- Need of integrity, confidentiality and work ethics among professionals
- Ethical and unethical behaviors
- Understanding service learning,

3.1 Genesis and meaning of values, morals and ethics

There is broad demarcation between Values, Morals and Ethics with considerable overlapping in meaning and sometimes used interchangeably. Summarily, Values are personal; Morals are more concerned with society whereas ethics are more applicable to Professions and professional life.

We give below some of the commonly understood meanings and definitions of these terms.

3.1.1 Genesis of Morals and Values

- Morals are generally taught by the society to the individual, whereas values come from within himself. Morals are related to one's religion, business or politics, whereas values are personal fundamental beliefs or principles. Morals act as a motivation for leading a good life while the values can be called as an *intuition* or the *call of the heart*.

- Morals have a greater social element as compared to values and tend to have a very broad acceptance. Morals and values are a part of the behavioral aspect of a person. A person is judged more for his moral character than the values.
- Morals are like commandments set by the elders, and to be followed by the younger people. One always treasures the morals and they refine with driven the other hand, values are not set by the society. Whatever is valuable for one person may not be valuable for the other. It is choice of inner personality.

3.1.2 What are the Values?

- Values are the inner standards of any person to judge the right or wrong, good or bad, just or unjust. They are the fundamental principles, giving guidance to a person to evaluate the merits and demerits of a thing. Values include sense of faith, patience, tolerance, integrity, responsibility, courage, respect, patriotism, honesty, compassion, and fairness, etc. All these are not mandatory by society but depend on individual's choice.
- Values are the moral imperatives of human conduct; attitudes are emotional reactions to social events. In the development of personality, values and attitudes merge together.

3.1.3 Morals or Moral Values?

- Morals are moral values, which we attribute to a system of beliefs, typically a religious system, but it could be a political system or some other set of beliefs. These moral values get their authority from something outside the individual- a higher being or higher authority (e.g. society). Many people find their moral values strongly influenced by their sense of morality- as defined by a higher authority. The moral code of the people is an indicator of their social and spiritual ways of life.
- Moral virtue in humans does not emanate from nature and need to be imbibed by habit. This habit has to be cultivated, individually and collectively.
- This is not merely a matter of cultural options or selective virtue; record shows that no nation has achieved greatness without attaining a high level of moral integrity in personal and social conduct.
- New norms and standards keep on evolving with changes in social situations. We cannot apply the traditional measuring rod of morality to the changed conditions. There is a need to refine our perception of morals in changed conditions.

- Upholding the rule of law is an essential requirement of the *public morality* in a modern democracy. John Locke's dictum *"...wherever law ends tyranny begins"* has universal validity.

3.1.4 What is Ethics?

- Ethics is a study of moral issues in the field of *individual* and *collective* interactions in professional life. The term is also sometimes used more generally, to describe issues in arts and sciences, religious beliefs and cultural priorities. The professional fields of engineering, medicine, trading, business, accountancy, law etc. deal with ethical issues in their professional conduct.
- Ethics are defined in the Oxford English Dictionary as the *science of morals, moral principles or code*. Ethics are considered the *moral standards* by which people judge behavior. Ethics are often summed up in what is considered the *golden rule*- do unto others as you would have them do unto you. The ethics are defined on societal basis. Defining what is ethical is not an individual exercise.
- In multicultural societies like India, where there is not a monolithic belief system, there can be very wide differences in opinion in society as to whether a given action is ethical (or moral) or not. Such differences are clearly visible in respect to marriage, status of women, type of education for children, religious edicts *vs.* constitutional provisions etc. The cultural obligation to look after one's family outweighs other concerns.
- Applied ethics is the branch of ethics which consists of the analysis of specific, controversial moral issues such as abortion, animal rights, euthanasia, infanticide, animal rights, environmental concerns, homosexuality, capital punishment, or nuclear war etc. In recent years issues of applied ethics have been subdivided into convenient groups such as medical ethics, business ethics, environmental ethics, sexual ethics etc.
- Ethics are not static propositions but are constantly in a state of dynamic flux. The older cultural stranglehold in a given society does not want to loosen easily its grip on their ethical principles. However, there evolves a progressive subset of voices, simultaneously pointing towards the dawn of new culture and morality.

What is not ethics?
- Ethics is not just following the law.
- Ethics is not religion, though most religions do advocate high ethical standards.
- Ethics is not following culturally accepted norms.

- Ethics is not science though social and natural science can provide an important tool to enable in better ethical choices.

3.1.5 Morality

Above definitions and descriptions of moral, values and ethics give fair idea of their genesis, need and scope of field of applications. However, in real life situations, most of the people are guided by conventional understanding of these terms. Generally, what morally correct is not always ethically correct also. Morals or the expression, *moral values* are generally associated with a personal view on societal values. They can reflect the influence of religion, culture, family and friends. These concepts and beliefs about right and wrong are often generalized and codified by a culture or group, and thus serve to regulate the behavior of its members. Conformity to such codification is called *morality*, and the group may depend, on widespread conformity to such codes, for its continued existence.

- **Common morality**

Common morality is the set of moral beliefs shared by almost everyone. It is the basis, or at least the reference point, for the other type of morality. When we think of ethics or common morality, we usually think of such precepts, for example it is wrong to murder, lie, cheat or steal, break promises, harm others physically, and so forth. It would be very difficult for us to question seriously any of these precepts.

Three characteristics of the common morality are mentioned here.

1. Many of the precepts of the common morality are negative. According to some moralists, the common morality is designed primarily to protect individuals from various types of violations or invasions of their personhood by others
2. Although the common morality, which one may call the *ground floor,* is primarily negative, it does contain a positive or aspirational component in such precepts as "prevent killing," "prevent deceit," "prevent cheating," and so forth. However, it might also include even more clearly positive precepts, such as *help the needy*, *promote human happiness* and *protect the natural environment,* etc. This distinction between the positive and negative aspects of common morality is important to further understand professional ethics.
3. Common morality makes a distinction between an evaluation of a person's actions, and an evaluation of his intentions. Evaluation of action is based on application of the type of moral precepts we have been considering so far, but an evaluation of the person himself is based on intentions. This distinction can be explained by examples from law, where also this distinction prevails.

For example, if a driver kills a pedestrian in his automobile accidentally, he/she may be charged with manslaughter (or nothing but not murder). Even though the pedestrian is dead as if murdered, but the driver's intention was not to kill him, and the law treats the driver differently, as long as he/she was not reckless. The result is the same, but the intent is different. To take another example, if you convey false information to another person with the intent to deceive, you are lying. If you convey the same false information because you do not know any better, you are not lying and not usually as morally culpable. Again, the result is the same (the person is misled), but the intent is different.

- **Personal morality**

Personal Ethics or Personal Morality is the set of *Moral Beliefs* that a person holds. For most of the persons, their *Personal Moral Beliefs* closely parallel the precepts of Common Morality. They believe that murder, lying, cheating, and stealing are wrong. However, their Personal Moral Beliefs may differ from Common Morality in some areas, especially where Common Morality seems to be unclear or in a state of change. For example, we may oppose stem cell research, even though common morality may not be clear on the issue (Common morality may be unclear at least partially because the issue did not arise until scientific advancement made stem cell research possible and ordinary people have yet to identify decisive arguments). A systematic study of morality is a branch of philosophy called Ethics.

3.2 Scope and Field of Moral Theories

Moral Education is more critical study of morals, ethics, and interrelationships along with overlap of their field of applications. Morality has three principal meanings.

3.2.1 Descriptive Ethics

In its *descriptive* sense, morality refers to personal or cultural values, codes of conduct or social mores that distinguish between right and wrong in the human society. Describing morality in this way is not making a claim about what is objectively right or wrong, but only referring to what is considered right or wrong by people. Mostly right and wrong acts are classified as such because they are thought to cause benefit or harm, but it is possible that many such moral beliefs are based on prejudice, ignorance or even hatred. In this sense of term, ethics is addressed as *descriptive ethics*.

3.2.2 Normative Ethics

In its *normative* sense, morality refers directly to what is right and wrong, regardless of what people think. It could be defined as the conduct of the ideal *moral* person in a certain situation. This usage of the term is characterized by *definitive* statements such as '*...that act is immoral*' rather than descriptive ones such as '*... Many believe that act is immoral*'. It is often challenged by a *moral skepticism*, where the unchanging existence of a rigid, universal, objective moral *truth* is rejected, but supported by *moral realism*, in which the existence of this *truth* is accepted. This type of normative usage of the term *morality* is also addressed as *normative ethics*.

3.2.3 Morality as synonymous with Ethics

Some social scientists define morality as synonymous with ethics because their field of application encompasses the above two meanings within a systematic philosophical study of the moral domain. Ethics seeks to address questions such as:
- How a moral outcome can be achieved in a specific situation (Applied Ethics)
- How moral values should be determined (Normative Ethics)
- What morals people actually abide by (Descriptive Ethics)
- What the fundamental nature of ethics or morality is, including whether it has any objective justification (Meta-Ethics)
- How moral capacity or moral agency develops and what its nature is (Moral Psychology).

3.2.4 Moral realism

Under *Moral Realism*, key issue is to look into meaning of the terms *moral* or *immoral*. Moral realism holds that there are *true moral statements* which report objective moral facts. Whereas *moral anti-realism* would hold that, morality is derived from any one of the *norms* prevalent in society (*cultural relativism*); the edicts of god (*divine command theory*); morality is merely an expression of the speakers' sentiments (*emotivism*); an implied imperative (*universal prescriptivism*); or falsely presupposes that there are objective moral facts (*error theory*).

3.2.5 Moral relativism

Some thinkers hold that there is no correct definition of right behavior, that morality can only be judged with respect to particular situations, within the standards of particular belief systems and socio-historical contexts. This position, known as *moral relativism*, often cites empirical evidence from anthropology as evidence to support its claims.

3.2.6 Moral universalism

Some have views which are opposite to Moral Relativism. Their view is that there are universal, eternal moral truths which are known as moral universalism. Moral Universalists might concede that forces of social conformity significantly shape moral decisions but deny that cultural norms and customs define morally right behavior.

3.3 Morals *vs.* Values

Morals and values are a part of the behavioral aspect of a person and both are correlated to each other. These are emotionally related for deciding right or wrong. Morals are a motivation or a key for leading a good life in right direction whereas values are good or bad, depending on the person's choice.

Morals can be related to one's religion, political system or a business society. Business morals include prompt service, excellence, quality and safety. One practices all the morals while running a business, but the values may not coincide with them. Therefore, these morals are taught by the social groups and have to be followed. Whereas values like courage, respect, patriotism, honesty, honor, compassion etc. coming from within, are not mandatory by society but depend on individual's choice.

3.4 Integrity and Confidentiality

Integrity is consistency of actions, values, methods, measures, principles, expectations and outcome. As a holistic concept, it judges the quality of a system in terms of its ability to achieve its own goals.

Integrity and confidentiality are two faces of the same coin. Integrity indicates that person is dependable as repository of confidential information of personal or professional nature. For engineers there come many instances in career when he/she confronts question of his professional integrity. "It is perfectly possible to make a decent living without compromising the integrity of the company or the individual", wrote business executive R. Holland, "Quite apart from the issues of rightness and wrongness, the fact is that ethical behavior in business serves the individual and the enterprise much better in long run", he/she added.

A person without integrity can misuse the truth not only by lying or otherwise distorting or withholding it, but also by disclosing it in inappropriate circumstances. For example, an engineer with poor integrity might be tempted to disclose confidential information of a client without his consent. Information may be confidential, if it is either given to the engineer by the client or discovered by the engineer in the process of work done for the client.

Most of the engineers are employees and come across many internal information of the company like designs, business deals, pricing policy, employees, clients, etc. which are of confidential nature. A competing company in general looks for such information, through some employees for their business intelligence. It is very common problem of industry. For engineers, even involving in the improper use of proprietary information of a former employer, is violation of integrity and confidentiality. Using designs and other proprietary information of a former employer is dishonesty and may result in litigation. Even using idea developed, while working for a former employer, can be questionable in new job, if those ideas involve trade secrets, Patents, or licensing arrangements.

For these engineers, there is an obligation to protect the confidentiality of the information of employers and clients as professional conduct of high integrity, just as with lawyers and physicians. Confidentiality would ordinarily cover both sensitive information given by the client, and information gained by the professional in the work paid for by the client.

An engineer can abuse Client-Professional-Confidentiality in two ways. First, he/she may break the confidentiality when it is not warranted. Second, he/she may refuse to break confidentiality, when the higher obligation to the public requires it. The protective privilege ends where the public interest dominates. The California court agrees with engineering codes in placing the interests of the public above those of clients or employers. The other extreme might be a case in which an engineer breaks confidentiality to promote his own financial interests. Between these two extremes are many other possible situations in which the decision on maintenance of confidentiality might be difficult.

3.4.1 How to maintain integrity?

- Stand up for your beliefs
- Follow your conscience
- Be honorable and upright
- Live by your principles no matter what others say
- Have the courage to do what is right
- Build and guard your reputation
- Don't do anything wrong
- Do not lose heart if you fail or don't get what you want

3.5 Work Ethics

Work ethic is a set of values based on hard work and diligence. An employee with good work ethics believes that it gives him some moral benefits and enhances personal character. Work ethic includes being reliable, having initiative and maintaining good social skills.

Work ethics are intrinsic and they come from within. However, one may ask if they come from within, how they germinate within? Philosophically, this may lead to various perspectives; it can be religious scriptures or religious personalities who preach various work ethics; or personalities whose life inspires us and who live a life of honesty, integrity, doing a job well, keeping things above board, and feel accountable.

Work ethics demonstrates how one feels about his job, career or vocation, and how one performs his/her job or responsibilities. This involves attitude, behavior, respect, communication, and interaction; how one gets along with others. Work ethics demonstrate many things about work culture and personality of a person. It involves such characteristics as honesty and accountability. Essentially, work ethics break down to what one does or would do in a particular situation. It involves a question about what is right and acceptable and above board, versus what is wrong.

In work ethics, it is vital that one practices honesty (not lying, cheating, and stealing), does a job well and values what he/she has done, has a sense of purpose and feeling/being a part of a greater vision or plan. Philosophically, if one does not have proper work ethics, then the person's conscience may be cluttered. People for the most part have good work ethics; they want to do the proper thing in a given situation.

There are two fundamental work ethics: *humility* and *the treatment with others*. Humility is being humble; no task is too demeaning. Humility involves attitude of service i.e. placing other peoples need before one's own and treating others with decency and respect. Workers exhibiting a good work ethic in theory (and practice) should be selected for better positions, given more responsibility and rewarded ultimately with promotion. The idea of a meritocracy is based somewhat on the work ethic. Under meritocracy, workers who possess a good work ethic (work hard and follow the rules) are to be rewarded and moved ahead and workers who do not have a good work ethics are to be counseled and not rewarded.

3.6 Working with Ethics

Many MNCs and reputed companies have adopted some guidelines to cultivate and maintain ethics in working and operations of the company. Some of such guideline are listed below:
1. A company and its employees should always believe that managing the ethics of the company is a continuous process and it is inherent like any other management function in the organization.
2. The ground of *ethics management* is relationship between working people and management. The collective behavior of all employees is the basic environment for working with the ethics. Thus, without

fair and just behavioral environment, an organization cannot make their employees follow the ethical practices.
3. The act of breaking the ethical norms/ code must be rooted out in its very initial stage, with immediate action in impersonal and consistent manner. The codes must be applicable to each and every employee without discrepancy.
4. Training programs must be conducted to educate the employee so that they develop awareness and feel that working in accordance with the ethics is as much necessary for the good health for the organization just as fresh air is necessary for human being.
5. A company may adopt different ways and methods to bring in work ethics in work life. Whether the circumstance is business or life, ethical values should be ground- rules for behavior. When we live by these values we are demonstrating that we are worthy of trust.

3.7 Ethical and Unethical behavior

Ethical behavior refers to that conduct that is beyond reproach and is in accordance to the laid down standards of a society, organization or institution.

3.7.1 Ethical behavior in the Society

This varies from place to place. The behaviors considered unethical in one society can be acceptable in another. For instance, it is unethical to have second wife for a married person in Hindu society but it is acceptable in some other societies.

3.7.2 Ethical behavior within the Workplace

This refers to the *ethical conduct* that the organizations expect their employees to hold while at work. Most organizations have formulated documents referred to as *codes of conduct* that set out the accepted behaviors within the workplace. They have set out the rules and regulations that need to be adhered to by the employees in their organization. This is mainly because of the requirement that all employees must conform to common behavior and conduct to maximize the overall performance of an organization.

3.7.3 Employee's Unethical behavior

In any organization, it is unethical of an employee to be corrupt. One is not supposed to accept or give out bribes in exchange for services or goods. An employee who engages in corruption is said to have acted in an unethical manner. Taking excessive breaks or repeated sick leave are also unethical behaviors. This should only happen when there is a serious personal need to do so. Again, taking office supplies home is extremely unethical. Office property should be kept separately from one's personal property. In some organizations, this conduct can be translated as theft.

3.7.4 Employers Unethical behavior

It is not only employees who can behave in unethical ways. Employers also have a common code of conduct and are required to act in a given manner. For instance, an employer is not supposed to use the company money for his personal expenses.

3.7.5 Ethical behavior in Academic Institutions

For students within learning institutions it is unethical behavior to cheat during examinations. Ragging is another serious unethical behavior. Ethical behavior is to be cultivated within an individual from an early age. Without strong moral convictions, one can be easily swayed to engage in contrary behaviors.

3.8 Service Learning

Service learning is a method of encouraging student learning through, development of volunteerism among them (for participation in community service); active participation in thoughtfully organized and conducted services that meet the needs of the community. *Service -learning-projects* are conducted for community service program, through involvement of students of educational institutions like elementary schools, secondary schools, institutions of higher education in the community. It helps foster civic responsibility among the students. It is integrated into the academic curriculum or the educational components of the community service program in which the participants are enrolled. It provides structured time for students or participants to acquire the community-service-experience.

Service-learning is more than just a buzzword for community service or volunteering. By participating in an environmental service learning project, students learn how they can make a difference in their future, and the future of our planet. Service-learning goes beyond what is learned in the classroom. It is a hands-on experience of students. Students gain new skills by working directly with the community. Service-learning enhances students' valuable academic skills, communication skills, team building skills and critical thinking; builds their self-esteem; and develops their sense of responsibility for decision-making. Examples of service-learning projects are like various aspects of safe solid waste management, such as recycling, composting, and reducing household hazardous waste etc.

Educational institutions, organizing service learning activities must identify a contact person (or office), who can before start of any program provide information on how to identify community need, design the project methodology and plan out funding resource. Service-learning projects are one of the best ways to make an environmental difference for people and their community.

3.8.1 Principles of Universalizability in conflicts on moral and ethical issues

In practical situations, sometimes a conflict or confusion arises on how to decide or act, when two or more moral and ethical considerations are applicable. To resolve such conflicts, one needs to follow certain principles explained below, that may provide guidance to decision making process.

There is a basic concept that is especially important to keep in mind in answering these questions. This is the idea of universalizability: Whatever is right (or wrong) in one situation is right (or wrong) in any relevantly similar situation. Although this does not by itself specify what is right or wrong, it requires us to be consistent in our thinking. Thought of universalization is good criteria but difficult to implement in many situations as many decisions of right or wrong are dependent on social, cultural and religious conditions. One can easily understand these dilemmas in family and marriage issues. However, in job situation and public services, higher degree of universalization is possible.

There are two general ways of thinking about moral issues that make use of the idea of universalizability and that attempt to provide underlying support for common morality while at the same time offering guidelines for resolving conflicts within it. The first appeals to the utilitarian ideal of maximizing good consequences and minimizing bad consequences. The second appeal to the ideal of *respect for persons*. Both these approaches can be helpful in framing much of our moral thinking about ethical issues in engineering.

3.9 Summary

There is broad demarcation between values, morals and ethics with considerable overlapping in meaning. Sometimes these terms are used interchangeably. Summarily, values are personal, Morals are more concerned with society whereas ethics are more applicable to professions and professional life.

Morals are generally taught by the society to the individual whereas values come from within. Morals are like commandments set by the elders and to be followed by the descendants. Morals are values which we attribute to a system of beliefs, typically a religious system, but it could be a political system or some other set of beliefs.

Values are the inner standards of any person to judge the right or wrong, good or bad, just or unjust. They are the fundamental principles that give guidance to a person to evaluate the merits and demerits of a thing. Values include sense of integrity, responsibility, courage, respect, patriotism, honesty, honor, compassion, respect, fairness, etc.

Ethics is a study of moral issues in the fields of individual and collective interactions in professional life. The professional fields that deal with ethical issues include engineering, medicine, trading, business, accountancy, law, etc. Ethics is not just following the law. Ethics is not religion, though most religions do advocate high ethical standards.

Integrity and Confidentiality: Integrity is consistency of actions, values, methods, measures, principles, expectations and outcome. Integrity and confidentiality are two faces of the same coin. Most of the engineers are employees and come across many internal information of the company like designs, business deals, pricing policy, employees, clients, etc. which are of confidential nature. They have an obligation to protect the confidentiality of the information of employers and clients as professional conduct of high integrity.

Work Ethics: Work ethic is a set of values based on hard work and diligence. An employee with good work ethics believes that work ethics gives some moral benefits and enhance personal character. Many MNCs and reputed companies adopt some guidelines to cultivate and maintain ethics in working life.

Service Learning: Service learning is a method of encouraging student learning and development of volunteerism among them. Service learning enhances students' valuable academic skills, including communication, team building and critical thinking; also builds their self-esteem and develops their sense of responsibility.

Review questions

1. Explain in detail what do you understand by values, morals, and ethics. elaborate on their field of applications
2. What is morality? What are types of morality?
3. What is scope of moral education? Is morality synonymous with ethics-explain?
4. Elaborate on morals *vs.* values.
5. Distinguish between integrity and confidentiality. What are their fields of application? How to maintain integrity?
6. What is work ethics? What are guidelines for working with ethics?
7. Elaborate on ethical behavior in the context of society, organization or institution. What is considered unethical behavior?

8. What are ethical considerations and general principles in various professions?

4 Ethical Values, Virtues and Character for Peaceful Happy Living

Learning objectives

In this chapter you will learn about

- Live Peacefully, Reduce Worries, Adopt Right Attitude and Change with Time
- Attributes of "Human Excellence", "Ethics of Caring" and "Global Commons"
- Moral duty towards Honesty, Value Time, Cooperation, Commitment and Empathy
- Courage, Self-Confidence, Spirituality and Character for professional success
- Civic virtues, and virtue ethics

4.1 Art of Living Peacefully

Majority of people think that talent, health, money, power, fame, etc. can bring them peace and joy. It is also observed that for many people experience inner tranquility even without much material support. Those who pursue material goals vigorously lose their inner peace. A person driven by ambition, torn between discords, is likely to develop psychic anxiety, emotional conflicts and economic in security. How can he/she live in peace? Personal unbalance of people never leads to social stability.

Peace of mind is sure to bring happiness. Social peace can come only when there is no unrest or turmoil in the individual's mind. That is why our ancestors introduced the practice of ending every meeting with the invocations of *Om Shanthi, Shanthi, Shanthi* (peace for the individual, peace for the society and peace in the world). A co-operative and fear-free world cannot be shaped by people who themselves have inner conflict, and infected with the poison of mutual suspicion and hate. Although peace and happiness are two evenly held scales, the scales stand slightly tilted in favor of peace! Happiness is a feeling of the mind. Peace is the experience of the soul.

4.1.1 Tips for reduction of worries for peaceful living

Peaceful living depends on our mental makeup, about how one relates himself with rest of the world. Any mismatch in his/her perception with realities of life in the world causes pain and worries. One can't change the world, but he can always rationalize his/her perception of the world by being more realistic rather than being an idealist. Instead of replaying the same old worries day after day, why don't we look at how to stop worrying and start living peacefully? Here are some tips for living peacefully with reduced level of worries.

1. **Check your thought pattern**: One need to first understand what makes him worried. It could be brooding over unpleasant thoughts that come to our mind. We tend to dwell, fixate, exaggerate and obsess with those thoughts. Be rational and ask yourself, "...are my worries realistic?" Through introspection and meditation practices, one can come out of these worries.
2. **Adopt Cleanliness in Physical living and Mental Thinking Habits:** Accumulation of unnecessary things and material possession around, disordered and cluttered living habits, indicate turmoiled state of mental priorities, which is root cause of worries and stress. By adopting a minimalist lifestyle, you can throw out what you don't need in order to focus on what you do need. If you start examining your thinking pattern, understand your goals and priorities, understand your resources, then it will be easy to get rid of clutters in the mind and a clear picture will evolve, resulting in peace of mind.
3. **Exercise and yoga are essential for good physical and mental health**: Have a safe place where you can relax through certain exercises like yoga, meditation, etc.
4. **Organize yourself and your time**: Make a routine of essential activities for effective use of your time; learn how to avoid those factors which disturb your peace.
5. **Have some daily physical exercise**: Exercise releases endorphins, which make the brain feel good. Exercise also reduces the body's stress hormones.
6. **Trust yourself**: Do you worry about whether you're on the right path or taken right decision? Look inside and ask your heart in silence. You can hear the small voice deep inside of you. Your inner GPS won't steer you wrong. Purity of heart is essential for getting right advice. Simply tune into your inner compass; it's guiding you in the right direction.

7. Remember these things:
   - Worrying accomplishes nothing
   - Worrying is bad for you
   - Worrying is the opposite of being peaceful
   - Worrying puts your attention in the wrong direction

4.1.2 Tips for right Attitude and Mindset for living peacefully

Living in peace is about living harmoniously with yourself, others, and all sentient beings around you. Living in peace is both an outward and an inward process. Outwardly, living in peace is a way of life in which we respect and love each other in spite of our cultural, religious and political differences. Inwardly, everybody needs to search their hearts and minds and understand the fear that causes the impulse of anger and violence. If anyone continues to ignore the discontent and rage within himself, the storm outside will never subside.

Peace without work or purposeful engagement is no peace. Peaceful living must promote human excellence to fulfill goal and mission of life. Human excellence is achieved by adopting certain attributes like:
- Honesty
- Discipline
- Will power
- Dedication
- Confidence
- Strength
- Self-control
- Compassion
- Self-reliance
- Concentration
- Knowledge
- Devotion

While one finds his/her own meaning of peaceful living, it largely depends on his/her attitude and mindset about the world around their life. Its outward manifestations will depend on their beliefs and lifestyle for being at peace. There are some basics principles for living in peace that cannot be overlooked, such as being non-violent, being tolerant, holding moderate views and celebrating wondrous-life. Here are some suggestions to help you to discover your journey to living in peace, a journey and way of life that ultimately depends on you.

1. **Give love and do not have hunger for power to control others**: Our desire, to dominate and seeking power to control and rule over other people, is the first culprit which need to be checked and controlled for living peacefully. Try to see their side of things.

Think peace before power. Power based on love is a thousand times more effective and permanent than the power gained through threat of punishment.
2. **Learn the skills of negotiation, conflict resolution and assertive communication:** These personal characteristic and skills are important. Constructive communication skills help you to avoid or effectively move through conflict with others. The clarity of the message is always vital to ensure peace, because conflict arises out of misunderstandings
3. **Moderate your convictions:** Thinking in absolutes, and holding to convictions without ever considering the viewpoints and perspectives of others, is a sure way to live a life without peace.
4. **Be tolerant:** Tolerance, in all that you think and do will, make a difference in your life and in the lives of others around you. Tolerance for others is about appreciating diversity, the plurality of modern society, and being willing to accept "live and let others live" principle of life.
5. **Be peaceful:** To be peaceful is to be able to act with compassion toward those who are violent.
6. **Reflect:** Reflection of thought is important – many times a hasty response has resulted in a tragic outcome; because time to think through all of the issues and angles has not been taken. Choose instead to respond peacefully.
7. **Learn forgiveness and not be revengeful**: Any thought or action of anger or revenge perpetuates anger, violence, and sorrow. Replace this with forgiveness to seek the way of living peacefully.
8. **Find inner peace, it depends on proper mindset:** Without inner peace, anyone will be in a constant state of conflict. Always struggling to fill your life with possessions will leave you perpetually unhappy.
9. **Learn to see positive side of things and enjoy them**: Joy brings peace in life. Habit of positive outlook, on what is good in others and the world brings peace of mind. Feel joy in watching wondrous aspects of life.
10. **Bring positive changes in your personality**: Be the change you wish to see in the others: It calls you to rise for appropriate actions from your side. Some of the proactive actions, by all individuals looking for peace in life, are given below:
    - Be positive and rationalize your outlook and attitude towards world.
    - Try to be part of the solution whenever any problem surfaces.
    - Do not be self-centered. Make sacrifices to help others

- Bring harmony to the world by championing love and peace for all
11. **Stop worrying about things beyond your control:** In family, society, and national context, there can many issues like social justice, communal harmony and economic disparities etc. which can disturb your peace. You have to insulate yourself from these issues unless you have reached to a position to change them.
12. **Broaden your understanding of peace**: You're free to choose your own path. Everything written above is suggestion to you. Finally living in peace will be your own conscious efforts.

Material prosperity has no meaning unless there is improvement in *moral standards*. The root of the troubles afflicting the human being today is unlimited selfishness bordering on greed. The seeds of war are in the hearts of the individuals. If anyone wants to reform the world, he/she should transform himself.

4.2 Motivating Employees to adopt organizational work culture

For peaceful living one should be ready to adopt changes in living and working conditions as well as structural changes coming in the family, society and industry.

One of the most debated topic and research in industry is Motivation of employees. How to motivate employees to do what an organization wants them to do, efficiently and effectively in workplace? By understanding motivational essentials, we can encourage them to be their best and do their best at work. Once the people are motivated to be successful and achieve the goal set for them, their confidence on themselves and their abilities grow, which makes them even more motivated.

When people are confident and motivated at work, it impacts positively on working ambience; and many other positive factors become operative in the working environment. For example, employees job satisfaction improves; commitment to organization increases; work environment improves; results become the focus point; better drive is created and role clarity improves; thus, promising better tapping of employee's full potential.

- **Personal Motivation**

Everybody has a desire to excel and achieve something great in his life. Being motivated to his goals means that he/she's able to raise his self-confidence; exercise self-discipline and, be realistic to what he/she can achieve; work for stretching beyond his perceived limits for reaching to set goals; and enjoy the recognition or perks associated with achieving the goals. The more one is able to achieve the more self-confident he/she becomes. Then the more self-confident one becomes, the more he/she is able to achieve. Understanding this relationship between motivation and self-confidence is important if anyone wants to be able to improve either trait in himself.

- **Personal change**

When anyone is motivated to make changes in his life, there are certain steps and phases that are common to follow. Steps required for personal change, process of change and how to set goals that will guide to success are discussed below. The general process of change (for raising motivation level) which an individual goes through is from denial phase to resistance to exploration and finally to commitment stage.

1. **Denial Stage:** The process begins with the required changes identified or suggested for betterment and improvements. One may not be ready to accept the change and surrounded by thoughts like "this isn't necessary" or "the way I have always done things" works just fine etc. In this way his focus is on the past (practices) and he/she's in denial mode. Other emotions one may experience could be, shock, discouragement, disbelief, anxiety, uncertainty etc.

2. **Resistance stage:** At this point, one may externally agree to the need for change, but internally still he/she might have resistance to change. One needs to look inside himself to what is happening there in order to successfully overcome his resistance. Some of the symptoms or behavior he/she might experience at this stage are suffering anger or stress, loss of productivity, confusion over roles or future, self-sabotage of the change, loss of commitment, lethargy etc.

3. **Exploration stage:** The next stage occurs when one begins to accept that the future will involve the change. He/ She may begin to consider what the change will actually mean to his life and life style. He/ She may begin getting some of the benefits of the change, even if he/she is not completely convinced. This is a sort of learning phase and at this stage he/she should try to focus on the good side of the change. Think what strengths the new change will bring to you? What benefits and opportunities will come from the change?

4. **Commitment for change:** In the final stage of the change process, he/she becomes committed to the change. Commitment is now the part of the environment in which he/she is operating and becoming the norm. He/ She may find that they are becoming the model for others.

4.3 Ethics of Caring

Quite often we hear the complaint from public that *nobody cares* for others. It seems obvious to know, why we should be interested in caring of people? Many times, ethics of *caring* suffer because of bureaucratic procedures and regulations. One can predict that the complaint *nobody cares* will continue to be heard unless people understand importance of *Ethics of caring*. As human being it is our natural trait that we want to *care* and be *cared* for. Caring is important in itself.

Caring is giving love and attention to people and things that matter to you. When you care about people, you help them. You do a careful job, giving your very best effort. Caring makes the world a safer place. Caring appears at first glance to be a simple, child-friendly virtue. It is often, one of the first ones that children can grasp and practice

Definition of Care Ethics: One of the most popular definitions construes care as "a species of activity that includes everything we do to maintain, contain, and repair our World, so that we can live comfortably in it, as far as possible. That world includes our bodies, ourselves, and our environment". Some other definitions are praised and widely accepted, because it admits to cultural variation and extends care beyond family and domestic spheres. There are many other definitions of *care ethics like* (Sander-Staudt, 2011).

- Care is understood as a virtue or motive
- Care ethics is a species of virtue ethics, with care as a central virtue
- Care with a kind of motivational attitude of empathy
- Care as styles of situational moral reasoning that involves listening and responding to others on their own terms

Overall, care continues to be an essentially contested concept, containing ambiguities but advantageous, revealing the complexity and diversity of the ethical possibilities of care.

4.3.1 Theory of Care giving as relationship

The moral theory known as the *ethics of care* implies that there is moral significance in the fundamental elements of relationships and dependencies in human life. Normally care ethics seeks to maintain relationships; promoting the well-being of *care-givers* and *care-receivers* in a network of social relations. It builds on the motivation to care for those who are dependent and vulnerable.

The greatest contribution of *care theory* is its emphasis on the *caring relations* and not individuals. Caring is used to describe a certain kind of relation or interaction. *Caring* is also construed as a virtue, as an attribute or disposition frequently exercised by a moral agent. "Caring is a relationship that contains another party i.e. the cared for, and both are reciprocally dependent". Reciprocity of caring relation is not contractual.

Care ethics is nowadays applied in relation to *motherhood*, *international relations* and in *political theory*. It is widely applied to a number of moral and ethical issues like caring for animals, caring the environment, caring as part of bioethics and more recently public policy.

4.3.2 Applied Care Ethics

Care ethics has been applied to a number of contemporary ethical debates, including reproductive technology, homosexuality and gay marriage, capital punishment, political agency, hospice care, HIV treatment, etc. It is increasingly applied in moral analysis of the professions, such as education, medicine, nursing, and business, throwing up new topics and modes of inquiry. It is used to provide moral assessment in other ethical fields, such as bioethics, business ethics, and environmental ethics. Perhaps because medicine is a profession that explicitly involves care for others, care ethics was quickly adopted in bioethics as a means for assessing relational care and embodied aspects of medical practices and policies on abortion etc. Ethic of care provides new insights into contraception and sterilization, artificial insemination and in vitro fertilization, surrogacy, and gene therapy. Care ethics is also applied by some authors to organ transplantation, the care of high risk patients, artificial womb technologies, advanced directives and the ideal relationships between medical practitioners and patients.

4.4 Global Commons and Sharing Ethics

On the planet Earth, there are lots of natural resources which are treated as common inheritance of mankind and are for use by entire humanity and are not for sale. Air (atmosphere), water (ocean), sky (space), sunshine, and all other natural resources, are called as *global commons*. These are shared by all. There are many men made resources developed for sharing by all nations. For example, Internet is shared globally. Similarly, open source software is freely available to anyone interested in its use. All governments create common infrastructure for general public which are to be used on shared basis.

In the field of science and technology, various agencies collect data for specific purposes which are globally shared among interested parties. Thus, remote sensing data, global warming data, pollution data, data on effectiveness of medicines in field trial or new techniques and procedure for treatment of diseases etc. are shared globally for further improvement of human life. *Interpol* works on the principle of cooperation among various nations to share crime data to control crimes of International order. Ethics of sharing is realization of joint efforts and responsibility by individuals and specialized agencies, for shared efforts to common goal of improving quality of life on the planet earth.

4.4.1 Preservation of Global Common Resources

The global commons are the set of natural resources, basic services, public spaces, cultural traditions, and other essentials of life. Behind the commons is the fundamental idea that life, information, human relationships, popular culture and the earth's riches are sacrosanct and not for sale.

Many of the global commons are non-renewable on human time scales. Thus, resource degradation is more likely to be the result of unintended consequences that are unforeseen, not immediately observable, or not easily understood. For example, the carbon dioxide emissions that drive climate change continue to do so for at least a millennium after they enter the atmosphere and whereas any extinction of species due to climate change is forever.

4.4.2 Sharing of National Common Resources

At national level a short list of wonderful elements of life which are actually protected parts of our commons includes: government hospitals, railways, national forests and rivers; the cultural treasures, bus services, metros, highway systems, the Internet, public schools and state universities, town parks, playgrounds, and the postal service etc. Here we share their collective use and enjoyment of these resources and services which seems so normal that we take it for granted

Time to time people agitate and try to ensure that society's and nature's wealth remains for the use of the community and for the sustenance of the earth. Collectively, the endeavors can be seen as the global commons movement.

4.4.3 Sharing of Open Source Software

Just like physical resources, there are common intellectual resources, freely shared by users. For example, encourage in intellectual commons is through the creation and distribution of open source software (free software giving users rights that would otherwise be prohibited by Copyright). The GNU general public license is one license for free software. Software developers can license their products with GNU to be free software and remain free forever, regardless of how the program gets changed or distributed. GNU employs copy left (opposite to Copyright), not to restrict users, but to empower them with what it calls *freedoms*. GNU defines these as "... the freedom to use the software for any purpose, the freedom to change the software to suit your needs, the freedom to share the software with your friends and neighbors, and the freedom to share the changes you make" Conard et al. (2012, pp.436). This system allows a wide range of programmers, tinkerers and hackers to adjust programs to run better, shore up security weaknesses and meet peoples' need in new and unexpected ways.

4.4.4 Sharing of Internet Resources

Other innovations, where global sharing is being practiced without problems, is creating city-wide wireless networks and nurturing Internet institutions like Wikipedia, the free encyclopedia supported by a non-profit foundation, collaboratively written by volunteers and open to editing (and monitoring of that editing) by any reader. These advances have trumped corporate monopolies on computing and the Internet.

4.4.5 Sharing of Data resources

Research requires authentic data to study and conclude on any phenomena. Normally many agencies (like hospitals) do research in any field. This requires sharing of data between them. Sharing of data resources depends upon professional culture of inter-organizational exchange of sharing behaviors. The patterns of information sharing may be influenced by a number of factors. Research institutions provide extensive guidance to researchers about ethical issues and requirements.

When research involves obtaining data from people, researchers are expected to maintain high ethical standards, both during research and while sharing data. Research data is even sensitive and confidential can be shared ethically and legally if researchers pay attention, from the beginning of research to four important aspects:
- including provision for data sharing when gaining informed consent
- protecting people's identities by anonymizing data where needed
- considering controlling access to data
- applying an appropriate license

These measures should be considered jointly. The same measures form part of good research practice and data management, even if data sharing is not envisioned. Data collected from and about people may hold personal, sensitive or confidential information.

Why share your data? There are many good reasons to share data and benefit you, your discipline (and possibly others) and the research institution in which you work. Sharing your data allows:
- New discoveries from existing data
- Integration of sets of data for new analysis
- Re-analysis of expensive, rare or unrepeatable investigations

4.5 Honesty as basic Moral and Ethical value

In order to explain role of Honesty in public life, we take example of India for the purpose of elaboration of the points of discussion.

Honesty is our moral duty. According to Kant, moral duties are *categorical imperatives*. As imperatives, they are injunctions or commands that we impose on ourselves as well as other rational beings. They require us to do what is right, unconditionally and without special incentives attached. For example, we should be honest because honesty is required by duty; it is required by our basic duty to respect the autonomy of others, rather than to deceive and exploit them for our own selfish purposes. Be honest, says, morality-not because doing so benefits us, but because honesty is our duty. Morality is not hypothetical (conditional) imperatives, such as *if you want to prosper, be honest*. A businessperson is not ethically honest, if he/she is honest solely because honesty pays-in terms of profits from customers, who return and recommend their services, as well as from avoiding jail for dishonesty if he/she fails to fully meet the requirements of morality.

Violating the responsibility for truthfulness undermines trust. Honesty has two primary meanings: (1) truthfulness, which centers on meeting responsibilities about truth, and (2) trustworthiness, which centers on meeting responsibilities about trust. The meanings are interwoven because untruthfulness violates trust, and because violations of trust typically involve deception.

4.5.1 For students need to practice Honesty and Academic Integrity

For students, honesty begins with practicing honesty during education while studying to become an Engineer. Academic dishonesty among students takes several forms.

- **Cheating:** intentionally violating the rules of fair play in any academic exercise, for example, by using crib notes or copying from another student during a test.
- **Fabrication**: intentionally falsifying or inventing information, for example, by faking the results of an experiment.
- **Plagiarism:** intentionally or negligently submitting others' work as one's own, for example, by quoting the words of others without using quotation marks and citing the source.
- **Facilitating academic dishonesty**: intentionally helping other students to engage in academic dishonesty, for example, by loading them your work.
- **Misrepresentation:** intentionally giving false information to an instructor, for example, by lying about why one missed a test.

- **Failure to contribute to a collaborative project**: failing to do one's fair share on a joint project.
- **Sabotage:** intentionally preventing others from doing their work, for example, by disrupting their lab experiment.
- **Theft:** Stealing, for example, stealing library books or another students' property.

4.5.2 You can't find Truth without Honesty

Honesty is the most fundamental value a person has by birth. Through honesty only one can know the truth and present the truth to others. It is even greater than truth because truth can never be found if people are not honest. For example, in legal profession a lawyer feels his professional duty to save his client in criminal or cheating cases. Even if he/she knows the truth, they do not help the court to find out the truth. Rather all sorts of distorted arguments are presented to misguide the judiciary. If professionals start practicing honesty then lakhs of pending legal cases in the courts can be solved quickly. By projecting false stories and cooking all sorts of probabilities in the case, fake witnesses, cooking and misinterpreting circumstantial evidences, etc. truth is sacrificed. Unfortunately, many educated persons and common man started believing that by honesty, you can't live a decent life.

4.5.3 Honesty sacrificed due to wrong emphasis on Group Identity

In India group identity is above national identity. Educated and uneducated persons have a group identity and they feel that their custom demands special consideration, which should be given to the members of the group, be it family, caste or tribe. As a result, personally upright individuals sometimes come across moral dilemma when confronted with choices on *complex public policy*. For example, while helping family, clan or community members is a good private moral, it would tantamount to an unacceptable public evil and be termed nepotism. These instances can be multiplied and add a nefarious dimension to the conduct of public policy. This becomes breeding point of dubious considerations at the cost of higher moral and ethical values of Honesty and Truth.

4.5.4 Poor Code of Conduct in public domain policies

As an example, in India we have in place a loosely structured code of conduct for the three sets of actors in the public service domain – civil service, legislature and the judiciary. There is need for a set of *public service values* and *a code of ethics* governing public service operations which should be stipulated by law. The need for a more purposeful, result oriented, approach is imperative.

Public morality demands honesty in pursuit and dispensation of justice in an impartial, quick and in an impersonal manner. Injustice is a powerful motivator of negative human emotions, like rebellion and destruction. Every scripture in our multi-religious society testifies to it.

Unfortunately, quality of politics is such that honesty is considered incompatible with survival. If public life attracts undesirable and corrupt elements, seeking private gain, then abuse of authority and corruption become the norm.

4.5.5 How to maintain Honesty

- Tell the truth and nothing but the truth
- Be sincere
- Be forthright and candid
- Don't Lie
- Don't Cheat
- Don't Steal
- Don't Be tricky, or deceptive

4.5.6 Honesty in Engineering Profession

The concern with truth telling extends far beyond the boundaries of the engineering profession. Religious and secular literature contains many injunctions to tell the truth. For example, *satyameva jayathey*, which means truth alone triumphs is national motto of India. One of the Ten Commandments forbids bearing false witness against one's neighbor. "...honesty is the best policy", was emphasized by George Washington in his 1796 farewell address.

In light of the strong emphasis on honesty in our moral tradition, it is not surprising that engineering codes contain many references to honesty. The third canon of the code of ethics of the Institute of Electrical and Electronics Engineers (IEEE) encourages all members "...to be honest and realistic in stating claims or estimates based on available data" (Mendelson, 2013, pp. 461). Canon 7 requires engineers "to seek, accept, and offer honest criticism of technical work." Details of Code of Ethics and Code of Conduct of IEEE are furnished in Appendix F. The American Society of Mechanical Engineers (ASME)Code of Ethics is equally straightforward. Fundamental Principle II states that engineers must practice the profession by "being honest and impartial." The seventh Fundamental Canon states, "Engineers shall issue public statements only in an objective and truthful manner." A subsection enjoins engineers not to "participate in the dissemination of untrue, unfair, or exaggerated statements regarding engineering".

4.6 Courage in Professions

Courage is the ability to do something that frightens one or is strength in the face of pain or grief. Other synonyms words are bravery, valor, fearlessness, daring, boldness. Standing up for something that is important to you, in the face of all the challenges and temptations that we face in the life, takes a great deal of courage. In professional life, many situations come up when an Engineer has to show courage to face seniors and management, on the question of his professional judgment and interest of management. There is a natural conflict between management and professionals, because of their differences in educational background, socialization, values, vocational interests, work habits and outlook.

Some situations are narrated below where an engineer has to show courage and conviction on his opinion and decisions.

1. Many managers are not engineers and do not have engineering expertise. They do not really understand the engineering issues. Engineers must show courage to adhere to their professional judgments. Decisions of managers and engineers are focused on different aspects of business process. Normally managers focus on business factors such as timing and cost, where engineers focus their attention on quality and safety.
2. Normally organizational ethos does not allow genuine moral commitments to play a part in the decisions of corporate managers, especially highly placed ones. Thus, an Engineer must learn to separate individual conscience from corporate actions. Managers, prefer to think in terms of trade-offs between moral principles, on the one hand, and expediency, on the other hand. What engineer might think, as genuine moral considerations, may play little part in managerial decisions? However, engineer must take courage to state his stand boldly. There is no moral or ethics involved in realization that faulty products are bad and will ultimately harm the company's public image; and environmental damage is bad for business; or will ultimately affect managers in their private role as consumers.
3. In engineer-oriented companies, quality of product and services takes priority over other considerations, except safety. There, normally engineers' resort to overdesigning the products to safeguard the reputation of the organization, even if it costs a little more. Here negotiation or arriving at consensus is prominent feature in relationship among engineers and managers. Managers may make the final decision, where issues as cost or marketing are

involved. Managers feel strong pressure to keep costs down and may believe that engineers sometimes go too far in pursuing safety; often to the detriment of such considerations as cost and marketability.

Finally, engineers may have to negotiate with concerned people with courage to justify their actions and views on goals. If professionals are committed to something important to them, they must have Courage to stand for it. Sometimes they have to show courage to say NO to things that attempt to dissuade them from their course.

4.7 Value of Time

Everybody must understand that he/she gets *time* of only 24 hours in a day whether they are rich or poor, educated or uneducated, child or adult, professional or businessman or any other class of person. Success depends on how effectively and efficiently one has used his time. Everybody must also know his resources for sustenance of successful life and should care to *value* them. For any person, the only resources are his health, time, thoughts, emotions, attitudes, motivations, dedication, vision of future and persistence to achieve his goals. It depends on him, how, why and where he/she invests his resources, because his success and growth in future will depend on that. Nobody can snatch these resources from him unless he/she allows others to disturb, consume or waste them.

Out of all above resources, *time* is most *inflexible* and *irreversible*. Time not utilized now cannot be used later on. It flows at uniform rate whether used or wasted. Value of time is very crucial and how much one cares for it, depends on the nature of activity where it is spent. In examination hall time is fixed for writing paper and students can have probably flexibility of five minutes. In job interviews, candidate's answers should be within minutes. In driving motorcycle, only fraction of few seconds will be available to avoid accidents. For Olympic runners a fraction of second makes difference between winner and loser. A dying man prays to God for a few breaths. So, one can understand how time factor is critical in different circumstances. Everybody should be sensitive to this time factor on each activity and spends his time judiciously. This sensitivity and alertness towards utilization of time will make or mar the success in the concerned activity. A cumulative aggregate of these individual successes will frame your future or career.

The same consideration will dominate in your profession. A project manager who controls the time of various activities and meets the targets within stipulated time is considered as efficient and, dependable taskmaster. He/she rises in the ladder of his career in any organization. Time factor is very important in multidisciplinary projects which are to be executed on turnkey basis, because any slippage in execution time increases the cost of the project, which in turn may reduce profit or result in losses. On the other side if the project is completed ahead of time schedule, cost of the project reduces and contributes to higher profit margin.

The net message is that engineers, professionals and managers must be very conscious about *value of time* in their operations.

4.8 Ethics of Cooperation

Cooperation is a kind of virtues which we all are taught by parents and learns it in childhood among family and friends. Cooperation refers to the process whereby individuals or groups work together to attain common goals. Cooperation is working together and sharing the load. When we cooperate, we join with others to do things that cannot be done alone. It is a universal process.

However, when we are grown up, our ego also grows. We enter into competitive world and at that time many of us struggle with cooperation in our workplaces and at home. Why is that? It is because cooperation calls for putting aside our ego and put the needs of the group above our own needs. Putting aside our ego is NOT an easy thing to do. It takes effort, determination and sacrifice on everyone's part, in order to truly come to a place of genuine cooperation and unity in a group.

In job situation or professions, cooperation calls for joint efforts on projects which normally involve expertise of multiple disciplines and can be successfully executed only by team of experts of respective fields, and by working together on the projects. In bigger projects, or projects which are geographically spread (sometimes global in nature) like launching of satellites, space probes, defense projects, environment monitoring, weather forecasting etc., cooperation of many, national and international agencies, research labs, professional bodies are called for success of the programs. An engineer within his job responsibilities has to learn the value of mutual cooperation for his success and growth, as well as growth of his team members.

Thus, reflecting on the virtue of cooperation reminds us our childhood story with the twigs and how one twig is so easy to break but when you have 50 twigs bound together, the bundle of them cannot be broken. That is the way it is with cooperation. Together, we create a powerful bond that is unbreakable.

Cooperation is a normative process, whereby human behavior is governed by rules and procedures. Cooperation exists in nature among plants and animalstoo.In informal modes of cooperation, like when few friends come together to achieve something, the norms of cooperation are implicit rather than explicit. In large, complex societies, cooperative work is often undertaken on voluntary basis. Socialist philosophy is based on cooperative thinking. Today, international cooperation is witnessed in many fields by organizations such as UNO, UNESCO, UNICEF, etc.

4.9 Ethics of Commitment

Commitment is defined as the state or quality of being dedicated to a cause, an activity, etc. for example *the company's commitment to quality* or *the teacher's commitment to students*. Commitment is like a pledge, a promise and an obligation to adhere to certain activity, value, responsibility or duty.

A commitment is what transforms the promise into reality. Our ability to commit will determine the ability to succeed, prevail and overcome. Many people start but only few commit to finish a task successfully. Among students, those who are committed to studies make good grades. Unless commitment to studies is undertaken by students themselves, they are only giving promises and hopes to parents and faculty without chalking out their plans for studies. An engineer not committed to quality and excellence will be liability to the company. Commitment is the difference between goal and a wish.

The quality of a person's life is in direct proportion to their commitment to excellence, regardless of their chosen field of endeavor. Desire is the key to motivation, but its determination and commitment to an unrelenting pursuit of your goal – a commitment to excellence – that will enable you to attain the success you seek.

There's a difference between interest and commitment. When anybody is interested in doing something, he/she will do it only when circumstance permit. When he/she is committed to something, he/ she will accept no excuses, only results. One should stay committed to his/ her decisions, but also stay flexible in his approach. Commitment unlocks the doors of imagination, allows vision and gives us the right stuff to turn our dream into reality.

4.9.1 Status of commitment of people to Moral and Ethical values

Many people are fairly aware of moral and ethical values of life and society. They may not know definitions of these values in an academic sense, but they are fairly clear and capable of discrimination between good or bad and right or wrong side of virtues. Even though meaning of virtues like honesty, integrity, truth, compassion, justice, equality, nonviolence, tolerance, secularity etc. are known to wide spectrum of the people; their faith and commitment to these values is not up to the mark. The result is over all lack of commitment to various ethical values like trustworthiness, reliability, commitment to duty, responsibility and accountability, self-control, fairness, justice, caring concern for others, citizenship, respect for authority and the law.

Among engineering students, campus violence and ragging of junior fellows is a scorn in our academic ambience. What will be commitment of students to civic and social virtues when they enter into job market? The question arises that when people know about these virtues, why they do not practice them in life i.e. within family, society and job situations. A genuine question arises, do educated people, technocrats, engineers and professionals believe in them and practice them in their profession. The answer is negative and lack of commitment is abundantly visible in their personal behavior, devoid of any commitment towards moral and ethical values, or commitment towards society or displaying good national character. This trait is widespread among people whether they are educated or uneducated, rich or poor, employees or entrepreneurs, professional or bureaucrats.

Personal commitments motivate, guide and give meaning to the work of professionals. Yet these commitments have yet to receive the attention, they deserve in thinking about professional ethics. When the virtue of commitment is considered in light of personal well-being, what comes to mind is how important it is for commitment to be paired with other traits like love, trust etc. Commitment without flexibility can be harsh and unyielding. Commitment without love can be cold and ineffective. Commitment without trust can be useless and daunting.

4.10 Empathy Ethics

The term *empathy* is used to describe a wide range of emotional experiences of concern about others in problem. Emotion researchers generally define empathy as the ability to sense other people's emotions, coupled with the ability to imagine what someone else might be thinking or feeling. Empathy is a form of receptivity to the other; it is also a form of understanding. Undertaking an ethical inquiry without empathy-sensitivity to what is happening to and with the other, would be like engaging in an epistemological inquiry without drawing on the resources of perception.

Having empathy doesn't necessarily mean we'll want to help someone in need, though it's often a vital first step toward compassionate action.

4.10.1 Empathy *vs.* Sympathy

People are more familiar with use of sympathy, whereas empathy ethics is a virtue of wider scope of application. The distinction between *empathy* and *sympathy* is a dynamic and challenging one, in the context of Ethics. The words *empathy* and *sympathy* can be distinguished in several ways. Some of these distinctions are controversial and work is needed to make them more precise. For example, *sympathy* is frequently used to mean one person's response to the negative effects (suffering) of another individual, leading to pro-social (helping) behavior towards the other. In contrast, *empathy* generally includes responding to positive affects as well as negative ones without, however, necessarily doing anything about it (no pro-social behavior required). *Sympathy* is understood to include agreement or approbation (an act of approving) whereas *empathy* is often, though by no means always, a relatively neutral form of data gathering about the experiences and effects of others. *Sympathy* means a specific affective response such as compassion or pity whereas *empathy* once again encompasses affects in general including negative ones such as anger, fear, or resentment.

In British version of utilitarianism, empathy was a necessary social bond, finds expression in current research on empathy, compassion and the morality of caring. With the arrival of the word *empathy*, the difference between a method of data gathering about the experiences (sensations, affects, emotions) of other individuals and the use of this experience for ethically relevant processing, decision making, and evaluations, was able to move into the foreground.

4.11 Virtues

In the beginning virtue used to mean manliness or valor, but over time it settled into the sense of moral excellence. Virtue is also referred for moral excellence, a good or admirable quality or character of a person, a behavior showing high moral standards, a quality considered morally good or desirable in a person. Virtue means conformity of one's life and conduct to moral and ethical principles. There are many virtues like truth, honesty, integrity, loyalty, compassion, sincerity, goodness, righteousness, rectitude, chastity, virginity etc. that are considered as moral and ethical principles.

4.11.1 Virtues in Public Service

There are some *ethical principles* that seem to apply objectively to all of us. For example:
- **Compassion**: Concern for the well-being of others.
- **Non-maleficence**: Avoiding inflicting suffering and hardship on others.
- **Beneficence:** Preventing and alleviating others' suffering; meeting the needs of the most vulnerable; promoting others' happiness (strongest toward our family and friends).
- **Fairness:** Treating people the way they deserve to be treated; as having equal rights unless merit or need justifies special treatment.
- **Courage:** Courage in opposing injustice.
- **Respect for individual autonomy**: Not manipulating rational individuals even for their own good.

- **Respect for the Constitution and other laws**: Laws enacted by legitimate governing bodies.
- **Honesty:** Not deceiving anyone who deserves to know the truth.
- **Promises:** Keeping promises that we made freely and not making promises that we don't intend to keep.
- **Integrity:** Upholding our obligations in spite of personal inconvenience.

Some Specific Virtues expected from Public Officials:
- Use impartial judgment in the service of all constituents.
- Avoid conflicts of interest that could undermine your objective judgment.
- Don't show favoritism toward family and friends in hiring.
- Don't solicit or accept bribes from people seeking to influence your official decisions.
- Don't invest in property or companies that could be affected by your official decisions.

4.11.2 Virtue Ethics

Ethical theories place the primary emphasis on *right acts* and *moral rules*. Other ethical theories shift the focus to the kinds of persons we should aspire to be and become. For example, Virtue ethics also focuses on *good character*. Self-realization ethics focuses on *self-fulfillment*. Persons are characterized by the pattern of *virtues* and *vices* they display or possess. Virtues are desirable habits or tendencies in action, commitment, motive, attitude, emotion, ways of reasoning, and ways of relating to others. Vices are morally undesirable habits or tendencies (Tiberius, 2015).

Familiar words expressing virtues, in engineering and in everyday life are, for example, competence, honesty, courage, fairness, loyalty, and humility. Similarly, Vices are expressed in familiar words: incompetence, dishonesty, cowardice, unfairness, disloyalty, and arrogance.

A List of important virtues for engineers and managers is furnished below.
- The most important virtue is ***practical wisdom*** that is morally good judgment, which enables us to discern the mean for all the other virtues.
- The most comprehensive virtue of engineers is responsible ***professionalism***. This umbrella virtue implies four (overlapping) categories of virtues: public well-being, professional competence, cooperative practices, and personal integrity.
- ***Public-spirited-virtues*** are focused on the good of clients and the general public.
- The minimum virtue is ***non-maleficence***, that is, the tendency not to harm others intentionally. In particular, one should not cause

avoidable or intentional harm. This includes avoiding even the risk of harm.
- *Justice* within corporations, government, and economic practices is an essential virtue in the profession of engineering.
- *Proficiency virtues* are the virtues of mastery of one's profession, in particular mastery of the technical skills that characterize good engineering practice.
- The most general proficiency virtue is **competence**: being well prepared for the jobs one undertakes.
- *Diligence* virtue which demands alertness to dangers and careful attention to detail in performing tasks by, for example, avoiding the deficiency of laziness and the excess of the workaholic.
- *Creativity* is especially desirable within a rapidly changing technological society.
- *Teamwork-virtues* are those that are especially important in enabling professionals to work successfully with other people. They include collegiality, cooperativeness, loyalty and respect for legitimate authority.
- *Leadership* qualities are important virtues that play key roles within authority-structured corporations, such as the responsible exercise of authority and the ability to motivate others to meet valuable goals.
- Finally, *self-governance-virtues* are those necessary in exercising moral responsibility. Some of them center on moral understanding and perception: for example, self-understanding and good moral judgment-what Aristotle calls *practical wisdom*. Other self-governance virtues center on commitment and on putting understanding into action: for example, courage, self-discipline, perseverance, conscientiousness, fidelity to commitments, self-respect and integrity. Honesty falls into both groups of self-governance virtues, for it implies both truthfulness in speech and belief and trustworthiness in commitments.

Virtue ethics seems vulnerable to the criticisms that it is incomplete and too vague. The meaning and requirements of virtues need to be spelled out in terms of at least rough guidelines or rules, lest the virtues fail to provide adequate moral guidance.

4.11.3 Empathy *vs.* Caring

The moral aspect of the ethics of caring is precisely empathy. However, empathy does not require that one do anything other than listen empathically and talk empathically in response, thus falling short of the practical caring (for example, serving dinner) intended. Indeed, a quiet, rich empathic silence is often sufficient. If one decides to act on the basis of empathy, then the action may be altruistic; if the beneficiary is a stranger the action may be caring; if the beneficiary is someone *near and dear*, there any how one is obligated to attend to in any case. Thus, it is important to distinguish between directly helping others, by caring for their physical needs like feeding the hungry, binding up the wounds of the injured, sheltering the injured traveler, and so on; and empathizing with the other in such a way, to allow the other to regain their emotional equilibrium when it has been lost or upset (admittedly by traumas and suffering).

4.11.4 Why to practice Empathy?

Empathy is a building block of morality for people to follow the golden rule. It helps if they can put themselves in someone else's shoes. It is also a key ingredient of successful relationships because it helps us understand the perspectives, needs, and intentions of others. Here are some of the ways that research has testified to the far-reaching importance of empathy.

- **Empathy *vs.* self-interest**: Studies have shown that people higher in empathy are more likely to help others in need, even when doing so cuts against their self-interest. Empathy reduces prejudice and racism.
- **Empathy is good in marriage relationship:** Research suggests being able to understand your partner's emotions deepens intimacy and boosts relationship satisfaction; it's also fundamental to resolving conflicts.
- **Empathy fights inequality:** Empathy encourages us to reach out and want to help people who are not in our social group, even those who belong to stigmatized groups, like the poor.
- **Empathy is good for the office**: Managers who demonstrate empathy have employees who fall sick less often and report greater happiness.
- **Empathy is good for health care:** A large-scale study found that doctors high in empathy have patients who enjoy better health; other research suggests training doctors to be more empathic improves patient satisfaction and the doctors' own emotional well-being.

4.12 Self-Confidence

Confidence, self-confidence, arrogance, overconfidence, self-esteem are related words indicating different hues of one's mental state of capability to achieve or perform an act successfully. Confidence is often equivalent to self-confidence, and generally described as a state of being certain about his thinking, idea, judgment, a hypothesis or prediction being correct, or that his chosen course of action is the best or most effective. Self-confidence is having confidence in oneself.

Arrogance shows about unmerited confidence, believing something or someone is capable or correct when they are not. Overconfidence is excessive belief in someone (or something) succeeding, without any consideration to likely chance of failure. Confidence can be a self-fulfilling prophecy, as those without it may fail or not try because they lack it and those with it may succeed because they have it.

Self-confidence can vary and be observed in a variety of dimensions. Lack of self-confidence in social and academic life of a person, effects the individual self-esteem. An individual's self-confidence can vary in different environments, such as at home or in school.

Self-confidence is extremely important in almost every aspect of our lives, yet so many people struggle to find it. This can be a vicious circle: people who lack self-confidence can find it difficult to become successful. A person with lack of self-confidence will appear nervous, fumbling, and overly apologetic, whereas a confident person will speak clearly, holds his or her head high, answer questions assuredly, and readily admits when he/she or she does not know something. Self-confident people inspire confidence in others: their audience, their peers, their bosses, their customers and their friends. And gaining the confidence of others is one of the key ways in which a self-confident person finds success. Person's level of self-confidence can show in many ways: his behavior, his body language, how he/she speaks, what he/she says, and so on.

Two main things contribute to self-confidence: self-efficacy and self-esteem. We gain a sense of self-efficacy when we see ourselves (and others similar to ourselves) mastering skills and achieving goals that matter in those skill areas. This is the confidence that, if we learn and work hard in a particular area, we'll succeed; and it's this type of confidence that leads people to accept difficult challenges and persist in the face of setbacks.

This overlaps with the idea of self-esteem, which is a more general sense that we can cope with what's going on in our lives, and that we have a right to be happy. It comes from the sense that we are behaving virtuously, that we're competent at what we do, and that we can compete successfully when we put our minds to it.

Some people believe that self-confidence can be built with affirmations and positive thinking. There's some truth in this, but actual self-confidence is built by setting and achieving goals, thereby building competence. Without this underlying competence, your self-confidence could be shallow over-confidence, without proven through some achievements and challenges undertaken.

In summary, confident people focus on their strength while managing their weakness, are not afraid to take risks, enjoy challenging jobs and setting high goals for themselves, look for self-improvement opportunities.

They are not afraid to admit when they make mistake, are not afraid to acknowledge when they don't know something, make good team leader or mentor, can relate to customers and company members at any level of organization and are honest to admit their shortcoming.

4.13 Spirituality

The most fundamental of all fundamental principles is that a Spirit, supreme and unchanging, pervades the entire universe; and the material world is merely manifestation of the spirit. Thousand years ago, India perceived this principle more clearly, and understood its implications even more deeply, than the most highly civilized nations do today. Swami Vivekananda had been among the foremost speaker of Indian spiritual wisdom and makers of modern India. He gave message of compassion, love, service, tolerance and harmony in the world that has universal acceptance and application. He fostered respect and understanding among religions, cultures, and nations. Religious ethics need to be interpreted anew in ongoing contexts

Spirituality develops feelings of oneness of the universe, universal belonging, love for humanity and openness to all. The idea of human coexistence demands a climate of mutual respect, and religious harmony, to favor peace between human beings and nations. God and spirituality reside in each of us and we can serve each other in that spirit. Solution of violence on the earth, killing of people in the name of religion, political ideology etc. lies in the change of hearts, minds and actions of all people.

Desire for peace and harmony is hidden in the heart of everyone, but we are unaware of this. Each one of us must try to discover this treasure within him, understand ways and means to promote peace and work for fostering global understanding. It is responsibility of each one of us to explore domain of human rights, plan effective action by us and share experiences to bring peace and harmony to the individuals as well as to the society. We should examine our ultimate goal and purpose of life, including the economic well-being. Instead of always thinking of financial matters we should also think associated moral issues. We must practice compassion, sharing and caring, love for fellow being, desire to serve others etc. and remember God who resides in all of us. Have genuine acceptance of other people's opinions to bring peace, understanding of real meaning of human rights and applying this in our own life.

Further, we should explore the relevance of religions and their spiritual messages, in addressing the critical issues of humanity like poverty, the empowerment of women, human rights and peace-making. Appendix-C gives brief details of major religions of India.

4.13.1 Why Spirituality to Engineers and Professionals

Modern science has positively influenced and refined general thinking and attitudes of people; their beliefs in ethical and social moral issues; but all is not well as far as the implementation of ethics and moral views in practice are concerned. Ethics has not produced the desired effect in eradicating material disparity between haves and have-nots. The plight of vast majority of poor people, in various sections of society world over, is most pathetic to say the least (Basis, 2009).

The question of unethical trends cannot be put directly on individual engineer or scientist, but there is no doubt that prevailing corporate culture, work culture or social culture are strongly influenced by *scientific development*, which is responsible to create disparity and discrepancy in distribution of scarce resources and their availability to all human being.

Hankering after materialistic gains by well to do people, groups and societies has pushed the nobility of ethics and morality into disrepute. Materialistic influence has also led to the general belief that gratification of senses is the only way of enjoyment. This has produced highly selfish mentality without spiritual concept of life.

Engineers and professionals have to collectively think on how to carry out their industrial and scientific activities, such that the skewed and diverse trends in distribution of prosperity, caused by scientific progress does not promote imbalance in distribution of prosperity, as this is a social moral and Ethical concern.

In the Internet age, global awareness is growing and cultural separations and isolations are dissolving. Along with this awareness, stress and agitation levels of human minds are increasing. As such our mind is fickle by nature. It should not be allowed to get wild. The senses may get restless, the body, however should be held in check, and not allowed to be impatient. Mind if kept under control is a wonderful servant to man, but without control it becomes terrible master over man and destroys the peace of mind. Being peaceful yourself is the first step if you want to live in a peaceful universe.

Spirituality trains the mental outlook and develops a realization that you never have to change what you see, only the way you see it. Spiritual practices range from yoga-asanas, pranayama, meditation, or combinations of these under different proprietary names. Extensive investigations have been done about such practices and the results support beneficial effects in favor of a sense of well-being.

A peaceful mind is essential for right thinking and judgment. Engineers and professionals are required to keep cool and composed when dealing with their professional duties, where they have to negotiate between multiple conflicting demands or prevailing considerations. A more skillful use of intellect is **CONTEMPLATION** which helps in finding optimum solutions. In work situations many times problems arise because of feelings of righteousness. Righteousness cuts you off from the flow of conversations and negotiations. Spirituality guides you to lead a life according to *dharma*(which is not a religion) and to walk in dharma is also to hear other human beings with compassion and without reservation. Dharma is ethics of senses.

4.13.2 Yoga for balance of mind

Spirituality prepares man with capacity of self-reflection, introspection, self-inquiry; whatever you may call it, to visualize the situations more objectively and clearly with an unbiased mind. The internal reflection can be seen as a process of witnessing or observing our own actions, thoughts, and emotions with an attitude of *tolerance* and *love*. With this shift in our inner identity, our external experiences become in closer alignment with our inner being. This is **YOGA** i.e. yoga of mind (*jnana yoga*), yoga of the heart (*bhakti yoga*) and yoga of selfless action (*karma yoga*).

Spirituality through practice of Yoga enables us to penetrate many layers of our inner being, from most mundane to pure awareness and unconditional love of oneness. Love is the doorway to oneness with all things, to being in harmony with the entire universe. The essence of *yoga* is union or becoming one with the universe. The reality of oneness is greater than what is available to you through your senses and thoughts.

Yoga means regulation, moderation and control of contents (mental tendencies, desires, liking, disliking, etc.) of your mind. The mind by nature is in constant agitation and purpose of yoga is to lead to a silence of the mind. The silence is the prerequisite for the mind to be able to accurately reflect on objective reality without introducing its own subjective distortions. Thus, aim of yoga is the transformation of human beings from their natural form to a perfected form. Through yoga a person develops balance within his inner and outer personality and thus no longer be wholly at the mercy of natural tendencies of mind and inclinations of sense organs. The practice of yoga invigorates the entire personality, resulting in a reshaping of mind, body and emotions.

4.13.3 Meditation for Inner Awakening

Meditation is essential for peace of mind, spiritual stability and inner awakening, because it blesses us with inner gifts beyond the reach of science: a sense of our true purpose in life, a feeling of relatedness to God, or shared warmth of fellowship and love. Enjoyment without possessiveness and renunciation without repression will lead to peace of mind according to our scriptures. This is confirmed by modern research in science and psychotherapy. Happiness is a condition of the mind. Peace has spiritual quality.

4.13.4 Understanding Spirituality

Spirituality can be understood as an internal quest to understand or explore the essence of own being, study of own nature, purpose of life, origin of life, etc. This internal exploration is often achieved through spiritual practices such as contemplation, study of scriptures, meditation, yoga, etc. with the intention to understand self and grow in depth internally. Spiritual experiences could be of various types; of different level of consciousness; like feeling of expansion, lightness, deeper connection with life; identity of self with other individuals or the entire humanity; or with the divine realm. Spirituality is often experienced as a source of inspiration or orientation in life. It can encompass belief in immaterial realities or experiences of the immanent or transcendent nature of the world.

Spirituality leads to feeling of love and kindness towards all forms of life, including your own, and sense of gratitude towards creator and his entire creation. Spirituality motivates to preserve and beautify the nature, encourages respecting all forms of life, to be forgiving, to be gentle and to be that which is supportive of life. You become instrumental to supports life, supports all endeavors, it becomes the energy of life itself.

Human spirituality is intimately related to a sense of purpose, which governs human concerns and motivations. Proper motivations are critically important for the responsible engineering and professional practices.

4.13.5 Differentiating Spirituality from Religion

Spirituality and religion are two different paths for almost the similar goals for human beings. Both emphasize on adoption of moral and ethical values of life. However, their perception of life, its purpose and goals as well as methods of practice are widely different. Being religious connotes belonging to and practicing a religious tradition. Being spiritual suggests a personal commitment to a process of inner development that engages us in our totality. Spirituality is a way of life that affects and includes every moment of existence. It is at once a contemplative attitude, a disposition to a life of depth, and the search for ultimate meaning, direction, and belonging. The spiritual person is committed to an essential ongoing goal of life. In this state of being, a practitioner starts identifying himself with all forms of life as himself. Followers of spiritual path start developing a feeling of oneness and unity with all, resulting in his or her action for welfare and service to all. Moral and ethical considerations become paramount for him. Spirituality unites the people.

Religion (see Appendix-C) divides the people into believers and non-believers. Believers develop a superiority complex and somewhat dislike to non-believers. Historically, so far religion has caused many wars between their followers, communities and nations, whereas there is no fight among spiritual persons at any time. Religion is called opium of people by Karl Marx, whereas spirituality is nectar of life for people. Religion is more of an institutionalized system with a lot of rules and processes that are required to be adhered to; whereas, spirituality is much more personal. Religiosity seems more outwardly oriented, doctrinal and authoritarian which inhibits some personal expression, whilst spirituality often implies more subjective, emotional, inward-orientation with the freedom to be freely expressive.

Cognitive (intellectual activity as thinking, reasoning, or remembering) flexibility is one outcome of being spiritual rather than religious, which as a powerful tool keep spiritual person healthy and motivated. Coping up with responses, that are built around fixed rules and inflexible strategies of religions, mean that you have to try harder to comply with them.

4.13.6 Spirituality and Engineering Education

Science and technology are study of external physical world. The mode of exploration or understanding is based on objective methods, analytical and experimental approach. It promotes an *ethic of competitive individualism*, where an engineer or professional thinks about others and the world, like an object and, tries to manipulate them for their own private ends. Due to this competitive objectivity embedded in the philosophy of education in science and technology, students are shaped into efficient scientists and engineers who tend to focus on making discoveries and producing effective products. While this worldview of efficiency is not necessarily bad and is certainly the means to a progressive end, but this perpetuates a fragmented form of community, in which members fight over resources under competitive individualism.

There is no problem with existing education of scientific methods and research. The problem is that existing system is one sided and not holistic for development of students with balanced outlook and personality. The problem is that under this type of education in the name of objectivity; students start believing that objectivity requires to eliminate or ignore the questions of purpose, value, and meaning; and to assume that we humans are only machines, call it biological, genetic machines, social machines, etc. The current education has ignored relationship with social dimension of human being. Students are not taught value of collective thinking and working together, using all of the talents offered, to reach a more complete and harmonious solutions.

Any engineering problem of industry or society or life requires collective approach to find an acceptable solution. For example, a project on health-related instrumentation may require team of engineers from biomedical engineering, mechanical engineering, electronics and electrical engineering, software engineering, faculty of psychology as well as panel of doctors etc., to execute the project satisfactorily. Thus, these engineers act as bridge to translate science and technology into applications useful to human beings and society at large. They should be able to understand the scientific knowledge as well as the needs of human beings and the society.

The role of faith in higher education, specifically in science and engineering has received more attention in recent years. Science and faith are more commonly being examined as an integral element to produce a balanced and whole worldview, i.e. develop a sound and coherent worldview to the intellectual and educated mind.

Courses in ethics typically provide students with positive understandings of moral duty and professional obligation. Spirituality can contribute in widening their worldview by developing in them awareness and mental orientation for services, capacities of listening, empathy, healing, social awareness, persuasion, conceptualization, foresight, commitment to the growth of people and building community. Recent studies are recognizing the importance of encouraging students to make connections between scientific knowledge and other ways of knowing such as direct experience, self-evident truths and wisdom which is the domain of spirituality.

4.14 Respect for Others

Everyone needs and deserves respect. Respect is a basic human need. We all crave respect and we all should give respect. Respect is the acts of showing someone that you value his or her feelings and thoughts. Respect is a universal value that each person desires not only to embody, but also to receive. Respect is not just what you say but also the way you act. Showing the people, that their feelings and thoughts are taken care of, is the way how one earns respect? If you demonstrate respect toward others, then others will respect you and listen to your opinions. Respect begins with self-respect and then extends to the respect of others.

The golden rule, do unto others as you would like others to do to you, is perfect example of respect. This famous saying means treat others as you would like yourself to be treated. People demand different amounts of respect, though not everyone is willing to give the amount needed. Respect is very important to a person because it can be the balancing factor of life. Respect is one of the keys to build or tear down ego.

For any person *social respect* plays a role in everyday life. When we go to school, there's respect. When we go to a restaurant, there's respect. When we go to our family, there is respect. You may not notice it, but that's only because they are being respectful to you.

4.15 Virtue of Character

Role of family on personality and character development has already discussed in chapter 2. Summarily, when a child grows up to adulthood and starts his independent life, makes family, finds good friends, etc. and interacts in society, he/she displays his character developed in the childhood. Although time brings many changes in his personality but the importance of family background remains there. The children who have a sound family background and strong family ties are almost always happier. Their values about life and society are stable and possess strong character. The family life adds a sense of responsibility to one's personality.

A person of character
- Is a good person, someone to look up to and admire?
- Knows the difference between right and wrong and always tries to do what is right.
- Sets a good example for everyone.
- Makes the world a better place.
- Lives according to the Six Pillars of Character:
  - Trustworthiness,
  - Respect,
  - Responsibility,
  - Fairness,
  - Caring and
  - Good Citizenship

4.15.1 Professional Character

Professionally speaking, the term *professional character* refers to those character traits that serve to define the kind of person one is. The *good engineer* is the engineer who has those traits of professional character that makes him or her best or ideal engineer. To be sure, the vocabulary of professional character can also be used to describe the engineer who would be a good exponent of preventive ethics.

We can use the term *professional character portrait* to refer to the set of character traits that would make an engineer a good engineer and especially an effective practitioner of aspirational ethics. Three-character traits that might be a part of such a *professional character portrait* are suggested.
- The first professional character trait is professional pride, particularly pride in technical excellence. If an engineer wants her work as a professional to contribute to public welfare, the first thing he/she/ she must do is, be sure that her professional expertise is at the highest possible level.

- The second professional character trait is social awareness, which is an awareness of the way in which technology affects and is affected by the larger social environment. In other words, engineers need an awareness of *social embeddedness* of technology. Engineers are often called on to make design decisions that are not socially neutral. This often requires sensitivities and commitments that cannot be incorporated into rules. We believe that such social awareness is an important aspect of a professional character that will take seriously the obligation to promote public welfare through professional work.
- A third professional character trait that can support aspirational ethics is an environmental consciousness. Environmental issues will increasingly play a crucial role in almost all aspects of engineering. Increasingly, human welfare will be seen as integral to preserving the integrity of the natural environment, that supports human and all other forms of life. Eventually, being environmentally conscious will be recognized as an important element in professional engineering character.

4.16 Summary

Living Peacefully: Majority of people think that health, money, love, fame, beauty, power and talent can bring them peace and joy. Those who pursue material goals vigorously lose their inner peace. Living in peace is about living harmoniously with yourself, others and all sentient beings around you. Peaceful living must promote human excellence to fulfill goal and mission of life. Human excellence is achieved by adopting certain attributes like honesty, discipline, dedication, confidence, self-control, compassion, knowledge, etc.

Motivation: One of the most debated topic and research in industry is motivation of employees. Objective of motivation of employees is to do what an organization wants them to do efficiently and effectively in workplace. When people are, confident and motivated at work, it impacts positively on working ambience and many other positive factors become operative in the working environment.

Ethics of Caring: All human beings want to care and be cared for. Caring is giving love and attention to people and things that matter to you. There are many definitions of *care ethics*. Normally care ethics seeks to maintain relationships and promoting the well-being of care-givers and care-receivers in a network of social relations. The greatest contribution of care theory is its emphasis on the caring relations and not individuals. Care is a kind of motivational attitude of empathy.

Global Common Resources: There are lots of natural resources on the planet earth like air (atmosphere), water (ocean), sky (space), sunshine etc.

which are called as *global commons* and treated as common inheritance of mankind for use by entire humanity. The global commons are sacrosanct and not for sale and shared by all. There are many manmade resources developed for sharing by all nations. For example, Internet, open source software, remote sensing data, global warming data, pollution data, data on effectiveness of medicines in field trial or new techniques and procedure for treatment of diseases etc. are freely shared globally.

Honesty: Morality demands to *be honest* because it is our moral duty. Students start practicing honesty during education. Academic dishonesty takes several forms like cheating in any academic exercise; Fabrication i.e. falsifying information; Plagiarism i.e. intentionally submitting others work as one's own, etc. *Code of ethics* and *code of conduct* of many professional bodies contain references to honesty. Public morality demands honesty in pursuit and dispensation of justice in an impartial, quick and in an impersonal manner. Every scripture in our multi-religious society emphasizes on being honest.

Courage: Courage is strength or ability to face the pain or grief. Other synonyms words are bravery, valor, fearlessness, daring, boldness. In professional life many conflicting situations come up between management and professionals because of their differences in educational background, socialization, values, vocational interests, work habits, outlook etc., when an engineer must take courage to state his stand boldly.

Value of Time: Success depends on how effectively and efficiently one has used his time. Your only resources are your health, time, thoughts, emotions, attitudes, motivations, dedication, and your persistence to achieve goals. Out of all above resources, time is most inflexible and irreversible. You have to be sensitive to time factor on each activity. This sensitivity and alertness towards utilization of time will make or mar your success in the concerned activity.

Cooperation: Cooperation refers to the process whereby individuals or groups work together to attain their goals. When we cooperate, we join with others to do things that cannot be done alone. It is a universal process. In job situation or professions, cooperation calls for joint efforts on projects which normally involve expertise of multiple disciplines and can be successfully executed only by team of experts of respective fields working together on the projects.

Commitment: Commitment is like a pledge, a promise, and an obligation to adhere to certain activity, value, responsibility or duty. Our ability to commit will determine our ability to succeed, prevail and overcome. Among students, those who are committed to studies make good grades. Even though meaning of virtues like honesty, integrity, truth, compassion, justice, equality, nonviolence, tolerance, secularity, etc. are known to many people, but often they lack faith and commitment to these values.

Empathy: Empathy is defined as the ability to sense other people's emotions, coupled with the ability to imagine what someone else might be thinking or feeling. Having empathy doesn't necessarily mean we'll want to help someone in need, though it's often a vital first step toward compassionate action. People are more familiar with use of sympathy whereas empathy ethics is a virtue of wider scope of application.

Confidence: Confidence, self-confidence, overconfidence, self-esteem are related words indicating different hues of one's mental state of capability to achieve or perform an act successfully. Self-confidence of any one is expressed in many ways: his behavior, his body language, how one speaks, what he/she says, and so on.

Spirituality: Spirituality can be understood as an internal quest to understand or explore the essence of own being, study of own nature, purpose of life, source of life, etc. This internal exploration is often achieved through spiritual practices, such as, contemplation, study, meditation and prayer with the intention to understand self and grow in depth internally. Spiritual practices range from *yogasanas*, *pranayama*, meditation or combinations of these under different proprietary names.

Virtue: Virtue is referred for moral excellence. Virtues are desirable habits or tendencies in action, commitment, motive, attitude, emotion, ways of reasoning and ways of relating to others. There are many virtues like truth, honesty, integrity, loyalty, compassion, sincerity, goodness, righteousness, rectitude, chastity, virginity, etc. considered as moral and ethical principles.

Respect: Everyone needs and deserves respect. Respect is a basic human need. We all crave respect and we all should give respect. Respect is the acts of showing someone that you value his or her feelings and thoughts. Respect is a universal value that each person desires not only to embody, but also to receive.

Review questions

1. New millennium along the path of material civilization has robbed of his inner peace of human beings-comment.
2. How can one reduce his worries for living peacefully-explain?
3. Explore how to develop right *attitude and mindset* for living peacefully?
4. How to improve motivation to adopt change among employees. What is the process of adaptation of change?
5. What are attributes of human beings required for achieving *human excellence*?
6. What do you understand by *ethics of caring*? What is theory of *care giving as relationship*?
7. Explain *sharing ethics* and what are *global common physical resources*? Justify need for their sharing.

8. What are *common intellectual resources* which are freely shared by users? Describe some of these important resources.
9. Discuss about honesty. How students learn about honesty in colleges. Relate honesty with academic integrity.
10. Explain how honesty is sacrificed due to wrong emphasis on group identity in public service domain.
11. Elaborate on importance of honesty in engineering profession.
12. Explain the importance *courage* and *value time* for engineers. How one can do better time management?
13. Cooperation and commitment are virtues for engineers-explain. What do you feel about status of commitment of people to moral and ethical values?
14. Compare virtues of empathy, sympathy and caring. How to cultivate and practice empathy?
15. Engineers must have self-confidence on their professional operations-comment.
16. Yoga being part of spirituality, justify how spirituality is helpful to engineers and professionals?
17. Differentiate spirituality from religion. Explain how spirituality makes engineering education holistic?
18. Throw light on civic virtues and ethical principles and virtues in public service
19. Describe virtue ethics and give details of important virtues for engineers and managers.
20. Explain important features of professional character.

Section 2: Engineering Ethics and Factors of Success, Growth and Personality Development

5 Historical development of Ethics, Ethical Theories and Kohlberg's Theory on Moral Development

Learning objectives

In this chapter you will learn about

- Development of ethics in India (based on Hinduism, Buddhism and Jainism)
- Development of ethics in western world
- Ethical principles of beneficence, least harm, autonomy and justice
- Ethical theories (duty ethics, utilitarianism) and applications (moral human rights)
- Types of ethical inquiries and tools of ethical analysis for professional ethics
- Kohlberg's theory- Gilligan's argument-Heinz's dilemma

In this chapter focus is on understanding of theoretical background of ethical and moral development and its utility to professional behavior. Professional and Engineering ethics deal with application of moral and ethical theories to identify some of the moral complexities in engineering. It tries to define engineering ethics and state the goals in studying it. Study of moral and ethical considerations will prepare the students, in understanding the importance and acceptance of sharing moral responsibility within the corporate setting, where today most engineering activity takes place. There is the need for a basic congruence between the goals of responsible Professionals, Professions, and the corporate world. Moral values are embedded in engineering projects, as standards of excellence, and not treated as external burdens.

5.1 Historical development of Ethics

Ethics (*niti-shastra*) is the branch of philosophy that examines right and wrong moral behavior, various moral concepts (such as *justice, virtue, duty*) and language of moral communication. Various *ethical theories* pose various answers to the question "...what is the greatest good?" and elaborate a complete set of proper behaviors for individuals and groups. All over the world in all civilizations, ethics has its origin in its religious and philosophical thinking. The moral code of the people is an indicator of their social and spiritual ways of life. All cultures have evolved and adopted an ordered moral system, practices and norms to guide proper conduct and behavior of its members

History of ethics in western world and eastern world has different streams of development but having common goal of human happiness and moral order in society.

In western world, ethics is the philosophical treatment of the moral order. The history of ethics is concerned solely with the various philosophical systems which in the course of time have been elaborated with reference to the moral order.

In eastern traditions ethics and religion are so closely related, that it is difficult to talk about ethics without influx of religion, which contains within itself some system of morality for the guidance to its followers. From time immemorial, various religious faiths have flourished in India. Every religious and philosophical system of India has a prominent component of moral and ethical considerations. Moral and Ethics are the core of teachings and injunctions of all these systems. In every religious tradition good moral conduct is considered essential for a happy and contented life.

Moral consciousness is an undeniable fact of human experience. The moral sensibility is something essential for the peaceful society. Ethics as a speculative science is based on the foundations of the moral behavior of man, but a substantial portion of the moral codes are based on religious beliefs, social customs and traditions.

5.1.1 History of Ethics in India

The Indian term for morality and ethics is *dharma* and the function of dharma is to hold the human society together for its stability and growth. Right conduct is essential if the human society is to survive. Dharma is understood in Vedas as duty par-excellence. Dharma is also generally understood as the duties of humans according to one's own caste and stage of life i.e. *varnashrama dharma*.

In Indian ethics, the morality is very much based on certain beliefs, customs and traditions of Indian religions. Foundations of Indian ethics can be sought in the metaphysical and the theological beliefs in the form of worship, prayers, ideals and principles that directed man's life in the society. By moral considerations one's actions might be branded as good or bad, right or wrong, praiseworthy or blameful, etc. Specifically speaking, morality is the awareness of a living based on a distinction between our animal demands and the demands of higher faculties of human beings, which make the human beings distinct from animals.

5.1.1.1 Scriptural background and sources of Ethical and Moral principles in India

In ancient times education was imparted by *Guru* and development of moral and ethical values among disciples had been part and parcel of his teachings and discourses. Guru used to impart *value education* whose content was derived from scriptures dealing with religion and philosophy. Epics *Ramayana* and *Mahabharata* and Scriptures like *Vedas, shruti, Smriti, Puranas, Upanishads*, etc., are all full of injunctions on moral and ethical behavior for *rulers* as well as general public. Scripture GEETA provides excellent discourse on logical approach towards personal values, duties and clarity on goal of life. Various schools of religions and philosophies like Buddhism, Jainism, Samkhya, Yoga, Nyaya, Memansa, Vedanta, Charvaka, etc. provide theoretical background and logical reasoning for their set of value injunctions. Major religions of India are briefly described in Appendix-C. A student must have some knowledge of these religions to understand relationship between religions and moral and ethics.

In India besides scriptures, practices of good people's conscience and reason also play a role in the matters of morality. In the history of Indian philosophy, ethics of inner conscience is also the source and test of morality. This means that even the desire arising out of the right *will* or *determination* may serve as a source or guide to morality. In recent times, especially in the thoughts of Gandhi and Aurobindo, conscience has been accorded a very important place as source of guidance, giving final verdict regarding questions of morality and immorality.

In Indian ethics, one of the central ethical concepts of the *Rig Veda* is a conception of *unifying order* or *moral law*, pervading all things. This concept has given rise to two other important concepts: *dharma* and *karma*. The concept of *dharma* has got different and divergent meanings; its meaning is close to the word called *duty*. The concept *karma* signifies that there is a uniform moral law governing the actions of man and deciding factor for the rewards and the punishments appropriate to their actions.

5.1.1.2 Hinduism based ethical and moral guidelines in India

The Hindu social morality is relativistic on several counts. Man's duties are accepted to be relative to time and place. The duties of a person are also strictly relative to his class (*varna*) and the stage of life (*ashram*). According to Dharma Edicts, certain virtues are universal. They are contentment, forgiveness, self-control, non-stealing, cleanliness, regulation and moderation of desires and the senses, wisdom to know the *Supreme Atman, truthfulness* and *abstention* from anger, etc. These virtues are important moral components of Dharma, having common and universal character, and usually termed as *morality*. Core component of Hinduism is centered on

- **Doctrine of karma**: The doctrine of *karma* states that whatever a man suffers or enjoys is the fruit of his own deed, a harvest sprung from his own actions, whether good or bad but committed in his previous and the present life. This *karma* must remind us that, whatever a man sows, he/she shall reap.
- **Transmigration of soul**: The doctrine of karma and transmigration of soul are closely bound together. After the death of the body, the life of the individual is continued in another body and so on in indefinite cycle of birth and death.
- **Supreme goals**: The dominant interest of the Hindu thought in this life is, in the realization of highest values of human life. There are four values which give meaning to the human life. They are called *Purusharthas* and they are: 1) *Dharma* 2) *Artha* 3) *Kama* 4) *Moksha*.

5.1.1.3 Ethics in Buddhism

Ethical and moral guidelines in Buddhism are prescribed as ten meritorious deeds which should be performed, ten de-meritorious deeds which should be avoided and five precepts to regulate behavior in society. The precepts are the basic practice in Buddhism. These five refrains are called as *Panchasila*.

5.1.1.4 Ten meritorious deeds

The Buddhism taught ten meritorious deeds which should be performed in order to gain a happy and peaceful life as well as to develop knowledge and understanding. The ten meritorious deeds are:
1. Charity
2. Morality
3. Mental culture
4. Reverence or respect
5. Service in helping others

6. Sharing merits with others
7. Rejoicing in the merits of others
8. Preaching and teaching Dhamma
9. Listening to Dhamma
10. Straightening one's views

Moral conduct benefits all Beings with whom one comes into contact. Mental culture brings peace to others and inspires them to practice Dhamma.

5.1.1.5 Ten de-meritorious deeds

There are ten de-meritorious deeds from which the Buddhist are advised to keep away. These deeds are rooted in greed, hatred, and delusion and they will bring suffering to others. These ten deeds are divided into three sets: 1) actions of the body 2) verbal actions 3) actions of mind.
- Bodily actions are killing of living beings, stealing, and unlawful sexual intercourse.
- Four verbal actions are: lying, slander, harsh speech and meaningless talk.
- The other three actions of the mind are: covetousness or being desirous especially of things belonging to others, ill-will, wrong views.

5.1.1.6 Five precepts

Telling about ten meritorious and ten evil actions, the Buddhism invites the lay Buddhists to adopt five precepts voluntarily to follow in order to live together in civilized communities with mutual trust and respect. A good Buddhist should remind himself to follow the five precepts daily. They are as follows:
1. To refrain from Killing living creatures
2. Not taking which is not given
3. Refrain from sexual misconduct
4. Refrain from False speech
5. Not to take intoxicating drugs and liquor.

5.1.1.7 Jain Ethics

Like Buddhism, Jainism also takes ahimsa to be the most important ethical virtue and consequently denounces the Vedic sacrifices. Ethics of Jain tradition focuses on right knowledge, right faith and right conduct which are known as Triratnas – or the three gems of Jainism. In Jainism, one must follow the five great vows namely the *panca-maha-vrata*for the perfection of right conduct. They are *ahimsa, satyam, asteyam,* *brahamacaryam* and *aparigraha*. People following Jainism should give up attachment for the objects of five senses.

Over all concepts of ethical behavior in India are complex and multi-faceted one, being constituted of divergent and several religious and philosophical traditions. This diversity of metaphysical beliefs and volitional attitudes is reflected in Indian morality. We need to choose those ethical aspects of Hindu-religious-culture, which are in harmony with modern human values and need to reject other ideals, which are contrary to modern values and ethics.

5.1.2 History of Ethics in Western World

- **Ethics of ancient Greek philosophy: Socrates, Plato, Aristotle**

Ethics was properly narrated among the Greeks, in the teaching of Socrates (470- 399 B.C.). According to Socrates, the ultimate object of human activity is happiness, and the necessary means to reach it is virtue. All evil arises from ignorance, and the virtues are so many kinds of prudence i.e. careful good judgment that allows someone to avoid danger or risks.

The disciple of Socrates, Plato (427-347 B.C.) declares that Virtue enables man to order his conduct according to the dictates of reason and acting thus he/she becomes like unto God. But Plato differed from Socrates in that he did not consider virtue to consist in wisdom alone, but also in justice, temperance, and fortitude as well, which constitute the proper harmony of man's activities.

Plato's illustrious disciple, Aristotle (384-322 B.C.), can be considered the real founder of systematic ethics. With characteristic keenness she solved in his ethical and political writings, most of the problems with which ethics concerns itself.

Aristotle chose to take the facts of experience as his starting-point and sought to trace their highest and ultimate causes to happiness. This happiness cannot consist in external goods, but only in the activity proper to human nature i.e. in the highest and most perfect activity of his reason, which springs in turn from virtue. Aristotle's findings and analysis, to a great extent are regarded correct even at the present time. The nature and role of the State and the family were rightly explained by him.

- **Ethics of Greek and Roman Philosophy: Hedonism, Epicurus, Cynics, Stoicism, Skeptics**

A more hedonistic (hedone, *pleasure*) turn in ethics begins with Democritus (about 460-370 B.C.), who considers a perpetually joyous and cheerful disposition as the highest good and happiness for man. The means, to achieve that is virtue, and it wisely discriminates between the pleasures to be sought after and that to be shunned. Aristippus of Cyrene (435-354 B.C.) taught that Hedonism or Pure Sensualism is the end and supreme good of human endeavor. Epicurus (341-270 B.C.) differed from

Aristippus and believed that man's highest good is in holding the largest possible sum total of spiritual and sensual enjoyments with the greatest possible freedom from displeasure and pain. Virtue is the proper directive norm in the attainment of this end.

The Cynics, Antisthenes (444-369 B.C.) and Diogenes of Sinope (414-324 B.C.) taught (contrary to Hedonism), that virtue alone suffices for happiness, and pleasure is an evil. The Stoics, Zeno (336-264 B.C.) and his disciples, Cleanthes, Chrysippus and others refined and perfected views of Antisthenes, saying that Virtue, in their opinion, consists in man's living according to the dictates of his rational and individual nature which is but a part of the entire natural order. Virtue nature is therefore the harmonious agreement with the divine reason.

- **Ethics: History of Christian Morality**

A new epoch in ethics begins with the dawn of Christianity. Pre-Christian religions belonging to a number of ancient cultures of Greece and Rome, etc. is referred as *paganism*. Ancient paganism never had a clear concept of the relation between God, and the unity of human race, of the destiny of man, of the nature and meaning of the moral laws. Christianity first shed full light on these and similar questions. St. Paul taught that God has written his moral law in the hearts of all men, this law manifests itself in the conscience of every man and is the norm according to which the whole human race will be judged on the day of reckoning. Thus, ethics received its richest and most fruitful stimulus from Christianity. Proper ethical methods were now unfolded and philosophy was in a position to follow up and develop these methods.

This ethical course was soon adopted in the early ages of the Church by the Fathers, ecclesiastical writers and especially the illustrious Doctors of the Church, Ambrose, Jerome, and Augustine, who, in the exposition and defense of Christian truth made use of the principles laid down by the pagan philosophers. St. Augustine thoroughly developed along the philosophical lines and established firmly most of the truths of Christian morality. The eternal law and source of all temporal laws, the natural law, conscience, the ultimate end of man, the cardinal virtues, sin, marriage, etc. were treated by him in the clearest and most penetrating manner.

- **Ethics: History of ethical philosophy: Kant, John Stuart Mill and Altruism**

A complete revolution in ethics was introduced by German philosopher Immanuel Kant (1724-1804). Immanuel Kant is the founder of deontological ethics. His ethics, which he mainly put forth in the *Groundwork of the Metaphysics of Morals* (1785), *Critique of Practical Reason* (1788) and *Metaphysics of Morals*(1797), is one of the most prominent and highly respected theories. Kant focused on practical reasoning than pure theoretical reasoning and found an absolute, universal and categorical moral law. It is rather the law of our own reason, which is, therefore, autonomous, that is, it must be observed for its own sake, without regard to any pleasure or utility arising there from. Only that will be morally good which obeys the moral law under the influence of such a subjective principle or motive as can be willed by the individual to become the universal law for all men.

The system of Cumberland, who maintained the common good of mankind to be the end and criterion of moral conduct, was renewed on a positive basis in the nineteenth century by Auguste Comte who had many adherents of his views. Historically speaking, Jeremy Bentham in his *Introduction to the Principles of Morals and Legislation* (1789) and John Stuart Mill in *Utilitarianism* (1863) are the founders of utilitarianism. Herbert Spencer (1820-1903) sought to bring a compromise between social Utilitarianism (Altruism) and private Utilitarianism (Egoism) in accordance with the theory of evolution.

- **Ethics: evolutionary philosophy, socialism, Nietzsche**

As the evolutionists, so too the socialists favor the theory of evolution from their ethical viewpoint; yet the latter do not base their observations on scientific principles, but on social and economic considerations. According to K. Marx, F. Engels, and other exponents of the so-called "materialistic interpretation of history", all moral, religious, juridical and philosophical concepts are but the reflex of the economic conditions of society in the minds of men. Now these social relations are subject to constant change; hence the ideas of morality, religion, etc. are also continually changing. Every age, every people, and even each class in a given group of people, form its moral and religious ideas in accordance with its own peculiar economic situation. Hence, no universal code of morality exists binding on all men at all times; the morality of the present day is not of Divine origin, but the product of history, and will soon have to make room for another system of morality as the time passes.

5.1.3　Ancient Ethics and Modern Morality

Modern morality, in particular contemporary morality, is characterized by the fact that quite a few important scholars elaborated modern versions of Aristotle's classical virtue ethics in the twentieth century. These scholars argue that virtue ethics was quite successful in solving ethical problems in Antiquity and they believe that adhering to a refined version of virtue ethics is not only useful but also superior in solving our modern moral problems. Among the most important neo-Aristotelian scholars claim that the traditional ethical theories such as deontological ethics (Kantianism) and consequentialism (*utilitarianism*) are doomed to failure.

It is commonly supposed that there is a vital difference between ancient ethics and modern morality (Gordon, 2012). For example, there appears to be a vital difference between virtue ethics and the modern moralities of deontological ethics (*Kantianism*) and consequentialism (*utilitarianism*). But when viewed in totality one finds that both ethical approaches have much more in common than their stereotypes may suggest. There are at least two main criteria that each moral theory must fulfill: first, the criterion of justification (that is, the particular moral theory should not contain any contradictions) and, second, the criterion of applicability (that is, the particular moral theory should solve concrete problems and offer ethical orientation). However, many (traditional) moral theories are unable to meet the second criterion, and simply fall short of the high demands of applied ethics, to solve the complex moral problems of our times. The main point is that the traditional moral theories are not sufficiently well equipped to deal with completely new problems such as issues concerning nuclear power, gene technology, and cloning and so forth. Therefore, there is constant interest in updating and enhancing a particular moral theory in order to make it compatible with the latest demands.

5.2 Ethical Principles

In third chapter we have discussed about moral and ethics without giving any theory or criteria for how to decide what is ethical? Here we discuss about ethical principles on the subject matter.

Ethical theories and principles are the foundations of ethical analysis because they are the viewpoints from which guidance can be obtained along the pathway to a decision. Each theory emphasizes different points, such as predicting the outcome and following one's duties to others in order to reach an ethically correct decision. However, in order for an ethical theory to be useful, the theory must be directed towards a common set of goals. These goals include beneficence, least harm, respect for autonomy and justice.

5.2.1 Beneficence

The principle of beneficence guides the ethical theory to examine from the point of *what is good to do*. This priority to *do good,* guides to possible solution to an ethical dilemma which is acceptable. This principle is also consistent with the principle of utility i.e. which says that our actions should attempt to maximize ratio of good over possible evil in the world. An example of *doing good* is found in the medical field where the health of an individual is bettered by treatment from physicians.

5.2.2 Least Harm

While applying the principle of beneficence sometimes we come across a situation in which neither choice is beneficial. In that case, a person should choose the path of action with least harm possible and to do harm to the fewest people.

5.2.3 Autonomy

This principle states that an ethical theory should respect autonomy of individuals and allow people to make decisions that apply to their lives. Each man deserves respect because only he/she has those exact life experiences intimately and understands his emotions and motivations. Issue of moral autonomy to engineers has been discussed in the sixth chapter with full details.

5.2.4 Justice

The justice principle states that ethical theories should prescribe actions that are fair to those involved. Ethical decisions should be consistent with the ethical theory unless justified extenuating circumstances exist in the case. An ethical decision should have a consistent logical basis to justify the decision. For example, *a fire truck* or *police van* is allowed to speed on the highway beyond prescribed speed limits because they must arrive at the scene of fire or crime as quickly as possible in order to control the situation. These vans are allowed to cross the speed limits because it is a justified under the extenuating circumstances.

5.3 Ethical Theories

We have discussed above historical development of ethics. Now we shall see what are these theories which are relevant to modern times? Ethical theories are used to evaluate actions, rules, and character. An important role of a sound ethical theory is to improve our moral insight into particular problems on ongoing basis. Hence, there is an ongoing checking of an ethical theory (or general principles and rules) against the judgments about specific situations (cases, dilemmas, issues), that we are most confident are correct, and on reverse order, a checking of our judgments about specific situations by reference to the ethical theory. Theories and specific judgments are continually adjusted to each other in a back-and-forth process until we reach what John Rawls calls a reflective equilibrium.

Two main *moral theories* of modern *virtue ethics* (or neo-Aristotelianism) are Kant's *Deontological ethics* and *Utilitarianism*. Both theories have been adopted and modified by many scholars in recent history in order to make them (more) compatible with the latest demands in ethical reasoning and decision-making, in particular, by meeting the objections raised by modern virtue ethics. The following briefly depicts Kantianism in its original form and the main features of Utilitarianism

5.3.1 Kantianism or Deontological Ethics or Duty ethics

Kant's ethics is deontological (meaning the normative ethical position that judges the morality of an action based on the action's adherence to a rule or rules) in the sense that one has to obey the duties and obligations, which derive from his supreme principle of morality, that is the Categorical Imperative: "Act only according to that maxim whereby you can at the same time opine that it should become a universal law" (Kant 1785). The categorical imperative is a test for maxims which, in turn determine, whether certain acts have moral worth or not. A maxim is an individual's subjective principle or rule of the *will*, which tells the individual, what to do in a given particular situation. If the maxim can be universalized, then it is valid and one must act upon it.

Kant's ethics are universal in the sense that the system of moral duties and obligations point at all rational human beings. Morality is not based in interests (such as social contract theories), emotions and intuitions, or conscience, but in reason alone. This is the reason why Kant's ethics is not heteronomous - by being a divine ethical theory in which God commands what human beings should do (for example, the Bible and ten commandments); or natural law conception in which nature itself commands, what human beings should do; by providing human beings with the faculty of reason; who in turn, detect what should be done in moral matters - but truly autonomous with regard to rational beings; making their moral decisions in the light of pure practical reason. The pure practical reason is not limited to the particular nature of human reasoning but is the source and the field of universal norms, which stem from a general notion of a rational being.

Deontology theory is based on the concept of what is considered *morally right* on universal laws that exist outside of a specific situation. It states that people should adhere to their obligations and duties to another individual or society when dealing with an ethical dilemma. Upholding one's obligations and duty is what is considered ethically correct. A deontologist will be very consistent in his ethical decisions since he/she adheres to set of duties.

Deontology provides for special duties and obligations to specific people, such as those within one's family like elder brother has an obligation to protect his little brothers and sisters whenever required. This theory praises those deontologists who exceed their duties and obligations, which is called *supererogation*.

5.3.2 Utilitarianism

John Stuart Mill the founders of utilitarianism in his book *Utilitarianism* (1863) gave basic formula of utilitarianism is as follows: The creed which accepts as the foundation of morals, utility, or the greatest happiness principle holds that actions are, right in proportion as they tend to promote happiness, wrong as they tend to produce the reverse of happiness. By happiness he intended pleasure and the absence of pain; by unhappiness, pain and the deprivation of pleasure.

There is widespread agreement, that there are numerous different utilitarian theories in modern ethics. Following four main aspects are typical for each utilitarian theory.

1. *The consequence principle:* Utilitarianism is not about actions but about the consequences of actions. This kind of theory is a form of consequentialism, which means that the moral worth of the particular action is determined by its outcome.
2. *Happiness:* Utilitarianism is a teleological (the philosophical doctrine that final causes, design, and purpose exist in nature) theory insofar as happiness is the main goal to be achieved. This particular goal can be identified with (I) the promotion of pleasure, (ii) the avoidance of pain or harm, (iii) the fulfillment of desires or considered preferences, or (iv)with meeting some objective criteria of well-being.
3. *Greatest Happiness Principle:* Utilitarianism is not about mere happiness but about "the greatest happiness" attainable. The moral rightness or wrongness of actions depends on the goal of achieving "the greatest happiness for the greatest number".
4. *Maximizing:* The collective amount of utility, regarding sentient beings affected by the action, should be maximized. This line of reasoning contains strong altruistic claims because, roughly speaking, one should only choose those actions which improve happiness of other sentient beings.

5.3.3 Ethical Theories having direct applications to Professionalism

Ethical theories and principles bring significant clarity to the decision-making process. All of the ethical theories attempt to follow the ethical principles in order to be applicable and valid by themselves. These varieties of ethical theories provide a substantial framework for trying to make ethically correct answers. Each ethical theory attempts to adhere to the ethical principles that lead to success when trying to reach the best decision. When one understands each individual theory, including its strengths and weaknesses, one can make the most informed decision, when trying to achieve an ethically correct answer to a dilemma.

Each of them emphasizes different aspects of an ethical dilemma and lead to the most appropriate ethical decision, satisfying the guidelines of the ethical theory. However, choice of ethical theory by people is usually based on their individual experiences of life.

- **Rights (Moral and Human Rights)**

Rights ethics is the most familiar ethical theory, for it provides the moral foundation of the political and legal system of any country. We hold certain truths to be self-evident, for example all men are created equal; that they are endowed with certain unalienable rights like right of life, liberty and the pursuit of happiness. These are unalienable natural human rights; that cannot be taken away (alienated) from us; although sometimes they are violated. Human rights have been appealed in all the major social movements of the twentieth century, including the women's movement, the civil rights movement, etc.

In the rights ethical theory the rights set forth by a society are protected and given the highest priority. Rights are considered to be ethically correct and valid since a large or ruling population endorses them. These rights are moral entitlements and valid moral claims that impose duties on other people. All ethical theories leave some room for rights, but the ethical theory called Rights Ethics is, distinctive moral bottom line, in that it makes human rights the ultimate appeal,

The idea of human rights is the single most powerful moral concept, in making cross-cultural moral judgments about customs and laws. As such, the notions of human rights and legal rights are distinct. Legal rights are simply those laws which society has granted to its members, whereas human rights are those we have as humans, whether the law recognizes them or not.

Human rights constitute a moral authority, to make legitimate moral demands on others to respect our choices; recognizing that others can make similar claims on us. At its core, rights ethics emphasizes respecting the inherent dignity and worth of individuals as they exercise their liberty.

In order for a society to determine what rights it wants to enact, it must decide about the society's goals and ethical priorities. Therefore, for the rights theory to be useful, it must be used in conjunction with another ethical theory that will consistently explain the goals of the society.

- **Casuist**

The *casuist ethical theory* is one that compares a current ethical dilemma with examples of similar ethical dilemmas and their outcomes. This is virtually search of precedence, which could be similar to the current dilemmas and how they were resolved. This allows the best possible solution according to others' experiences. Usually one will find paradigms that represent the extremes of the situation, so that a compromise can be reached, that will hopefully include the wisdom gained from the previous examples. One drawback to this ethical theory is that there may not be a set of similar examples for a given ethical dilemma.

- **Virtue**

In *virtue ethics theory* a person is judged by his character rather than by an action that may deviate from his normal behavior. Virtue ethics says that good character is central to morality. It considers the person's morals, reputation and motivation when rating his unusual and irregular behavior, sometime that is considered unethical. One weakness of this ethical theory is that it does not take into consideration a person's change in moral character.

5.3.4   Self-Realization

Each of the ethical theory leaves considerable room for self-interest that is for pursuing what is good for oneself. For example, utilitarianism says that self-interest should enter into our calculations of the overall good; rights ethics says we have rights to pursue our legitimate interests; duty ethics says we have duties to ourselves; and virtue ethics links our personal good with participating in communities and social practices. Self-realization ethics, however, gives greater prominence to self-interest and to personal commitments that individuals develop in pursuing self-fulfillment.

Individuals vary greatly in what they desire most strongly and also in their talents and virtues. Self-realization ethics points to the highly personal commitments that motivate, guide, and give meaning to the work of engineers and other professionals. These commitments enter into the core of an individual's character. Personal commitments are commitments that are not incumbent on everyone, for example, specific humanitarian, environmental, religious, political, aesthetic, supererogatory and family commitments. However, they also include commitments to obligatory professional standards, especially when these are linked to an individual's broader value perspective.

5.4   Types of Inquiry

Ethical issues and questions arise in all fields of human activities like the individual in society, the creative arts, business and economics, education, engineering, technology, environment, law and justice, medicine, etc.; with implications that may be personal, political, or even global. Our intent is to limit our discussions to Engineering field only and explore the complexity of some of the most vexing ethical questions.

Any set of conventions, whether *codes of ethics* or *actual conduct*, should be open to scrutiny in light of wider values. At the same time, *professional codes* should be taken very seriously. They express the good judgment of many morally concerned individuals and the collective wisdom of a profession at a given time. Certainly, codes are a proper starting place for an inquiry into professional ethics; they establish a framework for dialogue about moral issues and more often than not, they cast powerful light on the dilemmas confronting engineers.

Inquiry means an investigation and in engineering ethics it involves investigations into morals, ethical values, meaning and facts in practical engineering operations (Florman, 2002). These inquiries in the field of engineering ethics are of three types.
1. Normative Inquiries
2. Conceptual Inquiries
3. Factual or Descriptive Inquiries

5.4.1 Normative Inquiries

Normative ethics is interested in determining the content of our moral behavior. Normative ethical theories provide moral action-guidance i.e. inquiry methodology to find answer of the practical questions like what one should do in a particular situation. The moral theories of Kant and Bentham are examples of normative theories that seek to provide guidelines for determining a specific course of moral action.

Normative inquiries help to identify the values which guide in analyzing the issues and take the decision. In most of the cases, type of questions like the one stated below, normative theories are able to provide guidance to find answers and justify some norms and standards on moral basis:
1. How do the obligations of engineers protect the public safety in given situations?
2. When should an engineer have to alarm their employers on dangerous practices?
3. When the laws and organizational procedures affect engineering practice on moral issues?
4. What are the moral rights essential for engineers to fulfill their professional obligations?

5.4.2 Conceptual Inquiries

In engineering, process of product development encounters lot of inquiries of moral complexity at various stages, from a mental concept to physical completion of the product. Engineers face both moral and technical problems concerning variability in the materials available to them; the quality of work by coworkers at all levels; pressures imposed by the time and the whims of the marketplace; and relationships of authority within corporations etc.

During conceptual design phase, inquiries are meant for scrutinizing the description and meaning of the concepts, principles, and issues related to Engineering Ethics. These inquiries also verify whether the concepts and ideas are expressed with precision and clarity. The following are some of the questions of conceptual inquiries:
1. What is the safety measure adopted and how it is related to risks?
2. How the conformance to codes of ethics for engineers is ensured to protect the safety, health and welfare of the public?
3. How manufacturing, sales and marketing are planned to ensure safety from evils like bribery?
4. How professional ethics followed and *professionalism* maintained?

5.4.3 Factual / Descriptive Inquiries

To find solution of the moral problem, these types of inquiries adopt scientific methods of collecting all facts and figures; analyze and understand the role played by respective factors, their interrelatedness, etc. The facts connected with the ethical issue could be, prevailing engineering practices and business realities of that time and place; effectiveness of code of ethical conduct prescribed by professional societies; procedures of risk management; psychological background of connected people etc. The information and data about these facts help in understanding of background conditions which create moral background of the problem. These facts are also helpful in solving moral problems by using various alternative ways and tools to find appropriate solution.

5.5 Tools of Ethical Analysis

- **Exploration**

Analysis skills: Paying attention to moral and ethical values at play in the situation or issue.
Careful consideration: Factual issues and terms.

- **Getting unstuck**

Creativity/Application: The case may have multiplying options, shifting problems. Paying attention to values can open up new possibilities for integration. Ethical theory can be of some help here, but it is often limited.

- **Making a case Analysis: Finding explicit key values.**

Understanding and application: Making key values explicit. Defining and defending key factual claims and terms. Consider key objections arising from other theories. Ethical theories can be of help here to realize the key objections, and it also help us in making our key values explicit.

- **Deciding for yourself**

Prioritizing and integrating the key values. Search new and creative options. Check facts and inferences.

5.6 Use of Ethical Theories

Moral theories are one way to assist students in setting aside the feelings, desires, and ambitions that often tend to skew one's moral vision and look at a problem from a rational viewpoint. These moral theories should help the student develop a more systemized, rational scheme of thought through which they can reflect on the ethical decisions they will be required to make. In other words, these theories offer some different frameworks for thinking about ethical issues and potential for guiding discussions.

A moral theory is a mechanism for assessing whether a particular action or rule is ethically justified. More precisely, a moral theory can help us to sharpen our moral vision, it helps us determine whether an action or a rule is ethically right, wrong or permissible (which means that it may be but need not be acted or followed). While approaches of ethical theories on moral issues differ significantly, all moral theories have two things in common. For a moral theory to be helpful, it should provide us with the source of moral values, and it should provide us with a framework or strategy for ranking moral norms when we confront a dilemma.

Requirements of Ethical theories are built in engineering codes of ethics by reference to broader moral principles. In doing so, they illuminate connections between engineering ethics and everyday morality, that is the justified moral values that play a role in all areas of life. We discussed above ethical theories that have been especially influential: rights ethics, duty ethics, utilitarianism, virtue ethics, and self-realization ethics. Rights ethics says we ought to respect human rights, whereas duty ethics says we ought to respect individuals' rational autonomy. Utilitarianism says that we ought to maximize the overall good, taking into equal account of all those affected by our actions. Virtue ethics says that good character is central to morality. Self-realization ethics emphasizes the moral significance of self-fulfillment. None of these theories has won a consensus, although each has proven attractive to many people. At least in some of their versions, they widely agree in their practical implications.

Finally, ethical theories attempt to provide clarity and consistency, systematic and comprehensive understanding, and helpful practical guidance in moral matters. Main features of Sound ethical theories are as follows.
1. Sound ethical theories are clear and coherent. They rely on concepts (ideas) that are sufficiently clear to be applicable, and their various claims and principles are internally consistent.
2. Sound ethical theories organize basic moral values in a systematic and comprehensive way. They highlight important values and distinguish them from what is secondary. They apply to all circumstances that interest us, not merely to a limited range of examples.

3. Sound ethical theories provide helpful guidance that is compatible with our most carefully considered moral convictions (judgments, intuitions) about concrete situations.

Ethical theories like utilitarianism, rights ethics, duty ethics, virtue ethics, and self-realization ethics mostly satisfy above criteria to a large extent.

5.7 Kohlberg's Theory- Gilligan's argument-Heinz's dilemma

5.7.1 Theories on Moral Development

In western countries, systematic research and scholarship on moral development has been going on since last 80 years or so. Educators wishing to address the issues of moral development have been making use of what has been learned through that work and introducing it into education curriculum. The following overview introduces the main perspectives, which is guiding current work on the issue of stages and process of moral development of persons and education.

5.7.2 Piaget's Theory of Moral Development

Jean Piaget is among the first psychologists whose work remains directly relevant to contemporary theories of moral development. In his early writing, he focused specifically on the moral lives of children, studying the way children play games in order to learn more about children's beliefs about right and wrong. From his observations, Piaget concluded that children begin in a *heteronomous* stage of moral reasoning, characterized by a strict adherence to rules and duties, and obedience to authority. According to Piaget, all development emerges from action; that is to say, individuals construct and reconstruct their knowledge of the world as a result of interactions with the environment. Based on his observations of children's application of rules when playing, Piaget concluded that morality, too, can be considered a developmental process.

Piaget concluded from this work that schools should emphasize cooperative decision-making and problem solving, nurturing moral development by requiring students to work out common rules based on fairness.

Piaget rejected this belief that children simply learn and internalize the norms for a group; he believed individuals define morality individually; through their struggles to arrive at fair solutions. Given this view, Piaget suggested that a classroom teacher should perform a difficult task i.e. the educator must provide students with opportunities for personal discovery, through problem solving, rather than indoctrinating students with norms.

5.7.3 Kohlberg's Theory on Moral Development

Lawrence Kohlberg (1969) modified and elaborated Piaget's work and laid the groundwork for the current debate within psychology on moral development. Consistent with Piaget, he proposed that children form ways of thinking through their experiences, which include understandings of moral concepts such as justice, rights, equality and human welfare. Kohlberg followed the development of moral judgment beyond the age limits studied by Piaget and determined that the process of attaining moral maturity took longer and was more gradual than Piaget had proposed.

Kohlberg's stages of moral development are planes of moral adequacy to explain the development of moral reasoning. He said that our psychological theory of morality derives largely from Piaget, who claims that both logic and morality develop through stages, and each stage is a structure which is in better equilibrium than its predecessor. It assumes, that each new (logical or moral) stage is a new structure which includes elements of earlier structures; but transforms them in such a way as to present a more stable and extensive equilibrium. He wrote his doctoral dissertation in 1958, outlining what are now known as his stages of moral development.

This theory holds that moral reasoning, which is the basis for ethical behavior, has six identifiable developmental stages. He followed the development of moral judgment beyond the ages originally studied by Piaget, who claimed that logic and morality develop through constructive stages. Kohlberg expanded considerably on this groundwork, determining that the process of moral development was principally concerned with justice and that its development continued throughout the lifespan.

Kohlberg used stories about moral dilemmas in his studies and was interested in how people would act if they were put in a similar moral crux. He would then categorize and classify evoked responses into one of six distinct stages. They are distinguished by the degree of moral cognitive development, that is by the kinds of reasoning and motivation an individual adopts in response to moral questions. These six stages where broken into three levels: pre-conventional, conventional and post-conventional. His theory is based on constructive developmental stages; each stage and level are more adequate at responding to moral dilemmas.

Level 1 (Pre-Conventional): The pre-conventional level is most primitive level of moral reasoning and is especially common in children, although adults can also exhibit this level of reasoning. Reasoners in the pre-conventional level judge the morality of an action by its direct consequences. The pre-conventional level consists of the first and second stages of moral development and is purely concerned with the self (egocentric).

This is the level of development of all young children and a few adults also who follow:
1. Obedience and punishment orientation. In this stage individuals are motivated primarily by the desire to avoid punishment, by unquestioning deference to power and never like to go beyond it.
2. Self-interest orientation i.e. what's in it for me: In this stage primary desire is to satisfy one's own needs and right conduct is regarded as whatever directly benefits to oneself.

Level 2 (Conventional): The conventional level of moral reasoning is typical of adolescents and adults. Persons, who reason in a conventional way, judge the morality of actions by comparing these actions to societal views and expectations. Here the norms of one's family, group, or society are adopted uncritically as being correct because they represent authority.

The conventional level consists of the third and fourth stages of moral development.
3. Interpersonal accord and conformity i.e. the good boy/good girl attitude: Individuals at this level are motivated by the desire to please others and meet the expectations of the social units, regardless of immediate effects on their self- interest.
4. Authority and social-order maintaining orientation i.e. Law and order morality: In these individuals, loyalty and close identification with others have overriding importance.

Level 3 (Post-Conventional): The post-conventional level, also known as the principled level, consists of stages five and six of moral development. The level is attained when an individual comes to regard the standard of right and wrong as a set of principles having to do with rights and the general good that are not reducible to self-interest or to social conventions. Kohlberg calls these individuals autonomous because they think for themselves and do not assume that customs are always right. They also seek to reason and live by general principles such as the *golden rule*(do unto others as you would have them to do unto you) which apply universally to all people in all cultures. Their motivation is to do what is morally reasonable for its own sake (rather than solely from ulterior motives), together their desire to maintain their moral integrity, self-respect, and the respect of other autonomous individuals. Realization that individuals are separate entities from society now becomes salient. One's own perspective should be viewed before the societies. It is due to this "nature of self before others" that the post-conventional level, especially stage six, is sometimes mistaken for pre-conventional behaviors.
5. Social contract orientation: In this stage five, individuals are viewed as holding different opinions and values, and it is paramount that they be respected and honored impartially. Issues that are not regarded as relative like life and choice should never be withheld or inhibited. In fact, no single choice is correct or

absolute. Along a similar vein, laws are regarded as social contracts rather than rigid dictums. Those that do not promote general social welfare should be changed, when necessary to meet the greatest good for the greatest number of people. This is attained through majority decision, and inevitably compromise. In this way democratic government is ostensibly based on stage five reasoning.

6. Universal ethical principles i.e. principled conscience: In this stage six, moral reasoning is based on abstract reasoning using universal ethical principles. Laws are valid only insofar as they are grounded in justice; and that a commitment to justice carries with it an obligation to disobey unjust laws. Rights are unnecessary as social contracts are not essential for deontic moral action. Decisions are met categorically in an absolute way rather than hypothetically in a conditional way. This can be done by imagining what one would do being in anyone's shoes, who imagined what anyone would do thinking the same. The resulting consensus is the action taken.

Kohlberg's theory of moral development has as obvious connection with goals of studying ethics in the college. To be morally responsible, one must be able and willing to exercise moral reasoning, and this in turn requires overcoming passive acceptance of dominant conventions in one's society or in the group. Yet moral responsibility emerges from a foundation of early moral training by one's parents and culture. This early training, which involves submitting to the power of one's parents, makes possible later growth beyond complete self-centeredness (at the pre-conventional level) and uncritical acceptance of customs (at the conventional level) towards the respect of other people (at the post-conventional level).

According to Kohlberg, moral development of individual progresses gradually through these stages, one stage at a time, and jumping of a stage is not possible. They could only come to a comprehension of a moral rationale one stage above their own. Thus, according to Kohlberg, it was important to present engineering students with moral dilemmas for discussion on gradual progression of moral development to higher stages of morality maturity. He saw this as one of the ways in which moral development can be promoted through formal education.

5.7.4 Gilligan's Theory of Moral Development

Carol Gilligan, one of Kohlberg's former student and colleague, did not agree with Kohlberg's theory,on the basis that Kohlberg seems to make fundamental assumption that movement towards autonomy is morally desirable. This also assumes that moral autonomy is inherent general character trait, essential for exercising moral responsibility. Gilligan says that Kohlberg's studies are distorted by a male bias as he conducted his studies with male subjects only. Males normally focus on general *rules and rights* on moral issues.

Gilligan's own studies suggest that there is some tendency for men to be more interested in trying to solve moral problems by applying abstract moral principles. Males tend to resolve moral dilemmas by determining which moral rule is more important and should override other moral rules relevant to the dilemma. Women, by contrast, try harder to preserve personal relationships with people involved in a situation. Accordingly, women focus greater attention on the details of the context, in which dilemmas arises rather than invoking and trying to rank general rules. Gilligan refers this context-oriented emphasis on maintaining personal relationships as the *ethics of care* and contrast it with an *ethics of rules and rights*. Both male and females sometimes use both kinds of ethics. Gilligan wishes to draw attention only to difference in emphasis, not a strict difference based on gender.

5.7.5 Heinz's Dilemma

In order to make Gilligan's criticism of Kohlberg clearer, consider the most famous example that Kohlberg used in his questionnaires and interviews. This example, called Heinz's dilemma, involves a woman living in Europe, who will die from cancer unless she obtains an expensive drug, which the doctors think will help her. Her husband, Heinz, cannot afford to purchase the drug. The local pharmacist is charging 10 times the cost of making the drug. He also invented the drug and remains the sole source for obtaining it. The husband goes to everyone to borrow money, but he manages to raise only half the money needed to purchase the drug. When he asks the pharmacist to sell the drug at a cheaper price or let him pay for it later, the pharmacist refuses. In desperation, Heinz breaks into the pharmacy and steals the drug. Was the theft morally right or wrong?

Analysis of Heinz dilemma in the light of Kohlberg theory suggested six (6) stages of moral considerations:

1. Stage one (obedience): Heinz should not steal the medicine, because he will consequently be put in prison.
2. Stage two (self-interest): Heinz should steal the medicine, because he will be much happier if he saves life of his wife, even if he will have to serve a prison sentence.
3. Stage three (conformity): Heinz should steal the medicine, because his wife expects it; he wants to be a good husband.
4. Stage four (law-and-order): Heinz should not steal the medicine, because the law prohibits stealing and making it illegal.
5. Stage five (human rights): Heinz should steal the medicine, because everyone has a right to choose life, regardless of the law.

Or Heinz should not steal the medicine, because the scientist has a right to fair compensation.
6. Stage six (universal human ethics): Heinz should steal the medicine, because saving a human life is a more fundamental value than the property rights of another person. Or Heinz should not steal the medicine, because others may need the medicine just as badly, and their lives are equally significant.

Applying his theory of moral development, Kohlberg ranked experimental subjects according to the kinds of reasoning they used about the dilemma (and not depending on their specific answers or conclusions). For example, the subjects who said that Heinz did wrong, because he broke the law, are reasoning at the conventional level, in which right conduct is regarded as simply obeying the law. Also, those people are at this level, who said the husband did right because according to their religious beliefs, God commanded that human life is sacred and God should be obeyed. By contrast people, who said that the right to life of the wife is inherently more important than the property right of the pharmacist, are reasoning at the post-conventional level.

Women, interestingly enough, tended to cluster more frequently than men at Kohlberg's conventional level. This is because they showed greater hesitancy about stealing the drug and searched for alternative solution in term of the context. For example, they recommended further attention to reason with the pharmacist and to find creative ways to raise the Necessary money. Here even women were applying the general principles about the *right to live*.

Gilligan however, drew a very different conclusion from this data. She contended that it reveals a greater sensitivity to people and personal relationships, including the relationship with the pharmacist and the wife (who would not be helped if the husband ended up in the jail for stealing the drug). She also saw value in the context-oriented reasoning used by the women, who did not locate the solution of the dilemma in abstract general rules, ranked in order of importance.

Drawing on such reinterpretations of Kohlberg's experimental data and combining them with her own studies of women, Gilligan offered a strikingly different scheme of moral development. She recast Kohlberg's three levels of moral development as stages of growth towards an ethnic caring. Gilligan's recasting looked something like this:

- **The pre-conventional level**: This is roughly the same as Kohlberg's first level in that the person is preoccupied with self-centered reasoning. Right conduct is viewed in a selfish manner as solely what is good for oneself.
- **The conventional level:** Here there is the opposite preoccupation with not hurting others and with a willingness to sacrifice one's own interest in order to help or nurture others. Women are

especially prone to fall prey to the cultural stereotype that pressure them always to be willing to give up their personal interest in order to serve the needs of others.
- **The post-conventional level:** The individual becomes able to strike a reasoned balance between caring about other people and pursuing one's own self-interest while exercising one's right. The aim is to balance one's own needs with the needs of others, while maintaining relationship based on mutual caring. This is achieved through context-oriented reasoning, rather than by applying abstract rules ranked in a hierarchy of importance.

5.8 Summary

Ethics (*niti-shastra*) is the branch of philosophy that examines right and wrong moral behavior, moral concepts (such as justice, virtue, duty) and moral language. History of ethics in western world and eastern world has different streams of development but having common goal of human happiness and moral order in society.

In eastern traditions ethics and religion are so closely related that it is difficult to talk about ethics without influx of religion which contains within itself some system of morality for the guidance to its followers. Hinduism, Buddhism and Jainism are three major religions in India.

Ethics in Hinduism: In Hinduism morality and ethics are subset of *dharma* and the function of dharma is to hold the human society together for its stability and growth. Dharma is also generally understood as the duties of humans according to one's own caste and stage of life i.e. *varnashrama dharma*. In the history of Indian philosophy, ethics of inner conscience is also the source and test of morality. Ethical principles in Hinduism are derived from basic faith on *doctrine of karma* and *transmigration of soul*. There are four values, which give meaning to human life. They are called *purusharthas*. They are 1) *dharma* 2) *artha* 3) *kama* 4) *moksa*.

Ethics in Buddhism: Ethical and moral guidelines in Buddhism are prescribed as ten meritorious deeds which should be performed, ten demeritorious deeds which should be avoided and five precepts to regulate behavior in society. These five refrains are called as *Pancasila*.

Ethics in Jainism: Like Buddhism, Jainism also takes ahimsa to be the most important ethical virtue. Ethics of Jain tradition focuses on right knowledge, right faith and right conduct which are known as *Triratnas*. In Jainism one must follow the five great vows namely the panca-maha-vrata for the perfection of right conduct. They are *ahimsa, satyam, asteyam, brahamacaryam* and *aparigraha*.

Ethics in Western world: In Western world, Ethics is the philosophical treatment of the *moral order*. The history of ethics is concerned solely with the various philosophical systems which in the course of time have been elaborated with reference to the moral order. Ethics of ancient Greek philosophy was based on virtues which help to achieve *highest happiness*. Ethics of Roman Philosophy was focused on *Hedonism* (*hedone*, pleasure) with wide range of meaning given to Hedonism by different philosophers. For example, perpetually joyous and cheerful disposition, pure sensualism, largest possible sum total of spiritual and sensual enjoyment, etc. are different interpretation of Hedonism by different philosophers. Christianity first shed full light on clear and definite concept of the relation between God and the world, of the unity of the human race, of the destiny of man, of the nature and meaning of the moral laws. A complete revolution in ethics was introduced by German philosopher Immanuel Kant (1724-1804).

Ethical theories and principles: Ethical theories and principles are the foundations of ethical analysis. Ethical principles are the common goals that each theory tries to achieve in order to be successful. These goals include beneficence, least harm, respect for autonomy and justice. Ethical theories are used to evaluate actions, roles and character. An important role of a sound ethical theory is to improve our moral insight into particular problems on ongoing basis. Two main moral theories of modern virtue ethics are Kant's *Deontological* ethics and *Utilitarianism*. Deontology theory is based on the concept of what is considered *morally right* on universal laws that exist outside of a specific situation. There are numerous utilitarian theories in modern ethics. Following four main aspects are typical for each utilitarian theory. 1) The consequence principle or consequentialism i.e. the consequences of actions. 2) Happiness i.e. happiness is the main goal that should be achieved. 3) Greatest happiness principle i.e. the greatest happiness for the greatest number. 4) Maximizing i.e. the collective amount of utility should be maximized.

Ethical theories for professionals: Ethical theories ground their requirements in engineering codes of ethics by reference to broader moral principles and thus in one way assist professionals in setting aside the feelings, desires, and ambitions that often tend to skew one's moral vision and look at a problem from a rational viewpoint. Followingsethics are applied to professionalism.

Rights (Moral and Human Rights) Ethics: Rights ethics is the most familiar ethical theory, for it provides the moral foundation of the political and legal system of any country. The idea of human rights is the single most powerful moral concept in making cross-cultural moral judgments about customs and laws.

Inquiry in engineering ethics involves investigations into moral and ethical values, meaning and facts in practical operations (Harris et al. 2013). These inquiries in the field of engineering ethics are of three types, viz., 1) normative inquiries, 2) conceptual inquiries and 3) factual or descriptive inquiries.

Kohlberg's theory of moral development: Jean Piaget is among the first psychologists who proposed theory of moral development. Piaget concluded that children begin in a *heteronomous* stage of moral reasoning, characterized by a strict adherence to rules and duties, and obedience to authority. Lawrence Kohlberg (1969) modified and elaborated Piaget's work, and laid the groundwork for the current debate within psychology on moral development. Kohlberg's theory holds that moral reasoning, which is the basis for ethical behavior, has six identifiable developmental stages. These six stages are broken into three levels: pre-conventional, conventional and post-conventional. His theory is based on constructive developmental stages; each stage and level are more adequate at responding to moral dilemmas.

Review questions

1. Give bird eye view of history of Ethics and sources of ethical and moral Principles in India.
2. Explain various dharmas prescribed in our dharma-shastras for Ethical Life.
3. Describe ten meritorious, ten de-meritorious deeds and five precepts of Ethics in Buddhism.
4. Explain historical development of Ethics and history of Christian morality in western World.
5. Give an account of ancient Ethics and Modern Morality. What are distinguishing features of Ethics and Morality?
6. Justify that ethical theories and principles are the foundations of ethical analysis. Explain in detail ethical principles which are the common goals that each theory tries to achieve in order to be successful.
7. Give brief account of ethical theories like Deontological Ethics or Duty Ethics and Utilitarianism,
8. Explain ethical theories like of Moral and Human Rights, casuist ethical theory and virtue ethical theory. How are they having direct applications to Professionalism?
9. What are types of Inquiries used to analyze ethical issues and questions arising in all fields of human activities, Explain?
10. What is the Use of Ethical Theories? In social context what purpose they serve to humanity?
11. Explain salient features of theory of moral development proposed by Piaget and Kohlberg.
12. Kohlberg theory identifies three levels of constructive developmental stages. Explain that each stage and level is more adequate at responding to moral dilemmas.

13. Describe Gilligan's Theory of Moral Development. What was Heinz's Dilemma? Explain.

6 Role of Engineering and Professional Ethics in Industry and Business Operations

Learning objectives

In this chapter you will learn about

- Role of ethics in engineering profession to solve moral dilemmas
- Engineering and ethics of moral rights, autonomy and virtues
- Core values and important features of professional ethics
- Professional role of engineers on technical, non-technical and managerial issues
- Consensus and Controversies on ethical, technical and economic issues
- Ethical considerations in local and global Business

6.1 Purpose of Engineering Ethics

Globally Engineers play major role in implementation of technological development to modernize the world in all aspects of life. Technology and environment around him have profound effect on human life in the contemporary world. Thus, engineering profession is required to be morally committed to hold paramount the safety, health, and welfare of the public. Accordingly, engineers must be trained to deal with moral and ethical dilemmas they may confront in the process of their professional role. Introduction to ethics in engineering education is aimed to provide an exposure to engineers to understand the ethical issues arising in engineering practice. They must be explained about philosophical framework of moral and ethical issues arising out of implementation of technology, their social importance and intellectual challenge to convey benefits of technical solutions to general public. The educational goal is to stimulate engineer's thinking and reasoning capability on such issues/situations and equip them with the necessary conceptual tools for logical and rational decision making. Exposure to conflicting ethical approaches on an issue serves better our goal of encouraging responsible reasoning.

Studying engineering ethics should enable engineers and managers to wisely confront the issues and the questions arising due to application of technology. Further study of ethics is important for developing safe and useful technological products. In practice, ethical issues are quite complex and calls for serious reflections throughout the professional life. For example, chemical industry which provides many products like plastics, fertilizers, medical drugs etc., also produces water contamination and environment pollution. Ethical concern and impact of technology on society can be understood through I) college courses ii) continuing education iii) individual case studies and iv) research. Thus, primary objective of teaching ethical studies to engineers is to equip them for effectively dealing with moral complexities of engineering profession and to sensitize them about their moral duty, to solve the problems arising due to application of technology. The study of ethics strengthens their ability to reason clearly and carefully on moral and ethical questions. The unifying goal of engineering ethics is to increase moral autonomy of engineers.

Engineers are guided and empowered through suitably drawn code of conducts on ethical issues by professional bodies and legal framework, to express more effectively concern about dangers of technology and moral questions on risks and safety of employees, consumers and general public.

Under the scope of ethical studies, engineers are also taught about their obligations to society, to their clients, and to the profession. The field of ethical studies is closely related to such subjects like the philosophy of science, the philosophy of engineering, and the ethics of technology.

The purpose of studying *engineering ethics* is to give exposure to students on various dimensions of ethical problems arising during their engineering practice. An engineer must be aware of

1. Scope of engineering ethics applicable to his profession and professional responsibilities.
2. Ethical theories and moral reasoning behind them for effectiveness in profession and society.
3. Role of engineering as social experimentation and expected consequences of experimentation.
4. His obligations and responsibilities for safety of human beings in short term and long-term basis at micro and macro level.
5. His responsibility towards management, employees, clients, law, society etc.
6. His responsibilities in different roles like engineer, managers, consultants and project head etc.
7. Global issues are connected with- cross-cultural matters, environmental ethics, computer ethics, codes of ethics, ethical problems in research, Intellectual Property Rights, etc.

8. Rights of engineers.

Engineers sometimes face moral dilemmas on above referred roles or situations in their job or profession where a difficult choice has to be made between different conflicting requirements. Purpose of studying engineering ethics is to prepare him to face these moral dilemmas logically and professionally.

6.1.1 Moral Dilemmas

Moral dilemmas can also be called moral problems. Moral dilemmas have two or more conflicting requirements like -moral obligations, duties, rights, good and bad consideration or personal ideals, which disagree with each other. One moral principle can have two or more conflicting applications for a particular given situation.

Engineering ethics is not only teaching moral behavior in knowing about immoral and amoral in a set of beliefs, but also increasing the ability of engineers and other professionals to face boldly with the moral dilemmas arising from technological advancements, changes and other related activities. Compulsion of modern engineering practices requires that all the engineers should face boldly the moral dilemmas arising in their Professional careers.

Moral Dilemmas can be resolved by proceeding systematically by following steps which are interrelated and can also be used jointly.

1. Identify the relevant moral factors and reasons to understand conflict among them (i) the responsibilities (ii) the competing rights and (iii) the clashing of ideals involved etc.
2. Collect and gather all the available facts which are relevant to the moral factors for resolving the dilemma.
3. Organize above data or information in order of ranks of the moral considerations or principles on the basis of importance as applicable to the situation.
4. Examine alternative courses of action available within the limitation of time, space, money and impact, tracing the full implications of each factor for resolving the problem.
5. Discuss with the colleagues and team members about the problem for getting their suggestions and alternative ideas to consolidate the picture for arriving at the best solution to the moral problem supported by the facts or truths.

Thus, study of *engineering ethics* can inculcate required skills and attitudes among engineers and other professionals, by following above steps in resolving a moral problem. The case studies, classroom discussions, and debating on dilemmas, can sharpen their skill for resolving moral and ethical issues.

6.2 Engineering and Ethics

Engineering and Ethics are two different disciplines of study but in their application, they come together in all fields of engineer's activities and professional work. They are different because engineering profession faces unique problems quite different from other disciplines. The field of ethical studies is very wide and ethical problem arise almost in all fields of human activities. Problems similar to other fields of human activities are expected in engineering also and their solutions may provide guidance to solve the ethical problems in engineering professions.

Ethical theories, guide engineers and professionals in the search for a solution to ethical problems in engineering. Popular ethical theories like utilitarianism, Kantianism, rights theory, and virtue ethics are already discussed in chapter 5. In commonsense, *ethical theories* refer to general and systematic rules such as *maximize welfare* or "act only according to maxims that could be a universal law i.e. universalization of ethics" for engineering.

Engineering has many fields of disciplines like electronics, electrical, mechanical, civil, computer science, IT, Bio-Tech, etc. with each one having various lines of specializations. Thus, there cannot be a single uniform system, or standard, of ethical conduct across the entire spectrum of professional fields. Thus, ethical considerations for various fields of engineering, somewhat vary and differ based on the discipline and jurisdiction of operations. Moral and ethical considerations are most influenced by the way engineering services are provided. For example, engineers may be working independently and providing professional services to clients; or they may be employed in government service; or working as employees of an enterprise creating products for sale etc., their moral and ethical responsibilities will differ based on nature of engineering service provided by them.

Engineers keep on creating better and improved versions of products and processes in all fields of engineering activities like energy, communication, transportation, health, food production etc. and generate solutions against natural calamities like providing shelters, protection and rehabilitation to affected public. Engineers dedicate to enhance the convenience and beauty of our everyday lives. Most technologies are beneficial to the society but sometimes also give raise new moral challenges. For example, exploration of the moon and other planets are engineering triumphs but sometimes cause disastrous consequences like the explosions of the space shuttles. Tragic explosion of Challenger in 1986 and Columbia in 2003, were preventable, had urgent warnings voiced by experienced engineers been heeded.

All round improvement of conditions of human life, as well as dangers to human life and other cases of human error, call for considering the relationship of ethical dimension in the engineering profession. An engineer has to strike a balance between probable technological risks by minimizing it and should not allow the risks component to overshadow technological benefits. Ethics involves in promoting the positive dimensions of technology that so deeply enrich our lives.

6.3 Engineering Ethics

Engineering ethics is applied ethics, i.e. ethics applied to specific practical engineering problems or solution. Ethical considerations are applied to guide engineers what they should do when confronted with an ethical problem. Engineering ethics can exist as an independent field and can invoke ideas from the work of philosophers of different ethical theories.

Some people equate engineering ethics with the codes of conduct stipulated by different engineering and professional societies. Then *codes of conduct* become embodiment of what is right for engineers of that profession or field of activity. Actually, codes are essentially consensual in nature to guide and control the professionals working in the interest of the profession.

In light of wide range of engineering disciplines and moral complexity in each field of engineering branch, we attempt to define a common frame of engineering ethics and the purpose of studying it as follows.

1. The words ethics and engineering ethics have several meanings. Engineering ethics tries to define the responsibilities and rights of engineers that ought to be adhered by those engaged in engineering activity. It also stipulates desirable ideals and personal commitments towards the profession.
2. Ethics is study of moral justification of actions, goals, principles, policies, and laws from morality point of view. Accordingly, engineering ethics is the study of the values, policies and decisions, and their moral justification in engineering practice and research.

Above two senses of ethics are normative. They refer to justification of values, soundness of policies and rationality in choices. When applied to engineering ethics it refers to justified moral and ethical values to be adhered and practiced in engineering. About morals and morality, we have already discussed in Chapter 3. Summarily, morality is about right and wrong, good and bad values and what ought to be done.

6.3.1 Moral Rights in Engineering Profession

A strong ethical consideration in engineering and other professions is ethics of *moral responsibilities and rights*. Towards moral responsibilities, most of the engineering codes of ethics give special emphasis on the safety, health, and welfare of the public. This requirement amounts to, like an ethical edict for engineering disciplines to have respect for the public's rights to life, rights for safety from harmful and dangerous products, rights to privacy, and rights to fair deal and honest service in free market conditions.

Engineering professionals also enjoy human rights and special moral rights. For example, engineers and their employers have special moral rights for their respective roles which are specified in their contracts document. Special rights are basically drawn from their human rights, directly or indirectly. For example, when consumers buy a product, it is implied that the manufactures will ensure safe and useful product to the consumers.

Utilitarianism is one of the central principles in most the engineering codes: Transactions between manufacturers and consumers are built around the commitment of engineering activities producing good consequences, because such transactions revolve around utilitarian mode of thinking, where focus is on cost-benefit analysis. In engineering practice, one has to evaluate various options or proposals and their likely good and bad consequences, and then select that proposal which maximizes the overall good.

6.3.2   Ethics of Proficiency Virtue

Proficiency virtues demands mastery over one's profession, particularly command over the technical skills that leads to good decision making and engineering practice. Further, engineers are also required to enhance professional status by voluntarily giving their time, talent, and money to their professional societies and local communities. Further, engineers should demonstrate generosity in their attitudes, which means going beyond the minimum requirements in helping others. Engineers have to play crucial role of ensuring professional justice within corporations, government, and economic practices. Beneficence is another directive principle of engineering code which calls for prevention or removal of harm of any nature to others and, positive actions towards promoting the public safety, health, and welfare.

6.4   Moral Autonomy of Engineers

Autonomy means *self-ruling* or *independence for actions*. However, autonomy does not imply any kind of self-determining or independent reflection about ethics within the meaning of moral autonomy. Moral autonomy is essential for engineers for developing, expressing and acting on moral considerations. Moral autonomy includes habit of rational thinking on ethical issues with moral concern and commitment. Attitude of

general responsiveness, of an individual to his professional moral values, is attributed to basic training he/she receives in childhood when he/she develops sensitivity to his needs as well as rights of others. Moral autonomy may include the followings:
1. Capability to recognize moral issues in engineering and ability to differentiate as well as relate them to, problems in politics, law, economics, religious doctrine or administrative set up etc.
2. Skills in comprehending the views of opposite side and building consensus.
3. The ability to develop his viewpoint based on relevant facts / data.
4. Sensitivity to genuine difficulties and tolerance in making moral judgment or decisions.
5. Being aware of own moral integrity i.e. Recognition of the need of integrating one's professional life and personal convictions.

6.5 Professional Ethics

Role of engineers in industry, has already discussed in chapter 1. Broad spectrum of General Principles and Moral and Ethics in Various Professions were also discussed in chapter 3. Here we shall discuss ethical considerations of Professionalism in Engineering. A profession is one that requires extensive amount of education and field training before the trainees can be called a professional and it has wider field of applications than engineering. According to this definition, Engineering, Medicine, Law, Veterinary Medicine, Architecture, Accounting (at least certified public accountancy) etc., qualify to be called professions, and practitioners in these fields of specializations are called professionals of their respective areas. Important feature of *professional ethics* is discussed below.

Ethical commitment: Ethical commitment is the core value of professionalism. Professional ethics differ from profession to profession. For example, Ethical guidelines in medical profession are different from legal or accountancy profession. There are other types of ethics also like philosophical ethics, business ethics, personal ethics, and so on.

Compliance to professional ethics: Concept of professional ethics is partly composed of dos and don'ts of a professional in the workplace. Professionalism demands that any professional should adopt and conduct all of his dealings in accordance with ethics prescribed for his profession, as well as Ethical expectations and norms of behavior of the society. Commitment to Professional Ethics demands practice of showing respect to other professionals, avoidance of dishonest or fraudulent activities, and the professional development of other individuals. Professional ethics also commands for working towards the enhancement of the quality of professional services and image of the professional works.

***Specialized knowledge* to serve the public**: Because of the specialist knowledge possessed by professionals, professional ethics concerns on the moral issues that how the application of such knowledge should be governed in service to the public. Under professional ethics, a professional should try for "giving one's best" services which are in the interest of clients and the general public.

Compliance to code of professional ethics: Code of Professional Ethics guides the professionals on moral principles and standards of conduct, to be adopted in performing their professional duties and functions. Codes of professional ethics are established by professional institutions or organizations of professional bodies. Every profession like medicine, law, architecture, pharmacy and so forth has their own codes of professional ethics. A professional is subject to disciplinary action on violation of professional ethics. Departure from prescribed practice of professional ethics erodes the reputation of the profession and the confidence of the public.

Objectivity and integrity: In order to ensure objectivity and integrity of professional decisions, they should be based on rationality and independent of clients being served. The professionals must also maintain confidentiality of information obtained from the client in the course of a professional engagement. A professional while in public practice should not engage in any other incompatible occupation, where there could arise a conflict of interest.

6.5.1 Characteristic features of Professional Ethics

- Professional code of ethics is like a kind of mission statements for professional beings to live by. It flows out of the overriding necessity to ensure that any given task is undertaken and completed in conformity with the principles of accountability, equity, propriety, prudence, probity, rectitude, honesty, integrity and transparency, and paying due regard to the imperatives of national security, public safety, health and sanitation, environmental protection and ecological balance. These fundamental requirements admit of no compromise.
- Professional ethics must be considered above and free from cultural, religious, or ethnic considerations. Ethical values are framed taking a broader universal worldview.
- Sometimes, situation may arise where decisions or actions taken are legally correct but not morally, or may be ethically correct but not morally. Professionals at workplace have to strike proper balance between of morality, ethics and law in their professional activities.

- Professional ethics and excellence in professional activities go together as considerations of moral and ethical values permeate all phases of research and technological development.
- In order to provide guidelines for carrying out professional activities, organization frame rules, regulations, code of conduct, protocols, etc. These guidelines show how to walk, but do not show the correct path to walk on, which sometimes gives rise to ethical dilemma. Ethical dilemmas are often more real and highly complex. Quite often there are no clear guidelines either in law or in religion or in codes of conduct.

6.5.2 Ethical Assumption of Professional Organizations

Professional organizations work on five basic assumptions while dealing with ethical issues and human behavior.

1. Evolution of professional ethics is a dynamic process. It is not static or fixed like a textual matter to be learnt and practiced. It is a process of continuously reviewing changes in behavior against constantly changing standards. Something ethical today, or in some society, may be judged differently by other society or at other time.
2. Human behavior is the result of certain motivational factors like financial gain, power, compassion etc.
3. All actions have reactions and culminate into certain consequences.
4. Every individual has own views on what is ethical from his *point of view*. These views are formed by variety of factors like his social learning or media exposure, published codes, or statements of leading personalities etc.
5. Mutual trust, between manufacturers or suppliers of goods and services and consumers, is the backbone of successful *ethical business practices*. Mutual trust and respect rests on reciprocity of behavior and respect between each other. Respect is not a right and must be earned.

6.5.3 Professional Ethics *vs.* Personal Morality

1. Common morality and personal morality are based on social values and personal values. They are not formalized as a statement, whereas professional ethics is usually stated in a formal code. In fact, each profession prescribes his own codes and there are several such codes, promulgated by various professional bodies or institutions. These are usually referred as *codes of ethics* or *code of professional responsibility* or *code of professional conduct*. The content of these codes of ethics differ substantiality in some

important directions and principles, which the profession wants to emphasize. In engineering, for example, some of the codes have begun to emphasize concern on the environment and pollution.
2. In professional relationships with clients, personal morality is supposed to take back seat over professional ethics. This characteristic of professional ethics is important for the clients. For example, when a patient or client confides his problems with the doctor, he/she has justifiably expectations of a professional service with maintenance of confidentiality of his problems. Similarly, when an employer or a customer reveals details of a business relationship to an engineer, he/she expects maintenance of confidentiality of the details revealed by him. In the above examples, personal morality of the doctor or engineer should not play any role and only professional ethics of medicine and engineering professions should be paramount in mutual transactions.
3. Sometimes certain clauses of professional ethics conflict with individual's personal morality. For example, if personal morality of some engineer, who believes that war is an immoral activity, conflicts with his Job of designing military hardware and refuses to participate in such design activity, he/she is going against professional ethics. Here, the engineer's personal ethics is taking precedence over his professional ethics which is not right.

Conflicts between personal ethics and professional ethics can arise in other professions also. Quite often conflicts among common morality, personal morality, and professional ethics are complex in nature and difficult to resolve. In such conflicting scenario, clear answer in favor of professional ethics should be given priority. However, such cases of conflicts sometimes provoke profound moral controversy.

6.6 Professional Attitude in Engineering works and trade off with role of other Functionaries

With rise in professionalism, society becomes increasingly dependent on the services, knowledge and expertise of professionals in all fields of social functions. The public places more trust on engineers and professionals, as individuals and as members of teams working together. Engineers as professional must work to become trustworthy and display honesty, sincerity, integrity and confidentiality in their character while dealing with other professionals or public.

Nature of responsibility of engineers within the most of the production infrastructure in a factory consists of various stages of processing activities. The manufacturing processes are kept under rigid quality control to ensure final product quality. Large and complex products/ system like computers, automobile, railway wagons, airplanes, satellites, missiles etc. are produced in one location through assembly of thousands and lakhs of small and large components/ sub units received from ancillary industries engaged in their manufacturing. Quite often these ancillary industrial units are not co-located, but geographically located over widely spread locations or even in different countries. Final quality requirement and specifications of any product are used to define or translate into component level specifications, for procurement from ancillary units. Thus, job of all engineers, technologists and supporting technicians engaged in each respective ancillary unit; becomes to ensure compliance to quality requirement of each activity within their control; as per specifications laid down for the individual part/process, to ensure the quality of final production the final assembly stage.

It is worth noticing that the entire supply chain of components for any product is maintained by thousands of technical and non-technical persons at respective workstations. Clearly any laxity on the part of the working staff on quality measures like human error, material defect, deviance from prescribed process parameters etc. can cause disastrous results in the field performance of final product, process or mission.

6.6.1 Consequences of Responsibility without Ethical Concern

Many times, responsible professionals are not able to feel that they (as employee, entrepreneurs, employers or simply as a responsible citizen) and their job have their professional responsibility towards ultimate users or general public. Many engineering disasters happened due to this attitude of unconcern for risk and safety of public. Study and analysis of causes leading to engineering disasters reveal that many of these disasters were preventable if concerned professionals were alert, fearless and consciously concerned about welfare of the society and the fellow being. Such disasters take place due to lack of adequate understanding of few individuals about their responsibility, adherence to professional code of conduct, ethics and values and their role as an enlightened professional and citizen.

6.6.2 Engineer's roles of non-technical nature

At senior level and during execution of projects, an engineer has to perform many non-technical functions which are in the nature of, interrelationship and interdependence between subordinates, peer level colleagues, higher authorities, coordination on interdepartmental dealings and compliance to contractual requirements of customers/clients. Therefore, he/she should have very good aptitude and understanding of human behavior and their psychological make up for overall success and efficiency in execution of tasks.

Hershel should also have good understanding of human environment in which and for which he/she is working. To elaborate the point, an engineer should have clarity about role, type of person/group and situation he/she is responding:

1. **Personality Judgment**: From the point of view of moral ethical considerations, an engineer should have good understanding of human behavior, attitudes, motivations and personality traits of people with whom he/she is dealing in his professional interactions.
2. **Background Judgment**: In the context of working environment and functioning, an engineer should be familiar about the impact of back ground on behavior and value preferences ingrained in their team members, their locality, community and groupings based on, business, caste, language, region, religion, etc., which play role in successful delivery of product and services.
3. **Priority judgment among different values**: Understanding relative priorities of moral and ethical values in each domain from personal level to family and societal groupings mentioned above. An Engineer should have clear logical picture of demarcation of their boundaries, applicability and validity.
4. **Strong character**: A professional must be strong in character while playing different roles in life, as these roles have different set of values and different hierarchical emphasis.

6.6.3 Technical and Professional Competence

Professional competence Isa virtue ethics in any profession as discussed in Chapter 3. Therefore prior to undertaking any task/ jobs, an engineer must equip himself with required skills and knowledge of process involved in execution of task/job with confidence and perfection. For example, he/she must:

1. Understand his Task/ job in totality i.e. technically, operationally, application or conditions of utilization, testing and evaluation procedures, specifications of incoming material and qualification of outgoing product, reliability of process, methods of calibration, etc.
2. Be well versed in measurement techniques and achievable accuracy from them, new trends in evaluation techniques, statistical methods used in mass production, formats of data recording and reporting to ensure that accuracy of production process is under control.
3. Have knowledge of quality and reliability techniques to ensure wear and tear free operation of product i.e. he/she must be familiar

with prediction techniques like MTBF, MTTR, life or Fault free Mission time etc. in actual use of environment (i.e. under expected extreme environmental conditions of temperature, humidity, vibration, bumps and shocks, etc., and field of application indoor, outdoor, ground or airborne, high altitude space environment, etc.)
4. Understand working environments for the task/product like safety measures, air pollutant levels (in chemical industry/process), radiation level, temperature, vibration, noise, light level handling tools, dress code etc.
5. Train his team and develop team spirit and their skills under his control on the lines of above considerations. Understand human relations and ethical issues while dealing with staff (higher, lower and colleagues).
6. Holistic understanding of his professional role as well as role in the social environment within the ambit of professional role. He/ She must act as an educated person of higher and superior moral and ethical behavior. He/ She must act as an agent of social change and be role model in his profession. He/ She must act as an enlightened citizen.

6.6.4 Conflict in role of Engineering Professionals and Management

Management expert Raelin has analyzed value conflict in role of engineers and managers. He says that "...there is a natural conflict between management and professionals because of their differences in educational background, socialization, values, vocational interests, work habits, and outlook" (Raelin, 1986, pp.14).

Understanding conflict of roles and responsibilities between engineers and managers (or employers business objectives) as well as ways of their resolution is important in the interest of best service or products to the customers. Let us explore areas of conflict which engineers have to amicably resolve.
1. **Professional responsibility towards employer *vs.* high standards for quality and public safety:** Sometimes engineers come across conflict between loyalty to their profession and their employer. Employers look upon their engineers to be loyal employees, concerned about the financial well-being of the organization, and follow directions of their superiors. In the vocabulary of many engineering codes, they are required to be *faithful agents* of their employers for organization's well-being. At the same time, code of professional ethics requires engineers to have obligation to hold paramount the health, safety, and welfare of the public. This obligation requires engineers to establish high

standards for product and service qualityalong with safety features. However, higher quality and safety requirement pushes the cost of production high as high quality of inputs and tight control on production process becomes essential-which affects profitability of the company.

2. **Different qualification and background of Managers vs. Engineers**: Many managers are not engineers and communication with them on engineering and technical matters like design, quality and safety etc. is often difficult. Managers are normally concerned with planning, scheduling and profitability of product lines. Areas of emphasis of engineers and managers on business processes differ due to different areas of concern. This makes engineers task sometimes difficult and they find difficult to communicate with managers on points concern from engineering point of view.

3. **Dual role of manager and engineer:** In long run, many engineers aspire to management roles in the organization, where the financial rewards are better and span of control and command is wider, giving them higher social prestige. Some engineers do have dual roles of engineer and manager but many times this leads to internal conflicts.

6.6.5 Managers Trade-Off with conflicting situation

Above referred role conflicts between the engineers and managers are traded off by the managers in different ways as explained below.

1. Normally, decisions of senior corporate managers and top management team focus on organizational goals and ethos and do not care much for genuine moral commitments to play a role in the decision-making process. Engineers must learn to keep their individual conscience separate from corporate actions. Managers, look for a trade-off between moral principles, and expediency of corporate targets and goals. However, managers cannot limit their vision to short term goals alone and have to keep in view long term loyalty of customers, which if eroded, will bring down the image of the organization. There is no higher wisdom required for realization that faulty products are bad because they will ultimately harm the company's public image. Similarly, any environmental damage is bad for business in long run.

2. Loyalty towards management, superiors and peers is the characteristic of virtuous managers. A successful manager achieves his goals by creating team spirit among his staff and on that strength ready to accept more challenging jobs that reflects favorably upon him and others.

3. Sometimes managers purposefully keep lines of responsibility vague and diffused to protect oneself, one's peers, and one's superiors. In making difficult and controversial decisions, some manager tries to involve many people so that, in case of difficulties or failure, he/she can point his finger at others. Such managers work towards protecting and covering their boss, peers, and himself which supersedes all other considerations.

6.6.6 Models of Professional Roles

The main aim of the profession of engineering is to improve the public safety, health and welfare. In order to maximize his effectiveness in a working situation or problem, an engineer has to adopt various role models as the situation demands to achieve the objectives. These role models are as follows:

1. **Role of technical Leadership**
   Engineers, through technical development, are creating goods, products, systems and infrastructure for comfortable social habitation of human beings. Now everything is possible and achievable without much effort. Engineers should provide technological leadership to society at large to solve problems of poverty, inefficiency, waste and conditions of working of manual labor.

2. **Guardian**
   Engineers are aware of good and bad part of any technology. They can implement it with properly safe guarding against pitfalls and dangers of technology. Given proper authority based on their expertise skills they can decide and work in the best interests of the society. Here they are acting as guardians of technology.

3. **Bureaucratic Role**
   Many Engineers work in Government as policy makers and administrators. Their decisions have far reaching consequence in shaping and improving the society and support infrastructure. In Industry Engineer's role in the management is to some extent bureaucratic in nature who translates the directive of management for better achievements along with creating good industrial ambience and ensuring legal compliance to directives of Govt. agencies.

4. **Role of Agent of Social Change**
   Engineers are knowledgeable persons in the eye of common man. Their behavior, conduct and opinions about social matters carry lot of weight in society. They can induct scientific fervor in youths and motivate people in society against superstitions, unscientific beliefs and practices, unhygienic practices and living conditions

etc. This role of agent of social change falls upon engineers as their responsibility to the society.

6.7 Consensus and Controversies on work situations/business operations

Consensus is commonality of views or an *agreement* on the issue and *controversy* means divergent views or disagreement on any issue. The consensus and controversies arise on any problem due to conflicting divergent views and perceptions on ethical, technical, economic and commitment to schedule etc., among team members. Quite often such situations arise due to moral autonomy of engineers on the one hand and executive authority of managers and the management on the other hand.

Consensus and controversy have their root in professional role of engineers and managerial decision-making process, where adherence to morality views by professionals is digested reluctantly and a principled professional would appear to exhibit disobedience to authority. In practice it requires a broader understanding on type of business/service activities of the organizations and the rationale of the culture adopted by them for maintaining continuity and growth to sustain in their respective fields. Thus, there is need to scrutinize the likely areas of consensus and controversies where engineers are seen to have a much more concern towards productive relationship with the organizations.

There are two contrasting approaches to look at the issue of engineering ethics.
1. Microscopic view of day to day small petty moral problems and issues corresponding to immediate surroundings, but sometimes persistently nagging around.
2. The Macroscopic view of long term and larger social problems.

A professional is required to develop culture of consensus between controversies arising due to broad macroscopic view with specific microscopic circumstances of everyday settings.

An example of these types of tussles faced by engineers in their jobs could be like production of unsafe product or a product of less utility. This may be an intentional act or action under pressure or due to ignorance. There could be intentional design for limited life of utility, substitution of inferior material to reduce cost or a product of harmful nature in long term use. There could be other factors also at play like corruption, sabotage, bribery by competitors etc.

In large scale operations and projects employing latest techniques and technologies, many problems crop up which were not conceived earlier, or not fully understood, or neglected due to ignorance of their after-effects later on. For example, an engineer may notice deterioration in quality in production process but management may like him to continue production to meet targets. In a nuclear plant there could be different expert opinions on level of safety measures to be employed for human safety. In chemical plant there could be multiple solutions to deal with hazardous substances and waste disposal but none of them perfect from the human and environment safety point of view. In all such situation a consensus is required based on level of maturity of technology employed to minimize the controversies. A professional outlook on microscopic and macroscopic impacts, of issue under discussion, is necessary for a consensual solution with minimum controversies.

When an individual exercises moral autonomy, his conclusions and results may conflict from others who are also applying their moral autonomy. These differences lead to controversy of some moral differences for the results or verdicts. These kinds of disagreements are unavoidable and require better understanding and spirit of accommodation among individuals, who are autonomous and responsible professionals.

The purpose of engineering ethics is to promote tolerance while supporting moral autonomy of professionals so that there is more consensus than controversy on any issue.

Example of conflict between autonomy and authority:
Both the goals of engineering ethics and the goals of engineering courses have some similarities on aims of profession. But there arise conflicts also when exercising authority and autonomy is concerned in the field. For example, in the classroom, the teachers are having the authority over students and, in the workplace the managers are having the authority over engineers.

Relationship between autonomy and authority is complex on two counts.
1. Moral autonomy and respect for the authority co-exist in a working organizational set-up. They cannot be separated from each other in crystal clear fashion. Moral autonomy has good moral reasons for its recognition and is based on moral concern for other people. Whereas recognition of Authority is essential to provide a structure and the framework in which the organization is set up. Structure of authority pyramid is essential for functioning of an organization and its acceptance by both the engineers and the managers is unquestionably desirable.
2. However, consensus and controversies are bound to crop up due autonomy of both as well as difference in their roles. Generally, controversies arise because of pressure for need of consensus about authority and right of autonomy granted by code of ethics. The differences can always be narrowed down discussing openly regarding the autonomy and moral issue with the help of the intervention and facilitation of the authority.

Generally, conflicts between autonomy and authority are exaggerated when the authority is dictated and misused.

6.8 Ethics in Business

Events in corporate worlds, both in India and the west have demonstrated that when the leadership of a company does not behave ethically, company operations and image suffer and, litigation problems increase leading to legal battles. It is surprising, that highly educated, successful, and business savvy corporate professionals at Satyam, Mining Corporation, Enron, Tyco, WorldCom, Adelphia etc. got themselves into big mess. The reason is traced to profound lack of ethics in corporate functioning.

Conducting business ethically is good for business. Business ethics of any business is designed as the standards of conduct to be followed in business operations by individual businessman or the organization (Boylan, 2013).

Accordingly, to management experts, companies following ethical standards of their industries, have an advantage over their competitors. Ethical companies cash on customer loyalty, which is dream of most corporations, because ethical operation appeals to customers more than a product.

Today's marketplace is more conscience-focused and the customer's choice for companies following ethical business processes- known as Ethic is misincreasing. Simultaneously, there is pressure of new public initiatives and laws to improve business ethics in industry. Sometimes businesses can prosper on short-term gains by adopting unethical methods; but such behaviors are suicidal in long run and tend to harm the business as well as undermine the economy over time.

Historically, interest in business ethics gained momentum during the 1980s and 1990s in major corporations and academia. Most major corporate websites in western countries started propagating their commitment to the service to social sector, thus promoting non-economic parameters e.g. ethics codes, social responsibility charters, etc. Some corporations even redefined their core values in the light of ethical considerations on business objectives.

Parallelly, in compliance to business ethics program, many companies started formulating policies on the ethical conduct of their employees. These policies, typically called statement of corporate ethics, were in the nature of exhortations in broad, highly generalized language. The policies could be detailed out to the extent of specific behavioral requirements from the employees-typically called corporate code of ethics. These codes detail the company's expectations from employees and provide suitable guidelines on handling more common ethical issues which may crop up in the course of business operations. These policies and codes create better ethical awareness among employees and, consistency in their application which help in avoidance of ethical mishaps.

Another method adopted by companies, for sensitizing the employees on ethical matters, is organizing seminars for employees regarding business conduct, where company's policies, specific case studies, and legal requirements of the business are discussed and elaborated by experts. Some companies follow the route of signing agreements with employees as part of employment contract that they will abide by the company's rules of conduct.

To be successful in implementation of ethics policy, most ethicists suggest that the policy should:

1. Have unequivocal support of top management and demonstrated in words and actions.
2. Be conveyed to each employee orally and in writing. It also requires periodic checks and reinforcement for success in implementation.
3. Be doable which employees can both understand and adopt in practice.
4. Be monitored by top management, with routine inspections for compliance and improvement.
5. Incorporate in clear terms the consequences of disobedience.
6. Remain neutral to gender concern.

Applying ethics in business makes good sense. When a company applies ethics in its operations, it starts caring for stakeholders i.e. meeting all responsibilities to employees, customers and suppliers. In return the company receives high degree of loyalty, honesty, quality and productivity from stakeholders.

Ethics can be explained to employees but the best way to teach ethical behavior is by setting good examples because mere understanding of ethics does not necessarily result in ethical behavior. Personal values and ethical behavior are also taught at an early age by parents and educators.

Ethics are an essential part of the foundation on which of a civilized society is built. A business or society that lacks ethical principles is bound to fail sooner or later.

6.9 Global Business

Global companies want to earn consumers' confidence by assuring them that products manufactured by them, or their vendors, suppliers and licensees, are produced under best possible manufacturing plants and processes and in accordance with the sound principles of *business ethics*.

Business leaders differ in their views on whether ethics should be global in character or should adopt local ethics of foreign country also where the company is doing or wants to do the business. When a company adopts local ethics, sometimes business operation gets surrounded by scandals, thus risking the company's reputation. It may happen that in order to win a few overseas contracts, you risk permanently damaging your company reputation.

Some of the global business executives assert that a great global company can be built only with a single global standard of business practices. They argue that in favor of single global standard of the company business, because in absence of it, how company employees in far-flung locations decide on what to do in the interest of company business, when pressurized by customers or competitors to deviate from company standards? The counter argument against single global standard of company business is that, can company afford to miss the overseas business opportunity if the managers there adhere to strict ethical standards without compromise with local business environment, and then what happens to overseas financial targets. Management must be convinced within and must convey down the line that for them ethics and profits are complementary and not contradictory in their business.

Developing best practices for corporate conduct is a slow process and takes time to mature. However, there are some basic principles in operation which should be implemented from the beginning throughout the organization and practiced meticulously. Some of the arguments in favor and against the character on global ethical principles are presented below:

- **Ethics must be global not local**

Business Leaders of large MNCs prefer to adopt a global standard of ethical practices for their global business operation. However, many business executives believe that this is not a wise approach in global business. They argue that business ethics should adapt to the local environment and cannot be same throughout the world. They say that "...when in Rome, do as the Romans do" is a wise policy. In other words, follow local practices. This approach is named as *situation ethics*, based on flexibility in tailoring business operation as per local business culture. This approach is more pragmatic and avoids many complex dilemmas.

With globalization of the business world, debate on ethics has intensified. As an example, local business culture in many developing markets in Asia, Africa, the Middle East and Eastern Europe is making unethical payments, to obtain business. This being the common practice, many companies are tempted to oblige to make payments in various forms like gift, bribe, kickback, etc. to compete in the market for gaining business.

There is no common consensus on *situation ethics* principle. Some leaders of business organizations question that how a company have dual ethics standards i.e. one set of ethics principles in the home country and another for overseas market. They feel that scope of ethical operations has wider field of application than mere statements of code of conduct. Principles of ethical business must be clearly explained to employees around the world by CEO and top management and they must insist on transparency and compliance with them. If company follows principle of situation ethics, the management will remain in dark about what's happening on the ethics front, which sometimes may lead to problems. The company must build proper feedback system so that local marketing practices are monitored and audited regularly. Zero tolerance policy must be implemented to achieve high standards in global business operations.

- **Ethics could be local in global business- local considerations**

As many countries are integrating with global economy, it becomes possible to enter those markets and do business with high profitability, because those countries promise advantage of lower wage structure, better market potential, simple employment standards, affordable taxes, simpler environmental regulations, cheaper local infrastructure facilities, and abundant human resources. This scenario of overseas market is more conducive for global business as production can be organized where cost is lowest, and selling them in markets where profitability is high, and shift the resulting profits to countries where the tax rates are lowest.

However, global business also has its attendant problems which are nonexistent in the home land. For example, some problems arise due to differences in culture, values, and levels of economic development in those nations. Following points should be taken care of while operating in foreign land.

- **Abuse discrimination**–There should be dignity and respect for local employees. There should be no abuse and cruel treatment to employees. Disciplinary practices and employment conditions must be fair and justifiable. There should be no discrimination on the grounds of race, religion, origin, political affiliation, sexual preference, age or gender etc.
- **Acceptance of advantages** – Global companies should not engage with local supporting companies who practice unethical means to conduct business.
- **Environmental impact** – Global companies should comply with local environmental programs practices, and laws relating to the environment and disposal of toxic materials in a controlled and safe manner.
- **Compliance with applicable local laws**– Global companies must comply with the national laws of the country of their business including local laws, regulations and industry standards applicable to their business.

6.10 Summary

Purpose of subject of *engineering ethics* is to sensitize engineers on their role and responsibility within the job as well as indirect impact on common man as consumer of their products, service and their views as an expert.

Engineers should be empowered on ethical issues, through code of conducts drawn by professional bodies and legal framework, to express more effectively concern about dangers of technology and moral questions on risks and safety of employees, consumers and general public.

Moral dilemmas arise from technological advancements, changes and other related activities. Moral dilemmas are actually moral problems having two or more conflicting requirements like - moral obligations, duties, rights, goals or ideals which disagree with each other.

Engineering and Ethics: Engineering and ethics are two different disciplines of study but in application they come together in all fields of engineer's activities. All round improvement of human life, avoidance of dangers to life, cases of human error etc. require ethical considerations in the engineering profession. Engineering ethics is applied ethics, primarily dealing with rights and virtue ethics of engineers. Some people equate engineering ethics with the codes of conduct of the engineering societies.

Moral Rights: Rights ethics provides a powerful tool for enforcing ethical point in engineering and other professions. Most of the engineering codes of ethics hold paramount, the safety, health, and welfare of the public. Engineers and their employers have special moral rights that arise from their respective roles and the contracts they make with each other. Special rights are indirectly grounded in human rights.

Virtue Ethics: Virtue ethics demand many virtues from engineering professionals. For example, proficiency virtues i.e. mastery of technical skills of one's profession; generosity- meaning going beyond the minimum requirements in helping others; voluntarily giving their time, talent, and money to their professional societies and local communities; justice within corporations, government, and economic practices, beneficence i.e. preventing harm to others, promoting the public safety, health, welfare, etc.

Professional Ethics: A professional undergoes through extensive amount of education and field training. Professional ethics requires ethical commitment to the profession like adherence to code of ethics; norms of ethical behavior of the society; professional respect; avoidance of dishonest or fraudulent activity such as plagiarism and the professional development; enhancement of the profession and the related industry; Objectivity and Integrity in professional decisions, etc.

Professional Role of Engineers: The society has become increasingly professionalized and also became more dependent on the services of professionals for their knowledge and expertise. Engineers as professional must work to become trustworthy and display honesty, sincerity, integrity and confidentiality in their character in all their dealings. They should have good understanding of human environment and capacity to judge people or problems in their working situations.

Consensus and Controversies: Consensus is commonality of views or an *agreement* on the issue and *controversy* means divergent views or disagreement on any issue. The consensus and controversies arise on any problem among team members due to conflicting divergent views and perceptions on ethical, technical, economic and commitment to schedule etc. Such situations arise due to Moral Autonomy of engineers clashing with executive authority of managers and the management.

Ethics in Business: Running a business ethically is good for business. However, *business ethics* if properly interpreted means the standards of conduct of individual business people, not necessarily the standards of business as a whole. Global companies want its consumers to have confidence that products manufactured by them, or their vendors, suppliers and licensees, are produced in accordance with the principles of business ethics and are not made under inhumane or exploitative conditions. Experienced executives believe that the only way to build a great global company is with a single global standard of business practices, vigorously communicated and rigorously enforced.

Review questions

1. Explain Purpose of Engineering Ethics.
2. What is type of moral dilemmas an engineer faces in working situations?
3. Justify, that even though engineering must be ethical, engineering cannot have a single uniform system, or standard, of ethical conduct across the entire profession-Justify.
4. With wide range of engineering disciplines and moral complexity, how to define a common frame of engineering ethics?
5. What is scope of Engineering Ethics? Explain Rights, Moral and Virtue Ethics.
6. Explain 'Moral Autonomy' of Engineers and what features may include the Moral autonomy.
7. Explain Professional Ethics and its Core Values and Characteristic.
8. What are ethical assumptions of Professional Organizations and, give important features of Professional Ethics?
9. What is Professionalism and who is a Professional?
10. What do you perceive as 'Professional Role' to be played by engineers?
11. Justify natural Value Conflict in Role of Engineering Professionals and management.
12. Describe different role models of engineers to be played in their Professional Roles.
13. Explain how Consensus and Controversies arise among engineers and managers due to conflicting divergent views and perceptions on ethical, technical, economic and commitment to schedule etc.

14. Explain impact of Microscopic view of day to day small petty moral problems and, macroscopic view of long term and larger social problems on the issue of engineering ethics.
15. By giving example explain conflict between Autonomy and Authority in profession.
16. Why a business must adopt Ethical behavior in its operations? What happens if unethical practices creep into business?
17. Explain Ethical imperatives of Global Business? Justify that ethics in Global business must be Global and, not local.

7 Understanding our Personality, Potential, Motivations and Goals of Life

Learning objectives

In this chapter you will learn about

- Elements of Potential, internal Values, Basic Human values and Goal of life
- Understand Personality and important behavioral values
- Understanding *individual identity, self, who am I* and inner value system
- Positive thinking and its benefits, negative thinking and its harmful effects
- Understanding of happiness, unhappiness and holistic happiness
- *Self-Interest* for happiness, ambitions, personal life, economic life, social life etc.

7.1 Explore your Potential and Value System

All human beings have tremendous potential for the development and growth in any field of their choice. However, all are not able to harness this potential due to various reasons like ignorance, lack of enthusiasm and initiatives, too much dependence on others for help, lack of guidance, etc. To maximize your potential, you must understand that:
- It is up to you and only you to be responsible for maximizing your potential and making future. Your mother, father, brother, sister, friend, your company, your boss or even your coworker cannot maximize your potential or make your future.
- Every student should develop his mindset to learn and face difficulties with courage and confidence, which helps to reduce the resistance of the difficulty. Such mindset allows more options within his reach. Actually, improper mindset is the greatest roadblock preventing the achievements of the goal.

7.1.1 Tips for harnessing Potential of Growth and fulfilling goals of life

Every student wants to be successful in life and maximize his potential for achieving his goals of life. But they are unaware of their natural resources, talent, personality traits, level of determination and direction of efforts, attitudes, motivations, etc. required to achieve their goals. We give below few tips which can be useful for students in chartering their future goals and career.

1. **Make best use of Time and Thought power**: God has provided equal *resources* of *time* and *thought power* to everybody. Understand that everyone has 24 hours/day and 365 days/year to be successful. Success of any one is dependent on how effectively and efficiently he/sharpness's time for achieving his goals. Similarly, any one grows in that field only where he/ she invests his *thought power*. Too much fracturing of these resources of the time and thought power into many small bits is not going to be productive to achieve the goals. That shows that he/she is not focused on anything. Any skill development requires dedicated and focused efforts and attention.

2. **Take inspiration from life of successful persons you adore most:** Every student should identify few leading personalities from different walk of life which inspire him to shape his future. For example, life of Bill Gates, Steve Jobs, Stephen Hawking, Abdul Kalam, Narendra Modi, etc. could be inspiring to some of you. Reading biographies of such inspiring personalities of one's choice is very useful in understanding crucial factors of basic character, which made them successful. One can learn lot of things from their life and then emulate their good traits in his/her own personal, scholastic and professional life.

3. **Identify your uniqueness, area of strengths, and skills to exploit your potential:** Develop your communication skills along with presentation skills of technical knowledge and projects work. Participate in every hands-on, experiential learning opportunity to enrich your project portfolio. Remember that in this competitive world, everyone should possess some unique skill or excellence to show and impress the prospective employers or clients.

4. **Make best use of summer vacations for deepening your spectrum of skills**: Summer vacations provide opportunity to acquire knowledge and proficiency in some field of interest related with global business. Make summers more productive for handling future responsibilities. In selection process employers give tremendous weightage to practical experiences. Summer vacations can be utilized for internship opportunities during academic career.

5. **Understand your own aspirations and personality**: Understand your own aspirations and personality in holistic fashion and try to maximize your potential for success.

7.1.2 Understanding Internal Values System

We have ambitions, desires and feelings which are our inner responses based on our psychic constitution. We need to understand it for any rational value judgment. We need to understand holistic environment around us which plays role in shaping our *Self, Beliefs and Value System*. For example:

- Most of the people normally remain focused on external things and the world around them. Seldom they peep inside themselves to understand, *what is going on inside them* i.e. how their emotional responses are and how they visualize and interpret the things and happenings around them.
- We are living in an external environment consisting of human beings (family, friends, etc.), animals, plants, insects, etc. as well as things like air, water, soil, stones, metals, etc. All these things play roles and influence in shaping our life and values of life.
- We must also understand and, honestly observe and evaluate our own *beliefs and value system.*
- Finally, we must understand that our judgment about feeling of happiness or unhappiness, successful or unsuccessful, right or wrong, true or false, are shaped by our own *inner constitution, beliefs and value system.*

7.2 Basic Human Needs

Our wants can be categorized into two types, physical and non-physical. Physical requirements like bread, clothes, shelter, etc. are necessary for all human being. Besides physical needs, everybody wants non-physical emotional entities like love, affection, relationship, etc. Thus, we have two categories of our needs.

Physical needs: We require food clothes and shelter as the basic minimum facility for just survival. We are grown up in families and need to make families, acquire prosperities, do business or service to maintain decent life and standard of living in the society. For this purpose, we have to acquire suitable education, skills and employment. In societal context, to maintain social working conditions for the people, lot of civic facilities and infrastructure are required, which are arranged by the society and the Government. Government runs by taxes collected from public.

Emotional needs and relationship: Human beings are social being and have psychic requirement of the nature of emotional and relationship needs.

Human beings live in families and make societies. We want good relationships with other human beings and feel a sense of mutual fulfillment in these relationships. When relationship is uncomfortable it gives mental agony. Memory of such uneasy feelings stays with us for quite some time. Many times, relationships with human beings have problems, leading to unhappiness. We are unable to have fulfilling relationship all the time, within family, outside family, with society and the world at large.

Many times, accumulation of wealth and lot of physical facilities give feeling of prosperity, without sense of fulfillment. Quite often, when craze for prosperity occupies larger part of time and mental occupation, it starts developing strains in various relationships. Normally, such situation arises due to unproportionate ambitions, wrong assumptions about the purpose of life and false expectations from rosy picture of opportunities.

7.3 Understanding Personality and important behavioral values

Our personality consists of combination of certain characteristics or qualities, which decide what type of person we are. These characteristics constitute, what is called personality traits, and control our emotions, thoughts, feelings, actions, attitude and behavior. These traits make our personality unique and remain mostly consistent throughout our lives.

Our personality is like an armor, which is our greatest shield also; and also, potentially greatest prison. It is used to deal with outside world, but if required it can also keep us insulated from outside world and other people.

It is important to have clear understanding of one's own personality, personal likes and dislikes, strengths and weaknesses. The greater is this understanding about one*self*, it is more likely that he/she will make better choices in life and feel more satisfied and contented. We make better choices by understanding our personality traits. Therefore,

1. Everyone should know his personal desires and values i.e. to know about what is important to him and their hierarchical choices which should be fulfilled first. Knowing and doing what is important, makes his attention focused; motivates him and ultimately fulfils whatever he/she wanted.
2. We should nurture good values to become a better person. Our personal values need not be influenced by different opinions or perspective of his family, friends or society. One should be honest to himself and honor his values. Values need to be reviewed and refined based on experience gained. Feeding your passions and interests is good for your well-being and contentment.
3. Work is more enjoyable when one is doing something where he/she is good and capable. This requires having clear

understanding of one's own key strengths, skills, experiences, knowledge and interests.

7.3.1 Understanding Personal Values

For understanding true personal values, one should to be honest to himself. He/ She should listen to his/her heart and feelings that will reveal to him his own value system; then he/she will discover what he/she really wants. Personal values are those values which motivate you, give a sense of fulfillment to you; give energy and drive to work with dedication.

Some values may appear to convey the same or similar meaning in guiding our actions. For example, *freedom, autonomy,* and *independence* appear to convey similar meaning, but their actual message and content will be different for different people. So, to be effective, you need to have clarity about what they really mean to you and how hard you need to work to achieve them. Values often sit in our unconscious mind as we go about our daily business. Further, understand that over time texture of our values changes, as our priorities change through life.

7.3.2 Trustworthiness

Professionals must be trustworthy for which they must demonstrate following characteristics.
- **Reliability:** Implies that all professionals must adhere to their promises, keep their words, commitments and maintain timings, be dependable in financial transaction, etc.
- **Respect:** Implies that professionals must respect the dignity, privacy and freedom of all individuals; it suggests valuing and honoring all people, no matter what they do for you. They must commit to the *golden rule* of behavior which requires that *treat others the way you want to be treated* by others.
- **Respect others' Property:** Whenever tools, instruments or any other property is borrowed from others, you must use it properly and return to owner on the promised time. Don't take or use property of anyone without permission, respect the autonomy of others.
- **Tolerance and Acceptance**: Professionalism demands to be tolerant, respectful to others and an attitude of listening and accepting different views of others. You should judge others based on their character, abilities and conduct by giving no consideration to their race, religion, gender, or where they live, how they dress, or money they have.

- **Nonviolence:** Implies that disagreements, angers and insulting comments, etc. with any one must be dealt and resolved peacefully, without resorting to physical, verbal or emotional violence.
- **Courtesy:** Implies that one should cultivate good nature and manners, be courteous, polite and civilized to all whom one interacts in course of his daily life. Never try to use or manipulate others for your advantage. Maintain good positive language in communication and never demeanor mistreat anyone.
- **Responsibility and Duty:** Implies that all professionals must understand very clearly their responsibilities and duties in all fields of their involvement like family, jobs and society and needs to discharge them properly and timely. They should also clearly understand their professional, legal and moral obligations to discharge them honestly.
- **Accountability:** Everybody must be accountable for the consequences of their actions and decisions. Think about short term and long-term impact of the consequences on your professional image and career, as well as on others, before you decide to act. Professionals must be a role model for other and set good examples worth emulating.
- **Pursuit of Excellence**: Requires professionals to make best efforts and put maximum of their energy in pursuit of excellence in decisions, actions and operations in all walks of their life.
- **Self-Control**: Self-control means one should have his own control on his action, emotions, temperaments, etc. He/ She should be very realistic in setting his goals, be prudent and self-disciplined in all matters of life and have rational thinking i.e.do not act out of reason, anger, revenge or fear.
- **Fairness and Justice**: Professionals must be very fair and just in their commitments, promises and professional dealings. Treat everybody with dignity. Make decisions without favoritism or prejudice. Practice fairness in giving credits or blames.
- **Openness:** Requires transparency, open-mindedness and impartiality in all matters of professional dealings. Professional decisions should be objective and based on facts including opposing viewpoints and caring concern for others.
- **Charity:** Professionals should have mentality of being charitable and altruistic i.e. giving donations, time and support to worthy causes and be helpful to people in need.

7.3.3 Virtue of Contentment

Contentment is one of the basic qualities of ethical person. According to ancient Indian culture it is an Ideal or Aim to be achieved in life. However,

concept of contentment is misunderstood by many youths, particularly educated people who interpret contentment as something leading to complacency, or promoting passive acceptance of given state of affairs, or a compromise with the state of stagnated misery. Actually, contentment is an intensely dynamic acceptance of the results of efforts made to achieve something, or short-term and long-term actions and struggle of life. Contentment requires development of proper mindset on social realities which one encounters in life. For example, contentment requires that:
1. Every individual is duty bound to work for better future. He/ She has a legitimate right to work and must frame his goals for betterment in all aspects of life. This requirement is contained within the frame work of integrated social well-being.
2. In life one should accept gracefully failures or disappointments without losing his composure and dignity. One should not resort to blaming oneself or others, or regretting and brooding on the past, etc.
3. In case of failure one should review about what lessons could be learnt from the failure; what are one's goals and objectives; reassess one's abilities and limitations; scrutinize means and methods adopted, and what should be future course of action.

Thus, contentment is part of one's attitude towards world around him. It is a dynamic process based on respecting the process and accepting the result at any given time.

7.3.4 Motivational factors as we grow

Our personality is partly formed by nature and partly nurture through interactions within family, society, during education and professional jobs. Physically, it is product of our DNA. When we grow in life from childhood to adulthood and then to old age, we come across different common internal drivers with different vigor and motivational factors like ones given below, which keep on operating throughout the life with different intensity and priority:
1. **Hope:** Hope is internal driver which allows possibilities of learning and growth in all phases of life, like baby hopes to get everything from parents.
2. **Exploration**: Desire to explore and try to develop increasing degree of independence as we grow, while making sure that someone like parents, teachers, seniors, known elders are still around and give encouragement as well as support to activities.
3. **Identity:** At reaching to teenagers age, there are good amount of changes in physical and emotional make up of personality. Further, teenagers develop a craving for independence and establishing personal identity. A teenager looks for his acceptance more by

friends, rather than parents. There is emotional and psychological tension between one's separate identity and its acceptance by the group of friends.
4. **Establishment:** By the time boys or girls reach the age of 20s and 30s they develop the desire to establish themselves as individual, independent of their parents and desire to acquire all that is needed for an adult life. Many times, jobs force them to move out of the family, having their own earning for living, desire for finding a life partner, making their own family, etc. As an employee, now one establishes his own circles of colleagues and new friends rather than bosses and parents.
5. **Broadening:** In due course of time, the next phase of life begins when all needs and goals of life are fulfilled. This mid-life period slowly changes thinking with deep reflection and broadening of outlook towards life.
6. **Reflection:** Finally, in old age the priorities of life change. Here the work plays less important part and one looks for a new purpose and meaning to the life.

The above discussion show that our motivation and priorities change as we pass through different stages of life. These changes are mostly external changes in our personality, without much influence on our inner self; unless we are aware of and conscious of our inner self and have decided to refine and polish it. This refinement of our inner self will influence and reflect in our overall personality and value system.

Let us try to bring more clarity in understanding our inner self and associated development of value system.

7.3.5 Self-Management

1. Whatever you want to be, you have to work for it continuously at all times by mind, speech and action-like a seed which keeps on growing all the time to become a tree i.e. nonstop movements towards the goal.
2. To achieve anything consistency of efforts and direction is essential.

All actions and efforts have to start from *inner self* first in terms of WILL (i.e. *Sankalp*). These must be harmonized with goals, aims and objectives.

7.4 Understanding our Individual Identity

Personality is really reflection of our identity. The more awareness of our personality leads to better efforts and objectivity towards improving it and building our identity. It is important to understand about what shapes our individuality, and identity in the society.

Nature vs. Nurture: We must understand role of the *nature,* our *nurturing* during growth period and our personality development. The question is that whether it is our nature that decides our future, or the way of our nurturing has been done i.e. the way we are brought up; and the influences on and around us during that period, which dominate our future path and personality make up. The truth is that it is blend of both. However, nurturing is not a structured, concentrated, focused and consistent way of personality development. Nurturing is through encouragement (or pressure) from parents and near and dear, to accomplish something beyond natural capabilities or traits.

The desire for acceptance: Being loved and accepted by others works like tonic to development of personality for the vast majority of people and it pleases to know that they are good enough. The desire for acceptance induces to adopt sound beliefs, good values, a sense of right or wrong and actions acceptable to the society. These characteristics are partly inherited and partly acquired from friends, colleagues and society at large. They are absorbed slowly through osmosis process and not consciously taught to us.

Our desire of individuality is not in tune with the desire for being accepted by others. Usually the desire to be accepted is given preference because that is the only way society can operate, and most of the people can live together in peace. Desire of acceptance means sacrificing some individuality; so that to ensure sense of security coming through living together in the society.

Our identity: It is very likely that when we take a role and play that role intensively for quite some time, then that role become our identity. For example, a politician, a businessman, a doctor, a lawyer, etc. develop such an identity because of the role played by them most of the time. We identify with the role so much that the more we do things, the more they become our habit and we start thinking that way. These patterns of thoughts and behavior build our particular identity. Our identity through the role played by us gives us strength and self-confidence.

When the identity is derived from these external roles, our true identity based on inner personality is suppressed and the role becomes a mask to hide the true identity. When we are accustomed of living with these masks all the time and interacting in a safe, predictable way with others, we feel more at ease and secure about our life.

7.4.1 Shocks of Identity loss

When our identity built through external role is taken out of our hands like retirements from jobs, loss of any status in the society, etc.it shakes our sense of identity, self-confidence and purpose and status. A psychological shock is experienced by many people, with the end of such roles. There are many situations in life like when children leave home, a relationship breaks up or divorce; a redundancy or retirement, which cause shock and shatter the personality on loss of identity. Therefore, everybody must remember that our external identity exists only as long as these roles exist. Our true Identity is our inner Personality.

7.5 Formation idea of SELF or sense of "I" in an Individual and its Functional Reality

Evolution of man is psycho-social evolution and our cultural inheritance comes by birth from childhood onward. Whenever we study any aspect of human nature or life, we realize that it becomes more and more mysterious. We do not understand the vast universe in which our life is cast, simply because we do not understand ourselves.

For example, for a new born baby this world is a profound mystery. A just born baby is a very weak organic system. A little high or low temperature can destroy him. But he/she has vast potential of growth. He/She can become athlete, spiritual leader, a scientist or something very profound, having vast potential within himself. But his/her all the potentials are hidden inside his body. The purpose of education should be to bring out this potential of a child. The education should impart knowledge and skills of self- exploration which is so far neglected. Spirituality focuses on understanding and exploration of the *self*, which is source of our in-built desires, capabilities and potentials.

Spiritual nature of man is ignored in education. UNESCO pointed out in an education commission report titled *learning to be* where it noted that so far education world over has focused on *learning to do*. Man, through his own development of modern science and its discoveries has reduced himself into very small entity and devalued himself. Unless *learning to do* process is supplemented by *learning to be* process, *learning to* do alone will turn whole life into a disaster, as it is happening now.

The report says education is not just schooling i.e., going to college but a lifelong learning. This lifelong learning should not be limited to be expert on one dimension or master of many subjects but develop holistically deeper human dimension of being. This means shift in consciousness higher to higher level or intensifying the psychosocial evolutionary process. Out of that evolution process come out ethical awareness, moral awareness, deeper humanistic values etc.

Technique for this inward education is different from outward education. Greatest technique of penetrating layers of inner dimension of *being* is *meditation* where you are just *yourself*. Modern education focuses on work efficiency and neglects creativity. Creativity and utilitarian mind are opposite to each other.

Nature's *energy resources of human being* are organized in increasing subtlety, immensity, and inwardness (i.e. Muscles, nerves, psychic and intellectual power). Ultimately knowledge should rise to wisdom. You take a deeper look at the roles you play; your responsibilities towards your parents, children, friends, country, religion, *yourself* and job/ occupation; and to bring them into harmony with your deeper *being*.

7.5.1 Understanding Spiritual SELF identified as "I", the faculty of reason, rationality and emotional balance(also addressed as Third Eye of man)

Let us try to understand the mechanism of our perceptions, interpretation and inferences of the world around us. Any one perceives *reality* of objects and phenomena through his own eyes and sense organs. He/ She can't use any other person's eye or sense organs to know and comprehend the reality. Other's eye cannot become your eye. Other's observations, visions and perceptions cannot become your observations, visions and perceptions. Unless you have seen and experienced yourself personally and are convinced, you will not be able to absorb them in your behavior, thinking and psyche, which is actually the process of learning about human being, society, life and the world around. In this sense, we all are unique. The science and body functions of vision are same for all of us, but our experiences and conclusions of these visions and visualization including perceptions and inferences are not same. There is uniqueness in our process of inferencing on the same vision; and our experiences, perceptions and conclusions are different from all others.

Now think logically, who is really seeing the world, you or your eyes? Your eyes are only your organ of vision. They do not have any intelligence of their own to appreciate beauty and colors, distinguish, discriminate objects, etc. Eyes do not have memory and recognize anything. They do not interpret the objects. They do not attach values to the objects. All interpretations, perceptions, emotions, values and follow up actions are by *your inner self*, whom you refer as *I* e.g. *I* see, *I* interpret, *I* feel, *I* react, etc. This *I* is your *Third Eye*. Your *I* represent your *Self*, your *Consciousness*, your very *Being* and in pure state, it is also called *Soul* or *presence of God* in your heart.

All emotions, human desires and instincts of love, hate, fear, passion, anger, jealousy etc. are part of your *Inner Constitution* which is collectively referred as *I*. This is your *Third Eye* which is your *Instrument of Observations, Discrimination and Decisions*.

Working function of this *Third Eye* (now read *I*) is not limited to vision by physical organ of eyes but also integrates observations of other organs like ear (hearing), tongue (taste), skin (touch), etc. to gain knowledge and experience of phenomenal world. All education (formal and informal both) is to refine and awaken this *I* to higher plane of living and values than an animal's level and behavior. *I*is seat of intellect and emotions which differentiates us from animals. When awakened and cultured properly it uplift us to higher level of existence. This *I* is some total of your *personality*, your *identity*. It is embodiment of your values of life. Without *I* what are you? Remove this *I* from your vocabulary and you will be reduced to nothing.

You will agree that for truthful and correct observations and conclusions, the *instrument of observation* must be right and properly calibrated. Culture, religion and spirituality teach us methods and parameters (values) through which one can understand and calibrate the Instrument of Observation i.e. *I*. Some of these values are honesty, truthfulness, compassion, equanimity, fearlessness, justice, equality, self-control, sincerity, discipline, dedication, etc. One can use these and similar parameters to understand the world around as well as his own motives and attitudes.

With wrong map, you cannot reach to the right destination. No one can chart map of your future except you, because only you can know your inner strength, weakness, motives, attitudes, intentions and dynamics of your behavior with external world, provided you are honest to yourself.

God has gifted all of us with consciousness in the form of *I*nes. Consciousness can know about matter but matter cannot know about Consciousness. All scriptures talk about awakening of this consciousness which is *I* in purified form. Purification of *I* mean exercising control over yourself, your unwanted desires, unwanted inner detractions, tendencies, etc. *I* am a powerful vital force to be used to harness your strength and creative potential in the service of humanity at large.

Your *I* encompass five domains of your total personality and consist of 5 planes of existence like:
1. Physical body with all sensory organs
2. Intellectual faculty
3. Emotional constitution
4. Psychological constructs
5. Spiritual inclinations and tendencies

Your holistic *I* need to be developed and refined through education. Holistic education aims to develop your *I* through its five major objectives viz. development of 1) skill, 2) knowledge, 3) emotional, and moral balance, 4) vision and 5) identity.

Development and maturing of *I* is essential for better future and happy life. You must develop a better picture of your future and seriously work for that. Thus, for you it is necessary to open your *Third Eye*, i.e. *I* and culture it carefully. Knowledge of characteristics of *SELF* is essential to gain any other knowledge. To know your motives for actions you must question yourself like:
1. What I want?
2. Why I want?

3. When I want?
4. What are resources and support required to achieve it?
5. What is loss or repercussion, if I postpone it or don't get it?
6. How crucial it is for my goals and objectives?
7. How much I am committed?

If your answer in un-agitated mood is positive i.e. your *third eye* is able to give you clear picture. Open your *third eye* to chart map of your dreams, future plans and actions for your career. Dreams are source of powerful energy. Don't do outsourcing of your future. For everyone his future is more important than yours. Cultivate the heart; heart is the source of all humanistic feelings and impulses such as love, service, compassion, etc.

7.5.2 Few quotes to stimulate thinking about SELF

- You witness two universes. One external to you and one internal to you.
- The Universe, you see and react, is made of feelings, emotions, perceptions, stories, and not atoms.
- Behavior is largely a product of thinking (built around psychic beliefs and values).
- You must be the change agent for what change you want to see in the world.
- The world suffers a lot, not because of violence of bad people, but because of the silence of good people.

After analysis of various factors defining personality, motivations and SELF, next step is to understand *self-interest* which drives you to involve into various activities of personal life, profession, society and environment around you.

7.6 What is Positive Thinking?

A positive mind expects happy ending of his actions and activities in any situation. Positive thinking reflects mental attitude of expectations to achieve good and favorable results out of one's efforts and activities. It is the mental thinking process where thoughts are full of creative energy capable of transforming them into achievable reality.

People who are sad, worried, or disappointed with circumstances around them, or happenings in their life are advised to think positive and analyze their issues with positive attitude of expectancy. Positive thinking requires analyses of approach or thought process i.e. to distinguish between positive and negative thoughts and do not over emphasize negative possibilities beyond their probable happening. Thinking positive opens possibilities of many alternative paths or possibility of multiple and useful alternative solutions.

Professionals understand the need for positive thinking in their professions and they practice it among their clients and customers advantageously, for overall satisfaction, success and happiness. Successful people realize that one of the important factors behind their success is their positive way of looking at any problem or situation. Persons full of positive attitude are likely to be more successful professionally as well as personally in their life, than those who lack it.

Case study 1: The following story illustrates how power positive thinking works: In campus recruitment fair, many students including Anand and Raina both applied for jobs. Anand is a student with low self-esteem and didn't believe he will get the job, since he considered himself unprepared for interview and likely to fail in written test. He started seeing his failure even prior to written test and unlikely to succeed in job interview. He was full of negativity toward himself and strongly believed that other applicants were well prepared for the test. Anand's mind was perceiving failure, throughout the whole week preceding the job interview, because of his negative thoughts and fears concerning the job. As he was, anticipating failure, he did not do any advance preparations for interview day.

On the interview and selection day, he got up late. Because of that, he went for interview without proper dress, wearing a wrinkled shirt and even without taking breakfast. He was apprehensive and internally not at peace. He was mentally tense, with full of negative thoughts, hungry and worried about his dress. With these disturbances in the mind it was difficult for him to focus on the interview. His overall performance gave a bad impression and did not succeed in the interview. Actually, he materialized what he perceived mentally i.e. negativity of his mind.

Raina applied for the same job too but visualized the matter with different frame of mind. She was confident of her preparations and capabilities to get the job. She prepared well for the interview including her attire for that day. She visualized herself succeeding and making a good impression and finally getting the job.

In the evening prior to the interview day, she arranged her clothes properly and went to sleep a little earlier. Next day she woke up a bit early than usual days, gave ample time to eat breakfast and then arrived at the place of interview before the scheduled time. Raina created good impression in the interview and got the job.

What is the message from the mental attitude of Ananda and Raina? There was no magic. Everything happened the way Ananda and Raina visualized the event and the process. Positive thinking paid dividends.

7.6.1 Positive Thinking is a way of life

Positive and negative thinking are contagious. When people interact and communicate with each other, their communication instinctively and on a subconscious level affect each other, through words, thoughts, feelings and body language. Positive thing creates an environment of expectancy, hope and joy. Everybody likes to be with positive people and prefer to avoid people of negative temperament. Positive people display positivity and negative people broadcasting negativity. Generally, people dislike negativity and avoid interacting anyone full of negativity.

Negativity is reflected through negative attitude, thoughts and words produce unhappy feelings, moods and behavior. A mind full of negative thoughts gets affected by biochemistry of body by releasing harmful chemicals into the bloodstream, which cause more unhappiness and negativity. Getting trapped into mental attitude of negativity leads a person to failures, frustrations and disappointments.

7.6.2 Words inculcating Positive Thoughts

We came to the world to learn about life. The universe is the biggest school of learning. Through positive thinking our lives should become peaceful, useful, meaningful, purposeful and full of humility. Display of courage, honesty, wisdom, self-care, truthfulness, full of hopes, compassion, faithfulness, unselfishness and other positive traits in thinking and behavior indicates possession of positive thinking.

Develop positive mindset, it will help in enhancing skills, happiness, success of any person and make him a more sought-after individual. Positivity helps us to unfold our potential. Association with people with negative traits is always painful. Positive attitude empowers us to live joyfully, effectively and successfully. Habit of positive thing is like strengthening muscles by exercising; the more you practice it the stronger it will become. Researchers believe that your style of reasoning to visualize or explain is linked to whether you are an optimist or a pessimist. The optimist creed advises every person to become an optimist, which is important characteristic of positive thinking persons. It exhorts to promise you for the following:

- To be so strong that nothing can disturb your peace of mind.
- To talk health, happiness and prosperity to every person you meet.
- To make all your friends feel that there is something in them.
- To look at the sunny side of everything and make your optimism come true.
- To think only of the best, to work only for the best and to expect only the best.

- To be just as enthusiastic about the success of others as you are about your own.
- To forget the mistakes of the past and press on to the greater achievements of the future.
- To wear a cheerful countenance at all times and give every living creature you meet a smile.
- To give so much time to the improvement of yourself that you have no time to criticize others.
- To be too large for worry, too noble for anger, too strong for fear and too happy to permit the presence of trouble.

7.6.3 Benefits of Positive Thinking

Positive thinking has many health benefits also. Positive thinkers develop better skills to cope up with stress, improve immunity system of body and carry lower risk of cardiovascular disease. Taking an optimistic view of positive thinking rather than harboring on negative thoughts can improve overall mental well-being. Below are given just some of the benefits of positive thinking:
- It reduces stress level in daily life which has positive impact on health
- People with positive thinking develop strong confidence level
- With improved immunity one can expect to live comparatively longer life
- People with positive thinking are happier in their life and have reliable relationships
- It develops better management and decisions making skills

7.6.4 Strategies to cultivate Positive Thinking

"...see the positive side, the potential and make an effort" – Dalai Lama

Changing thinking pattern and mind set is not easy task. Implanting positive thinking in your brain from today and hoping that your thinking will become positive from now onwards in your life is impossible task. Change in thinking pattern and process to get rid of negativity is a slow process. One requires to go through some exercises and sincere practices to identify your negative traits in thinking patterns and then to travel towards positive thinking. Some of the recommendations for culturing positive thinking are given below.
1. Think and talk using positive words in conversation. If you often start your replies by NO or constantly say I cannot you are negative in your approach to the problems. You could convince

yourself that you are right but this is a narrow vision and you are not ready to broadening your vision or not open to consider possible alternatives. Replace negative words with positive ones. Assert to broaden your vision for other constrictive possibilities on problems or situations. This is positivity in addressing any issue.
2. Do not harbor or live in negative pattern of thinking. Do not allow negative thoughts to occupy your mental space. Try to replace negative thoughts and feelings with positive content. Be alert on your thoughts and practice to remain positive.
3. Practice to use those words that convey strength and success. Fill your mind stuff with thoughts and words giving feeling of strength, happiness and control over mood swings. Avoid attention to the words that suggest failure or incompetence.
4. Practice positive affirmations about self. Mentally reflection and repetition of positive phrases in thoughts, is the technique of positive thinking called positive affirmation. For example, repeating phrase like I am a happy person or I have a good personality or if God is with me who can be against me, etc. and genuinely believing these statements is the process of positive affirmation. One can construct his own positive phrases based on where he/she wants to improve through positive affirmation and practice it. This will generate mental picture of more positive opinion about himself.
5. Redirect your thoughts! This method is suggested by psychotherapists when someone feels negative emotions like depression or anxiety. Here to control your thoughts when you are in the grip of such emotion, start recollecting happy thoughts, happy moments, a positive image, or something that pleases you, to divert your attention away from those bad feelings.
6. Always think of succeeding. Self-confidence is elixir that creates a successful reality. Putting all doubts aside one should reinforce his/her belief that he/she will succeed in meeting the targets or objectives.
7. Analyze if things go wrong. Positive thinking does not mean that nothing can go wrong. If anything goes wrong instead of worrying or repenting on that, analyze what went wrong and avoid repetition of such mistakes in future. Look forward to be more positive.
8. Forgive and forget. People normally discuss and argue for things that went wrong. They should forgive and forget what happened as arguments will not change anything. Learning from mistakes they should move forward.
9. Think of a failure as an opportunity for learning. Failures give more data on deficiencies of thinking process, design process,

assumptions made, method, process of implementation, etc. They provide opportunity to learn and improve in future.
10. Use imagination and visualization power. All advance planning depends on imagination and visualization capability of the planner. Planning could also be for own career or future. Visualizing of what you want to achieve or be, can be a great motivating factor to plan out the distance or time one has to travel until the destination is reached.

Remember what you are today is due to your thinking and actions of the past and what you will be tomorrow or in future will be the result of your thoughts and action of today.

7.6.5 Overcome Negative Thoughts

Many people easily become victim of negative thinking. Negative thoughts drain out energy of a person and drive you away from the present moment. Thinking more about negative thoughts reinforces them and they become stronger by such pattern thinking. It is like the imagery of a stone ball rolling down from top of staircase towards ground and as it rolls it gains speed and momentum. Then it becomes very hard to stop it from rolling once it has gained speed and momentum. One small negative thought can get momentum like the strong speeding ball, bringing bad experiences, sad and ugly feelings. Similarly, a small positive thought can have the same effect and produce good feelings and experiences like blossoming of a beautiful flower.

Thus, one has to become a more positive thinker, taking help from the technique of auto suggestion to him. A few common strategies involve learning how to identify negative thoughts and replacing these thoughts with more positive ones.

7.6.6 Avoid Negative Self-Talk

Auto suggestion is like self-talk, which is suggesting to you mentally. It is like your inner voice inside your mind that analyzes how you perform and interact in the world around you. If a person engaged in self-talk is trapped into negative thoughts, his self-esteem will suffer. Therefore, one should always be alert and watchful of his thoughts. People are trapped in negativity unconsciously when they are not alert. When negative thoughts take over, suggest yourself mentally to stop and divert your thoughts to positive ones. It can help to break the negative thought pattern.

Try Humor: Try to be watchful for humor component in your communication and thinking pattern. A little humor or lightness in your communication can help you in staying positive. Even when things are serious and you are facing challenges, it is good remaining open to laughter and humor. Sometimes, simply humors in a situation can reduce stress levels and brighten chances of positive thoughts surfacing up.

Cultivate Optimism: Optimists tend to have a positive explanatory style. Pessimists on the other hand usually have a negative attributional style. If one does not blame himself for things outside of his control, then he/she is more optimistic person. When you are dwelling on negative thoughts, you can consciously try to minimize negative self-talk and cultivate a more optimistic outlook. In order to think positively, one needs to nurture himself using auto suggestion.1) Investing energy and time into things you enjoy, and 2) being around optimistic people are just two ways, fill life with positive thinking and energy.

7.6.7 Tips for maintaining Positive Attitude and overcome Negative Traits

Since attitude and thoughts do not change overnight, turning the mind toward the positivity requires some inner work. Here are suggestions to help you develop positive thinking and overcome negative thoughts.

1. Work on your thoughts: The power of thoughts is a mighty power that is always shaping our lives. This shaping is a subconscious process but it is possible to work on it consciously through auto suggestions.
2. Practice meditation or do yoga: Meditation and yoga techniques area very relaxing exercise for cooling the mind. It will facilitate to shift your attention away from negative thoughts. There are many meditation and yoga techniques and one have to learn it under guidance of a qualified teacher.
3. Keep smiling: Smiles create very relaxing environment to dissipate stress during discussions. One feels lighter because it takes fewer muscles to smile than to frown. Smile helps to think positively.
4. Surround yourself with positive people: When one is trapped in a negative spiral, it is best to talk to someone who can pull you out of negative spiral by conversing and putting things into proper perspective.
5. Cut spiral of negative thoughts: Diverting attention to something more pleasant breaks the negative spiral of thoughts. Take the focus away from you and do something nice for another person just like play with children.
6. Read positive quotes. You can place Post-It notes with positive quotes on your computer, fridge door and mirror as reminders to stay positive. On power of thoughts Gandhi ji said:
    - Watch your thoughts, they become words.
    - Watch your words, they become actions.
    - Watch your actions, they become habits.

- Watch your habits, they become your character.
- Watch your character, it becomes your destiny.

7. Actions for developing positivity: Remember that no one is perfect so allow you to move forward in positive direction. It's easy to dwell on mistakes. Learn from mistakes and move forward. The other actions like improving the power of concentration, willpower, self-discipline and peace of mind also contribute to the development of a positive mind.

7.7 Happiness

Surprisingly, everybody desires to be happy, but cannot define or tell with clarity what he/she means or understands by happiness. Some people feel that one is considered happy if he/she meets some standards objectives of the personal life. For some others, happiness is a subjective state of mind where one is pleased or satisfied with his life. No one is really responsible to make someone else happy. One can choose to be happy if he/she develops his mindset to be happy and see happiness around him. One should understand that he/she becomes whatever he/she chooses to be mentally.

The desire for happiness is natural choice of human nature. Happiness is a state of mind and it seems strange that many of us are putting it off, until something happens to give happiness. Happiness achieved through desires and selfish thoughts will not last. What would make you happy and keep you happy depends on your attitude, actions, choices and mindset. Acceptance of life without grudge or grumble is the first key condition to happiness. The second key to happiness is the conscious decision to live joyfully.

Happiness is the basic requirement of human beings and paraphernalia of physical and non-physical (i.e. emotional and relationship needs) facilities are means for fulfillment of the desire of happiness. But many times, accumulation of this paraphernalia does not result in happiness due to faulty assumptions. Happy people are at peace and harmony with themselves and surroundings even without much paraphernalia of facilities.

Happy people know that no one in this world can make them happy except themselves. They need to like themselves and achieve happiness from within. Nothing from outside can bring happiness in you. Your parents, friends, children, wife, husband, relatives, well-wishers can only add to your state of mind of being happy. Placing your happiness in the hands of others will lead to a lot of pain and disappointments.

Many people have wrong assumption that accumulation of wealth is the only thing we need for happiness and the rest will be taken care of automatically. Actually, man is a social animal and for him sweet and happy relationship with all concerned is essential for feeling of happiness.

A disturbed or unhappy relationship can disturb peace of mind of any person to a large extent. Our life is built within web of relationships and we spend significant time of our lives in relationships. Many times, our assumptions and expectations from relationship are wrong. For example, to be authoritative or bossing over in relationship matters is a wrong assumption for maximizing happiness. Happy life does not mean that everything in life around us is satisfactory and perfect. It means choosing to be happy in spite of the fact that it will never be perfect. People are happy as it is their nature and not that they have the best of everything. They just accept everything that comes their way and make best use of it.

Happiness is not about what happens to us, but it is how we perceive about what happens to us. It is the knack of finding a positive for every negative and view setback as a challenge. It is not wishing for what we don't have but enjoying what we have. Happiness is not the absence of conflict, but the ability to cope with it.

7.7.1 Understanding happiness through balloon analogy

Once in a management training seminar of a group of 50 people were asked to play a management game. This game was to teach them about happiness without any prior information. They were asked to assemble into a room which was already filled with 50balloons. Suddenly the speaker entered into the room and informed the participants that he wants them to play a game of group activity. He gave each participant a balloon and asked them to write his/her name on it. Afterwards all the balloons were collected and put into another room.

Now these participants were asked to go in that room and collect the balloon marked with their name within 5 minutes. Everyone was frantically searching for the balloon with their name. They were colliding among themselves and pushing around each other, thus creating utter chaos and confusion in the room.

No one could find his own balloon within the allotted time of 5 minutes. Then speaker asked participants that each one can randomly collect any balloon and hand it over to the person whose name was written on it. Everyone got his balloon within minutes.

Then speaker explained that in our lives also it happens exactly like this where everybody is frantically searching for happiness without knowing where it is.

People should understand that their happiness lies in the happiness of others. Handover their happiness (just like balloon in above example) to them; you will get your own happiness. Thus, the purpose of human life is to enable others in their pursuit of happiness. Happiness comes when your work and words are of benefit to yourself and others. Helping those less fortunate would also bring blessings and abundance along with happiness. Happiness never decreases by being shared.

7.7.2 Reasons of Unhappiness

Happy people know that anger, fear, jealousy, pride, deceit, worry and greed are the most powerful enemies which stimulate sinful deeds and must be renounced for the self-welfare and happiness. Happy people forgive all those who have offended them. They know that without forgiveness life will be governed by an endless cycle of resentments and retaliations which will never allow any body to live happily.

Happy people choose to be happy for what they have rather than sorrow and worry for what they do not have. To be happy we should examine following questions of good facilities *vs.* happy relationships to find out cause of unhappiness in life.
1. Is the unhappiness in the family is more due to lack of physical facilities or due to lack of emotional concern in relationship?
2. How much time is apportioned towards nurturing happy relationship and how much time is devoted to accumulation of physical facilities?

These questions require *right understanding* of all the factors having bearing on our happiness.

If we look around the world, we can see that there are three types of situations around people deciding about their state of happiness:
1. Those who do not have physical facilities/wealth and feel unhappy and deprived i.e. materially deficient and unhappy.
2. Those who have physical facilities/wealth i.e. materially affluent but still are unhappy and feel deprived of happiness.
3. Those who have moderate level of physical facilities, emotionally contented in relationship and feeling happy and prosperous.

7.7.3 Holistic Happiness

To understand how to be happy, we must first analyze how our life is structured. Our lives are structured in layers of existence where we spend most of our time. Our holistic happiness is broadly vector sum of our happiness in each of the life segments of human living as given below.
1. Living in myself i.e. personal life
2. Living in family i.e. family life
3. Living in society i.e. social life
4. Living in a profession i.e. professional life or life of economic activity

5. Living in Nature/existence i.e. dependence on natural resources, forces and cycles which governs life in all forms and stages of existence

From happiness point of view, if we look into life of common men, it appears that their life is full of conflicts and contradictions. In order to have happiness we need to bring harmony at all layers of our life as enumerated above. In order to be happy, we need to understand our role in all these five levels of living. We must also realize that these levels are having lot of human interactions, concern and transactions, overlapping between these levels. Thus, one has to have a holistic view of happiness vis-à-vis these levels of living, without much emphasis on rigid compartmentalization of life within these levels. It should be understood that if we ignore any of above levels, the happiness at that level cannot be sustained.

Thus, we must try to do introspection and self- analysis to develop an integrated view of our role which brings harmony in living through all these five levels, for our own happiness. The point is elaborated as follows for better understanding: basically, all of us are aspiring to be happy and whatever appears conducive to our happiness becomes valuable to us. Values form basis of our thoughts, behavior and actions. Values become source of sustenance of happiness. Without an appropriate value framework, we will not be able to decide whether a chosen action is desirable or undesirable, right or wrong. Our values at different level of living should not conflict with each other. The Golden rule or ethic of reciprocity like *treat others the way you want to be treated* can guide and harmonize our values at all levels of living and ensure continuous happiness i.e. happiness for one and all, at all times.

Rationalizing Our Values: We must ensure that our correct understanding of the *universal human values*. Most of the times we are driven by some of the ad-hoc values and beliefs that may or may not be true in reality. Sometimes these values may not be of universal in nature, or be contrary to the *golden rules*. For example, someone may believe that … a corporate job is best kind of job and other may feel government jobs are best. Similarly, opinions like … IITs are best institutions for studies; metro cities are best places to live in; money brings all happiness; with honest means one cannot make money; success by any good or foul means is OK. All these opinions have no rational basis. These biases deprive us from continuity of happiness and cause conflicts in our values and life. All of us live with such beliefs. These beliefs come to us from what we read, see, hear, what our parents tell us, our friends talk about, what magazines talk of, what we see in TV, etc. There is a whole body of belief-system that we live with at any given time, and these together constitute our world view. Such opinions, values and beliefs are usually not the same for everybody. They could be held by a small group or large group of people but they are not universal. These beliefs spread out far and wide into all our realms of living. Irrationality of these values and belief system lies in the fact that there is no universality in them and usually keep changing from person to person and time to time.

7.8 Self-Interest

Primary emphasis of ethical theories has been on *right acts* and *moral rules*. For establishing a social equilibrium, these theories try to prescribe desirable characteristics of the persons which should be aspired in the society. For example, good character is the focus of *virtue ethics* whereas *self-fulfillment* is aspired in *self-realization ethics*. In fact each of the ethical theories has ample space to support *Self-Interest* of a person i.e.to pursuing what he/she feels good for himself. Central focus of different ethical theories is briefly described below.

1. Utilitarianism prefers to argue that self-interest should be main consideration into our calculations of the overall good.
2. Rights ethics insists that it is our right to pursue our legitimate interests.
3. Duty ethics says that we have moral duty towards ourselves and others.
4. In Virtue ethics, our personal good is linked with our participation in communities and social practices.

Self-Interest is prime consideration in *Self-Realization* ethics and it values high the personal commitments of individuals in pursuing *self-fulfillment*.

We can consider two versions of ethical theories depending on meaning and scope of the way *Self* is understood.

1. In first version of ethical theory, the *Self* is considered a highly individualistic being and this theory is called *ethical egoism*.
2. In second version the *Self* is understood in terms of caring relationships of individual being with communities, thus the theory is identified as community-oriented version.

7.8.1 Diversity of Self-Interest in different ages and Professional Groups

Self and *Interest*, both are dynamic in nature. While the *self* is unitary and is evolving with time as personality develops. Self can be equated to *I* of a person, whereas his *interests* have multiplicity and keep on changing with time and age, education and profession. Some of them are short term interest whereas others have long term bearings. Any person at any time has multiple *self-interests*.

At present world population is around 7.3 billion, or we can that say that there are 7.3 billion s*elf's*, distributed over different age groups, like children, youths, professionals, business people, politicians, etc. Interests of each of the group will have lot of commonality throughout the globe. For example, broadly interests of all children or youths throughout the world are alike; but with some divergence based on their upbringing, social, cultural norms and religion. Further, for any individual in each group, the degree of specific interests and their priorities on different situation will be modulated by his background and education. For example, being a student, a householder, an employee, an entrepreneur, a professional, a social activist, a politician, etc. will have different spectrum of *self-interest* based on *Role* being played by him. A person can have multiple roles at a time which adds complexity of moral and ethical considerations to *self-interest* in harmonizing them with various roles being played by him.

7.8.2 Self-Interest at the core of happiness in life

A common core element among various hues and colors of *self-interest* is *happiness* in life. Man is a social animal and throughout his life he/she seeks for *happiness* as an end in itself. Happiness also includes healthy and prosperous life. Happiness is achieved through harmonious exercise of all his faculties. You may note that happiness is not necessarily dependent on money but money is required by majority of people to fulfill their *self-interest*. We find three classes of people whose *motivation* and *self-interests* are different from each other.

1. **Ambitious people**: Everyone has rights to pursue one's legitimate *self-interest*. For many people their primary *self-interest* is to acquire good source of income and amass wealth, which is essential to meet their family and social responsibilities throughout their life. Engineers and professionals are ambitious people whose *self-interest* is normally professional excellence, recognitions and good source of income through legitimate means and channels.
2. **Creative and hobbyist people**: There are other categories of people like the clergyman, the writers, the artist, poets, etc. whose self-interest is creativity in their field of activity and who may be poor because they want to devote all their time and energy in pursuit of their hobbies, and not to the business of earning money. The logic of their self-interest model is based on an aesthetic principle.
3. **Service oriented people**: Yet there are still others like priests, social workers, volunteers, etc. in the society whose self-interest is to serve their constituencies which are normally poor and deprived

people whom they seek to help and identify with them and their sufferings.

Self-interest though looks very simple term but in view of above discussion it is very complex issue governing total behavior of any person. *Self-Interest* of engineers will depend on various *roles* assumed by them in an organization, professional body and society.

7.8.3 Money centered Self-Interest to ensure financial well being

Many people in all walks of life have primary *self-interest* to earn or make enough money to fulfill their other *self-interest* and ensure their own financial well-being as well as well-being of their kith and kin for future also. People want to amass wealth to the extent that well-being of their future generations is also ensured. For this purpose, they sometimes are ready to adopt unethical means also.

Think of why students struggle for getting higher and higher education in engineering, medical, management, finance, law, etc.? These students do studies to get a decent job, be a professional, an entrepreneur or a businessman, etc. to acquire financial resources and social standing. In these roles, they will interact and transact with other persons or public and society and earn a decent salary, fees, commission or share of income as return of their services. The earnings from these jobs are meant to provide resource to fulfill their self-interest. The process of making money or wealth has lot of Moral and Ethical restraints. For engineers and professionals, *Moral Code of Conduct* is prescribed by professional bodies to regulate their behavior and dealings with clients or public.

There are moral and ethical considerations for any action involved in transaction with any individual i.e. SELF and another entity like a person, an organization, society or public at large. Moral and Ethical theories provide guidance to an individual to regulate their pursuit of *self-interest* in any role being played by them.

7.8.4 Self-Interest in economic context

The economic theory largely has been glorifying individual's pursuance of *self-interest* in economic field which was not questioned much by social scientists, especially from the ethical perspective. Some economists believe that *self-interest* explains virtually all behavior of individuals. The implication was growth of unethical traits in society which promoted few super-rich individuals (presumed to be benefactors of society) at the expense of the majority living under grinding poverty.

In the early days of modernization, the belief was that the pursuit of self-interest frees individuals from communal constraints and that it is the main reason for capitalistic prosperity. It is also alleged that *self-interest* is an individual vice, rather than virtues, which is the reason for the flourishing of wealth even by unethical means.

Modern economic theory of self-interest is based on the presumption that human economic relations are solely motivated by self-interest. Related to this presumption is the idea that individuals would promote the welfare of society through the pursuit of their *self-interests*. The problem with this theory of economic relations indicates towards unregulated pursuit of *self- interest*, which suggests an anarchic view of society, in the sense that there is a lack of concern for what *self-interest* would do to the whole social order.

Another claim that is made by late modern economic theorists is that motive of *self-interest* serves to generate and maximize our utilities and material comfort to the humanity at large. Further, actions of *self-interested* individuals automatically promote equilibrium to social, economic and political system better than attempts made to bringing order through any regulatory mechanism. To some people *self-interest* is basically centered on greed and is unethical because it does not account for the reality of our relationships with other human beings, sustenance of natural environment and, needs of the future generations.

We should realize that our human existence is intimately connected with the existence of others living and non-living entities in the nature. In broader sense, individual's interests are connected with interest of the community and imply that his *self-interest* should foster solidarity with community, rather than focused solely on the pursuit of *self-interest* without regard to welfare of the society.

7.8.5 Self-Interest in personal context

Self-interest is an important human motive. The question arises that selfishness is good or bad trait of human personality. Many thinkers argue that it is not good from social point of view. Social and cultural norms require that one should set aside *self-interest* in favor of some greater good to the society? On the other hand, a counter logic is forwarded that the world is bitterly competitive and if one does not take care of his *self-interest* he/she is likely to be left behind as compared to others who do care their *self-interest*. Motive of *self-interest* is very strongly rooted in human psyche.

Whilst *self-interest* of individuals motivates him to maximize his own gains, his actions and activities do results in socio-economic gains of those directly or indirectly associated or use those utilities. The problem, in this approach to the economy, is that given primacy to *self-interest*, the issue of morality is ignored in business and human economic relations. If *self-interest* of human beings is assumed as the sole purpose of human activity than it is impossible to support the idea of society or community which are indispensable for survival of individual's growth and well-being.

7.8.6 Self-Interest and Ambitions

Ambitious people are *self-driven*. They take initiative more earnestly to fulfill their *self- interest*. They are producers and achievers. Ambition is not inherently bad, though *over-ambitious* people are not liked by many. Similarly, people also do not like un-ambitious people who fail to make good use of their talents. Looking and making use of opportunities is one trait of ambitious people. To wait for others, to guide an individual or take the initiative, is one characteristic of un-ambitious person. It is dereliction of one's obligations not to play any role in society by being rational agent of change. Using talent and cash on opportunities to make money through rightful means is one of the main motives of self-interested people. They possess a competitive spirit in tapping the opportunities. Ambitious man tries to maximize returns from his efforts.

7.8.7 Self-Interest and Morality

Self-Interest with human face is good for society. It should not be pursued at the cost of *Morality*. Morality does not contradict self-interest. Morality lies in a genuine concern for others. For example, one should love one's neighbor for his own sake and not after calculation of expectations or any favor in return.

Arguments in favor of self-interest are often put forward above morality on the pretext of practicality. For example, it is argued that *honesty* is the best moral policy but it may not work all the time in your self-interest. A politician can't be honest to reveal all sources of his funding. A lawyer has to professionally argue in favor of his client without too much bothering about truth (even if he/she knows the real facts). However, this type of skepticism about morality is a very narrow approach and not wholly justified once professional responsibilities are also considered to judge an action. The more humanized self-interest becomes, the closer it becomes to morality (Oommen and Venugopal, 1993).

Our discomfort on tussle between *self-interest* and*morality* is partly logical. The reason is that one feels that he/she is being forced into buying morality against self-interest on spurious grounds which is not the case. For example, to a sales man it is good to deal with customers honestly in the long term, but in the short term, it may not be advisable to accept some sales returns of defective goods and replace them just before the end of the accounting year. Business realities are complex and it is not possible that every conflict between morality and self-interest is smoothly resolved.

7.8.8 Self-Interest in Business

Business is always with other person, organization or general public. These entities are often concerned with moral and transparent behavior and dealings. Therefore, *self-interest* in business is linked with moral and ethical expectations of society for business to prosper. Business people may feel pinch that there is no room for maneuvering or freedom to do anything other than what market dictates. But think of market is made up of what? It is customer in the form of individual, organization or general public and none of them would like to support *self-interest* devoid of moral and ethical considerations in their dealings.

However, many businessmen are shy of any ethical consideration to their decision-making process. They fear that it may land them with burden of impractical obligations and responsibilities. However, they should understand that the morality required in the market is to avoid unethical practices and it is just like the morality requirement of ordinary life for happiness of all in social life. It demands only a reasonable regard for the rights and interests of others. Our duties towards others do not demand total abandonment of all our own interests and rights.

A responsible businessman knows that he/she cannot alter the world, but he/she can make his business safer, stable and prosperous by serving his *self-interest* through responding to market forces in accordance to prevailing moral and ethical norms and customs.

7.9 Summary

Most people dream to be successful and achieve goal of life. But they are unaware of importance of their natural resources of time, will power, talent, personality traits, attitudes, motivations, etc. to achieve those goals. Engineering students to be a successful, should additionally need to develop good communication skills, presentation skills, technical knowledge, leadership and human networking skills. One should also do introspection on internal fears, inhibitions, weaknesses, negative personality traits and tendencies which become impediments for success.

Personality and Identity: When we say *I*, this I connotes some total of our personality and our identity. Our personality consists of combination of certain characteristics called personality traits, which decide what type of person we are. These personality traits control our emotions, thoughts, feelings, actions, attitude and behavior. These traits make our personality unique. Our personality is partly *nature* and partly *nurture*. It is partly genetic and partly developed from our experience of the world. It is important to have clear understanding of personal likes and dislikes, strengths and weaknesses of your own personality.

Personality is our sense of identity. It shapes us, as individuals and gives us an identity in the society. Our desire of individuality conflicts with the desire to be accepted. Desire of acceptance means sacrificing some individuality, which ensures security that comes with living together in community.

Trustworthiness: Professionals must be trustworthy for which they must demonstrate few important characteristics like reliability implying adherence to promises made, honoring commitments and be dependable; respect implying commitment to the golden rule of behavior that says that treat others the way you want to be treated; tolerance and acceptance implying that judge others on their character, abilities and conduct without regard to race, religion, gender, where they live, etc. accountability implying that you must accept responsibility for the consequences of your choices, not only for what you do but what you don't do; demonstrate self-control, fairness and justice etc.

Understanding S*elf*: The spiritual nature of a man is ignored in current education system. Spirituality focuses on understanding and exploration of *Self* and our in-built desires, capabilities and potentials. Modern education focuses on work efficiency and neglects creativity. But purpose of education (formal and informal both) should be to refine and awaken the *Self* or *I*to higher plane of living and values then animals' level and behavior. We have ambitions, desires and, feelings which are our inner responses based on our psychic constitution and, we need to understand them for any rational value judgment.

Multiple roles in life: We all have to play different roles in our lives and these roles keep on changing as we grow and mature. We all start life as a son or daughter, then add to that progressively new multiple roles like, within family sister or brother, husband or wife, father or mother, aunt or uncle etc.; and in society like friend, teammate, student, employee, partner, manager, etc. Everybody has some kind of perception of each of them, how to behave or not to behave in those roles. These multiple roles also cause role conflict. Impact of urbanization often creates role conflict in family and relationships.

Positive Thinking: Positive thinking is a mental attitude of good and favorable results. Display of courage, honesty, wisdom, self-care, truthfulness, full of hopes, compassion, faithfulness, unselfishness and other positive traits in thinking and behavior indicates possession of positive thinking. A person with a positive attitude will be more successful in life both professionally and personally. A positive thinking professional does not entertain negative thoughts. Positivity helps us to unfold our potential. Positive thinkers have better stress coping skills, stronger immunity and a lower risk of cardiovascular disease.

Happiness: Everyone wants to be happy, but no one can define happiness with precision. Happiness is the basic requirement of human beings. Physical and non-physical (i.e. emotional entities like love, affection and relationship needs) facilities are means for fulfillment of happiness. We live a significant portion of our lives in relationships. Problems in relationship can disturb and deprive us from happiness. Many people have wrong assumption that wealth is the only thing we need for happiness and the rest will be taken care of automatically. Most of the times, we are driven by similar ad-hoc values and beliefs. Theymay or may not be true in reality.

Self-Interest: Ethical theories place the primary emphasis on right acts and moral rules. Each of the ethical theory leaves considerable room for self-interest, which is pursuing what is good for oneself. *Self* and *Interest*, both are dynamic in nature. While the *Self* is unitary and is evolving with time as personality develops. *Self-Interest* in personal context represents our values which are highly constitutive of our identity. Thus, *Self* can be equated to *I* of a person, whereas his *Interests* have multiplicity and keep on changing with time, age, education and profession. Self-interest is at the core of happiness in life. Self-interest with human face is good for society. Self-interest in business is linked with moral and ethical expectations of society for business to prosper.

Review questions

1. How you can you better charter your future career?
2. What are basic Human Aspirations and how can you maximize your potential for the development and growth?
3. What are the combinations of certain characteristics or qualities which define our personality?
4. How can you understand your person values?
5. Explain why Contentment constitutes one of the basics of ancient Indian ideal?
6. Explain different internal drivers or motivational factors as we grow from childhood to adulthood to old age.
7. How our Individual Identity crystallizes into our personality. What happens when we get shock of Identity Loss?
8. Explain that exploration of 'Self' involves understanding of our in-built desires, capabilities and potentials.
9. Elaborate on 'Our third Eye- The faculty of reason, rationality and emotional balance' is key to understand 'Self'
10. Explain different roles played by all of us in different stages of life as we grow and mature. What is impact of Family on these Roles?
11. What are salient features of Research studies and findings on positive thinking?

12. What do you understand by happiness? Give an example to clarify your point.
13. Analyze what is happiness and how one can get happiness? What is holistic happiness?
14. What is scope of self-interest in different ethical theories which place their emphasis on different aspects of human conduct like right acts, moral rules, virtues, good character etc.?
15. Self-Interest is at the core of happiness in life, explain.
16. Elaborate with examples on 'self-interest reins all aspects of Human activities'.

8 Understanding Behavior, Moral and Ethical Values, to match with the External Environment

Learning objectives

In this chapter you will learn about

- Ethical impact of family and urbanization on different roles being played in life
- Customs, culture and cardinal values, religion and religious pluralism in India
- Modern Humanism, attitude toward ethical behavior and trustworthiness
- Changing corporate culture and present values of Indian-state

8.1 Tips for success in the professional career

An engineer for being successful and effective has to understand global requirements of engineering practice and develop global outlook in his operations, engineering decisions, etc. In engineering practice interactions with labor, subordinates, peers, seniors, managers and management, customers, society, Govt. agencies, etc. is quite common. Many of these interactions are in the nature of human relations where a good understanding of human behavior and moral and ethical issues are essential for the success in the profession. Therefore, it is essential to consciously work to inculcate following behavioral skills in your dealings.

1. Excel in skills of team work, human relations and networking: Sometimes in the career path, students have to play role of a project leaders, where they have to lead teams, consisting of many experts from different fields of technology. So, every student, to be a successful leader, must understand value of human relationship and their Networking, thus learn the skill of team working in the school days. Remember, throughout the career, as engineers you will work in teams and the skills developed in college days helps later on to become a successful team leader in jobs.

2. Grab leadership opportunities in any job or task undertaken: To mature in leadership skills, seek informal leadership roles wherever possible i.e. during student life, social life or in career jobs. Anybody can develop leadership qualities through his conscious decision for that. Starting from any position in an organization, one can grow and develop leadership qualities by influencing people and their decisions and working together with proactive participation.

3. Understand your internal make up and weaknesses, and be open for any feedback: Every student should introspect on his internal fears, inhibitions, weaknesses, negative traits and tendencies. Find the flaws and work to fix them. Just like with any skill, leadership qualities need refinements with continuous improvement. As part of a team, encourage and accept feedback from team members, group leaders, and professors. This feedback can be used to further improve the skills, including communication and leadership.

4. Develop managerial skills along with technical skills: Take interest in a business management-oriented course also. For an engineer, it's not enough for to be technically sound and proficient in work. He/She should also take interest in business matters and be business savvy. Engineers after reaching middle and top levels of an organization have to understand P&L statements, type of organization structures; develop skill to negotiate contracts and familiarity with other functions of administration.

5. Think Globally: Start globalizing your thinking and professional outlook right at the college days, as tomorrow's leaders will be required to engage with MNCs and global business houses. These leaders must be confident to communicate effectively with global companies. They should be familiar with other cultures and develop proficiency in any one foreign language.

Further, In the context of working environment and its functioning, an engineer should be familiar about the background of their team members and clients; because it plays an important role on their behavior and value preferences; which are ingrained in them from their locality, community and business class, caste, language, region, religion, etc. Therefore, we discuss below Customs, Culture and Religion in the context of India, which has wide diversity of these casual factors influencing professional service and Industrial environment. Engineers and professionals must be aware of their role and impact in public services and behavior.

8.2 Customs

Customs, Cultures, Religions are country and community specific. These topics are discussed with reference to India as an example. In eastern traditions ethics and religion are very closely related, and it is difficult to talk about ethics without influx of religion, culture and Customs, which contains within itself some system of morality for the guidance to its followers. In Indian ethics, the morality is very much based on certain beliefs, customs and traditions of Indian religions. By moral considerations one's actions might be branded as good or bad, right or wrong, praiseworthy or blameful, etc.

Engineers and professionals have primarily shaped contemporary world characterized by high level technology, mass communication systems and means-end relationship in all aspects of social life. The decline of religion in industrial societies has resulted in a secular view of life. The urban industrial centers have witnessed vast improvements in the quality of life in terms of civic facilities and comfort.

However, from customs point of view, life of general public is still anchored in primordial loyalty structures such as religion, caste, linguistic groups, variety of ethnic and territorial groupings, etc. There are lot of incompatibilities between personalities, groups and their social institutions vis-à-vis professional life and services. Frequently we come across the conflicts between doctors and patients, teachers and students, bureaucrats and citizens, etc.

In second chapter we have discussed role of engineers as agent of social change, where it was emphasized that educated persons in general and scientists, technologist and engineers in particular have an important social role to modernize the traditions, social customs, biases, norms and practices including the prevailing superstitions, unscientific beliefs, etc.

An engineer must be familiar with customs and religions of people and locality where he/she has to work as professional i.e.as designer, manager and project-in-charge or independent entrepreneur. People in marketing and business development must have fair knowledge of various religions prevalent among their clientele or consumers. Religion caters to the intellectual and emotional adjustment of individuals and groups which in turn promotes social order and stability.

8.2.1 Culture and Customs

Culture means over all totality of present social institutions governing life, values, beliefs, customs, behavior patterns, arts, science, literature, etc. and all other products of human work and thought having continuity with the past generations. The predominating attitudes and behavior that characterize the functioning of a group or organization is reflected in their culture. Indian culture is one of the most ancient cultures of the world. It is dynamic and flexible. It has great virtue of its power of assimilation and represents fusion of different cultural trends and strands.

Custom connotes long established social practices that have been followed for generations. Customs are the basis of rights and duties, as envisaged in law and are also the foundation of ethics in society. Societies are built around complex web of norms and behavior; regulating social activities and social interaction between its members. Societies are regulated by customs, traditions, laws, etc. Fore examples, each social unit like family, sect, cult, political party, industrial organization, trade union, government offices, schools and colleges, voluntary cultural associations, etc. have their own web of customs and traditions, regulating their identities, activities as well as interaction with other social units. The customs of these social units do undergo changes but very slowly, sometimes taking years and generations for adaptation. To impress about survival strength of society and its customs, it can be said that a nation may disappear in history much faster but societies continue. Society is more pervasive and more basic unit of human existence than a state. State and society are independent but society is the ultimate arbiter of people's destiny.

To modernize the customs and practices prevalent in any society is a real challenge to educated peoples and professionals of all hues and colors. Educational training only can correct existing deficiencies in social customs and quality of life. Enlightened professional behavior and commitment of educated people towards modernizing society as responsible citizens can induce general public to adopt reformation of outdated customs and practices. Enlightened citizenship is necessary perquisite for healthy all-round progress and growth of any nation. Democracy emphasizes equality of opportunity to all its citizens. It assumes existence of autonomous and independent individuals capable of participation in the decision-making process.

8.2.2 India and its Cardinal Values

A society must maintain a *social equilibrium*, which implies that units of society are well integrated with the whole of social structure and function with little or no friction. The effective functioning of the society rests on consensus about values and shared interests.

The Indian society is heterogeneous and it is a highly evolved organic whole. A fundamental cultural unity underlies its limitless diversities of languages and dialects, sects and religions. The teeming millions of India profess several faiths and cults and observe different customs and rites. There are apparent and endless diversities in India. In spite of that, India had always been culturally one and organically whole. In India there is a great diversity in traditions, manners, habits and customs. Though we speak different languages yet we are one Nation and all Indians.

The three Cardinal values of traditional society in India are hierarchy, pluralism and holism:

- **Hierarchy:** It implies graded structure of society in superior-inferior units, thus building institutionalized inequality in the

social system. It allocated a secure and definite place to each individual and caste group. Further, the caste system provided as institutional basis for reinforcing the pluralistic tradition of Hinduism. Due to linguistic diversities and cultural differences, caste system operated essentially as regional entities.
- **Pluralism:** As an ideology, it implied tolerance of others style of life while preserving one's own. Hinduism, the dominant religion of India was essentially tolerant. The faith of Muslim conquerors, Christian colonial rulers, Parsee merchants and traders not only survived but prospered and coexisted with relative harmony for centuries in India.
- **Holism:** It means a relationship between individual and group in which the later had primacy over the former; the individual was expected to perform his duties and claim rights always keeping in mind the wider interest of the community.

8.3 Religion

Religion is an important source of integration of general masses/people. The major religions of the world such as Hinduism, Buddhism, Christianity and Islam have provided enduring general values to millions of people. In spite of religious wars and persecutions, religions have inculcated certain universal values and norms among people. Basic to all these religions is the common belief in the unity and oneness of mankind. The belief that the world is originated from an unknown source called God was the central idea behind origin of religion which means to trace and relate the individual life's principle back to its source. The shortest path to reach the source is for one to observe the basic tenets of one's own religion.

Religion is expected to remake the individual refashion his attitude to life and things, make him look within himself; cleanse him of all evil tendencies; transform him and raise him to a higher plane. Science will triumph over ignorance and superstition and religion will triumph over selfishness and fear. Together they can bring a better world order and happier life for mankind. Real knowledge is found not in *knowing* the source but *being* with the source. Bookish or intellectual knowledge is different from experiential knowledge.

Broadly all religions teach imbibing of qualities such as truthfulness, humility, tolerance, nonviolence, obedience, honesty, righteousness, punctuality, confidence, courage, compassion, patience, kindness, courtesy, integrity, etc. These qualities make one's own character and lead people to a moral and ethical life. In a healthy body lives a healthy mind; a healthy mind does not have place for wickedness, anger, greediness, jealousy, arrogance and such negative qualities. Religion functionally reinforces social solidarity. Religious norms and the values transform the individual aspirations into a collective way of life.

8.3.1 Religious Pluralism

Indian religious pluralism is one of the most complexes in the world and may trace the main sources of its complexity to three factors: religious doctrines, historical antecedents and social composition of the believers. The social life requires *collective conscience* of shared values and moral beliefs. Religion is an important vehicle through which collective conscience is expressed. That which is perceived as *sacred* also strengthens social solidarity. This solidarity is often maintained through common beliefs and collective worship (Thompson, 1998).

Scriptures and sacred books are the basic source of societal values. By prescribing general principles, moral beliefs and code of conduct, they act as the fountain head of *value-consensus* in society, which is a prerequisite for establishing order and stability in the society.

Notwithstanding substantial advancement in science and technology there are questions which science cannot answer to man's satisfaction. Religion provides a range of answers, even rationalizations to deal with these questions and issues which make sense to a substantial proportion of people in any society. Hinduism, Islam, Buddhism, Jainism, Sikhism and Christianity are major religions in India (for details see Appendix-C).

Thus, Hinduism is the native religion of India, Islam is an alien religion although it existed in India for the last seven Centuries and Christianity is a colonial importation.

Heterogeneous structure of population contributed to religious pluralism due to cultural diversity, techno-economic development, societal stratification, etc. For example, people belonging to the same religious faith are distributed across different linguistic groups and social complexity as compared with situation when religious and linguistic identities coincide.

It is widely held that along with techno-economic development a process of secularization sets in to different religions with differing consequences such as erosion of religiosity, questioning the legitimacy of religious values and institutions, development of greater tolerance to other faiths, etc.

8.4 Holistic view of Humanity

Understanding psycho-social dimension of man is focus of modern Humanism. Study of man beyond organic dimension is part of spiritual philosophy in India. Conflict of science and spirituality in primarily a western phenomenon, it is not there in eastern traditions where knowledge was considered as one, just like ocean is one but for the purpose of study it is divided into Pacific, Atlantic. In the same sense knowledge is one but for the purpose of studies it can be divided into secular and transcendental, Physical and non-physical. Holistic view of universe is essence of spirituality in India which projects a unified vision of man and nature, something which comes within the purview of senses and something beyond senses. This view of *unity* in the universal existence is now gaining ground in physical sciences also. As a consequence of *holistic view of humanity* focus from religion (i.e. God and Heaven) has shifted to social conditions and welfare of human being on the Earth.

8.4.1 Contemporary meaning and scope of Human Values

In classical literature, there is no distinction between values and human values. But in the present century *theory of values* became a separate branch of modern philosophy called axiology. When this *theory of values* deals with areas of human concern like ethics, religion, art, science, social science, law, etc. it is referred as *human values*.

The theistic view of value system is based on a metaphysical belief system. This value system accepts the existence of a divine cosmic order created by God. It has faith in the authority of a creator God who is the upholder of all values. In spite of differences in their beliefs, rituals and customs, the great world religions also have agreement in large area of basic moral values. These religions have commonality in concept of personal virtues and desired behavior by social groups in the society. The commonality of the virtues and the behavior is called *human values*, which consist of a group of values like love, brotherhood, caring, sharing, etc. The term *human values* are used for this theistic approach to value system and highlight the universal nature of human values.

Many leaders of India like Swami Vivekananda, Sri Aurobindo, Rabindranath Tagore, Mahatma Gandhi, etc. were inspired by the absolutist-theistic value system. They used this value system as the basis of their programs for the spiritual, social and political rejuvenation of the Indian society.

Human value approach is very much holistic in scope and application as compared to the so-called scientific approach to human values. Scientific approach to define human values is quite narrow, because it does not consider divine nature of man or his spiritual nature, emotions and feelings in human relationships. Scientific approach reduces man to a biological organism of a random collection of atoms. It does not give any value to the question of purpose of life. In scientific reasoning there is no value to faith, belief, feeling and intuitive religious perceptions. This type of mechanistic and deterministic interpretation of human being robs him of all his dignity of divine nature and reduces him to merely a malleable automaton, which can be trained to meet the demands of the existing socio-technological order.

Different approaches to study human values can also be classified based on the level of aggregation like at *individual level, the sociological* level and the *ecological level*.

1. **Individual Level Values**: At first level the individual human being can be taken as an independent entity whereat this level some illustrative value are survival values, character, personal virtues, aesthetic appreciation, human rights, self-realization, etc.
2. **Sociological Level Values:** At the second level, individual values are treated subordinate to the sociological values. These values are concerned with those which are relevant at the collective level of human society. The term sociological values include values associated with family as well as other institutions and professions. These values are caring and sharing, sense of social responsibility, social and economic justice, human interconnectedness, etc.
3. **Ecological Level Values:** The values of second level are subordinated to the values of third level i.e. ecological level. These values consist of values from the standpoint of ecological system, where human being and the society are sub system of it. At ecological level, main concern of social scientists and world leaders is
    - to make the world conscious of the need for developing a new system of ethics in the use of material resources
    - for an attitudinal change towards nature based on harmony with nature rather than on the concept of conquering the nature
    - a concern for the survival of future generations if natural resources are exhausted;
    - to avoid global catastrophe caused by unrestrained economic growth

The demand for an ethical change is not as a consequence of ethical belief but as the rational economic analysis of rate of consumption of natural resources vs. rate of replenishment by nature. Human values from this perspective focus on the interdependency of human beings on the nature; propagate to respect the harmony with nature; apply the concept of *Mother Earth* sustainability, conservation etc. in dealing with earth resources.

8.5 Technology forcing fast changes in corporate culture

In ICT and Internet age, market and corporate functioning is changing so fast that before an organization absorbs the changes and finish getting adjusted, it is hit with several other waves of changes. Today the business environment is facing a period of constant transition, and the shelf life of business solutions keeps getting shorter. What solution works today becomes history very soon.

There is growing crowd of new generation of people who are coming up armed with another source of change i.e. *technology*; and technology feeds on itself. Look at what's happening in the area of science, inventions and technology in general. It is said more than 80% of our technological inventions have occurred just since 1900 and speed of technology changes has picked up from 1960 onward i.e. after World War II.

Internet, ICT and mobile communication are recent phenomena of first 15 years of 20th century. It is estimated that technological advances of last 15 years of the twentieth century have done as much technological changes as there was in the whole of 19th Century. Changes do not add up but multiply. Still another source of change is information and knowledge causing *information anxiety*, which doubles every 5 years. Waves of change have no heart or conscience to play favors for anyone and take no prisoners.

Change ruthlessly destroys organizations with cultures that don't adapt. The world of high speed change requires matching agility or radical shift in organizational behavior. No one in modern times can afford to ignore change and think to do what comes naturally. Engineers must face reality and do what works. Be agile to adopt change i.e. speed up response to change.

Under today's market and business conditions, slowing down is the most hazardous move a professional can think off. Therefore, don't resist change because that's drag on the organization. Cultural changes depend on professionals to give it a sense of urgency.

8.6 Role of Attitude and environmental factors on Ethical Behavior

Attitude is an individual's response on favorable or unfavorable evolution of ethical values or behavior. Bommer et al. (1987) proposed an ethical decision-making model with several environmental factors that could explain general ethical behavior (i.e. an individual's attitude toward the behavior). These environmental factors are belief system of personal, professional and societal origin as well as legal and business environment, as explained below:
1. **Societal Environment**: The societal environment means the social and cultural values that impact the individual's attitude and behavior.
2. **Belief system**: Belief system refers to religious values and beliefs developed in an individual's spiritual or religious environment in

which he/she has grown up from childhood i.e. family, society and education.
3. **Personal Values**: Personal values are an individual's choice of personal goals, values acquired through experiences, and his moral considerations, views and sensitivity.
4. **Personal Environment**: Personal environment is the influence of family, peers and significant others. In jobs an individual's environmental influences, moral obligation and consequences of one's behavior that influences an individual's attitude toward ethical behavior.
5. **Professional Environment**: Professional environment refers to work culture of place of work, professional codes of conduct and professional expectations of an individual's profession.
6. **Legal Environment:** Legal environment means environment of working culture in the field of the law, the legislation, and the government which imparts a list of do and don'ts to regulate the individual attitude and behavior.
7. **Business Environment**: Corporate business environment includes corporate goals, profit motive of the company, corporate policies on ethics, employees, customer service, etc. where the individual works. A company's stated policies may increase the probability of ethical behavior
8. **Moral Obligation**: Personal normative beliefs and consequently behavior of an individual towards the moral obligation one feels to perform or not to perform.
9. **Consequences:** Consequences of an unethical behavior alert an individual's awareness about the penalty a decision maker and/or other have to pay. Consequences influence ethical decision-making.

8.6.1 Social learning from life around us

- Life in school and college is very much focused on education and skill development. Here final goal is getting through education and making a good career or jobs. This is the time when we visualize the purpose of education as source of fulfillment of our future goals. During education period, we spend lot of time with family and friends also. Life with family and friends is virtually a period of training and experience in development of network of relationships. The relationship with parents and friends is an important aspect of our lives. We love these relationships but sometimes come across conflicting situations also. We learn a lot through these relationships.

- We learn a lot about relationships, life styles and values from social media like Internet, TV, radio, newspapers, magazines, etc. We get exposures about global issues like environment pollution, deforestation, global warming, demographic changes, etc. We also learn about scientific developments, politics, economy, legal frameworks, religious issues, etc.
- Through information from these channels and, our analysis and understanding of these matters, we develop maturity to evaluate their relevance and utility. They also help us in framing our goals. This learning from *life around us* is a lifelong process.

8.7 Institution of Family and influence of Urbanization and Globalization

We all have to play different roles in our lives and these roles keep on changing as we grow and mature. There are different stages of life that we go through and each one has its own priorities. These stages may demand us to play roles accordingly to the stage we are in.

Our life starts as a son or daughter of our parents. With time, new roles are added as role of brother, sister, friend, teammate, student, employee, husband or wife and later on as father or mother, aunt or uncle, grandparent and the list go on. One can visualize these roles in advance and prepare to play them when time for that comes. Similarly, when we are in the job, we perform different roles like role of an employee, or manager, or engineer, etc. After office hours, we again take up our roles within the family, society, etc.

Playing different roles is incumbent on us for smooth operation of society. The role can be visualized as some sort of functional relationship and broadly these functions and roles are standardized in the society. They are defined within a broad area of agreement and provide some sort of stability and security to all within that functional relationship. It gives a feeling of certainty on what to expect in any particular role.

Role Conflict: Multiplicity of roles at the same time for an individual does not imply that all these roles will be compatible with each other. Most often that will not be the case. For example, a good mother is required to spend quality time with her children. However, the role of mother is not compatible with her role as an employee, dedicated and committed to her role in the office. There are many such pairs of roles that are conflicting with each other and their compatibility requirement is difficult to meet.

8.7.1 Marriage and the Family

Marriage is key determinant for formation of a family and family values. It plays important role in building harmony in the family. Marriage among

Hindus is regarded as a sacrosanct that carries with it some supernatural sanctions. Marriage among Hindus and Christians is sacred, while among Muslims it is a contract which can be terminated unilaterally or by mutual consent.

Family is the basic unit of human interactions and a healthy understanding of the *Institution of Marriage* is essential for harmonious living and stable society. It is an important source of building relationship between family members. Family is also a very important primary group in the society. A family could be a small nuclear family or big extended family consisting of three or four generations, such as grandparents, parents and grandchildren and other male and female relatives.

The family is vested with important functions of bringing up children and imparting family values; look after their education and socialization needs. Family, as social unit is also engaged in various other important activities of economic, political, social and religious nature, having greater impact and implications in upbringing of children.

8.7.2 Shrinking of family units and impact on values and relationships

Heightened prospects of employment in towns led to a large-scale migration from the village, causing the breakup of the large joint family system. Further, higher education, urban occupations, desire for higher standards of living, desire for individuality and independence have made way for smaller family units.

Exposure of urban life is also causing shift in initially cherished values of family and community to which a person belongs. There is perceptible shift in importance of family unit in today's world which creates a big social problem. Family is the fundamental unit of any society world over. But the time of individuals spent with the family, or with the people living together as family, is shrinking in many societies world over. There is shift in cultural status of family units. *Institution of Marriage* is becoming more fragile, which can be seen in frequent breaking of relationship. Numbers of divorce cases are on rise resulting in more broken families. Divorced families have very bad impact on children who suffer from insecurity in their early ages, which in turn creates psychological problem of fears and lack of courage among these children. Now-a-days, such children are not as stable as they used to be in unbroken families in earlier times.

Therefore, it is pertinent for youths and professionals, who are aspiring for making stable family, to understand in advance about nature of responsibilities of family and relationship. They must become aware of stipulations of existing social and legal principles and practices of marriage, divorce, and inheritance to avoid pitfalls in family relationship in future.

8.7.3 Impact of Urbanization on family and relationship

Urban life is less compulsive for the observance of traditional norms. It also creates need for interaction between persons of different religion, race, cultural and caste backgrounds. The urban situation demands or forces people to adapt non-traditional occupations. Urban life is more cosmopolitan in nature, where people of different background meet, interact and work together. This change of social environment leads the redefinition of relationship between individuals and groups.

Further, unregulated growth of urban centers indirectly created a large number of problems like overcrowding, congestion, poor housing and sanitary conditions, leading to delinquency and crime in society.

Other Consequence of social change is steep rise in expectations, resulting in the lower class to copy and follow life style of middle class, and anxiety of middle class to ape the upper class.

Exploiting this rise in expectations, political parties offer lot of unviable and unrealizable promises during elections which are rarely fulfilled, and consequently breed frustration in the society and family life.

8.7.4 Life with family and friends

Students spend lot of time in schools and much bigger part of lives at home with family and friends. The network of relationship, with colleagues, parents, other siblings, and friends, is an important aspect of our lives. We love and enjoy these relationships, where sometimes conflicts of interest, views and opinions also arise.

At any moment, our *life or living* has five domains of existence or areas of concern. Each domain has its own choices, compulsions and priorities. These domains of concern are as follows:

- **Myself:** Concerned with individuals' choices, thoughts and desires i.e. his perceptions, thinking and wants.
- **Family:** Concerned with expectations of the family and our duties and responsibilities towards them.
- **Society**: Concerns with responding to various cultural and obligatory demands of the society and comprehensive goals of human being.
- **Professional**: Concerns with professional life, career or activities of economic nature.
- **Nature/Environment**: Need to understand human dependence on nature and Environment.

We need to understand interdependence and interconnectedness of above domains of concern for holistic life. It is essential to build harmony among all above domains.

Since we all live in these domains all the time, we need to understand them more clearly for our better adaptation and behavioral responses. Institution of *family* assures security and happiness to Individuals in the society. Let us examine, what do we understand by happiness?

8.8 Responsibilities as Good Citizen

Everybody in society should be and act as good responsible citizen. One should be good to neighbors. Nurture volunteer-ship and be caring person pursuing the common good. Student should participate as volunteer within their school and the community to make it better, cleaner, and safer. Every citizen should work for protecting the environment, conserving resources, reducing pollution and promoting clean living conditions. All citizens should become vocal for making things better by voicing their opinion, voting, serving on committees, reporting wrongdoing and paying taxes.

All citizens should inculcate respect for *authority* and the *law*. You should observe and follow the rules and comply with the laws. You should respect authority, be it parents, teachers, coaches and others who have been given authority. In your dealings with other persons and the society at large, honor and respect principles of democracy.

8.9 Direction of Indian State

Values of Indian nation-state are embedded in the constitution. The goals are socialism, secularism and democracy. Opinions differ on the primacy and order of priority among these goals. Thus, notwithstanding the overall consensus about the basic values, disagreement exists over their importance or the mode and sequence of their realization. Indian socialism is different in theory and practice as compared with socialism elsewhere. Indian socialism does not attempt collectivization of private property but only seeks to limit it.

Secularism means coexistence and tolerance of other communities, particularly religious communities. Secularism means non-interference in their affairs and a positive appreciation for their distinct style of life.

Democracy emphasizes equality of opportunity to all its citizens. It assumes existence of autonomous and independent individuals capable of participation in the decision-making process. But Indian democracy is anchored in primordial loyalty structures such as religion, caste, linguistic groups, etc. Majority in the population is still governed by traditional social values and rigid institutional structures where the individual as an autonomous entity making decisions for him is to some extent non-existent.

It can be seen that there is lot of contradiction between value package of hierarchy, pluralism and holism of traditional India, with value package of socialism, secularism and democracy of modern Indian-state.

8.10 Summary

Customs: *Custom* connotes long established social practices that have been followed for generations. Customs are the basis of rights and duties, as envisaged in law and are also the foundation of ethics in society. Societies are built around complex web of norms and behavior regulating social activities. Social interactions between its members are regulated by customs, laws, etc.
The decline of religion in industrial societies has promoted secular view of life and contributed vast improvements in their quality of life. However, from customs point of view, life of general public is still anchored in primordial loyalty structures such as religion, caste, linguistic groups, variety of ethnic and territorial groupings etc.
Culture: Culture means holistic working in totality of present social institutions governing life, values, beliefs, customs, behavior patterns, arts, science, literature, etc. having continuity with the values and beliefs of past generations. Indian culture is both dynamic and flexible. It has great virtue of its power of assimilation and represents fusion of different cultural trends and strands.

The Indian society is heterogeneous and it is a highly evolved organic whole. A fundamental cultural unity underlies its limitless diversities of languages and dialects, sects and religions. The Three cardinal values of traditional society in India are hierarchy, pluralism and holism.
Religion: Basic tenets of any religion for purposeful life are right conduct, truthfulness, love, nonviolence and peace. Religion functionally reinforces social solidarity. Science will triumph over ignorance and superstition and religion will triumph over selfishness and fear. Together they can bring a better world order and happier life for mankind. The social life requires *collective conscience*, of shared values and moral beliefs. Religion is an important means of expressing collective conscience of people. The multi-religious character of Indian society is of utmost importance in considering the state commitment to maintain religious pluralism in India
Modern Humanism: Understanding psycho-social dimension of man is focus of *modern Humanism*. Study of man beyond organic dimension is part of spiritual philosophy in India. Although differing in their belief systems, rituals and customs, the great world religions have a large area of agreement on the basic moral values, conceptions of personal virtues and social group behavior based on humanistic values of love, brotherhood, caring and sharing. In recent times the term *human values* have been used for this theistic approach to value system. Human value approach is very much holistic compared to, so-called scientific approach to human phenomena and associated values.

In the present century theory of values cover all areas of human concern like ethics, religion, art, science, social science, law,etc. arequite often called as *human values*. Different approaches to study human values can also be classified in terms of their attention focused on the level of aggregation like attention on the individual, the sociological and the ecological level.

Technology based changes in Corporate Culture: In ICT and Internet age changes in market and corporate functioning keep picking up speed. Before an organization can finish getting adjusted to one change, it gets hit with several others. We're living in a period of constant transition. *What works* today becomes history very soon. There is growing crowd of new generation of people who are coming up armed with another source of change- technology and technology feeds on itself. Change ruthlessly destroys organizations with cultures that don't adapt. Thus, corporate world has to adopt radical shift in behavior, think differently, reorder priorities and develop faster reflexes.

Direction of IndianState: Values of Indian nation are embedded in our constitution. The goals are socialism, secularism and democracy. Opinions differ on the primacy and order of priority among these goals. Values enshrined in the Indian constitution are not fully translated into practice. Even though secularism is fundamental goal of Indian state, its institutionalization is far from achieved because of soft approach towards communal, linguistic and caste-based mobilizations. It can be seen that there is lot of contradiction between value package of hierarchy, pluralism and holism of traditional India with value package of socialism, secularism and democracy of modern Indian state.

Review questions

1. What type of mindset or disposition displays positive thinking or positive attitude? What is exhortation of the *optimist creed*?
2. How one can cultivate positive thinking and overcome negative thoughts?
3. What do you understand by negative self-talk? Give practical suggestions for maintaining positive attitude and overcome negative traits.
4. Why an engineer must be familiar with customs and religions of people and locality where he/she has to works as professional?
5. Explain difference between culture and customs.
6. Explain basic diversities of society in India and its Cardinal values.
7. What role religion plays in shaping moral and ethical values of society?
8. What moral and ethical issues arise due to religious pluralism in India?

9. Explain how as a consequence of rise in modern Humanism, focus from Religion has shifted to social conditions and, welfare of human being on the earth?
10. What is contemporary meaning and scope of human values?
11. Give an account of changing corporate culture from human values point of view.
12. Explain how environment influences societal belief system, personal, professional, legal, as well as business practices?
13. What are characteristics of trustworthy which an engineer or professional must demonstrate in his behavior or dealings.

Section 3: Engineering as Social Experimentation and Engineers Roles and Responsibilities

9 Engineering as Social Experimentation

Learning objectives

In this chapter you will learn about

- Social responsibility of engineers for products and projects executed for society
- Uncertainties of design and development make engineering as social experimentation
- Experiential learning, knowledge gained through experimentation, informed consent
- Complexity of mega engineering projects from the point of social engineering
- Impact of industrialization, industrial pollution and effects

9.1 Social Responsibility of Engineers

In engineering works, there are inherent uncertainties, sometimes grave in nature, which is a unique feature of engineering. Even then responsibility of engineers to ensure public safety and good in their operations does not get diluted. The general public cannot usually comprehend the social risks and implications inherently present in the engineering works and projects. For example, airplane passengers do not know aerospace engineering and risks involved in it well enough when they board an airplane. Similarly, an automobile driver is not an automobile engineer to know well enough risks involved in driving a newly designed vehicle, nor public is aware of built in risks in civil engineering works to understand the risks taken a drive over a new bridge. Similar level of ignorance exists in general public about the knowledge of risks involved in the use of virtually any product or project of engineering design.

In medical profession, there is direct contact between doctor and the patient; and patients are required to give their consent to medical procedures used on them without knowing implication and risks involved. Therefore, the physician has obligation towards patient and sometimes to his near and dear relatives, to explain the risks associated in the procedures in spite of all care taken by doctors. In engineering the situation is different. Engineers do not directly deal with the general public; therefore, chance of this type of explanation is impossible to general public about risks involved in their products, projects or engineering works.

Based on level of complexity and multiplicity of technologies involved, engineering marvels can be broadly classified as

1. **Engineering Products**: Like mobile phone, camera, laptop, car, engines, generators, house, buildings, etc. which are standalone units of use and applications
2. **System Engineering based Standalone mega Products**: Like railway trains, ships, aero planes, satellite, rocket, missiles, radar units, drilling platforms, etc. which have high level of complexities than small size products, and require System-engineering based design approach using multiple specialized technologies.
3. **Plant Type Engineering Projects**: Like, power plants, fertilizer plants, steel plants, airports, nuclear plants, etc. which require lot of space and infrastructures for their operations as one unit.
4. **Network Type Megaprojects:** Like dams, bridges, railway lines, launch sites of missiles, rocket and satellite, etc.

All above engineering marvels have multiple levels of uncertainties during concept to final stage and their expected performance in the operational fields or sites, which requires experimentations of various nature and levels, to gain knowledge at each stage and phase of engineering works. The ultimate user of any engineering works, directly or indirectly are human beings. Hence engineers have obligation and responsibility to ensure public safety and good performance in their products, projects and operations. Wherever experimentation has direct impact on public, it is called *social experimentation* (Schinzinger and Martin, 2000). Nature of these uncertainties is discussed below.

9.2 Experimentation during Engineering Product-Design Process

Technology advances only by innovation and experimentation at various levels, operating conditions and degree of control on the environment of ultimate use.

1. **In-door Experimentation in controlled environment like R&D lab, design department or manufacturing plant/factory**: Engineering products/ projects, whether small consumer products, or larger one like bridges, buildings, communication network, power plants, launch of a rocket, etc. require specific designs, and have an experimental content in design, implementation and their field performance, whenever they are executed for the first time.

The Experimental content, in products/ projects is to assess short term or long-term impact of its design and success in field performance as well as customer satisfaction, irrespective of whether the experimentation level involved is small or big, simple or complex. In engineering, however, most of the time the ultimate users are general public who utilize the products, services or infrastructure developed by engineers.

2. **Out-door Experimentation in uncontrolled environment like actual operating field:** Engineering works are always associated with an element of uncertainty about the desired outcome and performance of any design work or concept. After careful design and development; when such lab model or a test bench-based product, is taken up for field trials, or field performance or to verify its applications; many new issues related to working environment of application prop up; which are new factors of operating conditions; introducing lot of unknown and uncertain factors and were not accounted at the initial design phase. These new factors experienced during environmental performance assessment necessitate improvement in initial design, and retesting of improved model of the product. Thus, a new cycle of engineering experimentation starts for a better mature product.

   For example, a cellular mobile set developed in the lab to prove the technology is not engineered and optimized from the point of view of compactness, weight, size, case design, electronic packaging, electromagnetic coupling between its components, internal heat generation and dissipation, battery power consumption, screen size, keypad, camera, input/ out port location. To optimize these issues a team of engineers from different related fields have to work together like an experimenter in their respective domain to develop production worthy model of cellular phone. Similarly, automobile, mechanical, electrical and metallurgy engineers, who are mostly involved in design of a new vehicle, but during design phase they are not fully sure about how well a new vehicle will perform on the road. Similarly, civil and structural engineers do not fully know, whether a new building designed by them will withstand a hurricane. However, it must be understood that there is a necessity of gaining new knowledge to circumvent current issues of risk factors and for that further experimentation is essential by engineers, to develop new more robust designs.

3. **Engineers Advanced visualization of various activities and processes involved in design, manufacturing, testing, marketing, ultimate use, and user profile:** However, in spite of uncertainties and gap in scientific or technological knowledge,

engineers have to take responsibility for their experiments at product level and also at project level. They must foresee and think about the possible consequences, both good and bad in different situations of use and application; an attempt must be made to eliminate as many bad consequences as possible right from design stage to production process level, till it reaches to ultimate user.

9.3 Example of Engineering as Social Experimentation

Many of you might have seen Titanic movie. Titanic was proclaimed the greatest engineering achievement of that time. It was the largest ship so far manufactured in the world at that time. It had a length of almost three times of a football field. Titanic had sixteen watertight compartments and in case of collision, it was designed to remain floating even with any of the four compartments flooded. The Titanic was believed fully safe ship and virtually unsinkable. It had a capacity to accommodate 3,547 passengers and crew.

With such confidence, the Titanic sailed on its voyage in April 1912 and the captain allowed the ship to sail with full speed. The ship collided at night with an iceberg which ruptured it and created a large gap in the ship's side, causing flooding of five compartments. Even though there was time available to evacuate the ship, the life boats in ship were not enough to save the passengers. The Disaster resulted in death of 1,522 passengers (drowned or frozen) out of the 2,227 on board. Titanic remains an example of technological complacency and overconfidence without perceiving the risk factors of the travel route.

Many technological products carry potential dangers during implementation in the field and different operating conditions. This is because of limitation to perceive all possible conditions prevailing in the field of application which cross the safety limits of design and manufacturing. Therefore, engineering is regarded as an inherently risky activity. Because of uncertainties and exploratory nature of engineering, ethical implications surface up and engineering is ethically viewed as an experimental process. Engineering experiments are not limited to experiment conducted solely in a laboratory under controlled conditions. They also have component of experimentation, outside the laboratory i.e. in the field without any control on the environment of experimentation but having ethical implications on a social scale involving human subjects.

9.3.1 Engineers Responsibilities with regard to Technology

The concept of engineering as social experimentation requires a fresh look at engineer's responsibilities with regard to technology. Most of these responsibilities of engineers are summarized below.

Chapter 9: Engineer as Social Experimentation

1. Engineers have to understand that technology is not socially neutral and has ethical implications because of its impact on human lives. It is embedded in the social life in cyclic fashion of both as cause and effect.
2. There is a continuous debate between technological optimists and pessimists without any conclusion. But both agree that technology has contributed to a large extent in making human life comfortable in many senses, but it also raised new issues that demand solutions and many of these problematic issues have to be solved by engineers. Therefore, engineers must examine very critically overall impact of technology on society in holistic fashion.
3. Especially engineering societies have a responsibility to educate the public about the dangers and risks involved in application of particular technology. They must also alert and advise government agencies and industry on the policy issues regarding use and limitations of technology.
4. Engineers are the primary source of implementation of technology for different applications. They have major responsibility to design their technical solutions with due consideration to minimize the risk factors and impact on the social and value implications of their designs.

9.4 Process of Engineering Development of Products or Projects

As explained above, experimentation is part and parcel of engineering works from the design stage to final product/ project. In design process, preliminary tests or simulations are conducted to examine feasibility and realizability of the new engineering concept. Prototypes are made of different materials and processes are tried out, employing formal experimental techniques. Such tests serve as the basis for pilot production stage where more detailed design features and specifications including test plans are chalked out. At the production stage, further tests are run until a finished product evolves. The normal design process is thus iterative with multiple trials in designs process. Beyond those specific tests and experiments, each engineering project taken as a whole can be treated as chain of experiments.

9.4.1 Knowledge-Gaps in Engineering of new Products/Projects or improving the existing one to compete in the market, requires experimentation

In development of concept in any engineering project, initially at conceptualization stage there is always certain degree of vagueness and uncertainties, about final detailed parameters of design or technical data, quality of input material to be used, appropriate production process, reliability of final project or outcome, etc. Due to these common features, practically any kind of project engineering can be viewed as an engineering experiment. Some of these features are elaborated below.

In the beginning there is always some degree of ignorance and lack of clarity about the shape, size, final specifications and application of the project. There are many uncertainties in

- the abstract model used for the design calculations
- the precise characteristics of the materials to be used
- the precision of materials processing and fabrication
- the nature of direct and indirect infrastructure support
- the uncertainties about the nature of the stresses on and of the finished product
- the uncertainties about total volume, weight, shape, size, power consumption, cost and final utility

Further, there is always a time and cost constraint. Thus, an engineer has to do tight rope walking due to these constraints and cannot have the luxury of waiting until all the relevant facts are available to start the work. He/ She has to try alternative techniques or temporary arrangements or scaffold with alternative substitutes till correct inputs are available. Sometimes, he/she may have to bypass certain tests for the sake of moving ahead on a project. Indeed, one talent crucial to an engineer's success lies precisely in the ability to accomplish the tasks safely with only a partial knowledge of scientific laws about the nature and user expectation and response.

The final outcomes of engineering projects carry certain uncertainties which are revealed in field during actual use and after some lapse of time. Launch of a satellite or missile or space probe or an aircraft of new design or earthquake proof building or bridge, etc. are examples which carry uncertainties of outcome in spite of best talent and technology employed. Even on small scale products like new mobile set, new drug, new software, new home appliances, etc. carry lot of uncertainties of field performance (many mobile phones have blasted in the field due to battery heating), safety features, customer acceptance and market penetration. Often engineering projects like dams, bridges, roads, etc. are built with long gestation period for the benefit to public. It is not even possible to know what will be the hidden negative outcomes (damage) they carry at great risks to public.

Improving the current products and creating better ones is essential in a competitive market. For this, continuous research and development of technology is essential. Feedback data for improving the product and process cannot depend on in-house development or testing only. Field feedback on product is much more important for ruggedization of the product and such data is available only after clients' usage. In engineering experiments, both the intermediate and final results of the product or project must be analyzed to take correct lessons for maturation of the product/ project and technology.

9.4.2 Experiential Learning

Experience is a great trainer. Engineers learn by practically doing some design and execute the project based on such design. Their experience matures when operating results match with expected performance of their designs. They also learn from design experience of other engineers whose design documents are published/ found in technical reports. But there are occasions when past mistakes are repeated because of lack of communication within the product or project teams in sharing the information or misplaced pride of individual or the department in not seeking necessary clarification/ information or feelings of embarrassment for the failure or fear of litigation or simply neglect of feedback by someone (less experienced) in the team.

It is necessary for senior engineers and project managers to keep watch on overall operations to guard against repetition of known mistakes and ensure updating of checklists and working manuals promptly at the earliest. They must be imaginative in visualizing all possible situations/ conditions, which can induce failure or damage to the equipment/products. Frequent and regular review meetings do help in guarding against weak points of workflow/process. Handbooks, computer programs, operating limits specified in the calibration tables, algorithms must be routinely checked/ recalibrated. Good engineering practice requires that engineers/ managers too must be alert and well informed of every stage of a project history and frequently exchange relevant date and ideas with colleagues of all other project related departments.

9.5 Complexity of Megaprojects from the point of Social Engineering

Building a smart city, new airport, a ring road to ease traffic congestion, metro line, laying a new railway line, setting up a nuclear plant, setting up missile or satellite launch site, building a dam for hydroelectric power generation, setting up a petrochemical complex, etc. are examples of engineering megaprojects of national importance. Such projects are real social engineering experiments as they are executed only once with no feasibility technology demonstration or building a prototype or pilot model before starting the execution. However, execution requires various studies prior to starting the project. Such projects are characterized by
- The requirement of large land sites

- Roads for transportation of man and material to site, availability of water resources
- Electrical power, communication facility, etc.

Site selection for such projects is a cumbersome process involving
- Legal issues and terrain condition
- Consent of public whose land is acquired or affected and issues of their displacement
- Rehabilitation, compensation, etc.
- Suitability from the point of deforestation, environment, climatic considerations, etc.
- Studies of soil condition and characteristic (soft or hard or uneven with hillocks and ditches, Load bearing capacity), etc. Many of these studies are conducted by engineers or under their supervision.

The problems of concern for people around the project sites and neighboring areas is about environmental pollution, excessive noise level, radiation hazards, water and air contaminations, etc. are the areas of direct concern to engineers to find the solution.

From the above description of the nature of engineering efforts required on *megaprojects*, it must be clear that such Projects have a large component of *experimentation in design features as well as its social impact* and because of those features *project engineering* is treated as *social experimentation*. It is also clear that experimentation of project engineering differs widely from standard experimentation process of product engineering. These differences highlight the additional responsibilities imposed by megaprojects on engineers towards society and human beings. Analysis of differences in complexity of product and project engineering can also make engineers aware of their moral responsibilities towards public and all those engaged in the engineering and execution of the megaprojects.

9.6 Impact of Industrialization and Industrial Pollution

The world entered into 21st century with rapid industrialization of almost all major economies. Rapid development of industries brought scourge of industrial pollution. Any form of pollution, traceable to industry or to industrial practices is known as *industrial pollution*. In fact, industrial pollution has become alarming and of grave concern to agencies fighting for environmental protection and prevention of further degradation. Those countries, which are growing rapidly and industrializing their economies, are contributing to sudden and rapid growth of industrial pollution. It is a serious problem which has to be brought under control immediately. Industrial pollution takes on many faces like pollution of sources of drinking water; pollution of the air quality by industries releasing unwanted toxins into the air; reduction in fertility and the quality of soil, etc. Thus, this is impacting the healthy environment for human habitation all over the world. Below are few of the causes of industrial pollution that have resulted in environment degradation.

Causes of Industrial Pollution
1. Many countries do not have adequate policies and legal framework to control pollution.
2. With unplanned industrial growth, pollution issue is neglected in selection of pollution efficient technology.
3. Outdated technologies, which contribute to high pollution, are cheaply exported to underdeveloped countries.
4. Presence of large number of small scale industries who are not conscious of pollution issue and unable to manage their pollutants.
5. Absence of efficient waste disposal system in many societies and countries.

Effects of industrial pollution
1. Water Pollution
2. Soil Pollution
3. Air Pollution
4. Wildlife Extinction
5. Global Warming

Pollution monitoring and control: It is difficult to predict precisely quantum of industrial pollution from project site. Engineers are required to establish regular monitoring of level of emanating Industrial pollutants and conduct test experiments on quality and quantity of these pollutants. Similarly, monitoring is required for noise and radiation level present in working environment of employees and other workers.

There are elaborate standard recommendations on emission of industrial pollutants, noise and radiation level to which human beings can be exposed during their duty hours. Engineers are required to establish monitoring and control mechanism to control these levels and ensure safe operating environment to workmen. He reengineering experiments are conducted on projects/products whereas final success of experiments is measured by safety of human being and its satisfaction.

9.7 Informed Consent

Engineering basically has content of experimentation to deal with multiple technologies applied in any product or project. In the end, all the technologies applied together culminate into a product or project where the final trial or experiment is performed on persons, not on inanimate objects. These experiments on a societal scale place the focus on human beings affected by technology. Thus, engineering parallels medical science where testing of new drugs or procedures is done on human beings.

Recently society has placed emphasis and recognized the primacy of the human safety and freedom of choice to participate or not participate in medical experiments, moral and legal rights of human beings have been accepted as fundamental. Thus, to conduct a medical experiment on human being, it is mandatory to take informed consent from participants. In similar fashion, engineering practice has also started recognizing those human rights and treats, informed consent of people affected by the experiment, very vital to the concept of a properly conducted experiment. This practice should be the keystone in the interaction between engineers and the general public for the conduct of experiment of the engineering projects affecting people.

When a manufacturer sells a new device of technological innovation to another firm, they both come to an agreement regarding the sharing of risks and benefits of trying out the new technology. Here informed consent, in the form of an agreement, implies two main elements *viz.* knowledge and voluntariness. In the agreement, first both parties should be agreeing to provide not only the information they request, but all the information needed to make a reasonable decision. Second, they must enter into the experiment without being subjected to force, fraud, or deception. Mere purchase of a product does not amount to having an informed consent. The public and clients must be given operating instructions and information about the practical risks and benefits of the process or product in the language they can understand.

Informed consent is treated valid when:
- The consent is given voluntarily without any pressure or force.
- The consent was based on the information provided to the participant, together with any other information requested by him.
- The consenter is competent (not too young or mentally ill for instance) to process the information and capable of making rational decisions.

9.8 Knowledge Gained

Effective engineering relies on knowledge gained by executing projects and products during production process and after the execution or field feedback. This learning provides knowledge, for further improving the projects/ products execution and quality in future. Growth and success in engineering depends on gaining new knowledge, through experimentation on unresolved problems and issues. The ultimate test of a product's quality and improvements rests on its efficiency, safety, cost-effectiveness, environmental impact, aesthetic value and how well it performs in the field applications. Building product or project history by monitoring of their performances in the field over long time gives an important data on ageing and de-rating phenomena of the product life.

Scientific experiments are conducted to gain new knowledge and engineering field deals with experiments based on such scientific and technological knowledge to execute new projects and products for benefiting human life. Their focus is on application rather than designed to produce new scientific knowledge. When we conduct an engineering activity, it is like an experiment on application of technology where we do expect some unexpected outcomes. Unexpected outcomes trigger search for reasons and explanations of such outcomes, thus gaining new knowledge possibly involving conduct of another experiment to confirm the conclusions of new knowledge. However, the distinction between engineering experiments and scientific experiments is not vital because we are concerned only the manner in which the experiment is conducted and not the rigor of conduct of experimental process. Along with working force of the engineering projects, general public is also involved in the project, because they are the final beneficiary of the project and their valid consent is sought, safety measures are taken and means for exist or terminating the experiment at any time are planned with arrangement of providing safe exit of all participants.

9.9 Summary

Social Responsibility of Engineers: In engineering works there are inherent uncertainties, sometimes grave in nature, which is a unique feature of engineering. Engineering works, whether consumer products, bridges, buildings, communication network, power plants, launch of a rocket, etc. have some degree of experimental content. Wherever engineering experimentation has direct impact on public we call it *social experimentation.*

For example, building Titanic ship was a case of engineering as social experimentation. Titanic ship was proclaimed the greatest engineering achievement of that time. The Titanic was believed fully safe ship-virtually unsinkable. However, the ship collided with an iceberg and broke. The Titanic remains a haunting image of technological complacency. So many products of technology present potential dangers that engineering can be regarded as an inherently risky activity.

The ultimate user of any engineering works directly or indirectly is human beings and most of them are usually not aware of the risks and social implications inherent in an engineering work. Therefore, engineers have obligation to ensure public safety and, must assume responsibility for their experiments.

The concept of engineering as social experimentation requires a fresh look at engineer's responsibilities with regard to technology. Engineers and engineering societies must adopt a critical attitude toward technology and take the responsibility to alert the public to the dangers and risks imposed by technology.

In fact, any engineering development of product or project has some degree of uncertainties about design parameters, input parameters and technical data of material to be used, production process etc. Similarly, the final products or projects carry some degree of uncertainties on performance which are revealed after use in the fieldfor some time. For example, launch of a satellite or missile or space probe or an aircraft of new design, etc. always carry uncertainties on final performance in spite of best talent and technology employed.

Experience is a great trainer. Engineers learn by practically doing design and execute the project based on such design. The whole design and engineering process are improved by regular review meetings on workflow/processes, operating handbooks, computer programs, limits of the tables, algorithms underlying their favorite tools and routine checked/ calibration of test setups.

Complexity of Megaprojects from the point of Social Engineering: Building a smart city, building new airport, building a ring road or metro line or a new railway line, setting up a nuclear plant, setting up missile or satellite launch site or petrochemical complex, building a dam for power generation, etc. are examples of mega engineering projects. Such projects are real social engineering experiments as they are executed only once with no feasibility technology demonstration or building a prototype or pilot model before starting the execution. The problems of concern for peoples, around the project sites and neighboring areas, is about environmental pollution, excessive noise level, radiation hazards, water and air contaminations, etc. which are areas of direct concern to engineers to find the solution.

Rapid development of industries brought along with it scourge of industrial pollution. Most of the pollution on the planet can be traced back to industries of some kind. Industrial pollution takes on many faces. It contaminates many sources of drinking water, releases unwanted toxins into the air and reduces the quality of soil. Major environmental disasters have been caused due to industrial mishaps, which have yet to be brought under control.

Informed Consent: Viewing engineering as an experiment on a societal scale places the focus on human beings affected by technology, because the experiment is performed on persons, not on inanimate objects. In this respect, engineering closely parallels medical science where testing of new drugs or procedures is done on human beings. In medical practice, moral and legal rights of human beings have been accepted as fundamental to give informed consent before participating in an experiment. Similarly engineering practice has also started recognizing those rights. It treats informed consent very vital to the concept of a properly conducted experiment involving human beings and should be the keystone in the interaction between engineers and the general public.

Knowledge Gained: Effective engineering relies on knowledge gained, by executing projects and products, both before and after the execution. This new knowledge gained facilitates improving the current projects/ products and creating better ones in future. Ongoing success in engineering depends on gaining new knowledge, through the ongoing success in experimentation. The focus of experimentation in engineering project is to gain knowledge on application rather than design to produce new scientific knowledge.

Review questions

1. Why there is social responsibility on engineers for their engineering works.
2. Explain nature of uncertainty in engineering works.
3. Explain engineer's responsibilities with regard to technology.
4. Explain that experimentation is part and parcel of engineering works from the design stage to final product/ project stage.
5. Compare features of engineering experimentation with standard experimental process.
6. What do you understand by *experiential learning*?
7. Explain the nature of complexity in social engineering experiments.
8. What do you understand by industrial pollution and how industrialization causes it?
9. Explain how engineering works contribute to knowledge gained?

10 Engineer as Manager, Consultant, Leader and Responsible Social Experimenter

Learning objectives

In this chapter you will learn about

- Functional roles of engineers, engineers as managers and their nature of authority
- Role and responsibilities of engineers as consultants
- Leadership qualities required by engineers, clarity of role as leader *vs* manager
- Engineer's responsibility as social experimenter

10.1 Typical Growth profile of a fresh engineer in industry

When an engineering graduate comes out of college, he/she has basic theoretical knowledge of wide ranging subjects in his discipline of study. He/ She does not have any worthwhile practical or industrial experience. His knowledge is somewhat 5-10-year-old then the contemporary prevailing technologies in industry. He/ She is full of dreams for bright future but does not have any exposure or experience with regard to various in-house activities in industry, like design and development, manufacturing, production, sales and marketing, purchase activity of various inputs, prevalent standards, quality control methods, etc. which are regularly carried out in an industrial organization.

A fresh engineer is not aware of how total business or service activities of various organizations, corporations, and multinationals are managed? How they are regulated by the governments and other regulatory agencies? His condition is like a child who does not know how family and society is running and integrated with rest of the world. However, like a child he/she has lot of dreams and potential to grow in any field of his choice and be leader or expert in that field. He/ She can acquire a lot of experience and has freedom to rise to any level in status and position with his hard work and dedication.

When a fresh engineer joins any company or industry, he/she works as individual or part of small team. He/ She start learning depth of technology and industrial processes of that particular industry. As time passes he/she gains experience, and starts growing in organizational hierarchy from individual level to a team leader, project in charge, departmental head, etc. In due course of time, with rise in hierarchy within the organization, engineers learn managerial skills, share and control higher level of responsibility to command and control larger group of activities.

10.2 Organizational Roles and Authority of Engineers and Managers

Many engineers who are not managers aspire to the management role in the future. Some engineers play both these roles as they have dual roles both as engineers and as managers. Respect for authority is important in meeting organizational goals. Clear lines of authority are required to fix and identify areas of personal responsibility and accountability. A manager is normally provided with executive authority whereas an engineer enjoys expert authority.

10.2.1 Functional Roles of Engineers and Managers

In an organization engineers and managers work as a team. However, their roles are quite different for the same task or project. Sometimes they face conflict between roles of each other because of their differences in educational background, socialization, values, vocational interests, work habits and outlook. It is very difficult for the management to define precisely their roles to demarcate and establish the boundaries of area and operations for decisions making by them, i.e. where decisions should be made by engineers and where manager should take decisions. However, still the answer lies in degree of role clarity on functions of engineers and managers in an organization.

10.2.2 Role of Engineers

Engineers have a special responsibility and concern for quality and safety. The primary function of engineers is to apply their technical knowledge and training to design and develop, products and processes as well as production infrastructure that are required by the organization to satisfy market demand and its customers. But engineers are also professionals bound by professional ethics and code of conduct and they must uphold the engineering standards that their profession has decided. These standards draw an operational boundary to guide them on use of their technical knowledge to enhance the respect of the profession in the society. Thus, engineers have a dual loyalty to the organization and to their profession. Their professional loyalties are more important and go beyond their immediate loyalty to the employer.

Professional obligations include, maintaining the quality and the standards established by professional and standardization organizations, usually associated with good design and accepted in good engineering practice. These standards are evolved with consideration to take care of efficiency, economy of design, vulnerability to improper manufacturing and operation, and the extent to which state-of-the-art technology to be used safely for the benefit of the society.

10.2.3 Functionality of decision making by Managers and Engineers

The well-being of an organization is primarily measured in terms of economic performance, but it also includes other parameters like public image, employee morale, etc. Manager's function is to keep focus towards the organization's operational activities and goals, which includes directing the activities of engineers also (without interfering with their technical matters).Strictly managers are not professionals and they work within the frame work of codes of ethical standards and procedures defined by the organization. Managers are not having any professional binding with code of conduct or code of ethics imposed by professional bodies external to the organization. Managers virtually act as custodians of functioning of the organization and are concerned with current and future plans and state of affairs.

This perspective of manager's role differs from that of engineers. Managers tend to count on all the relevant factors having bearing on the goals and objectives of the program and then make a balanced calculation or assessment before coming to any conclusion. Managers are under strong pressure to control the costs and work to bring it down. They believe that engineers are less sensitive to cost factor than safety considerations and push the cost up to make a robust design. Pursuance of safety features by engineers is quite often to the detriment of cost consideration and consequently marketability of the product. By contrast, engineers give weight to the various considerations relevant to design with compliance to the minimal standards of safety and quality before any other considerations. Engineers believe that they have a special obligation to uphold safety and quality standards while negotiating with managers to resolve the conflict. They insist that a product or process must comply with the accepted engineering standards.

These considerations suggest that decisions on proper engineering decision (PED) be made by engineers from an engineering perspective and proper management decision (PMD) should be made by managers from the manager perspective. Some features of characterizing these two types of decision procedure are as follows:

- **PED** refers to the decisions which engineers should make to take care of professional engineering standards because it either involves technical matters requiring engineering expertise of engineers or falls within the professional ethical codes, especially those that require protection of the public health and safety.
- **PMD** refers to the decision which managers should make taking care of management considerations which involves issues of organizational well-being such as cost, scheduling, marketing, and employee morale or welfare and other matters which does not pressurize engineers (or other professionals) to make unacceptable compromises with their own technical or ethical standards.

Finally, engineers who work in large organizations may have limited autonomy and are subject to the authority of managers and employers.

10.3 Engineer as a Consultant

Engineering consultants are normally private practitioner. After gaining sufficient experience in a particular field some engineers start their own consultancy, where they can operate as individuals or start a consulting company- recruiting many other engineers.

As individual, a consultant has greater freedom to make decisions about the projects undertaken. Yet their freedom is not absolute and shared with salaried engineers. Their services are normally either for certain aspect of project activity or association with the project for responsibilities of overall supervision and certification of completions. The compensation for services could be a lump-sum payment or percentage of cost of the project.

Bigger projects require many consultants for execution of the projects. For example, for a project of building sports complex, the main company may take the services of many consultants for different jobs like an architect, a site planner, structural design and analysis, construction supervision, electrical and lighting structure, supervision of sports ground, etc. In bigger project consultants could be an individual engineer or a consultancy firm.

Many professionals after retirement take up the job of consultants. Some field of engineering has provision of certification of consultants like civil engineering and architecture. Here we shall discuss few lines of consultancy and special responsibilities of consulting engineers. In safety matters consulting engineers may have greater responsibility than salaried engineers.

10.3.1 Responsibilities of Consultants in promotion of business

We consider the case of advertising to highlight the responsibilities of consultants. Design of advertising material, content and message is primarily through consulting firms and independent professionals. Advertising plays a role of educating public about products and services of any industry or company. Many health and hygiene advertisement provide information about cleanliness and educate general public. Much information about mother and child care is provided through advertisements. Many drugs and life style information, real-estate information, growth and development news, etc. come through advertisements. Internet and social media carry advertisements virtually on all popular issues.

The question of moral and ethical values arises whether advertisement is conveying truth or it is deceptive, it has exaggerated the facts or suppressed important information, etc. Deceptive advertising implies when products or services are made to look better than they actually are. For example, a consulting firm claims to have played major role in a well-known project when it played a very minor role or shows a picture of a major project without any claim, implying his role without quantifying the contribution. Similarly, in electronics a photograph of engineering product used to convey the impression that the item is routinely manufactured and available for purchase, when actually picture belongs to a prototype or mockup model under development. These types of advertisements mislead the buyers.

Similar misleading content can be projected in commercial bids of engineering projects. In major projects, main bidding firms take support of many consulting engineers and firms to prepare final bid where many claims are exaggerated by participating consultants. This amounts to misguide the project authority on real capacity of bidding firms which is unethical. This type of practice is irresponsible engineering as inaccurate bids will encourage either cutting safety and quality (in case of low bids) or padding and over designing (in case of high bids).

10.4 Engineer as a Leader

One of the purposes of value education is to motivate the college going youth in activities that encourage leadership qualities in them to play constructive roles in the environment they live and work. Leadership skills will open him to articulate their views, assert their own identity, and claim their individual space to step out into the world with confidence.

Engineers normally work in the team where teamwork enables them to work successfully with other people. Teamwork requires virtues of collegiality, cooperativeness, loyalty and respect for legitimate authority. It also provides an opportunity to develop important quality of leadership as part of his personality development. As leader, he/she must learn to play key role in the team and demonstrate ability to motivate others also to meet the set goals. Leadership is a crucial step in career growth where one can influence and change whole working environment for better performance of the team. Engineers should develop high moral ethical character and leadership qualities with attitude of selfless service.

> *"... leadership is not about being great but it's about getting others to be great"*
> – President Ronald Reagan

10.4.1 Role of Leaders

Leadership is the inner process of visualizing and influencing team members for a positive change to ensure achievement of desired goals through joint efforts of colleagues. The leadership qualities can be developed with conscious efforts by mastering following steps:
- Developing capability to envision in advance what is to be accomplished.
- To be responsible to organization and the teams working on the project and motivate them to achieve the goals.
- Influence and motivate people in supporting facilities to get involved in the task to be achieved.
- Coach all the team members and supporting staff and empower them to achieve success.

All above steps are for fulfillment of the quest to produce a positive change

10.4.2 Leaders *vs.* Managers

Good leaders are very sensitive to emotional needs of people such as need for belonging, need for security, need of self-esteem, need of self-actualization, etc. and they work hard to satisfy them. Leaders articulate the Mission and convey the core Purpose.

Leading is different from managing. A leader requires vision. He/ She must set a direction and have the capability of convincing and influencing team members. He/ She must inspire people and try to achieve goal through delegating, empowering and coaching. His focus should be developing relationships which are necessary to produce positive change in mindset of team members.

A manager normally focuses attention to detailed planning, defining actions and steps to be initiated by team members. He/She tries to organize the activity and exercise control over them. His attempts are for bringing stability in the operating setup.

The success of leadership is measured by the achievement of desired results and goals within allocated time and resources. Leaders work for improvement in morale and working knowledge of people associated in the task. Leaders are role models to the team members, who set the example with their actions and behavior. The leaders demonstrate through adopting qualities of
- Becoming role model for others to emulate
- Possess quality of a visionary person
- Capability to motivate people and infuse enthusiasm for performing the best
- Capability to coach people on how they can contribute best at their level of operations and improve themselves
- Act as a change agent in the organization or the people with whom they interact and command

By setting the example leader creates an environment of trust. Trust creates an environment of cooperation by team members or general public. Without trust, a leader cannot lead. Trust is at the foundation of leadership quality where one can influence others to get positive results. Showing competence and character in what one does; and how he/she cares for others is a basic ingredient to build trust with people.

Leaders articulate the mission and convey the core purpose? They explain who our customers are and what value the team brings to them? Leaders work for controlling and removing the common causes of de-motivation. Some of these causes are a dull, spiritless, toxic, dysfunctional work environment. Such working environment could be the result of lack of opportunity for growth, no individual recognitions, no concern for one's personal problems, etc.

10.5 Engineers as responsible Social Experimenter

Industries serve the society through their products, projects and services. They are responsible to the society. Industries are run by team of managers, engineers, other supporting employees and labor. Out of all engineers are the main technical sources or facilitators whose idea with joint efforts of all others is developed into concrete industrial output. Clearly major moral responsibility of performance of outputs of industry or impact of technology on society falls on them as they are the sole experimenters of technology. However, in wider sense management, public and others also share their responsibility as they are beneficiary of technology being experimented by engineers with all good intentions. With their technical expertise, engineers are solely responsible to monitor the projects to identify risks and to provide information to clients and the public on their reasonable decisions to prevent any risk factor.

From the social experimentation perspective a responsible engineer must demonstrate four characteristics *viz.*

1. A conscientious commitment to moral values i.e. an obligation to ensure the safety of human beings and honor their right of consent.
2. A comprehensive perspective and visualization i.e. awareness of the experimental content of the projects and forecasting of its possible deleterious effects. There should be a reasonable effort to monitor them also.
3. Autonomy i.e. with personal responsibility his involvement in all stages of the project.
4. Accountability i.e. accepting accountability for the good or bad consequences of the project.

These topics are discussed in detail in succeeding chapters.

10.6 Summary

A fresh engineering graduate has basic theoretical knowledge of wide ranging subjects in his discipline of study. But he/she does not have any practical or industrial experience i.e. functional operations of industry. When he/she joins any company or industry, he/she starts learning depth of technology and industrial processes of that particular industry. With time, he/she gains experience and grows in the organizational hierarchy from individual to a team leader, project-in-charge, departmental head, etc. In the process, he/she also learns managerial skills, takes higher level of responsibilities and command larger group of activities.

Many engineers aspire for the management role in the future, and in due course of their career growth, start occupying dual roles of engineer and manager. A manager role is equipped with executive authority whereas role of an engineer enjoys expert authority.

The primary function of engineers within an organization is to use their technical knowledge and training to create structures, products, and processes that are of value to the organization and its customers. But engineers are also professionals, and they must uphold the standards prescribed for their profession. Thus, the engineers have a dual loyalty to the organization and to their profession.

Manager's function is to direct the activities of the organization, including the activities of engineers. Managers, in general are not professionals in the strict sense. Managers view themselves as custodians of the organization and are primarily concerned with its current and future well-being. By contrast, engineers tend to assign importance to the various considerations relevant to design to ensure that minimal standards of safety and quality are met. Engineers believe that they have a special obligation to uphold safety and quality standards in negotiations with managers.

Engineer as Consultant: Engineering consultants are normally private practitioner. After gaining sufficient experience in a particular field, some engineers start their own consultancy firms. A consultant has greater freedom to make decisions about the projects undertaken. Their services are normally for certain aspect of project activity. Bigger projects require many consultants for execution of the projects. For example, consultants for different jobs like an architect, a site planner, structural design and analysis, construction supervision etc. are contracted in a megaproject.

Leadership quality among Engineers: One of the purposes of value education is, to motivate the college-going youth in activities that encourage leadership qualities in them. When in job, quite often they have to work in teams. Teamwork requires virtues of collegiality, cooperativeness, loyalty, and respect for legitimate authority. It also provides an opportunity to develop important quality of leadership as part of his personality development. As leader he/she must learn to play key role in the team and demonstrate ability to motivate others to meet goals. Leadership is a crucial step in career growth where one can influence and change whole working environment for better performance of the team.

Leaders *vs.* Managers: Leading is different from Managing. A leader requires vision. He/ She must set direction, must have capability of convincing and influencing team members. He/ She must inspire people and try to achieve goal through delegating, empowering and coaching. His focus should be developing relationships which are necessary to produce positive change in mindset of team members. Leaders articulate the Mission and convey the core Purpose.

A Manager normally focuses attention to detailed planning; defining actions and steps to be initiated by team members. He/ She tries to organize the activity and exercise control over them. His attempts are for bringing stability in the operating setup.

Engineers as responsible Social Experimenter: Industries serve the society through their products, projects and services. They are responsible to the society. Industries are run by team of managers, engineers, other supporting employees and labor. Out of all engineers are the main technical enablers or facilitators, whose idea with joint efforts of all others, is developed into concrete industrial output. Clearly major moral responsibility of performance of outputs of industry or impact of technology on society falls on them as they are the sole experimenters of technology.

Review questions

1. Explain how a fresh engineer moves gradually towards managerial roles?
2. Many engineers have to play dual role as engineer as well as manager-explain.
3. Explain functional role of engineer as manager
4. Distinguish between functional roles of engineers and managers in an organization.
5. Explain Role and responsibilities of engineers as consultants
6. An engineer must develop leadership qualities in his field of work. Why?
7. Elaborate on engineer's role as leader *vs* manager.
8. Explain engineer's role as leader.
9. Explain Engineer's role as responsible social experimenter.

11 Engineers Personality Trait, Big Five Personality Model, Conscientiousness

Learning objectives

In this chapter you will learn about

- Behavioral trait of employees, moral and ethics issues for professionals
- Role and personality trait of engineers to promote innovation and technology
- Big five personality model and self-governance virtues
- Conscientiousness and characteristics of conscientious individuals in workplace
- Moral responsibility of engineers

11.1 Understanding Personality Traits of Employees

For any employer, its employees are as important to the company as its operations and processes. Understanding what personality components drive the behavior of employees is a highly useful informational data for management. This data can be used to determine what type of assignments should be set, how motivation should be pursued, and what team dynamics should prevail and how-to best resolve conflict situations.

Employees are sometimes tested on the big *five personality model* in collaborative situations, to determine what strong personality traits they possess, which is useful to the group dynamics. Personality tests can also be part of the behavioral interview process when a company is hiring to determine an individual's ability to act with certain personality characteristics.

One of the important jobs of human resource (HR) manager in the organization is to identify and keep track of pattern of employee's individual behaviors, so that they can understand their different personality traits. Personality is reflected in the individual's behavior and is a relatively stable characteristic. Understanding these personalities' traits of employees, HR manager can use their personality traits and skills in the right job or avenue, where they are likely to be more creative and productive. HR manager can also further train the employees according to their trait and enhance skills for making them still more effective in their jobs.

11.2 Personality Traits required in Engineering Profession

One of the personality traits required by an engineer is to look for a challenging career where he/ she can transform his intellectual accomplishments into practical achievements. The challenge could be in any field like more efficient machinery, ingenious electronic gadgetry, new wonder chemicals, fantasizing about designing beautiful homes, environmentally-friendly heating or cooling systems, more economical industrial processes or cutting-edge software programs, etc. It could be any of a thousand things, depending on where his creative instincts lead you.

Nowadays, desirable personality traits of engineers required by employers or the companies are undergoing dramatic changes. An engineer is expected to compete in today's market, where rate of obsolescence for products is high, because of fast changing technologies and innovations. In competitive global market, maximum emphasis is on continuous innovation and rapid adaptation of newer technologies in product designs and features. These market pressures demands engineers to develop matching attitude to play more consequential roles in the innovation process to compete in the global market. To prepare for such roles, engineers require up-to-date knowledge, skills and appropriate personality traits.

Now engineers must function more entrepreneurially in their companies. The core competencies of engineers should be to think himself like being an entrepreneur, which requires a mindset with number of new qualities not found in job descriptions of traditional engineering. Now engineers are required to embrace revolutionary changes in working environment characterized by working with teams of other disciplines, being visionary in thinking style, good problem-solving abilities, and capability of risk assessment and comfortable with uncertainties in the process of design and development of product or execution of projects. Further, engineers are required to possess personality trait of creativity and curiosity, intuition and emotional balance and control, etc.

11.3 Understanding Personality Traits

Earlier terms such as *hard-working, reliable* and *persevering* described the desirable characteristics of character in moral evaluation of a person, but conscientiousness was overlooked as a real psychological attribute. During study of psychological aspect of personality traits, psychologists observed that personality traits could be categorized into two traits *viz.* temperament and character. Temperament is basically a biologically formed trait, whereas a character trait is learned during childhood as well as throughout the life. With the advent of the FFM (five-factor model), behavior scientist studied the full range of personality traits and found that all five factors are substantially inherited. In a study of identical twins, who were separated at birth and raised apart, it was found that even than they showed very similar personality traits for both character traits and temperament traits.

11.3.1 Big Five-Factors Personality Model

Behind all personality traits, five factors discussed below are assumed to represent the basic structure. Many personality psychologists propose that personality has five basic dimensions, often referred to as the *Big-5personality traits*. Studies on personality traits help in understanding the behaviors of employees at work. Behavior patterns of people can be analyzed by applying big five personality model (also known as OCEAN) which will help HR managers of a company to place the employees on proper jobs based on their personality traits. The big five personality traits are *Openness, Conscientiousness, Extraversion, Agreeableness and Neuroticism.*

It is also found in psychological studies that the big five traits are also universal in nature. In one study across more than 50 different cultures, it was observed that the five dimensions of *big five model* accurately describe the personality trait of people. Now many psychologists believe that the five personality dimensions also have biological origins. These five categories are usually described as follows:

- **Openness:** People with this trait have openness to experience and characteristics like imagination and insight. They also normally have tendency for wide range of interests. People with this trait are highly cultured and have creative and intellectually curious nature.
- **Conscientiousness:** People with this dimension of personality show high levels of thoughtfulness, with good level of self-control and goal-directed behaviors. Conscientiousness is discussed in detail later on in this chapter.
- **Extraversion:** People with this trait are emotionally quite expressive possess high degree of positivity, talkative nature, good at socialization and assertive behavior. People with these traits tend to be satisfied with things around them and their careers. This trait is very common among most of the talented and successful managers.
- **Agreeableness**: Agreeableness is the dimension of personality trait to be compassionate and cooperative towards others. Personal characteristics like being trustworthy, kindness to others altruism,

affection to colleagues and team members, and very sociable behavior are virtues under dimension of agreeableness.
- **Neuroticism:** Neuroticism is indication of an individual's level of emotional stability and impulse control. People with high level of neuroticism show symptoms of emotional instability, full of sadness, anxiety neurosis, mood swings and irritable nature. They are prone to suffer from anger, anxiety and depression.

It is important to understand that each of the five personality factors represents a wide range of possible behavior traits. For example, personality trait of extraversion and introversion are two extremes of a continuous spectrum of behavior trait. In practice actually, most people lie somewhere in between the two extreme ends of each dimension. Behavior of any person is governed by person's underlying personality and situational variables. The situation in which a person finds himself determines how he/she will react or respond, which most probably will be in accordance to his underlying personality traits. Personality is a complex phenomenon with very large domain of behavior spectrum. Behavior of each person may fall somewhere in between, across the several of these dimensions. Personality traits modulated by ethical considerations leads to *self-governance virtues*.

11.4   Self-Governance Virtues

Sometimes engineers face ethical dilemmas in jobs while discharging their duties. For handling ethical dilemmas, engineers should possess good moral judgment along with their expertise in technical field and both these skills should go together in solving the problems or in making moral choices.

Self-governance virtues require good understanding about the *Self, Motives, Interests*, etc. Some of the self-governance virtues are centered on other virtues like courage, self-discipline, perseverance, conscientiousness, fidelity, commitments, self-respect and integrity. These virtues are necessary for discharging moral responsibilities towards others and the society. The degree of *self-understanding* and *good moral judgment* is what Aristotle calls *practical wisdom*. Other important virtue is *honesty* which implies both *truthfulness* in speech and belief and *trustworthiness* in commitments.

11.5   Conscientiousness

In five factor model of personality *conscientiousness* is one of the five traits. It has been traditionally referred as one aspect of the virtue called *character*. This dimension of personality trait expects people to be thorough, careful, or vigilant in their performances and jobs they undertake.

Conscientious-people always want to do any task very well and look for perfection in actions.

Conscientious people have mental frame of self-discipline, they are duty conscious, and dedicated to achieve their targets and goals. People with conscientiousness always prefer planning for the jobs undertaken, good at building organization and dependable teams to achieve desired goals. They are themselves hardworking, organized and dependable.

11.5.1 Characteristics of Conscientious Individuals

Conscientiousness is further divided into *two aspects* of personality trait *viz. orderliness* and *industrious*. The *orderliness* implies the nature for keeping things in organized fashion and the *industrious* is more closely related to the nature of focusing on productivity and work ethic.

Conscientious people are well organized in their work ethics and are efficient in work skills. They have tendency to be self-disciplined, act dutifully, focus on achievements, display planning in working and are generally organized and dependable. On behavior front conscientious people display their behavior in characteristic like being neat and systematic; careful and thorough in their operations. Conscientious people are likely to be conformists, generally hard-working and reliable. On the extreme of behavior spectrum, they may be *workaholics*, *perfectionists* and *compulsive* in their behavior.

Tests of *big five personality traits* are conducted in collaborative situations on employees, to determine their strong personality traits and to place them in proper teams and tasks, so that they can add best to the group functioning. The test scores on all five dimensions of *big five personality trait* for individuals are frequently presented as percentile scores. People getting low score on conscientiousness are rated to be less goal-oriented and less driven by success. Such employees are more likely to possess personality trait of being antisocial with criminal behavior. Individuals, low on conscientiousness score are not motivated to accomplish the tasks.

11.5.2 Conscientiousness in academic and workplace performance

High level of conscientiousness is assurance for successful academic performance of students and high performance of managers and workers at the workplace. If someone has low levels of conscientiousness, he/she will display nature of procrastination.

Conscientious students or employees are more reliable, highly motivated and hardworking compared to their counterpart of low level of conscientiousness. Such students or employees record high percentage of attendance in schools or on the workplace. Dimension of conscientiousness in personality trait is the only one that is associated with the performance across all types of jobs. However, in jobs involving considerable amount of social interaction, other dimensions of personality trait like agreeableness and emotional stability also become equally important.

11.5.3 Characteristics of conscientious engineers

The word conscientiousness contains the central essence of engineering ethics, which combines virtue of competence and loyalty to the profession. Competence requires one to perform with requisite skill and experience, where one is expected to take due care, show persistence and diligence, work honestly and creatively with adequate attention to detail. Conscientiousness implies consciousness, open eyes, open ears and an open mind.

Openness and conscientiousness are two dimensions of personality trait, most vital for a prospective engineer that he/she must possess. In big complicated engineering projects an engineer should be rich on the dimension of agreeableness also along with openness and conscientiousness, to make sure that he/she is on the same plane as everyone else of the project. In big projects a team of expert from different background like designers, architects, surveyors, managers, safety inspectors, team of engineers, technicians, laborers are involved through whom engineering concepts are translated into real world applications. Clearly here an engineer cannot afford to act as an autocrat while directing the activities of such a diverse group of experts. Thus, creating a spirit of teamwork and cooperation are essential in such projects and engineers are responsible to create that environment.

11.6 Moral responsibility of engineers

Normally engineers as employees have narrow outlook on their moral responsibility, which is limited to the obligations towards the employer. Professionally, more than 90 percent of engineers are salaried employees. For them working environment within organizations is quite bureaucratic in nature and they work under great pressure within the organization. Their primary moral duty is limited obligation to one's employer. Scope of their duties by the organization is reduced to minimal duties, such as truthful reporting of data, not violating Patent rights and not breaching confidentiality, etc. as responsibility of moral duty.

But professionally, as engineering is conceived as social experimentation, engineers become guardians of the public interest and their professional responsibility becomes to ensure the safety, health and welfare of those affected by engineering projects. This professional commitment assumes that for the need of business profitability or in experimentation of their quest for new knowledge, they should not undermine safety and welfare of people affected by their projects. Even if the purpose of their experimentation or the project is for the benefit of the society, even then their role, as agent of social change, does not imply that engineers force their own views of the social good on the society. Here also, just like with medical experimentation on humans, the social experimentation in engineering should be as far as possible based on the informed consent of the affected public.

11.6.1 Engineers must take comprehensive perspective of their works

Conscientiousness does not have any meaning without relevant valid factual information. Therefore, any moral concern anticipates a commitment to gather and evaluate all available information that is important to meet the moral obligations. Obviously the first prerequisite to anyone is to have clear understanding of the context of one's work and associated moral considerations for the activity. For example, it amounts to lack of moral concern, when one involves in developing software for financial data analysis, which will be used to illegally manipulate status of financial health of a company. Thus, a conscientious engineer must be aware of the wider implications of one's work, whether it is going to be used or applied to immoral activities. This may sometimes be a convenient argument for engineers to ignore the need for knowing the wider context of their activities, which if known may be against his conscience.

It is also possible that reason for avoiding knowing the context of the assignment, may be due to ever-increasing specialization and division of labor that restricts one to limit his concern and operations to the task assigned to him. For example, one may argue that a product using components of inferior quality (like battery in mobile phones), may sometime harm the user or give service of poor quality, but it is not his concern; as it should be the concern of design or purchase or sales departments. It may appear natural to rationalize one's neglect of concern for public safety, but definitely this lack of concern is morally unethical and against professionalism. These ways of reasoning about job works leads to general unconcern for broader perspective on the nature of one's work. It also prevents self-efforts for acquiring full perspective of the consequences of his work, including moral and ethical concern. Because of this type of limited concern by engineers, focus on engineering as social experimentation emphasizes on the importance of context and urges the engineer to look his involvement in a project, which have wide range of impact on the society.

Thus, an extensive training in disciplines related to moral and ethical perspective of engineering profession is essential for students of engineering, so that they develop sensitivity for moral issues associated with their professional life in future. They must develop capacity to visualize and foresee the probability of dangers during production process or applications in the field. This training is just for exposing the students to the goal of practice of *preventive technology* in engineering, similar to the idea of preventive medicine in medical field. However, it should be understood that no amount of training and imagination can visualize or anticipate all dangers because engineering projects are inherently experimental in nature.

11.7 Complexity of Moral and Ethics issues for Engineering professionals

The definition of professional morality is not static in nature and must change with changes taking place in the world around. Actually, time to time there has been meaningful change taking place in engineering ethics and shall continue to change in future also. For example, simple prescriptions of engineering ethics in earlier times are no longer adequate and capable of providing satisfactory solutions to the complexities of the current day professions. The essence of engineering ethics is in development of holistic view of engineering works, where professionalism includes moral and ethical concern towards society along with engineering expertise. Conscientiousness is single word very close to define the holistic expression for ethics. Engineers should always be conscious of the fact that their fellow citizens are directly or indirectly ultimate customers of their products, services and repose trust on their professional services. While serving the fellow human beings with dedication through their professional duties they are acting righteously. The conscientious engineer by definition must possess qualities of being truthful, factual, alert, accurate and display ethical behavior during professional interactions.

11.8 Summary

Understanding Personality Traits of Employees: Personality is a relatively stable set of characteristics that influence an individual's behavior. HR manager will be able to motivate and train new employees better if he/she has a picture of their personality traits. For any employer, its employees are as important to the company as its operations and processes. Understanding personality traits of employees is a highly useful informational data for management. This data can be used to determine what type of assignments should be set, how motivation should be pursued, what team dynamics should prevail and how-to best resolve conflict situations.

Personality Traits required in Engineering Profession: One of the personality traits required by an engineer is to look for a challenging career where he/she can turn his intellectual accomplishments into practical achievements. Now engineers must function more entrepreneurially in their companies. An engineer is expected to deal with today's fiercely competitive global market with emphasis on continuous innovation and rapid ongoing adaptation. Engineers are required to embrace revolutionary changes in working environment, characterized by teaming with other disciplines, visionary thinking style, flexible problem-solving, risk-taking and comfort with uncertainties. Similarly, while working on innovation or new product development project engineers are expected to possess personality trait of curiosity, self-motivation, intuition, emotion management, self-awareness and creativity. While working in technical marketing engineers should possess competencies in people skills, social networking, team facilitation, risk management, customer responsiveness, etc.

Understanding Personality Traits: During most of the 20th century, psychologists believed that personality traits could be divided into two categories: *temperament* and *character*. Temperament traits were thought to be biologically based, whereas character traits were thought to be learned either during childhood or throughout life. With the advent of the FFM, behavior geneticists began systematic studies of the full range of personality traits and it soon became clear that all five factors are substantially heritable.

Big Five Factors Personality Model: Many contemporary personality psychologists believe that there are five basic dimensions of personality, often referred to as the *big 5 personality traits* include: openness, conscientiousness, extraversion, agreeableness and neuroticism. Psychologists have also found that the big five traits are also remarkably universal and they also have biological origins. The situation that a person finds himself or herself in plays a major role in how the person reacts. However, in most cases, people offer responses that are consistent with their underlying personality traits. These dimensions represent broad areas of personality. Personality traits modulated by ethical considerations leads to *self-governance virtues*.

Self-Governance Virtues: Self-governance virtues are those necessary in exercising moral responsibility. In engineering, excellence and ethics go together in the long run. Technical skills and morally good judgment needed to go together in solving ethical dilemmas and in making moral choices. So, do competence and conscientiousness, creativity and good character. Other self-governance virtues are courage, self-discipline, perseverance, conscientiousness, fidelity to commitments, self-respect and integrity. Honesty falls into both groups of self-governance virtues, for it implies both truthfulness in speech and belief and trustworthiness in commitments.

Conscientiousness: It is one of the five traits of the FFM of personality and is an aspect of traditionally referred as character. It is the personality trait of being thorough, careful, or vigilant. Conscientiousness implies a desire to do a task well. Conscientiousness is a tendency to show self-discipline, act dutifully and aim for achievement. Conscientiousness also refers to planning, organization and dependability. Those high in conscientiousness tend to be organized and mindful of details. They are hardworking, organized and dependable. Recently, conscientiousness has been broken down further into two aspects: *orderliness* and *industrious*. The orderliness is associated with the desire to keep things organized and tidy and the industrious is associated more closely with productivity and work ethic. Conscientiousness is importantly related to successful academic performance in students and workplace performance among managers and workers. Low levels of conscientiousness are strongly associated with procrastination.

Moral Responsibility of Engineers: At present working as an employee, engineers tend to have narrow moral vision of their responsibility limited to the obligations towards employer. Primary obligation to one's employer is justified in terms of prudent self-interest and concern for one's family. The moral obligations are limited to the minimal duties, such as not falsifying data, not violating Patent rights and not breaching confidentiality. Conceiving engineering as social experimentation restores the vision of engineers as guardians of the public interest whose professional duty it is to hold paramount the safety, health and welfare of those affected by engineering projects. This view assumes that they should not undermine public safety and welfare in their quest for new knowledge, the rush for profits, a narrow adherence to rules, or a concern over benefits for the many.

Further, as the world changes, the definition of professional morality must change with it. The essence of engineering ethics is something different when viewed in holistic fashion. There is no single word that defines this *something*, but conscientiousness is very close to holistic expression for ethics. The conscientious engineer must be by definition, truthful, factual, alert and accurate - all key elements of any definition of ethical behavior.

Review questions

1. Why understanding behavioral trait of employees is essential for employers.
2. What type of new role as personality traits of engineers is required to support innovation and technology development in business?

3. What do you understand by 'personality model'? Explain 'big five personality model'.
4. Explain conscientiousness and characteristics of conscientious engineers.
5. What do you feel should be moral responsibility of engineers?
6. What is moral autonomy and how it is relevant to engineers?

12 Accountability, Roles of Codes and Experimental Nature of Engineering

Learning objectives

In this chapter you will learn about

- Accountability and culture of accountability, engineers' accountability in big projects
- Role of codes- code of ethics, code of conduct, code of practice and moral codes
- General principles of NSPE code of ethics for engineers
- Various type of dilemmas faced by engineers in their jobs and roles
- Practice of building industrial standards for products and processes

12.1 Accountability in Engineering Profession

Accountability of a person to an organization or institution means that he/she is required to account for being answerable, being responsible and justify his actions or decisions. We all are aware that, issue of accountability is raised to guard against the consequences for bad results or poor performance. Quite often *accountable* in normal sense implies of being culpable and blameworthy for misdeeds. Thus, working under any authority creates in many people some sort of fear for accountability for the consequences of their actions and they become extra cautious in their dealings in the organization. But when things are running well and successfully in the organization no one asks about who is accountable for this success?

Responsible people normally accept moral responsibility for their actions without any reservation. For them accountability conveys a disposition of willingness to openly submit account of their actions for moral scrutiny and take responsibility even if assessments are done by others. As engineers are social experimenters, above meaning of accountability is not applicable in that sense for them, because all experiments carry certain amount of uncertainty or unknown factors involved. However, they have to develop positive attitude to be responsible and accountable for their actions and decisions affecting the society. For them accountability implies a positive connotation which means accountability being their personal choice and take up the work in the sense of the ownership, necessary for achieving desired results with full dedication. This definition requires an attitude of self-introspection and try to do the best possible, rising above the personal circumstances to achieve the results. With this new definition of accountability, an engineer is supposed to try all possible morally permitted ways and means to overcome difficulties arising in the working process and achieve the desired results.

Ownership attitude of engineers towards accountability can galvanize the operation of whole team or the organization with much better results. Such mind set promotes cross-functional communication for feedback between various teams, organizations or departments like design and development, execution and operations, installation and commissioning, quality assurance, certification, consultants and user agency etc. to execute contracts or supply orders and other services to the customers and the public. Such a networking of interactions between various departments creates an environment that motivates everyone for greater cooperation among themselves. There people analyze and identify the problem collectively and think about how they could solve it with mutual efforts. Motivated employees also overcome the natural barriers of functional expertise and preferences. They easily connect themselves for the common good.

12.1.1 Creating culture of Accountability

For creating a culture of accountability, the first thing management has to do is to define the goals of the organization and communicate them to all levels within the organization. The goals should be defined in very specific terms like a sales figure, a specified delivery schedule for the products or minimum return on investment etc. Then convey these goals clearly with all staff, managers, engineers and other employees from top to bottom ranks. Everybody within the company should be explained clearly about what they're working for and how their job will help in the growth of the company. Then the management must generate joint accountability between various departments by translating company targets into measurable goals of various departments involved and fix their targets. In an environment of joint accountability, no one can think that he/she has done his job if the team has not achieved targets fixed for the group.

For an engineer to direct his own career or goal, he/she has to assume full accountability for his ideas, plans, and ways of involvement in the operations, actions and results. Otherwise somebody or something else will play the role to decide his career or goal. The real benefit of accountability comes from the predictability of cost and contribution from each employee of the departments, which enables the management to keep measurable control on its functioning. With new definition of accountability, a company can gain more from a proactive posture of employees than from a reactive one. This new approach to accountability through making employees proactive can revitalize the business character, enhance the global competitiveness, strengthen the efforts for innovation and improve the quality of products and services produced by organizations.

12.1.2 Problems of Accountability fixation for engineers in Big Projects

In business and professions, separation between causal influences on a person and his sense of moral accountability is common, and engineering is no exception. Such a psychological shift on moral accountability is result of several important features of contemporary engineering practice as listed below.
1. Large-scale engineering projects are executed by dividing the total project into several modules based on expertise required like civil works, electrical works, communication module, civic amenities, transport, etc. In such scenario, contribution of each employee is only towards a small function or part of some module, which is a component of something much larger. Moreover, the final assembly of the product or execution of the project is done at places often far off away from one's immediate workplace. This separation between person's place of work and the final product or project location creates a kind of emotional distance, which reduces his sense of personal accountability.
2. Due to the fragmentation of work of large projects into many small pockets of activity, there is vast diffusion of accountability within large institutions. Normally the project management structures or the administrative set up for large projects becomes bureaucratic and hierarchical in operation; where large numbers of engineers and other staff work with various departments or disciplines. Within such hierarchical structure of authority, individual engineer's responsibility and personal accountability become limited to their areas of involvement.
3. Engineers by being an important resource of any organization, an advance planning is required to maximize their utilization for various products or projects. This result in their assignments to engage in more than one project at any time because of multiple projects being executed simultaneously. Thus, pressure of

schedules of different tasks among engineers leads to multi-tasking or tight rope walking through various schedules. This causes limiting of engineer's sense of accountability for meeting schedules, thereby affecting his accountability in wider context prescribed under professional codes.
4. In certain projects or products, their operations are directly of concern of health of employee's as well as general public. Working on, high power microwave devices, microwave ovens, x-ray machines, nuclear radiation units, production of chemicals like pesticides, insecticides, poisonous gases, many other industrial products, etc. are dangerous in handling to employees during production and to public in their use. They require lot of careful handling and can lead to legal battles in case of mishaps. This probability of crippling preoccupation with legalities makes engineers to shirk the responsibility of becoming morally involved in works beyond one's strictly defined role.

In spite of above problems engineer is a social experimenter and only he/she can find solutions of the problems. Whatever industrial development is happening in the world is due to scientists, technologists and engineers; these professionals are the main contributors in this growth. It becomes their moral responsibility to find solutions of bad side of industrial development concerning with health and safety of public at large. Engineers, who accept that engineering practice has a component of social experimentation, will readily accept moral responsibility for their work and associate themselves psychologically with this perspective of accountability of engineering profession.

12.2 Role of Codes

A professional society prescribes *codes of ethics*(CE) to its members stating their moral responsibilities during their professional practices. Some of the *code of ethics* and *code of conducts*(CC) from professional bodies like IETE, institution of engineers (India),Indian society for technical education (ISTE) and university grants commission (UGC) from India are furnished in Appendix-E. Engineers must understand meaning and implications of code of conduct of their profession and code of ethics of their companies as well as responsibility towards society as experimenter. These codes are statements on the profession's collective commitment to ethics. The codes lay stress on engineers' responsibilities while supporting the freedom essential to meet those responsibilities. Codes provide guidance and advice concerning the main obligations of engineers. They also give positive stimulus for ethical conduct in professional activities.

Code of ethics of IEEE and NSPE from USA are already framed long back to guide engineers in their professional conduct. These codes can be downloaded from their respective websites. For quick reference to students the code of ethics of these organizations are furnished in Appendix-F and G.

A number of companies have instituted their own codes. These tend to concentrate on the code of practice and moral and ethical issues in dealing with vendors and clients as well as compliance to statutory requirements.

Most of the *codes of ethics* stipulate eight essential roles to be played by professionals: 1) service and protection of public interest, 2) professional guidance on ethics, 3) inspiration to conduct ethically, 4) establishing shared standards, 5) support to responsible professionals, 6) contributing to education, 7) deterring wrongdoing and 8) strengthening of respective profession's image.

12.2.1 Examples to illustrate the Gravity of Engineer's Responsibility for Safety and Risk

1. **Civil engineering Safety issues:** Any civil engineering project must take care of following factors in structural design
   - Load
   - Environment
   - Structural Engineer's must understand causes of damage and structural failures. They should have a better understanding of geological faults on big structures and buildings.

Here are two examples of Bridge collapse:

I: TACOMA narrow bridge (1940) collapse-in USA

TACOMA narrow bridge was the one of this type of suspension bridge in the U.S. state of Washington that spanned the TACOMA Narrows strait of Puget Sound between TACOMA and the Kitsap Peninsula. Construction on the bridge began in September 1938. From the time the deck was built, it began to move vertically in windy conditions. The motion was observed even when the bridge opened to the public in 1940. The bridge's main span finally collapsed on the morning of November 7, 1940under wind conditions of 40-mile-per-hour (64 km/h). The bridge was the third longest suspension bridge in the world in terms of main span length behind the Golden Gate Bridge and the George Washington Bridge. The bridge's collapse had a lasting effect on science and engineering. In many physics textbooks, the event is presented as an example of elementary forced resonance with the wind providing an external periodic frequency that matched the bridge's natural structural frequency, though the actual cause of failure was aeroelastic flutter. Its failure also boosted research in the field of bridge aerodynamics-aeroelastic, the study of which has influenced the designs of the entire world's great long-span bridges built since 1940.

II: King Street Bridge (1962) - in Australia

The bridge was designed in 1959 for Country Roads Board Australia by an Australian construction company and construction was over the next two years. It was of a welded, deck-girder, suspended-span construction with spans up to 160 feet (49 m) long. Soon after completion on July 10, 1962, one span collapsed under the weight of a 47-ton semi-trailer, though the weight was within the bridge limits. The inquiry commission found that bridge failed with a brittle fracture on a very cold Melbourne winter day. The Commission identified the cause of girder failure was due to cracked welds. The fabricator was not familiar with welding low-alloy steel and the steel supplied was high in carbon, making it difficult to weld even for an experienced fabricator. The cracks in the welds were not discovered by inspectors of both the fabricator and the Country Roads Board.

2. Aviation Industry Safety Problems

General public is aware of plenty of cases of air disaster of aero planes. But what caused these problems is normally not in public knowledge. For example, a case like this where a commercial airline pilot enrooted to San Diego International Airport looks out a window at 10,800 feet height and sees another plane coming right at him. The captain quickly pulled up on the control column to avoid hitting the other plane. The two planes passed within about 100 feet of each other and a major air disaster was avoided. This is just one of thousands of examples of near-misses, bad communications, equipment failures, wildlife hits and sometimes just silly but dangerous errors contained in an aviation safety database collected and analyzed by NASA.

While flight-related fatalities are limited and commercial airlines suppress such reports because of bad publicity. The investigative journalists group reports thousands of repeated errors that point to potentially serious flaws in the safeguards set up for the aviation industry. On the average commercial pilots file 62 percent of the reports, while private pilots file 26 percent and air-traffic controllers file 10 percent. Some typical reports are like:
- Communications breakdowns: The pilot of a small plane landing at a particular airport noticed a larger air taxi bearing down from behind, less than a mile away and descending fast; a likely recipe for the two planes to collide on the runway. It turned out the air taxi had not been handed off as required to a local air traffic controller by a regional controller. To make matters worse the

local tower had no radar to show the large plane and the pilot of the small plane wrote in his report to NASA. Both planes aborted their landings.
- Equipment failures: Many of the reports to NASA concern problems on various aircraft, as when a B777 crew had to make an emergency landing in 2009 because of a foam liner between the fuel tank and an engine had worn away, causing what appeared to be a fuel leak.
- The relatively low level of training and experience among private pilots, compared to commercial pilots. For example, a flight instructor showing a student pilot how to use a cockpit computer in 2008 was jarred into reality by a call from the local tower with control-tower crash-avoidance alarms raging in the background. Just in time to look out of the cockpit to see another small plane pass a bare 400 feet overhead.
- Issues such as runway safety and adequate pilot training require closer scrutiny for air safety. The NASA data could be an important source to plan strategy for averting such tragedies in the future.

3. Future issues of aero safety in India

Air travel is catching up in India and has large potential for growth. Much has been reported recently concerning aviation issues in India. Safety, security and cost reductions have dominated the stories. The issue of safety and risk management in air travel directly calls for *engineer's responsibility for safety and risk*.

Purchasing of aero planes is easy job to meet the growing demand. But simultaneous matching of improvements in the civil aviation infrastructure like airports, navigation and flight control network, training of air and ground staff, engineering and maintenance staff etc. is a daunting challenge to airport authorities because infrastructure development and staff trainings are more strenuous and time-consuming processes.

Authorities in international air transport association (IATA) are concerned about how to overcome some of the major issues faced by the aviation community. A number of safety issues remain daunting challenges for the country and its civil aviation authority. India's fiercely competitive aviation sector will have to become more stable to support a quickly growing domestic demand for air transportation. As the demand for air travel increases, India will face growing pains related to the upgrading of country's existing airport and air traffic infrastructure. Taken above two issues together with rapidly expanding air carriers, lead to a situation with potential for a very high operating risk.

Runway safety is another area of big concern from safety and risk point of view. Basic items associated with runways such as adequate markings, signage and lighting need to be standardized and installed at all airports that support commercial and business air traffic.

Civil Aviation Administration (CAA) work hard to ensure that the standards and recommended practices of international civil aviation organization (ICAO) are followed in aviation sector. However, development and training of qualified engineers and personnel for aviation sector is of paramount importance to improve safety risk level which is inherently high in air travel.

Engineers have especially high responsibility for safety in aerospace industry because:

- Millions of passengers fly in commercial airlines every day. Engineers are responsible for safely getting these people to wherever they want to go.
- Aerospace and aeronautical engineers develop new technologies for aviation sector as well as for defense and space exploration. Range of products being developed are aircrafts including commercial, military jets, helicopters, spacecrafts, missiles and rockets etc. Many people are dependent on quality and safety of these products. Engineers are responsible for making sure these products run and operate correctly and safely.
- Aerospace engineers are mostly responsible for the continued operational safety of aviation products. Some aerospace Engineers work on aircraft testing; others investigate crashes to determine causes and prevent future accidents.

12.2.2 Understanding scope of Codes of Ethics, Conduct, Practice and Moral Codes

A document of *code of ethics* may outline the mission and values of the business or organization, the ethical principles of the organization, organization's core values, the standards to which the employees will be held responsible and how they are supposed to approach problems.

Organizations frame ethical codes to make employees or customers understand the difference between *right* and *wrong* for the organization and following them during their operations in the organization. An ethical code generally implies documents at three levels:

1. *Codes of business ethics*: containing ethical principles followed by the business.
2. *Codes of conduct*: for employees to guide and regulate their conduct in business operations.

Chapter 12: Accountability, Roles of Codes and Experimental Nature of Engineering

3. ***Codes of professional practice***: as stipulated for the particular profession by professional bodies.

Code of Ethics *vs.* Code of Conduct (Corporate or Business Ethics): The terms ethical code and code of conduct are used interchangeably in many companies. However, they have different connotation.

A code of ethics is prescribed for companies or organizations. It sets out the values that are put in the form of code which describes a company's obligation to its stakeholders. The code of ethics is a publicly available document which anyone can access who is interested in the company's activities and the way it does business.

A code of conduct is intended for employees alone. It usually sets out rules and regulations for employees conduct and restrictions on behavior. Document of code of conduct is focused on compliance or rules to be observed rather than focused on value or principle of the company or business

Code of Practice (Professional Ethics): A *code of practice* (CP) is adopted to regulate a profession. It may be adopted by a professional body or by a governmental or non-governmental organization. It may be like a *code of professional responsibility* which will describe clearly what behavior is considered *ethical* or *correct* or *right* in the circumstances. If a member fails to comply with a CP, it can result in expulsion of the member from the professional organization.

Ethical Codes are adopted by management as they are necessary for running an organization in a complex society in which moral concepts play an important part. However, ethical codes are distinct from moral codes that apply to the culture, education, and religion of a whole society.

12.3 Spectrum of Codes

12.3.1 NSPE Code of Ethics for engineers- general principles

Entry of science and technology in human society is of very recent origin, hardly 150 years of past centuries. They have developed many branches of knowledge and have brought together revolutionary changes in Human life, knowledge, faiths and beliefs. National Society of Professional Engineers (NSPE) in America has prescribed professional duties of engineers which are given below in brief.

Preamble: Engineering is an important and learned profession. As members of this profession, engineers are expected to exhibit the highest standards of honesty and integrity. Engineering has a direct and vital impact on the quality of life for all people. Accordingly, the services provided by engineers require honesty, impartiality, fairness, and equity; and must be dedicated to the protection of the public health, safety and welfare. Engineers must perform under a standard of professional behavior that requires adherence to the highest principles of ethical conduct.

Fundamental Canons: Engineers, in the fulfillment of their professional duties, shall:

- Hold paramount the safety, health, and welfare of the public.
- Perform services only in areas of their competence.
- Issue public statements only in an objective and truthful manner.
- Act for each employer or client as faithful agents or trustees.
- Avoid deceptive acts.
- Conduct themselves honorably, responsibly, ethically, and lawfully so as to enhance the honor, reputation, and usefulness of the profession.

NSPE code of ethics explains in detail all points of *fundamental canons* under *rules of practice* and *professional obligations*. Details of NSPE Code of Ethics are furnished in Appendix-G.

The NSPE code of ethics is evolved through the collective efforts of members of one particular professional body of engineers but actually addresses to ethical responsibilities of wide range of practicing engineers, even for those engineers who are not members of NSPE. The NSPE code attempts to emphasize on the role that engineering plays in society and the standards of conduct that is expected from engineers to reasonably comply with the role anticipated by the code. It suggests that, engineers have foremost responsibility to apply their specialized technical knowledge and skills for the benefit of clients and the public in the spirit of service and in response to trust placed in them. This type of responsibility is some referred as obligation-responsibility having the feature of positive and forward-looking concept on responsibility.

12.3.2 Engineering Codes, Standards and Responsibilities for Engineers

Engineering codes specify standards of responsibility for engineers which are quite demanding and should be undertaken seriously. Engineers must take up their responsibility with best efforts in accordance to the codes and not with an attitude of minimum compliance.

Some of the engineering codes are regulatory standards that specify technical requirements for specific kinds of engineering design in the nature of Dos and Don'ts. For example, safety standards of electrical wiring, standards of Internet networking, and certain standards of safety are met by bridges or buildings, etc. In sum total these standards are formulated to ensure quality, safety and efficiency in engineering with standardization of engineering practices in particular industry or business segment. It is important to realize that in spite of considerable standardization in engineering industry, there is considerable room for professional discretion in design and its implementation.

Engineering standards may also standardize certain procedures to be adopted, for testing and qualifying limits of variances within the specific, measurable levels to ensure and guarantee the quality or safety of products and services.

Ethics of Engineering codes also stipulate that engineers to comply with those standards which are being followed for quite some time and commonly accepted in engineering training and practice.

12.3.3 Responsibility for compliance to Codes of Practice

Many times, people look for clear guidelines and ethical limits of the professional's responsibility and how power and authority should be used in service to the client and society. Many professions already have codes of practice to prevent exploitation of the client and preserve the integrity of the profession. These codes are internally enforced in the organization on the members of the profession that must be followed meticulously. This not only benefits the client but enhances the reputation of the profession, thus benefiting to those belonging to the profession. Sometimes less scrupulous professional may act against the code of practice on the pretext of false morality of avoiding rejections of slightly poor-quality product to reduce wastage or save time or to meet the demand or schedule, etc. Here disciplinary codes allow the professional bodies to draw a standard of conduct and ensure that individual practitioners meet this standard by disciplining them. In this way public's trust is maintained in the profession. Here are some tips which professionals should practice

Things to Do
1. Do return value to your customer (internal and external) in all business decisions.
2. Do return value to your community locally and globally.
3. Do deliver quality in a timely fashion.
4. Be honest in your work content and schedule. Have courage to inform the client, customer, or boss if tasks or targets or project will not meet the target date as scheduled.
5. Do ask for help in order to meet the project or task deadline. A professional will not feel shy if he/she acknowledges that he/she needs help.
6. Promote reputation of your profession.

Things Not to Do
1. Do not tell the client, customer, or boss that you can do something when you cannot.
2. Do not waste resources of the organization.
3. Do not undermine your capabilities.

12.3.4 Purpose of Codes of Ethics

One purpose of the code is to guard against certain pressures and protect each professional so that others in the profession do not take advantage of good conduct. A code of professional ethics is a kind of morally permissible convention. For example, preference is given to safety overriding the wishes of the employer. Under any kind of circumstances professional should not think of making exceptions to the code of ethics. The need for a code of ethics is justified for the following reasons.

- To perform duties with objectivity and provide professional care as per professional standards and best practices.
- To serve honestly in the interest of the stakeholders and in compliance to legal requirements. Professional should also maintain high standards of conduct and character in his dealings and not to act against the professional injunctions.
- To maintain the privacy and confidentiality of information received during professional duties unless disclosure is sought by a legal authority. However, in no case such information to be used for personal benefit or released to improper channels.
- To maintain professional competency, undertake only those activities which can be reasonably completed with competence within the required frame of schedule.
- To support the implementation of all the rules and the regulations of the institution.
- All significant information to be revealed to the appropriate parties.

12.4 Engineers Dilemmas on Duty Ethics of engineering practice

We have already discussed in chapter 6 about *moral dilemmas of* engineers in general faced during engineering practice. Here we focus on duty ethics of engineering practice. If there is any possible danger or risk to others, from any client or employer, first of all the engineer is supposed to advice or warn them about such risk or danger. If the client or the employer fail to take note of or direction given by the engineer to avoid or tackle the possible danger, a basic ethical dilemma arises for the engineer, that he/she has the duty to report about such risk and noncompliance to his advice or warnings to the appropriate authority, even outside the organization.

According to first principles, this duty overrides the duty to a client and/or employer. If engineer fails to discharge this duty, even if the failure to report the danger is not to life or health, he/she likely to be disciplined or his license is revoked. This duty can be discharged by proper advice to the client about the nature of risk or danger and its consequences in a forthright manner and making sure that the client has understood it. The engineer must also make sure that appropriate corrective measures are taken and if not, the situation must be reported to the appropriate authority. Sometimes engineer's advice or warning about the risk or danger falls into deaf ears of authorities or even a governmental authority may not act and then engineer can only discharge the duty by going public or media. This action of engineer is called whistle blowing. Whistleblowing by professional engineers is not unusual and protected by law. In many cases courts have overruled duties to employers and confidentiality considerations that otherwise would have prevented the engineer from speaking out about risky and dangerous situations.

12.4.1 General Ethical Issues

There are many ethical issues which are not related to the area of professional expertise that engineers may face. These issues are connected with broader considerations of business conduct. These include:
- Relationships with clients, consultants, competitors, and contractors.
- Legal compliance by clients, client's contractors, and others.
- Conflict of interest of various agencies involved in the project or business.
- Issues arising due to local business practices like bribery and kickbacks, gifts, meals, services and entertainment.
- Issues associated with confidential or proprietary information.
- Issues concerning use, preservation and protection of the employer's assets.
- Issue of career growth and outside employment/activities.

Some engineering societies are addressing environmental protection as a stand-alone question of ethics.

12.5 Limitations of Codes

Codes do not give answer to all type of dilemmas which an engineer faces or likely to face in future. They are not substitute for individual's responsibility while encountering real dilemmas. Most codes are described in general wording and contain substantial areas of vagueness. Therefore, they do not address all situations and do not give a strait forward solution to specific dilemma or conflict of values. Vagueness of wording is a desirable feature of codes so as to allow and accommodate possibility new technical developments, and shifting social and organizational structures, happening all the time and everywhere in society and industry.

Uncertainties can also arise when different clauses in codes carry conflicting connotation while interpreting them in relation to a situation.

Usually codes do not provide any clue or guidance about which clause should be given priority in such cases. For example, sometimes engineers face a conflicting situation between their responsibilities to the employer and to the wider public. Similarly, duties are to tell and demonstrate morally relevant truths which sometimes conflict with duties towards confidentiality.

Despite authority of codes in guiding professional conduct, they are not always the complete and final in the changing world of technology. For example, till recently most codes were silent on the issue of professional responsibilities towards the environment because awareness about environment is a recent phenomenon. Therefore, codes should not be regarded as unchanging sacred canon to silence healthy moral debates including debate about how to improve codes and make them more versatile in application.

12.6 Industrial Product, Process and Interface Standards

Standards help industry to grow and expand with universalization of their products and services. Product standards facilitate the interchangeability of components manufactured by different industries spread all over the globe. Standard components and products serve as readymade substitutes against everyone trying to manufacture them through their own lengthy design procedures and specifications. Standards allow bulk production and reduce the production costs.

Standards consist of explicit design diagrams, material specifications and process of manufacturing, that when followed with care, ensure that stated criteria for interchangeability and quality will be attained. Examples range from mechanical and electrical hardware, batteries, various tools and automobile components like tire sizes and their load ratings, to computer hardware and protocols etc.

Some Standards are established by companies for in-house use and are company specific. But many standards, initially evolved by some company or institution are adopted and accepted by professional associations and trade associations for industry-wide usage. Some standards may also be enforced by law and official regulations and are called mandatory standards, which often arise from lack of adherence to voluntary standards.

Standards not only help the manufacturers but they also benefit the client and the public. Standards facilitate competitiveness in industry by removing emphasis on brands name and promoting the smaller manufacturers a chance to compete. International standards are becoming a necessity in global trade and promote integration of economies. International Standards Organization (ISO)has adopted an interesting approach that replaces the detailed national specifications for a plethora of products, with statements of procedures that a manufacturer guarantees to carry out to assure quality products.

12.7   Summary

Accountability in Engineering Profession: Accountability of any one means being accountable, answerable, responsible and justify one's actions or decisions. Thus, engineers as social experimenters should develop a positive attitude to be responsible and accountable for their actions and decisions. For creating a culture of accountability, the first step is to define the goals and communicate to all levels of managers and employees within the organization. Everyone must know what they're working for and how their job pushes the company forward.

Large-scale engineering projects involve fragmentation of work. Each person makes only a small contribution to something much larger. Moreover, the final product is often physically removed from one's immediate workplace, creating the kind of "distancing" with a lessened sense of personal accountability, thus resulting into vast diffusion of accountability within large institutions.

Role of Codes in Engineering: A professional society prescribes to its members, profession's collective commitment to ethics as codes of ethics, stating moral responsibilities during their professional practices. A number of companies have their own codes as code of practice and moral and ethical issues in dealing with vendors and clients as well as compliance to statutory requirements. An ethical code generally implies documents at three levels: codes of business ethics, codes of conduct for employees and codes of professional practice.

Standards of responsibility expressed in engineering codes typically call for engineers to follow these standards meticulously. NSPE code requires that the work of engineers conform to *applicable engineering standards*. These may be regulatory standards that specify technical requirements for specific kinds of engineering design. For example, that certain standard of safety is met by bridges or buildings.

Duty-Ethics of Engineering Practice: An engineer has the duty to report to the appropriate authority, any possible danger or risk to others, from any client or employer, who fail to take note of his advice or direction to avoid the possible danger or risk. This duty overrides the duty to serve a client and/or employer. Failure to this *Duty-Ethics* the engineer may be disciplined, or have their license revoked, even if the failure to report such a danger does not result in the loss of life or health.

Industrial Product, Process and Interface Standards: There is one area in which industry usually welcomes greater specificity, and that is in regard to standards. Product standards facilitate the interchange of components as readymade substitutes and decrease production costs.

Standards consist of explicit specifications that, when followed with care, ensure that stated criteria for interchangeability and quality will be attained. Examples range from automobile tire sizes and load ratings to computer protocols. Standards are established by companies for in-house use and by professional associations and trade associations for industry-wide usage.

Review questions

1. Explain what do you understand by accountability of a person? How to create 'culture of accountability' in an organization?
2. Explain how defining individual accountability and role diffuses overall responsibility in big projects.
3. Elaborate scope of code of ethics, code of conduct, code of practice and moral codes.
4. Explain points of *fundamental canons* stipulated in NSPE code of ethics for engineers.
5. Justify that satisfying the standards which the codes endorse for engineers to approach their work, if taken seriously, are quite demanding.
6. While practicing codes in profession, what are the things to do and what not to do?
7. Give the reasons which justify the need for professional code of ethics-a kind of morally permissible convention.
8. Give an account of several types of ethical issues that engineers face during their technical role and also many others issues with broader considerations of business conduct.
9. Codes are no substitute for individual responsibility in grappling with concrete dilemmas. What are limitations of codes as most codes use general wording, and hence contain substantial areas of vagueness?
10. What is utility of industrial standards?

Section 4: Engineer's Responsibility for Design with Safety Features, Risks control, Quality and Reliability

13 Engineers Responsibility for Safety and Risk

Learning objectives

In this chapter you will learn about

- Engineers responsibility in industry for safety and risk
- Stipulations of IEEE and NSPE code of ethics for engineers on risk and safety
- Few examples to illustrate the gravity of engineer's responsibility for safety and risk
- Example of types of safety problems in aviation industry and future issues of safety
- Technical concepts of safety and risks including types of risks

13.1 Risks Factors in engineering profession and activities

Each one of us faces risks in our daily life. Students face risks of accident in their academic life while travelling from home to college and back, risks of physical and mental health during academics, risk of future career, etc.

Everyone tries to assess these risks and deal with them in multiple ways based on the situation. For example, risks of health issues can be reduced by controlling intake of certain foods; accidents risk by driving carefully and using safety gadgets, avoiding visit to places or activities prone to have danger of some risk, etc. Everyone determines the risk factor himself, for example, whether to use tobacco, alcohol, drugs, etc. or not.

At personal level, everyone finds his own ways to deal with these risks like travelling in groups to places of high danger, carry documents of insurance and enough funds to help when bad things happen. Dealing with these risks is *risk management*.

We spend much of our time, money and other resources to deal with risks for safety in life which includes our personal life, family life, professional life, as well as risks in business organizations, social, religious and voluntary activities etc.

All engineering disciplines have their own risks particularly related to that discipline; but some risks are very common to all disciplines or professions like health and safety risks, risk associated with travelling, etc. and some risks are specific to particular application like risk of design liability, etc. Some risks are uniquely associated with individual disciplines. For examples: risk of electrical hazards, fire hazards, mechanical risks in shop floor, risk during structural fabrication, risks during installation, risks of civil engineering structures, computer networks, Internet, software glitches, chemical processes, aeronautics sector, nuclear energy, space program, etc.

13.2 Engineers Responsibility for Safety and Risk

Engineer's responsibility for safety and risks is multi-dimensional and multi-directional. Safety and risk management in air and train travel, nuclear plants, power plants, transport vehicles, multi-story buildings etc. directly fall on engineer's responsibility for safety and risk. Engineers not only have to demonstrate technical excellence in their professional jobs but also take care of social and regulatory requirement of the profession. In case of safety and risk issues, sometimes engineers and their employer's advance argument against failure to provide safety and quality under the logic that they have complied with the existing regulatory standards, but such logic is not necessarily acceptable to the courts. The engineers are expected to meet the *standard of care*, which under tort law (which is concerned with wrongful injury) is not restricted to regulatory standards alone.

The responsibility of an engineer or architect is essentially of the same nature as that of lawyer to his client, or the physician to his patient, or for that sake any professional who offers his services to the public on account of his professional skill and ability.

The responsibility of an engineer or an architect implies that he/she will exercise and apply his skill, ability and judgment for reasonable care to the service of his client or public without neglect. What counts as reasonable care depends on what the public can reasonably expect and what is acceptable practice in the opinion of experienced and competent engineers. Due to innovative nature of engineering designs, they are bound to see some failures and mishaps, but at the same time, it is incumbent on engineers to do their best to anticipate and avoid failures and mishaps.

Virtually all engineering codes give a prominent place to safety while fixing the responsibility of engineers. Engineers must hold paramount the safety, health and welfare of the public. The risk concept has very close relationship with safety concept. If products, structures, processes and substances are unsafe, it implies that humans and the environment are

exposed to undue risk. Therefore, the statements in the codes of professional ethics about safety become relevant to the topic of risk also.
NSPE Code of Ethics stipulates that
- II.1.a. If engineers' judgment is overruled under circumstances that endanger life or property; they shall notify their employer or client and such other authority as may be appropriate.
- II.1.b. Engineers shall approve only those engineering documents that are in conformity with applicable standards.
- III.2.a. Engineers shall not complete, sign, or seal plans and/or specifications that are not in conformity with applicable engineering standards. If the client or employer insists on such unprofessional conduct, they shall notify the proper authorities and withdraw from further service on the project.

Many other engineering codes give similar instructions to engineers. For example, the IEEE Code of Ethics emphasizes member's responsibility for the public's health and safety in three ways.
1. Electrical engineer agrees "... to accept responsibility in making engineering decisions consistent with the safety, health, and welfare of the public, and to disclose promptly factors that might endanger the public or the environment".
2. They agree "... to improve the understanding of technology, it's appropriate application and potential consequences".
3. They agree "... to maintain and improve our technical competence and to undertake technological tasks for others only if qualified by training or experience, or after full disclosure of pertinent limitations." These last two items emphasize the importance of informed consent.

13.2.1 Engineering necessarily and inherently involves risk

Engineers have created marvelous master pieces of technology like airplanes, communications gadgets, Internet, power plants, chemical plants, nuclear plants, civil engineering marvels like bridges, dams, flyovers, etc. We all are daily users of these infrastructures of public utilities. We are also aware that all of these engineering marvels can create havoc to public if not designed, operated and maintained properly within the strict safety and control parameters.

Engineering designs must take care of actual working conditions and working environments as well as possible extremes of stresses and strains encountered in widespread situations of application, for example stability of civil engineering structures during nature's fury like cyclones, earthquakes etc. We see during natural calamities like floods, cyclone, tornado, hurricane, etc. many lives are lost and large-scale loss of properties takes place. Road bridges collapse, communication towers bend down, electricity, water, communication and transportation systems come to stand still. We cannot control natural calamities but engineering designs can always be improved and modified to take care of probable peaks of stresses on structures because natural phenomena are quite cyclic and geographically specific. Thus, engineer's responsibility towards public safety is very high.

Risks are also associated with use of products, structures, variety of materials and substances developed by engineers. New hazards could be traced in products, processes and chemicals when they are employed for new applications; whereas so far, they were considered to be safe for earlier applications. As engineers are constantly involved in innovation, risk component increases with development of technology. Creation of new machines, synthesis of new compounds, development of new applications, etc. carry new type of risks, as their long-term effects on humans or the environment are so far unknown or without full knowledge.

13.3 Safety and Risk

Safety is achieved through combined approach of several groups, each with its own interests at stake. If within each group people have differences of opinion about what is safe and what is not, then *Safety* becomes an elusive term, and so also *Risk*. Thus, let us first be clear with the concept of risk and safety, then we may turn to safety and risk assessment methods of reducing risk. Finally, by examining a case of the nuclear power plant accident at Three Mile Island, we will consider the concept of *Safe Exit* in an ever-growing complexity in big engineered systems; i.e. designs and procedures, for building big and complex engineered systems, need to ensure that if a product fails, it will fail safely and the user is safe from any kind of *harm*.

13.3.1 The Concept of Risk

Concept of risk in any product or system involves undesirable adverse effect or harm to users. Harm is considered as a limitation on the user's freedom or well-being while using or operating the product or the system. Some of the most important types of well-being referred above are physical well-being, psychological well-being and economic well-being, etc. However, under engineering risks we are mostly concerned with physical and economic well-being. Engineering work can carry risks of health and accident or physical injury, which affects our economic well-being. For example, faulty design and construction of a building can cause it to subsequent collapse, resulting in economic loss and may even result

Chapter 13: Engineers Responsibility for Safety and Risk

into deaths for the inhabitants (Johnston et al. 2007). Similarly, faulty design of a chemical plant can cause accidents and economic disaster.

Ethical consideration in concept of risk analysis is to *respect every person's prima facie right, not to be exposed to risks*. Concept of risk includes probabilistic happenings which may occur or may not occur, like:
- An unwanted event.
- The cause of an unwanted event.
- The probability of an unwanted event.
- The statistical expectation value of unwanted events.

And the fact that decisions have to be made by engineers under conditions of known probabilities of unwanted events. It must be clarified that *risk* does not have a single well-defined meaning. Further, *Risk Assessments* are not always based only on well-established scientific facts. Lowrance defined risk as "... *a compound measure of the probability and magnitude of adverse effect*" as cited inSchwing and Albers (2013, pp.5). To assess a risk the first job of an engineer is to identify the risk. To identify a risk, one must know what a risk is. The concept of risk involves the notion of *Adverse Effect* or *Harm*. Harm can be defined as adverse action on a person's freedom or well-being.

13.3.2 The Concept of Safety

Safety is the demand of all users in any product or service because nobody wants to take risk of any type or any potential harm. However, safety is also subjective to some extent. Any product or service considered safe by someone may not be considered safe by someone else, because of variety of perceptions people have about safety and risk. For example, any sharp object like knife, etc. in the hands of a child is more hazardous to child safety then in the hands of adults and seniors. To general public safety and risk are the two things which are understood differently by them, but both are related to each other. If there is low safety then risk is high and vice versa, implying that if lower the risk, higher the safety. Absolute safety which can satisfy views of everybody or groups in all circumstances is neither attainable nor affordable.

Engineers come across two types of public conceptions with safety. One is the overly optimistic attitude about the things that are familiar to us, and which have not hurt us before and where we have some level of control, that present no real risks. On the other extreme, people are dreaded of the situation whereat some place or occasion an accident killed large numbers of people or harmed them, whom we know, even though statistically speaking such accidents might occur very infrequently or rarely.

According to Lowrance "...*a thing is safe if its risks are judged to be acceptable*" as cited in Boylan (2013). This approach of defining safety supports the notion, that safety is a subjective matter as it depends on what risks a person judges to be acceptable. This approach suggests that judgments about safety are perceptual value judgments, and it depends on what is considered as acceptable risk to a given person or group. Differences in perceptions of safety are thus reflecting differences in values.

The concept of acceptability of risk in above definition makes definition of safety very vague as it depends on individual's value judgment and prevents any objective assessment of risk. Once we settle on what constitutes an acceptable risk, we start a search of at least some objective point of reference outside ourselves that allows us to decide whether our judgments about safety are correct. A new definition of safety can be formulated, that could capture this element without omitting the fact already noted, that safety judgments are relative to people's value perspectives. One simple option could be to equate safety with the absence of risk. In life and engineering the risks are always present. Safety is high if risks are low, i.e. below certain predetermined levels. A new definition of safety according to Schinzinger and Martin (2000, pp.109) says "... *a thing is safe if its risks were fully known; those risks should be judged acceptable by reasonable persons in light of their settled value principles*". However, Rowe says that "... *a risk is acceptable when those affected are generally no longer (or not) apprehensive about it*". Being apprehensive about risk largely depends on how the risk is perceived by people. This perception is influenced by factors such as

1. Whether the acceptance of risk is voluntary
2. The impacts of knowledge on how the probabilities of harm are known or perceived
3. When the risks are related to jobs or any other type of pressures that cause people to be aware of the risk or to overlook risks
4. Whether the effects of a risky activity or situation are immediately noticeable
5. Whether the probable victims of risk are identifiable beforehand.

13.3.3 Magnitude and Proximity

Our reaction to risk largely depends on the dread of a possible mishap, in terms of its magnitude and the personal identification or relationship with the potential victims. For example, a single major airplane crash in a remote country or the specter of a person we know or observe on the television screen trapped in a cave-in or any similar case of sufferings in person or group of people, these happenings affect our concern for them more acutely than the ongoing; but anonymous carnage or accident on the highways where no one involved in carnage is known to me. This is called *proximity effect*.

The magnitude of proximity effect is a measure of depth of feeling of concern about the affected persons or group. For example, we feel much more keenly about a potential risk of one of us out of a group of 20 intimate friends, compared to say 50 strangers out of a proportionally larger group of 1,000. This proximity effect arises in perceptions of risk over time in future as well. A future risk is easily dismissed by various rationalizations including

1. General attitude towards events in future having feelings like *out of sight, out of mind*.
2. Common assumption that the future predictions should be discounted by assigning lower probabilities for occurrence of risk factor.
3. General belief that an appropriate solution to reduce risk factor will come up in time.

13.4 Type of Risks

Type of risks depends on the way we look at the domain of risks. They can be classified as follows:

1. **Financial and non-financial**
   It is common knowledge that wherever financial transactions or matters are involved, there is a scope for mismanagement, fraud, misappropriation, etc. Banking and insurance sectors deal with risks of financial nature. Trading in stock market is full of risks. Non-financial risks are there when a project over shoots time frame, does not fulfill the mission. Industrial designs fail in the field, market does not accept the product as forecasted, a new drug introduced in medical field proved ineffective in treatment or having bad side effects.
2. **Static and dynamic**
   Dynamic risks are result of changes in the economy (e.g., changes in price levels, consumer taste, income, and output). In the long run, economic changes benefits society by readjustments of allocations of resources. Static risks would exist even in the absence of economic change (from perils of nature or human dishonesty). This causes loss to society.
3. **Fundamental and particular**
   Fundamental risks are impersonal in origin and consequences. They are societal risks. It is held that society (rather than the individual) should deal with them. Particular risks involve losses that arise out of individual events and are felt by individuals rather than the entire group. Particular risks are considered the individual's own responsibility that is properly addressed by the individual.

4. **Pure and speculative**
   Speculative risks involve the possibility of loss or gain. They are voluntarily accepted because of the possibility of gain. Pure risks involve the possibility of loss or no loss only. In general, insurance deals with pure risks only.

Risks in engineering and corporate sector can be classified as:
1. **Engineer's personal risks**: physical, mental, social, credibility, financial, etc.
2. **Organizational property rights and confidential data risks**: Theft or sabotage of designs, process, Patents, confidential data/records, etc.
3. **Legal contractual liability risks**: Business contracts, government regulations, professional mandatory requirement, etc.
4. **Risks arising out of failure of others:** Unions, strikes sabotage, etc.
5. **Job-related risks:** Not only the people who deals with hazardous materials but even other working staff like clerical and managerial staff are exposed to risk. Exposure to high voltages, strong radiations, toxic substances, harmful chemicals, fumes; materials like asbestos, etc. are risk factors to all employees.

13.5 Voluntary *vs.* Involuntary Risk

Ordinary people seem to perceive voluntarily incurred risks as less troublesome than involuntarily incurred risks. Consider the diverse public reactions to airplane crashes and automobile crashes. Or consider the fact that tobacco is by far the largest source of preventable deaths in the United States. Why do we not devote much more of our regulatory effort to reducing smoking? The reason seems to lie in a judgment that smoking is a voluntary activity and hence the resulting deaths are less troublesome than are other sorts of deaths. People have voluntarily assumed the relevant risks. This idea helps account for the fact that the government devotes relatively little in the way of resources to control not only smoking, but also to combat the habits of poor diet and insufficient exercise, which produce at least 300,000 premature deaths every year.

It has been found that many times individuals voluntarily accept risk up to three orders of magnitude (1,000 times) routinely for sport, money, thrill, loyalty, glory and duty. Some adventurous people voluntarily accept risk up to six orders of magnitude for these reasons.

On the other hand, people showed involuntary acceptance of risk even to much lower levels of risk when the risks were imposed upon them from others. It has been found that acceptance level for *known risks* is generally three orders or magnitude below the base. Whereas for Unknown or greatly feared risks acceptance level is generally found to be six orders of magnitude below the base.

The distinction between voluntary and involuntary risk may well be the central element in the difference between lay and expert judgments about risk. Experts tend to focus on aggregate lives at stake; lay people care a great deal whether a risk is undertaken voluntarily.

Voluntarism and Control

Let us consider two cases: first case of voluntary choice of risk and second case of involuntary situation of risk.

Case 1: Voluntary choice of risk

Many students enjoy high speed crisscross rough driving of motorcycle for amusement. Many local train passengers prefer to stand at the door, peeping and hanging outward from the door side, even though they may have place to go inside the compartment. Many students stand on foot steps of city bus and hang outward. Many of them ride or get down from a running bus near the bus stands. They all know the risk involved to their body or life in case any mishap happens, even then they take the voluntary risks for engaging in such a potentially dangerous position in moving vehicles. They do not expect the manufacturers of these bikes or buses to adhere to the standards of safety for such driving or places of public entry points. For example, the bikes should be sturdy but guards covering exposed parts of the engine, padded instrument panels, collapsible steering mechanisms or emergency brakes are clearly unnecessary, if not inappropriate.

Case 2: Situation of involuntary risk

Human habitation and industrial plants are mostly static settlements. Many people do not have choice of house or place of residence. Most of the people like to live close to their workplace (Sunstein, 1977). If there is a chemical plant, a coal-based power plant, a cement plant, stone crushing plant or any other air polluting industry nearby and because of that they suffer from some air pollution, and some toxic wastes in the ground. Municipal inspectors tell them not to worry. Nevertheless, they do and they think they have reason to complain. They are worried about being exposed to risks from a chemical plant on an involuntary basis.

Most of us would under above two cases/ circumstances show up less apprehensive about the risks to which we expose ourselves voluntarily than about those to which we are exposed to involuntarily. In terms of our *engineering as social experimentation* paradigm, people are more willing to be the subjects of their own experiments (social or not) than of someone else's.

Intimately connected with this notion of voluntarism is the matter of control. In the first case people have selected their own transport media/ machines and they feel confident on how well they control risk environment or think they can. They are aware of accident possibility, but they tell themselves that those apply to other travelers and not to them. In this manner, most of the people may display the characteristically unrealistic confidence when they believe hazards to be under their control. But still riding motorbikes, skiing, hang gliding, bungee jump, horseback riding, boxing and other hazardous sports are usually carried out under the assumed control of the participants. Enthusiasts worry less about their risks than the dangers of, say, air pollution or airline safety. Another reason for not worrying so much about the consequences of these sports is that rarely does anyone accident injures innocent bystanders.

13.6 Short Term *vs.* Long Term consequences

Risk is the potential of losing something of value in short time frame or over a long exposure to risky environment. Values such as physical health, social status, emotional well-being or financial wealth generally get affected over a comparatively long time compared to accidental risks or sudden body sickness due foreseen or unforeseen causes or uncertainties. *Uncertainty* is a potential, unpredictable, immeasurable and uncontrollable factor; whereas risk is a consequence of action under uncertainty.

We say a thing is not safe means it implies that it exposes us to unacceptable risk; but what is meant by *risk*? A risk means that there is a possibility of something harmful that may happen. Rowe defines risk as "*... a potential for the realization of unwanted consequences from impending events*" as cited in Schinzinger and Martin (2000, pp.110). Thus, it assumes that in future some occurrence of harm is possible. The prospective harm in future could be visible over a short period or show up its consequences after a long period.

Risk like harm is a broad concept covering many different types of harmful occurrences. In connection to technology and engineering, risk implies dangers of bodily harm (physical as well as mental) or economic loss or of environmental degradation which could cascade into delay in job execution or faulty products or systems or economically or environmentally injurious outcomes while solving a technological problem.

Good engineering practice has always been concerned with safety. But as technology and engineering modernized the society, it also injected higher level of risk factors in the society. Now public awareness and concern on harmful factors of technology and consequent risks has also increased. The hazards of many consumer products and industrial processes are identifiable and measurable. Now the public is conscious about the short term and long-term consequences of these harmful effects of some of the technologies.

Many risks appear to be new risks but they were in existence since quite some time and became measurable now. They are new only in the sense that they are now identifiable because of changes in the magnitude of the risks they present because they have passed a certain threshold of accumulation in our environment, or because of a change in measuring techniques. Further, the public's perception of them has changed because of education, experience and media attention.

A more analytical discussion on Risk Perception and Probability of Risk, Threshold Levels for Delayed Risk *vs.* Immediate Risk etc. is discussed in Chapter 14.

13.7 Summary

Risks Factors in Engineering Activities: Risks are part of our daily life. A student, an engineer, an employee and a professional, all have risks in their activities and jobs. We assess these risks intuitively or by formal assessment and spend much of our time, money and other resources to deal with risks for safety in life. All engineering disciplines have their own risks. Some are common to all like health and safety risks, travel risks, design liability risks etc. Some risks are unique to individual disciplines for examples: electrical hazards, fire hazards, shop floor risks, risk during structural fabrication, civil engineering structures, etc.

Risks arise from engineering substances, products and structures created by engineers. New hazards could be found in products, processes and chemicals that were once thought to be safe.Further, new risks may come to light after long-term effects on humans or the environment. Normallylong-term risks of new machines and new compounds synthesized by engineers are not known initially.

Engineer's responsibility for Safety and Risk: The relationship of risk and safety is very close. Virtually all engineering codes give a prominent place to safety stating that engineers must hold paramount the safety, health and welfare of the public. Engineers have to demonstrate technical excellence in their professional jobs and also take care of social and regulatory requirement of the profession. Engineering designs must take care of actual working conditions and working environments as well as possible extremes of stresses and strains on the operating conditions. We cannot control natural calamities but engineering designs can always be improved and modified to take care of probable peaks of stresses on structures because natural phenomena are quite cyclic and geographically specific.

Safety, Risk and Safe-Exit: Concept of risk involves adverse effect or harm. Harm is a broad concept covering many different types of harmful occurrences. Risk assessments are not always based on well-established scientific facts. In any project several groups of people are involved in safety issues, each group with its own interests and concern at stake. Faulty design of a building can cause it to collapse. Faulty design of a chemical plant can cause accidents and economic disaster. In examining engineering disasters, emphasis should be on the ultimate need for Safe-Exits through proper designs and procedures ensuring that if a product fails it will fail safely and harm to the user is avoided.

Safety and risk are subjective because of variety of perceptions about what is safety and risk. Good engineering practice has always been concerned with safety. To general public safety and risk are the two things, which are understood differently by them. But both are related to each other. Differences in appraisals of safety are seen as reflecting differences in values. A new definition of safety could be a thing is safe if, its risks were fully known; those risks should be judged acceptable by reasonable persons in light of their settled value principle.

Types of Risks: Types of risks depends on the way we look at the domain of risks. They can be classified as financial and non-financial, static and dynamic, fundamental and particular, pure and speculative. The other way of classification of risk could be engineer's personal risks i.e. physical, mental, social, credibility, financial, etc.; or risks of organizations like property rights, Patents, confidential data/records etc. Risk of theft of confidential technical details, drawings, designs and process; legal contractual liability risks; risk from unions, strikes, sabotage, etc.

Ordinary people seem to perceive voluntarily incurred risks as less troublesome than involuntarily incurred risks. It has been found that many times individuals voluntarily accept risk of much higher level (up to three to six orders of magnitude) routinely for sport, money, thrill, loyalty, glory and duty or some adventures. But the same people showed involuntary acceptance of risk even to much lower levels of risk when the risks were imposed upon them from others.

Short Term *vs.* Long Term consequences: Risk is the potential of losing something of value in short time frame or over a long-term use and exposure to risky environment. Values such as physical health, social status, emotional well-being or financial wealth generally get affected over a comparatively long time compared to accidental risks or sudden body sickness due foreseen or unforeseen causes or uncertainties. Uncertainty is a potential, unpredictable, immeasurable and uncontrollable factor; however, risk is a consequence of action under uncertainty.

Review questions

1. Comment on the statement that "Risk is everywhere, whatever you do".
2. Explain multi-dimensional nature of engineer's responsibility for safety and risk.
3. What is the purpose of codes of ethics of professional bodies?
4. What are likely future issues on aero safety in India? Explain engineer's responsibility for safety in aerospace industry

5. Give basic concepts of safety and risk and elaborate on relationship between them.
6. Explain different type of risks and how they are classified?
7. What do you understand from voluntary and involuntary risks- explain?
8. Explain short term and long-term consequences of risks

14 Risk Perceptions and Risk Assessment Analysis

Learning objectives

In this chapter you will learn about

- Risk perception, probability of risk, delayed risks, hazard, harm and uncertainty
- Risk threshold, risk appetite, risk management and sources of risk
- Process and methods of risk identification, quantifying the risk assessment
- Risks of financial losses, risks in project management, risk in public health
- Risks in high reliability organizations, risks in IT field

14.1 Risk Perception and Probability of Risk

Risk perception is the subjective judgment of people about the severity and/or probability of a risk, and the assessment may vary for person to person. All human activities carry some risk but some activities are much riskier than others.

Engineers and technologists work for defining and quantifying the risk which can be measured or predicted in probabilistic terms. This study of probability pattern of risks facilitates *risk assessment* which is used in designing better products and systems with lesser risks. Risk can be analyzed in terms of a chance or situation involving exposure to the possibility of injury, loss or any other adverse effect. Some risk perceptions from different field of activities are given below:

1. **Risk of uncertain event or condition:** For engineers involved in a project work, an uncertain event or condition is a risk that if occurs has an adverse impact on at least one of the project objectives. As a risk factor it is the probability of something happening (even causing delay in program schedule) multiplied by the resulting cost or loss.
2. **Probability of Quantifiable damage:** The probability of occurrence or chance of quantifiable damage in the form of injury,

liability, loss or any other adverse occurrence caused by external or internal forces, that may be avoidable through preemptive action.
3. **Finance:** The possibility of reduction of actual return on an investment than the expected return.
4. **Insurance:** A situation where the probability of occurrence of an event (for example a car accident) is known but the mode of occurrence or the actual extent of the damage or loss (to a particular car) is not known.
5. **Workplace risk**: It is the product of the risk factor and probability of a hazardous event or phenomenon.

Risk is a condition where a possibility of an adverse deviation exists for different or negative outcome than the desired one. The *degree of risk* is a measurable quantity which indicates whether risk is more or less. It varies with the probability of deviation from what is expected in case of aggregate data or from what is hoped for in case of individual.

14.1.1 Delayed *vs.* Immediate Risk

Health, safety and environment (HSE) are separate areas of practice by professionals. However, they are quite often linked with each other on the aspect of risk. This linkage of risk element between these areas may have impacts in all three areas, albeit over different timescales. For example, the risk of uncontrolled release of radiation or a toxic chemical in any process, reservoir or plant may have immediate short-term safety consequences but comparatively impact on health matter over longer time and much longer-term environmental impacts.

One may argue that many times exposure to risks (like chemicals, fumes, materials like asbestos, etc.) on a job situation is in a sense voluntary activity of workers because one can always refuse to work in such risky jobs. But due to jobs scarcity often workers have very little choice on job matter and are compelled by circumstances to stick to risky jobs and do work as they are asked to do. Quite often workers are not aware of seriousness of risk factors as they are not told about how their exposure to toxic substances can affect them with their delayed long-term dangers. Further, the risk of toxic exposure becomes complicated as very often these long-term dangers cannot be readily seen, smelled, heard or otherwise sensed in short term period.

Workers education on occupational health and safety regulations (such as right-to-know rules regarding toxics) can alleviate the worst situations to some extent. But standards regulating conditions like air quality etc., around workers engaged in risky situations in the workplace, are generally still far below the standard conditions used to regulate environment for our general public. Factory workers are seldom carefully screened for exposure level during their work. Disasters like Chernobyl are good example to understand seriousness of impact of risky exposures of workers and the environment where there were immediate deaths, long-term deaths from cancers and lasting impact on environment leading to birth defects, impacts on wildlife, etc. To study this type of widespread impact on workers and the environment, a form of risk analysis called *environmental-risk-analysis* has been developed which attempts to understand events and activities that bring risk to human health or the environment.

14.2 Understanding Risk, Hazard, Harm and Uncertainty

Anything that can cause harm can be called a hazard. The risk is the consequence of the chance of harm taking place. The harm is opposite to safety or a negative safety and may occur in many forms like health consequence (e.g. injury, ill health, or death) or financial risk, etc. Risks can occur due to various uncertainties coming from different sources; such as uncertainty in financial markets; problems in project execution due to deficiencies in any phase like design, development, production, or field operations; legal liabilities of business, credit risk, accidents, natural causes and disasters as well as deliberate attack from unsocial elements, etc. Different risk management standards have been evolved by various agencies like the project management institute (PMI), the national institute of standards and technology (NIST), actuarial societies and ISO standards. Methods, definitions and goals of these organizations involved in development of risk management standards have wide variation according to the context like project management, security, engineering, public health and safety, etc.

14.2.1 Definitions of Risk

Uncertainty is a potential, unpredictable, unmeasurable and uncontrollable factor. The widely-accepted meaning of uncertainty refers to a state of mind characterized by a lack of knowledge or doubt about the future. Risk is a consequence of actions under uncertainty. A risk is not analogous to uncertainty where neither the probability nor the mode of occurrence is known. It is like a cause of loss or a hazard or it is a condition that creates or increases the chance of loss.

The ISO 31000 (2009) / ISO Guide 73:2002 definition of risk is "*... the effect of uncertainty on objectives*". In this definition, uncertainties include events which may or may not happen and also uncertainties caused by ambiguity or a lack of information. Risk can be seen as relating to the probability of uncertain future events. For example, according to factor analysis of information risk, risk is the probable frequency and probable magnitude of future loss. In computer science, this definition is used by *The Open Group* (which is a vendor and technology-neutral industry consortium with over five hundred member-organizations. It was formed in 1996 when X/Open merged with the Open Software Foundation).

OHSAS (occupational health & safety advisory services) defines risk as "... *the combination of the probability of a hazard resulting in an adverse event, times the severity of the event*". In *information security* risk is defined as "... *the potential that a given threat will exploit vulnerabilities of an asset or group of assets and thereby cause harm to the organization*" (Wright and DeHert, 2012, pp.2).

Financial risk is often defined as the unpredictable variability or volatility of returns and this would include both potential better-than-expected and worse-than-expected returns. The related terms *threat* and *hazard* are often used to mean something that could cause harm.

14.3 Risk Threshold and Risk Appetite

For many types of effects there is a minimum exposure required before the effect surfaces up and becomes visible or measurable. This is called the threshold level. Exposure to levels below threshold level in any risk study is not risky. For example, exposure to a dangerous chemical substance below the threshold level is not a risk, because no effect will occur. For other types of effects, such as many cancers, no threshold level is known and all exposures are associated with some risk.

The easiest way to define risk appetite can be likened with eating food. When we eat our regular meal like dinner, a time comes when we start getting feeling of fullness that is threshold level of our appetite. Eating more than threshold level starts beginning of risk and risk of discomfort will keep on rising as more and more we continue to eat, which may lead to some more complication of higher level of risk.

Similarly, when we go to work without breakfast on an empty stomach, a number of other factors come up, such as tolerance level of feeling hungry which is another level of threshold when individual performance start affecting his productivity.

The same concept is applicable to business organizations also. Risk Appetite for an organization means the cost that it is willing to sacrifice over a specified period in pursuit of some other business gain. For sustenance of organizational growth, it is essential for any organization to establish a level of risk appetite to achieve the desired gain and maintain balance between spending initiatives vis-à-vis becoming very cautious to investments and therefore stifling the growth initiative. Organizations need to review their risk appetite regularly to tailor it in accordance to business requirement and keeping risk threshold within control.

14.3.1 Relationship between Risk Appetite and Risk Threshold

Risk thresholds area sort of indicators or points calling for risks triggering action where a decisive action is required by management executive or board intervention. When the organization has established extent of risk appetite, risk thresholds level (also known as tolerance or benchmark) can be conveniently established in relation to the risk appetite. Risk Threshold levels can vary from department to department, division to division, business unit to business unit as the case may be within the organization.

By cumulative measurements against these thresholds, an organization can understand the nature of risk appetite being followed within the organization, whether it is averse or aggressive. It is important to understand that when threshold levels are exceeded, effectiveness of the risk response(s) undertaken to address the risks most likely will be decided by the type of risk appetite present.

Most organizations depend on insurance to guard against losses due to some risks which is likely to have high premiums in absence of risk management framework in place. On the other hand, some insurance companies reduce the insurance premiums when there is an effective risk management framework in place.

14.4 Risk Management and Sources of Risk

Original sources of risks are often identified and located in infrastructural or technological assets, tangible variables and sometimes even within human factor variables, mental states and decision-making aptitude.

Risk management is the identification, assessment and prioritization of risks. It is followed by judicious deployment of resources to minimize, monitor and control the probability and/or impact of risky events. Risk management also attempts to maximize the realization of opportunities. Objective of risk management is to ensure that any uncertainty does not result into deviation of the endeavors from the business goals. It also includes both negative and positive impacts on objectives.

14.5 Quantifying the Risk Assessment

In all types of engineering of complex systems, sophisticated risk assessments are often made within safety engineering and reliability engineering, when it concerns threats to life, environment or machine functioning. The nuclear, aerospace, oil, rail and military industries have a long history of dealing with risk assessment. Also, medical, hospital, social service and food industries control risks and perform risk assessments on a continual basis. Methods for assessment of risk may differ between industries; whether it pertains to general financial decisions or environmental, ecological, or public health risk assessment.

The fundamental difficulty in risk assessment is determining the rate of occurrence since statistical information is not available on all kinds of past incidents. Furthermore, evaluating the severity of the consequences (impact) is often quite difficult for intangible assets. Asset valuation is another question that needs to be addressed. Thus, best educated opinions and available statistics are the primary sources of information. Nevertheless, risk assessment should produce such information for the management of the organization that the primary risks are easy to understand and that the risk management decisions may be prioritized. Thus, there have been several theories and attempts to quantify risks. Numerous different risk formulae exist but perhaps the most widely accepted formula for risk quantification is rate (or probability) of occurrence multiplied by the impact of the event equals risk magnitude.

Risk assessment is the determination of quantitative or qualitative value of risk related to a concrete situation and a recognized threat (also called hazard). Quantitative risk assessment requires calculations of two components of risk (R) 1) the magnitude of the potential loss (L) and 2) the probability (P) that the loss will occur. Then,

$$Composite\ Risk\ Index = Impact\ of\ Risk\ event \times Probability\ of\ Occurrence.$$

Once risks have been identified, they must then be assessed as to their potential severity of impact (generally a negative impact such as damage or loss) and to the probability of occurrence. These quantities can be either simple to measure in the case of value of a lost building or impossible to know for sure in the case of the probability of an unlikely event occurring.

Often the probability of a negative event is estimated by using the frequency of past similar events. Probabilities for rare failures may be difficult to estimate. This makes risk assessment difficult in hazardous industries. For example, nuclear energy, where the frequency of failures is rare, while harmful consequences of failure is severe.

Risk is often measured as the expected value of an undesirable outcome. This combines the probabilities of various possible events and some assessment of the corresponding harm into a single value. The simplest case is a binary possibility of accident or no accident. The associated formula for calculating risk is given by:

$$R = Probability\ of\ the\ accident\ occurring \times Expected\ loss\ in\ case\ of\ the\ accident$$

For example, if performing activity X has a probability of 0.01 of suffering an accident of A, with a loss of 1000 then total risk is a loss of 10, the product of 0.01 and 1000.

Chapter 14: Risk Perceptions and Risk Assessment Analysis

Situations are sometimes more complex than the simple binary possibility case. In a situation with several possible accidents, total risk is the sum of the risks for each different accident, provided that the outcomes are comparable:

$$R = \Sigma \begin{pmatrix} \text{Probability of the accident occurring} \\ \times \text{ expected loss in case of the accident} \end{pmatrix} \text{For all accidents}$$

For example, if performing activity X has a probability of 0.01 of suffering an accident of A, with a loss of 1000 and a probability of 0.000001 of suffering an accident of type B, with a loss of 2,000,000, then total loss expectancy is 12, which is equal to a loss of 10 from an accident of type A and 2 from an accident of type B.

This kind of risk analysis is common in fields like nuclear power, aerospace and the chemical industry.

14.6 Risk Assessment in various fields of activity

14.6.1 Methodology

The term methodology means an organized set of principles and rules that drive action in a particular field of knowledge. A methodology does not describe specific methods; nevertheless, it does specify several processes that need to be followed. These processes constitute a generic framework. They may be broken down in sub-processes, they may be combined or their sequence may change. However, any risk management exercise must carry out these processes in one form or another.

For the most part, these methods consist of the following elements, performed, more or less in the following order.
1. Identify and characterize threats
2. Assess the vulnerability of critical assets to specific threats
3. Determine the risks (i.e. the expected likelihood and consequences of specific types of attacks on specific assets)
4. Identify ways to reduce those risks
5. Prioritize risk reduction measures based on a strategy

14.6.2 Risks in terms of financial losses

Financial risks in most of the economic activities are expressed in terms of a currency of the country concerned or US dollars, which is universally accepted currency. Decisions on risks in banking sector, commerce and trade, stock exchanges, insurance sectors and industrial activity, etc. are expressed as losses in terms of a currency like dollar amounts or equivalent in another currency.

Many times, for consumption of general public or for the sake of comparison between risks of different types like accidents, fire, faulty structures, etc. are translated in terms of financial figures (losses or liabilities) even though actual risk may be in terms of deaths, disabilities, collapse of structures, etc.

14.6.3 Risks in project management

In project management, risk assessment is an integral part of the risk management plan, studying the probability, the impact and the effect of every known risk on the project, as well as the corrective action to take in case of that risk occurs. Of special consideration in this area, the relevant codes of practice that are enforced in the specific jurisdiction. Understanding the regime of regulations that risk management must abide by is integral to formulating safe and compliant risk assessment practices.

Megaprojects: Megaprojects (sometimes also called *major programs*) are extremely large-scale investment projects, typically costing lot more Rs. 500 Crores per project. Megaprojects include bridges, tunnels, highways, railways, airports, seaports, power plants, dams, wastewater projects, coastal flood protection, oil and natural gas extraction projects, IT Networks, aerospace projects and defense projects etc. Megaprojects have been shown to be particularly risky in terms of finance, safety and social and environmental impacts.

14.6.4 Risks in High Reliability Organizations

A high reliability organization (HRO) is an organization that has succeeded in avoiding catastrophes in an environment where normal accidents can be expected due to risk factors and complexity. Most studies of HROs involve areas such as nuclear aircraft carriers, air traffic control, aerospace and nuclear power stations. Organizations such as these, share in common, the ability to consistently operate safely in complex, interconnected environments where a single failure in one component could lead to catastrophe. Essentially, they are organizations which appear to operate in spite of an enormous range of risks.

Some of these industries manage risk in a highly quantified and enumerated way. These include the nuclear power and aircraft industries where the possible failure of a complex series of engineered systems could result in highly undesirable outcomes. The usual measure of risk for a class of events is then given by

$$R = probability\ of\ the\ event \times the\ severity\ of\ the\ consequence$$

14.6.5 Enterprise Risk Management

In enterprise risk management, a risk is defined as a possible event or circumstance that can have negative influences on the enterprise in question. Its impact can be on the very existence, the resources (human and capital), the products and services, or the customers of the enterprise, as well as external impacts on society, markets, or the environment. In a financial institution, enterprise risk management is normally thought of as the combination of credit risk, interest rate risk or asset liability management, liquidity risk, market risk and operational risk. In the more general case, every probable risk can have a pre-formulated plan to deal with its possible consequences (to ensure contingency if the risk becomes a liability).

14.6.6 Risk Assessment in public health

When risk assessment is used for public health or environmental decisions, loss can be quantified in a common metric such as a country's currency or some numerical measure of a location's quality of life. For public health and environmental decisions, loss is simply a verbal description of the outcome, such as increased cancer incidence or incidence of birth defects etc. In that case, the *risk* is expressed as $R = L \times P$; where, L is risk (loss) potential and P is probability of occurrence

If the risk estimate considers information on the number of individuals exposed, it is termed as a *population risk* and is in units of expected increased cases per a time period. If the risk estimate does not consider the number of individuals exposed, it is termed an *individual risk* and is in units of incidence rate per a time period. Population risks are of more use for cost/benefit analysis; individual risks are of more use for evaluating whether risks to individuals are *acceptable*.

14.6.7 Risks in IT field

Information technology risk or IT risk is a risk related to information technology. This relatively new term due to an increasing awareness, that information security is simply one facet of a multitude of risks, that are relevant to IT and the real-world processes it supports. The increasing dependencies of modern society on information and computers networks (both in private and public sectors, including military), has led to a new term like IT risk, for example, risk of cyber–attack and cyber warfare.

The IT risks are the risks that are involved in the applications of information technology to all sectors of economy and business; i.e. the risk associated with the use, ownership, operation, influence and adoption of IT within an enterprise. IT risk management can be considered as a component of a wider enterprise risk management system.

The establishment, maintenance and continuous update of an information security management system (ISMS) provide a strong indication that a company is using a systematic approach for the identification, assessment and management of information security risks (Conrad et al. 2012).

The Certified Information Systems Auditor Review Manual 2006 provides the following definition of risk management: "...*risk management is the process of identifying vulnerabilities and threats to the information resources used by an organization in achieving business objectives, and deciding what countermeasures, if any, to take in reducing risk to an acceptable level, based on the value of the information resource to the organization*" (Raggad, 2010, pp.23).

14.6.7.1 Risks in Software Evolution

Studies have shown that early parts of the system development cycle such as requirements and design specifications are especially prone to error. This effect is particularly notorious in projects, involving multiple stakeholders with different points of view. Evolutionary software engineering processes offer an iterative approach to requirement to alleviate the problems of uncertainty, ambiguity and inconsistency inherent in software developments.

14.6.7.2 Information Assurance and Information Security

Information security means protecting information and information systems from unauthorized access, use, disclosure, disruption, modification, perusal, inspection, recording or destruction. Information security grew out of practices and procedures of computer security.

Information security has grown to information assurance (IA) i.e. the practice of managing risks related to the use, processing, storage and transmission of information or data and the systems and processes used for those purposes.

Information assurance is interdisciplinary and draws expertise from multiple fields, including accounting, fraud examination, forensic science, management science, systems engineering, security engineering and criminology, in addition to computer science.

14.7 Summary

Risk Perception: For general public *risk* perception is the subjective judgment of the severity and/or probability of a risk. Engineers and technologists work for defining and quantifying the risk which can be measured or predicted in probabilistic terms. This study of probability pattern of risks facilitates *risk assessment* which is used in designing better products and systems with lesser risks.

Health, Safety, and Environment (HSE) are separate practice areas. However, they are often linked. The strongest link between these is that a single risk event may have impacts in all three areas, albeit over different timescales. For example, single disaster like Chernobyl, caused immediate

Chapter 14: Risk Perceptions and Risk Assessment Analysis

deaths and in the longer term, deaths from cancers and left a lasting environmental impact leading to birth defects, impacts on wildlife, etc.

Defining Risk, Hazard, Harm and Uncertainty: A *Hazard* is anything that can cause harm. The *Risk* is the probability of harm being done. The H*arm* is a negative safety and may have health consequence (e.g. injury, ill health, or death) or financial risk etc. OHSAS defines risk as the combination of the probability of a hazard resulting in an adverse event, times the severity of the event. *Uncertainty* is a potential, unpredictable, unmeasurable and uncontrollable factor and risk is a consequence of action under uncertainty.

Risk Threshold, Risk Appetite: *Threshold* is a level beyond which the adverse effect becomes visible. For example, exposure to a dangerous chemical substance at levels below the threshold level is not a risk, because no effect will occur.

Risk Appetite can be understood by analogy with our eating food. While we eat our regular meal, our threshold level of appetite is when we start getting feeling of fullness. Eating more than threshold level starts beginning of risk of discomfort and the risk will keep on increasing if we continue to eat. The same concept is applicable to business organizations also. When there is an established *risk appetite, risk thresholds* can be set in relation to the risk appetite.

Risk Management and Sources of Risk: Risk management is the *identification, assessment,* and *prioritization* of risks followed by coordinated and economical application of resources to minimize and control the probability and/or impact of unfortunate events or to maximize the realization of opportunities. Several risk management standards have been developed by various agencies including the project management institute, the national institute of standards and technology, actuarial societies and the ISO standards. Methods definitions and goals vary widely according to whether the risk management method is in the context of project management, security, engineering, industrial processes, financial portfolios, actuarial assessments, or public health and safety.

Risks can come from different sources e.g. uncertainty in financial markets, threats from project failures, legal liabilities, credit risk, accidents, natural disasters as well as deliberate attack from an adversary, or events of uncertain or unpredictable root-cause.

Risk Assessment: *Risk Assessment* is the determination of quantitative or qualitative value of risk that is related to a concrete situation and which is a recognized threat (also called hazard). In all types of engineering of complex systems, sophisticated *risk assessments* are often made within safety engineering and reliability engineering. The nuclear, aerospace, oil, rail and military industries have a long history of dealing with risk assessment.

Any risk management exercise must first carry out risk assessment. The analytical steps followed are more or less in this order: Identify, characterize threats; assess the vulnerability of critical assets to specific threats; determine the risk (i.e. the expected likelihood and consequences of specific types of attacks on specific assets); identify ways to reduce those risks; prioritize risk reduction measures based on a strategy.

In project management, risk assessment is an integral part of the risk management plan, studying the probability, the impact and the effect of every known risk on the project, as well as the corrective action to take that risk. Megaprojects have been shown to be particularly risky in terms of finance, safety and social and environmental impacts.

Review questions

1. How risk perception is different from risk probability? Give examples of risk perception in different fields of activity.
2. Explain Delayed and Immediate Risk by giving examples.
3. Clarify meaning of terms Risk, Hazard, Harm and Uncertainty in connection of project management.
4. What do you understand by Risk Threshold and Risk Appetite? Explain by giving example.
5. What is relationship between Risk Appetite and Risk Threshold? When defining Risk Appetite, what type of total risk exposure' should be considered.
6. Explain Risk Management process and Sources of Risk. What is Process of Risk Identification?
7. How risk assessment is quantified? What are methods of Risk Assessment in various fields of activity?
8. Explain type of Risks in IT risk Field.

15 Engineering Design for Safety and Reliability

Learning objectives

In this chapter you will learn about

- Engineers role for safety in engineering designs and workplace safety
- Reliability, product safety and liability, categories of claims on product liability
- Engineers responsibility, criteria for safe designs, elements of safety engineering
- Design for reliability, reliability assessment, elements of reliability engineering
- Distinction between reliability and quality, mission (operational) reliability

15.1 Safety Issue in Engineering Designs

Let us take an example to illustrate the gravity of engineer's responsibility for safety and risk. On January 16, 2003 the Columbia spacecraft lifted off at Kennedy Space Center, USA for a 16-day mission in space. Columbia had a crew of seven persons and was scheduled to conduct numerous scientific experiments and return to Earth on February 1, 2003. Only 81.7 seconds after lift-off, a briefcase-size piece of insulating foam that covered the large external tank broke off and hit the leading edge of the orbiter's left wing. Unknown to the Columbia crew or the ground support staff, the foam knocked a small hole in the leading edge of the wing. For NASA engineers foam strike was a known problem and they felt that it could not cause significant damage and was not a safety-of-flight issue.

Upon re-entry into the earth's atmosphere, destruction of the spacecraft began when the bottom surface of the left wing began to cave upwards into the interior of the wing, finally causing Columbia to go out of control and disintegrate. The entire crew along with the spacecraft was lost.

This tragic event had many striking similarities with the Challenger disaster 17 years earlier. World over many disasters in the sky and also on ground have occurred which were due to technical design or operational faults. These disasters illustrate many of the issues surrounding the notion of responsibility in the engineering profession. The concept of responsibility is many-faceted. As a notion of accountability, it may be applied to individual engineers, teams of engineers, divisions or units within the organizations, or even organizations themselves. It may focus primarily on legal liabilities, job-defined roles or moral accountability. Our focus in this chapter will be mainly on the moral accountability of individual engineers and other connected facets of responsibility. As professionals, engineers are expected to commit themselves to high standards of moral accountability and conduct.

Safety is also linked with professional duties. In megaprojects engineers, city designers, architects, planners, etc. in their professional responsibility have to ensure measures of safety for infrastructure, operational process and equipment as well as the safety of working staff from incidents which may take all of sudden. Safety is quite precise term because in many cases we can readily distinguish a safe design from an unsafe one. Risk is a key element in any engineering design. However, it is quite difficult to design anything to be completely risk free. In megaprojects, always there is some risk during execution, operation and finishing the scheduled work.

15.1.1 Engineers Duty for Safe Designs

While involved in design activity an engineer should also be concerned about following factors along with safety issue.
- **Ethical Responsibility:** Any product must be safe for all those who are using and working in the same environment. Value of human life is always more than any amount of money. Engineers must be watchful on the design aspect of any product being used in their knowledge or the project. He/ She should have courage to admit any mistake happened in the design and point out likelihood of all subsequent problems due to faulty design
- **Well-being of Employer**: An employee engineer while designing a product should always keep in mind that design should be perfect and he/she should do everything possible to prevent potential lawsuits on the company. Remember that damage to reputation of employer or the company is costlier.
- **Well-being of Engineer**: Whenever an engineer designs something, he/she carries a risk to his career. Too many small mistakes or one big one can cause you to lose the job. For example, an engineer lost his license to practice structural engineering after collapse of a hotel building.

15.1.2 OSHA and Workplace Safety

OSHA: You have the right to a safe workplace. The occupational safety and health act of 1970 (OSH Act of USA) was passed to prevent workers from being killed or seriously harmed at work. The law requires employers to provide their employees with working conditions that are free of known dangers. The act created the occupational safety and health administration (OSHA) in 1971, which sets and enforces protective workplace safety and health standards. OSHA also provides information, training and assistance to workers and employers. Workers may file a complaint to have OSHA inspect their workplace if they believe that their employer is not following OSHA standards or that there are serious hazards.

15.2 Safety and Reliability

Safety is not reliability. If a medical device fails, it should fail safely and other alternatives will be available to the surgeon to cope with the failure. But if an aircraft fly-by-wire control system fails, there is no backup. Hence it must be designed both for safety and reliability. Similarly, electrical power grids are designed for both safety and reliability. Telephone systems are designed for reliability.

Probabilistic risk assessment has created a close relationship between safety and reliability. *Component reliability*, generally defined in terms of *component failure rate* and external *event probability;* both are used in quantitative safety assessment methods such as FTA *(fault tree analysis)*. Related probabilistic methods are used to determine system *mean time between failure* (MTBF), *system availability* or *probability of mission success or failure*. *Reliability analysis* has a broader scope than *safety analysis* in which non-critical failures are considered. On the other hand, higher failure rates are considered acceptable for non-critical systems.

Safety generally cannot be achieved through component reliability alone. Catastrophic failure probabilities of 10^{-9} per hour correspond to the failure rates of very simple components such as resistors or capacitors. A complex system containing hundreds or thousands of components might be able to achieve a MTBF of 10,000 to 100,000 hours, meaning it would fail at 10^{-4} or 10^{-5} per hour. If a system failure is catastrophic, usually the only practical way to achieve 10^{-9} per hour failure rate is through redundancy. Two redundant systems with independent failure modes, each having an MTBF of 100,000 hours, could achieve a failure rate on the order of 10^{-10} per hour because of the multiplication rule for independent events.

The typical approach is to arrange the system so that ordinary single failures cause the mechanism to shut down in a safe way (for nuclear power plants, this is termed a passively safe design, although more than ordinary failures are covered). Alternately, if the system contains a hazard source such as a battery or rotor, then it may be possible to remove the hazard from the system so that its failure modes cannot be catastrophic. The U.S. Department of Defense Standard Practice for System Safety (MIL–STD–882) places the highest priority on elimination of hazards through design selection.

One of the most common *Fail-Safe* systems is the overflow tube in baths and kitchen sinks. If the valve sticks open rather than causing an overflow and damage, the tank spills into an overflow. Another common example is that in an elevator the cable supporting the car keeps spring-loaded brakes open. If the cable breaks, the brakes grab rails and the elevator cabin does not fall.

15.3 Responsibility and Liability of Unsafe Designs

In engineering, "... *the one choice engineers, designers and their employers no longer have is whether or not to pursue safety goals. To ignore or pay only lip service to safety can jeopardize corporate survival*" (Kolb and Rose, 1980; Florman, 2002, pp.2).

An industrial firm can be held liable for defective product design, defective manufacture, inadequate labeling and faulty packaging. Liability losses can be suffered by companies that fail to keep proper records of product sales and distribution or fail to keep adequate records of project failures and customer complaints.

Product safety is no longer a matter of conscience and good will. It is a professional specialty founded in knowledge of prediction techniques, *fault tree analysis, failure mode effects analysis* and the *operator-design interface*. When it comes to establishing liability all worthy intentions no longer count. Tort law traditionally required that negligence be proved as a *proximate* cause of an injury. But, since the 1960s, courts have been imposing *strict liability* for injuries caused by dangerous products whether or not negligence was involved. Similarly, industrial pollution is not mainly a matter of ethical integrity as it once was earlier. Most of the major environmental protection laws include provisions that permit private suits to pull the culprit tothe court. In addition to penalties that can be imposed by government agencies the increasingly powerful environmental organizations also have easy access to the courts.

Attempt to fix the responsibilities and liabilities in new fields of activities are becoming difficult. For example, in the *information age* there are many problems which are elusive to solutions, because of uncertainty to understand or define the problem or who should control the Internet and how, because these are still too new to predict their resolution. This is also the case with genetic engineering, terrorism and other technological problems that seem to arise almost daily. But it is clear that all of our old assumptions and beliefs including engineering ethics will be subjected to continual challenges and reevaluations.

It must be remembered that from liability point of view, a court is not always concerned with the stupidity of the user and may pass severe strictures and impose heavy penalty against defaulters, if it feels that a product was not properly defined or designed; and placing a warning label on products is not sufficient. Thus, engineers must do the extra engineering works required to produce a safe design.

15.4 Product Safety and Liability for consumers

We demand safe products and services but we also realize that we may have to pay for this safety. Absolute safety, in the senses of (a) entirely risk-free activities and products, or (b) a degree of safety that satisfies all individuals or groups under all conditions is neither attainable nor affordable. Yet it is important that we come to some understanding of what we mean by safety and what is associated liability for unsafe products.

Product liability is the area of law in which manufacturers, distributors, suppliers, retailers and others, who make products available to the public; and all of them are held responsible for the injuries those products cause to consumer. Although the word *product* has broad connotations, product liability as an area of law is traditionally limited to products in the form of tangible personal property.

It is very important for the entrepreneur to assess their product before marketing them they comply with all the regulations under the relevant consumer product safety act of the country. In India consumer's *right to safety* is governed by the consumer protection act 1986, where the consumer right is referred to as "... *right to be protected against marketing of goods and services which are hazardous to life and property*" (Fernando, 2011, pp. 305). It is applicable to specific areas like healthcare, pharmaceuticals and food processing etc. This right is spread across the wide range of products and services that can have a serious effect on the health of the consumers or their well-being viz. automobiles, housing, domestic appliances, travel, etc. In USA, the consumer product safety act was passed in 1972 and created a five-member commission that has the power to prescribe safety standards for more than 15,000 types of consumer products.

In addition to setting safety standards for products, the commission also has a great deal of responsibility and power to identify what it considers to be substantial hazardous and bar those products which it considers unsafe. It is especially active in recognizing whether possible product defects may be hazardous to consumers. When this is the case, the commission will request the manufacturer in writing to take corrective action.

The act was amended and signed into law in 1990. The amended law establishes stricter guidelines, for reporting product defects and any injury or death resulting from such defects, which could be subjected to fine up to $1.25 million for product liability settlements or court awards.

Any new product that is responsible for the entrepreneur's entry into a business should be assessed to ascertain whether it falls under the consumer product safety act. If it does, the entrepreneur will have to follow the appropriate procedures to ensure that he/she or she has met all the necessary requirements.

15.4.1 Problems of launching New Products

Product liability problems are complex and continue to be an important consideration for entrepreneurs. Changes in the legislation were felt necessary to address many longtime concerns of businesses; such as the amount of punitive damages allowed in certain cases; and the application of the product liability laws to durable goods that have been in use for more than 15 years.

Changes in the global market have also contributed to the need for reform. Technology is moving at a fast pace and new products are being put in market by startup companies. Startup companies do not have track record of product and safety issues. Risk managers claim that without new reform legislation, start-up companies that do not have a product liability track record, may not have this type of legal liability coverage.

Categories of claims regarding Product Liability
1. **Manufacturing defect:** Manufacturing defects are those that occur in the manufacturing process and usually involve poor-quality materials or shoddy workmanship.
2. **Design defect**: Design defects occur where the product design is inherently dangerous or useless (and hence defective) no matter how carefully manufactured; this may be demonstrated either by showing that the product fails to satisfy ordinary consumer expectations as to what constitutes a safe product, or that the risks of the product outweigh its benefits.
3. **Negligence**: It extends to all parts of the production and marketing process. It involves being negligent in the way a product is presented to a client, such as using deficient labels, false advertising and so on.
4. **Strict liability**: Rather than focus on the behavior of the manufacturer (as in negligence), strict liability claims focus on the product itself. Under strict liability, the manufacturer is liable if the product is defective, even if the manufacturer was not negligent in making that product defective.

Chapter 15: Engineering Design and Safety 277

5. **Breach of warranty**: Warranties are statements by a manufacturer or seller concerning a product during a commercial transaction. Warranty claims commonly require priority between the injured party and the manufacturer or seller i.e. they must be dealing with each other directly. Various implied warranties cover those expectations common to all products (e.g., that a tool is not unreasonably dangerous when used for its proper purpose), unless specifically disclaimed by the manufacturer or the seller. Consumers may sue if advertising or information overstates the benefits of a product or if the product does not perform as stated.
6. **Misrepresentation:** This occurs when advertising, labels or other information misrepresent material facts concerning the character or quality of the product. The best protection against product liability is to produce safe products and to warn consumers of any potential hazards. It is impossible to expect zero defects, so entrepreneurs should be sensitive to what kinds of product liability problems may occur.

15.5 Engineering guidelines for Safe Designs

Since safety is an essential aspect of our duties as engineers, how can we be sure that our designs are safe? For safe designs, the following design process should be adopted.

1. Define the problem: includes determining the needs, requirements and the constraints.
2. Generate several solutions
3. Analyze each solution to determine the pros and cons of each. Examine in detail what is involved in each to determine the consequences of each design solution and find out whether it solves the problem. Critically test the results of each probable solution.
4. Select the best results for further analysis on following aspects.

Four criteria to ensure a Safe Design:
1. The minimum requirement is that a design must comply with the applicable laws. This requirement should be easy to meet since legal standards for product safety are generally well known and are published and easily accessible.
2. An acceptable design must meet the standard of accepted engineering practice. You cannot create a design that is less safe than what everyone else in the profession understands to be acceptable in contemporary practice. To address this issue an engineer must continually upgrade his/her skills with information on the current state of the art in the field.

3. Alternative design solutions as suggested above, which are potentially safe and must be explored if required. This requirement is somewhat difficult to meet since it requires a certain amount of creativity in seeking safe alternative solutions. The best way to know if your design is the safest available, is to compare it with other potential designs.
4. Finally, the engineer must attempt to foresee potential misuses of the product by the consumer and must design to avoid these problems. Again, this requires a certain amount of creativity and research. An engineer should execute designs in such a way as to protect even someone who misuses the product.

For any engineering design problems, there is rarely, if ever, a uniquely correct solution or response, or indeed, any predetermined number of correct responses. *Absolutely safe* is not an attainable engineering goal. Furthermore, safety, affordability, efficiency and usability are different and often competing criteria for a good product. For example, one of the most common conflicts faced by engineers is the one (like safety and reliability vs. price) in which an engineer's obligations to an employer seem to conflict with obligations to the public. However, these dual obligations are stated in NSPE code of engineering codes.

To be ethically and professionally responsible, an engineer should spend a considerable amount of time thinking about his options. He/ She should attempt to find a course of action that honors both his obligation to protect the public and his obligation to his employer. It is also completely legitimate for the engineer to try for protecting and promoting his own career insofar as he/she can, while still protecting the public.

15.5.1 Safety Engineering

Safety engineering is an engineering discipline which assures that engineered systems provide acceptable levels of safety. It is strongly related to systems engineering, industrial engineering and the subset system-safety engineering. Task of Safety engineering is to ensure that life-critical systems behave as needed, even when some components fail during its use.

- **Analysis Techniques** can be split into two categories: qualitative and quantitative methods. Both approaches share the goal of finding causal dependencies between a hazard on system level and failures of individual components. Qualitative approaches focus on the question: what must go wrong such that a system hazard may occur? While quantitative methods aim at providing estimations about probabilities, rates and/or severity of consequences.

    Traditionally, safety analysis techniques rely solely on skills and expertise of the safety engineer. In the last decade model-based approaches have become prominent. In contrast to traditional methods, model-based techniques try to derive relationships between causes and consequences from some sort of modeling of the system.

- **Traditional methods for Safety Analysis:** The two most common fault modeling techniques are called *failure modern defects analysis* and *fault tree analysis*. These techniques are just ways of finding problems and of making plans to cope with failures as in probabilistic risk assessment. One of the earliest complete studies using this technique on a commercial nuclear plant was the WASH-1400 study, also known as the reactor safety study or the Rasmussen report.
- **Failure Modes and Effects Analysis (FMEA)** is a bottom-up inductive analytical method which may be performed at either the functional or piece-part level. For functional FMEA failure modes are identified for each function in a system or equipment item, usually with the help of a functional block diagram. For piece-part FMEA, failure modes are identified for each piece-part component (such as a valve, connector, resistor, or diode). The effects of the failure mode are described and assigned a probability based on the failure rate and failure mode ratio of the function or component.
- **Fault Tree Analysis (FTA)** is a top-down deductive analytical method. In FTA, initiating primary events such as component failures, human errors and external events are traced through Boolean logic gates to an undesired top event such as an aircraft crash or nuclear reactor core melt etc. The intent is to identify ways to make top events less probable and verify that the safety goals have been achieved.

15.5.2 Design for Reliability

Reliability design begins with the development of a *system model*. Reliability and availability models use block diagrams and fault tree analysis to provide a graphical means of evaluating the relationships between different parts of the system. These models may incorporate predictions-based failure rates taken from historical data. While the predictions (input data) are often not accurate in an absolute sense, they are valuable to assess relative differences in design alternatives. Maintainability parameters for example MTTR (Mean-Time-To-Repair) are other inputs for these models.

One of the most important design techniques is redundancy. This means that if one part of the system fails there is an alternate success path, such as a backup system available to allow uninterrupted function. The reason why this is the ultimate design choice is related to the fact that high confidence reliability evidence for new parts/ items is often not available or extremely expensive to obtain. By creating redundancy together with a high level of failure monitoring and the avoidance of common cause failures, even a system with relative bad single channel (part) reliability, can be made highly reliable (mission reliability) on system level.

Another design technique to prevent failures is called *physics of failure*. This technique relies on understanding the physical static and dynamic failure mechanisms. It accounts for variation in load, strength and stress leading to failure at high level of detail, possible with use of modern Finite-Element-Method (FEM) software programs that may handle complex geometries and mechanisms like creep, stress relaxation, fatigue and probabilistic design (Monte Carlo simulations / DOE). The material or component can be redesigned to reduce the probability of failure and to make it more robust against variation.

Another common design technique is *component derating*. Selecting components whose tolerance significantly exceeds the expected stress, as using a heavier gauge wire that exceeds the normal specification for the expected electrical current.

Another effective way to deal with unreliability issues is, to perform analysis to be able to predict degradation, and being able to prevent unscheduled down events/ failures from occurring. RCM (Reliability Centered Maintenance) programs can be used for this.

15.5.3 Techniques of Reliability Assessment

Many engineering techniques are used in reliability risk assessments, such as *reliability hazard analysis, failure mode and effects analysis* (FMEA), *fault tree analysis* (FTA), *reliability centered maintenance, material stress and wear calculations, fatigue and creep analysis, human error analysis, reliability testing*, etc. Because of the large number of reliability techniques, their expense and the varying degrees of reliability required for different situations, most projects develop a reliability program plan to specify the reliability tasks that will be performed for that specific system.

Consistent with the creation of database of safety cases, the goal of reliability assessments is to provide a robust set of qualitative and quantitative evidence, that use of a component or system will not be associated with unacceptable risk.

15.6 Reliability Engineering

Reliability is defined as the probability that a device will perform its intended function during a specified period of time under stated conditions. Mathematically, this may be expressed as

Chapter 15: Engineering Design and Safety

$$R(t) = P\{T > t\} = \int_t^\infty f(t)$$

Where, $f(t)$ is the failure probability density function and is the length of the period of time (which is assumed to start from time zero?).

There are a few key elements of this definition:
1. **Reliability is predicated on *intended function*:** Generally, this is taken to mean operation without failure. However, even if no individual part of the system fails, but the system as a whole does not do what was intended, then it is still charged against the system reliability. The system specifications and functional requirement is the criterion against which reliability is measured.
2. **Reliability applies to a specified period of time:** In practical terms, this means that a system has a specified chance that it will operate without failure before time. Reliability engineering ensures that components and materials will meet the requirements during the specified time.
3. **Reliability is restricted to operation under stated (or explicitly defined) conditions:** This constraint is necessary because it is impossible to design a system for unlimited conditions. A Mars Rover will have different specified conditions than a family car. The operating environment must be addressed during design and testing.

15.6.1 Parameters of System Reliability

Quantitative Requirements are specified using reliability parameters. The most common reliability parameter is the Mean-Time-To-Failure (MTTF), which can also be specified as the failure rate; this is expressed as a frequency or conditional probability density function (PDF) or the number of failures during a given period. These parameters may be useful for higher system levels and systems that are operated frequently, such as most vehicles, machinery, and electronic equipment. Reliability increases as the MTTF increases. The MTTF is usually specified in hours but can also be used with other units of measurement such as miles or cycles.

In other cases, reliability is specified as the probability of *Mission-Success*. For example, reliability of a scheduled aircraft flight can be specified as a dimensionless probability or a percentage, as in system safety engineering.

A special case of mission success is the single-shot device or system which only operates once. Examples include automobile airbags, thermal batteries and missiles. Single-shot reliability is specified as a probability of one-time success. Single-shot missile reliability may be specified as a requirement for the probability of a hit.

For repairable systems it is obtained from failure rate and Mean-Time-To-Repair (MTTR) and test interval. In addition to system level requirements, a separate reliability requirement may be specified for critical subsystems.

The desired level of statistical confidence also plays a role in reliability testing. Statistical confidence is increased by increasing either the test time or the number of items tested. Reliability test plans are designed to achieve the specified reliability at the specified confidence level with the minimum number of test units and test time.

15.6.2 Accelerated Testing

The purpose of accelerated life testing (ALT test) is to induce field failure in the laboratory at a much faster rate by providing a harsher, but nonetheless representative environment. In such a test the product is expected to fail in the lab just as it would have failed in the field, but in much less time. The main objective of an accelerated test is either of the following: to discover failure modes or to predict the normal field life from the high-level stress testing and survival in the lab.

Stress testing is a form of deliberately intense or thorough testing used to determine the stability of a given system or entity. It involves testing beyond normal operational capacity, often to a breaking point in order to observe the results. Reasons can include:
- To determine breaking points or safe usage limits
- To confirm intended specifications are being met
- To determine modes of failure (how exactly a system fails)
- To test stable operation of a part or system outside standard usage

The term *stress* may have a more specific meaning in certain industries, such as material sciences. Therefore, stress testing may sometimes have a technical meaning – For example fatigue testing for materials.

15.6.3 Software Reliability

Software reliability is a special aspect of reliability engineering. System reliability, by definition includes all parts of the system including hardware, software, supporting infrastructure (including critical external interfaces), operators and procedures. Traditionally reliability engineering focuses on critical hardware parts of the system. After computerization of many products, systems, Internet, communication networks, business operations, etc. software has become an increasingly critical part of most of the present-day systems.

There are significant differences in the behavior of software and hardware. In most of the hardware unreliability is the result of a component or material failure that results in misappropriate functioning of the system. Repairing or replacing the hardware component restores the system to its original operating state.

However, software does not fail in the same sense that hardware fails. Instead software unreliability is the result of unanticipated results of software operations. Even relatively small software programs can have astronomically large combinations of inputs and states that are infeasible to exhaustively test. Software reliability engineering must take this into account.

15.6.4 Reliability Engineering *vs.* Safety Engineering

Reliability engineering differs from safety engineering with respect to the kind of hazards that are considered. Reliability engineering is in the end only concerned with cost. It relates to all Reliability hazards that could transform into incidents with a particular level of loss of revenue for the company or the customer. These may cost us due to loss of production and due to system unavailability, unexpected high or low demands for spares, repair costs, man hours, multiple time redesigns, interruptions on normal production (e.g. due to high repair times or due to unexpected demands for non-stocked spares) and many other indirect costs.

Safety engineering on the other hand, is more specific and regulated. It relates to only very specific and system safety hazards that could potentially lead to severe accidents and is primarily concerned with loss of life, loss of equipment or environmental damage. It deals with unwanted dangerous events (for life, property and environment) in the same sense as reliability engineering but does normally not directly look at cost and is not concerned with repair actions after failure/ accidents (on system level). Another difference is the level of impact of failures on society and the control of governments. Safety engineering is often strictly controlled by governments (e.g. nuclear, aerospace, defense, railways, and oil industries).

Furthermore, safety engineering and reliability engineering may even have contradicting requirements. This relates to system level architecture choices. For example, in train signal control systems, it is common practice to use a fail-safe system design concept. In this concept the wrong-side failure needs to be fully controlled to an extreme low failure rate. These failures are related to possible severe effects, like frontal collisions ($2\times$ GREEN lights). Systems are designed in a way that the far majority of failures will simply result in a temporary or total loss of signals or open contacts of relays and generate RED lights for all trains, which is the safe state. All trains are stopped immediately. This fail-safe logic might unfortunately lower the reliability of the system. The reason for this is the higher risk of false tripping as any full or temporary, intermittent failure is quickly latched in a shut-down (safe) state.

15.7 Reliability *vs.* Quality

Six-Sigma is a set of techniques and tools for manufacturing process improvement. It was developed by Motorola in 1986. Today it is used in many industrial sectors. Six-Sigma seeks to improve the quality output of process by identifying and removing the causes of defects (errors) and minimizing variability in manufacturing and business processes.

Six-Sigma, having its roots in manufacturing and reliability engineering, is more related to systems engineering. The system engineering process is a discovery process that is quite unlike a manufacturing process. A manufacturing process is focused on repetitive activities that achieve high quality outputs with minimum cost and time. The system engineering process must begin by discovering the real (potential) problem that needs to be solved.

The everyday usage term *quality of a product* is loosely taken to mean its inherent degree of excellence. In industry, this is made more precise by defining quality to be "conformance to requirements at the start of use". Assuming the product specifications adequately capture customer (or rest of system) needs, the quality level of these parts can now be precisely measured by the fraction of units shipped that meet the detailed product specifications.

From reliability point of view the question arises that how many of these systems still meet function and fulfill the needs after a week of operation? What performance losses occurred? Did full system failure occur? What happens after the end of a one-year warranty period? And what happens after 50 years (common lifetime for aircraft, trains, nuclear systems, etc.)? That is where *reliability* comes in.

Quality is a snapshot at the start of life and mainly related to control of lower level product specifications; and reliability is (as part of systems engineering) more like a *system-level-motion-picture* of the day-by-day operation for many years. Time-Zero defects are manufacturing mistakes that escaped final test (i.e. final stage quality control checks and test). The additional defects due to worn out items and systems, by general wear, fatigue or corrosion mechanisms, debris accumulation or due to maintenance induced failures that appear over a time of use, are *reliability defects* or reliability fallout. These reliability issues may just occur due to inherent design issues, which may have nothing to do with non-conformance against product specifications.

Quality is therefore related to manufacturing and reliability is more related to the validation of sub-system or due to inherent design and life cycle issue of system or part of it.

15.8 Summary

Safety Issue in Engineering Design: Like Columbia and Challenger spacecraft disasters, many disasters world over have occurred in the sky and also on ground which were due to technical design or operational faults. These disasters illustrate many of the issues surrounding the notion of responsibility in the engineering profession. As a notion of accountability, it may be applied to individual engineers, teams of engineers, divisions or units within organizations or even organizations themselves. This chapter is focused mainly on the moral accountability and responsibility of individual engineers. While involved in design activity, an engineer should also be concerned about ethics, well-being of employer and well-being of engineer himself along with safety issue. Safety is also linked with professional duties. In megaprojects, engineers, city designers, architects, planners, etc. have to ensure measures of safety for infrastructure, operational process, equipment as well as the working staff from incidents which may take all of sudden.

Safety and Reliability: *Safety* is not *Reliability*. If a medical device fails it should fail safely and other alternatives will be available to the surgeon to cope with the failure. But if in an aircraft fly-by-wire control system fails, there is no backup; therefore it should be designed for both safety and reliability. Electrical power grids are designed for both safety and reliability. Telephone systems are designed for reliability. Probabilistic risk assessment has created a close relationship between safety and reliability. Safety generally cannot be achieved through component reliability alone.

When substitution of additional equipment is impractical (usually because of expense) then the least expensive form of solution is often to make design *inherently fail-safe*. That is to change the system design so that its failure modes are not catastrophic. Inherent fail-safe features are common in medical equipment, traffic and railway signals, communications equipment and safety equipment.

Safety and Product Liability: *Product safety* is no longer a matter of conscience and good will. It is a professional specialty founded in knowledge of prediction techniques like, fault tree analysis, failure modes effects analysis and the operator-design interface. *Product liability* is the area of law in which s, distributors, suppliers, retailers and others who make products available to the public are held responsible for the injuries which those products cause. Categories of claims regarding product liability are viz. manufacturing defects, design defects, negligence, strict liability, breach of warranty and misrepresentation of facts.

Engineer's Responsibility for Safe Designs: Safety in design is ensured through design process by first defining the problem then generating several solutions and analyzing each solution to determine the pros and cons of each and identifying the solution which solves the problem effectively. Four criteria used to choose the safe design are:1) the designs must comply with the applicable laws; 2) an acceptable design must meet the standard of accepted engineering practice;3) alternative designs as suggested above which are potentially safer must be explored; 4) the engineer must attempt to foresee potential misuses of the product by the consumer and must design to avoid these problems.

Safety Engineering: Safety engineering is an engineering discipline which assures that engineered systems provide acceptable levels of safety. It is strongly related to systems engineering, industrial engineering and the subset System-Safety engineering. Analysis techniques used are split into two categories - qualitative and quantitative methods. Qualitative approaches focus on the question: What must go wrong, such that a system hazard may occur? While quantitative methods aim at providing estimations about probabilities, rates and/or severity of consequences. In traditional methods for safety analysis, two most common fault modeling techniques called *failure mode and effects analysis* and *fault tree analysis* are used. These techniques are just ways of finding problems and of making plans to cope with failures, as in probabilistic risk assessment.

Design for Reliability: Reliability is defined as the probability that a device will perform its intended function during a specified period of time under stated conditions. The most common reliability parameter for higher system levels is the mean time to failure (MTTF), which is the failure rate or the number of failures during a given period. Reliability increases as the MTTF increases. For repairable systems, reliability is obtained from failure rate and mean-time-to-repair (MTTR).

Reliability design begins with the development of a (system) model. Reliability and availability models use block diagrams and fault tree analysis to provide a graphical means of evaluating the relationships between different parts of the system. One of the most important design techniques to improve reliability is redundancy. Another common design technique is component derating.

Reliability engineering differs from safety engineering with respect to the kind of hazards that are considered. Reliability engineering is in the end only concerned with cost. Safety engineering, on the other hand, is more specific and regulated. It relates to only very specific system safety hazards that could potentially lead to severe accidents and is primarily concerned with loss of life, loss of equipment, or environmental damage.

Reliability versus Quality: The everyday usage term *quality of a product* is loosely taken to mean its inherent degree of excellence. In industry, this is made more precise by defining quality to be "... *conformance to requirements at the start of use*". From reliability point of view, the question arises that how many of these systems still meet function and fulfill the needs after few days or weeks of operation? What happens after the end of a one-year warranty period? And what happens after 50 years (common lifetime for aircraft, trains, nuclear systems, etc.)? That is where *reliability* comes in.

Review questions

1. Explain what role an engineer plays for safe design. What are other factors which he/she must take care in safe design exercise?
2. How safety and reliability are interconnected in product quality considerations.
3. If safety features in design are not adequate, what are the ramifications? Who bears the liability of unsafe design and how?
4. Legally who are responsible for bearing liability of unsafe products? What are the categories of claims regarding product liability?
5. What are the criteria to ensure a safe design? What is the design process to ensure a safe design?
6. What are the analysis techniques employed in "Safety Engineering" field?
7. What is of reliability engineering? Explain its purpose, scope and methods used to predict reliability of any product.
8. What are parameters used to express reliability of a product? What reliability measures are used to predict software reliability?
9. Write a short note on Reliability engineering *vs.* safety engineering. Distinguish between basic reliability and mission (operational) reliability.
10. Explain relationship between reliability and quality of a product.

16 Risk Benefit Analysis and Accidents

Learning objectives

In this chapter you will learn about

- Risk and cost benefits analysis, technology evaluation and alternate solutions
- Complexity in evaluation of future risks and benefits of large engineering projects
- Focus beyond risk-benefit analysis and design alternatives for optimum solution
- Major disasters, importance of risk and safety for workers and general public
- Building improved safety features in products of daily use

16.1 Risk-Benefit Analysis

It's a method that helps engineers to analyze risk and determine whether a project should proceed or not. *Risk-Benefit-Analysis* (RBA) is the comparison of the risk of a situation to its related benefits. We accept a certain level of risk in our lives as necessary to achieve certain benefits. We assigned dollar amount for the risks and benefits. Then we select the most favorable ratio between risks and benefits. Thus, a risk-benefit ratio is the ratio of the risk of an action to its potential benefits. Here we must consider that those who are taking the risks are also those who are benefiting by it.

In practice the task of quantifying the risks and benefits and fixing a value in terms of a currency (Rupees or Dollars) is difficult, but still it is a useful technique to evaluate the worth of any new development of drug, a product or undertaking of a project which carries risks to individuals or public at large including environmental impact.

16.2 Technology Evaluation and Risk-Benefit Analysis for New Venture or Product

Nowadays new ventures or products have technology component which are considered a winning factor for start-up companies. Technology evaluation is one of the most significant methodologies in innovation and technology adaptation or transfer, utilized in screening new ideas, assessing innovative or not innovative products and technologies. This helps an organization in examining new ideas, identifying and analyze causes or potential change, develop and plan possible solutions and finally select and implement a proposed technology.

Cost-Benefits-Analysis aims to facilitate decision makers choose between alternative solutions in a way that the chosen alternative is the most cost-effective within the context of budgetary and political considerations. For *risk-benefit-analysis* one should also evaluate the potential risks, fixed costs, operational costs and benefits of the project. Compare the outcomes of two or more alternative *cost-benefit* scenarios of the same project to take appropriate decision.

A risk benefit analysis is necessary for any new venture or product launch to guard against the risk of shortfall of the actual benefits than the projected or estimated benefits. If for instance, a company is launching a new product or service and projected sales of 40 million dollars per year, whereas actual annual sales turn out to be only 30 million dollars, then the benefit shortfall is said to be 25 percent. Sometimes the terms *demand shortfall* or *revenue shortfall* are used instead of *benefit shortfall*.

Without proper planning and analysis, both public and private enterprises can be victim to benefit shortfalls. Prudent planning of new ventures will include the risk of benefit shortfalls in risk assessment and risk management.

The discipline of *benefits realization management* within an organization seeks to identify any benefits shortfall as early as possible in a project or programs delivery in order to allow corrective action to be taken about costs to be controlled and proportionate benefits realized.

16.3 Risk-Benefit Analyses of Large Engineering Projects

Many large projects and especially public works are justified on the basis of a risk-benefit analysis. The questions, to be answered by such a study, are the following: Is the product worth the risks connected with its use? What are the benefits? Do they outweigh the risks?

We are willing to take on certain levels of risk as long as the project (activity, product or system) promises sufficient benefit or gain. If risk and benefit can both be readily expressed in a common set of units (say, lives or rupees), it is relatively easy to carry out a risk-benefit analysis. For example, an inoculation program may produce some deaths, but it is worth the risk if many more lives are saved by suppressing an imminent epidemic.

As there are always some uncertainties associated with large projects, we should know their expected values. Risks may be converted into rupee value by multiplying the magnitude of the potential loss by the probability of its occurrence. Same process can be adopted to work out benefit analysis. The procedure of calculation looks very simple but question arises about who establishes these values, and how?

Further if the benefits are about to be realized in the near future but the risks are far off, we need to convert risks and benefit amounts to common time frame of present values. The question to be answered is how the future to be discounted, for example in terms of say an interest rate, so we can compare their present values?

In large projects, another difficulty is encountered in decision making process if the benefits accrue to one party and the risks are incurred by another party.

16.3.1 Complexity of Risk-Benefit analysis

Many projects or products have multiplicity of objectives in design. It is not only the operations but also weightage, volume, power, reliability, effect on health plus ergonomics, aesthetics considerations, etc. to be considered in design as they all introduce some risk factors. How should one proceed when risks or benefits are composites of these ingredients that cannot be added in a common set of units like rupees? At most, one can compare designs that satisfy some constraints in the form of "rupees not to exceed X, health not to drop below Y" and try to compare aesthetic values with those constraints. Or when all the risks can be expressed and measured in one set of units (*viz.* deaths on the highway) and all the benefits in another (speed of travel), we can employ the ratio of risks to benefits for different designs when comparing the designs.

16.3.2 Engineers to look beyond Risk-Benefit complex

It should be noted that risk-benefit analysis, like cost-benefit analysis, is concerned with the advisability of undertaking a project. When we judge the relative merits of different designs, however, we move away from this concern. Instead, we are dealing with something similar to *cost-effectiveness-analysis*, which raises the question about what design has the greater merit, given that the project is actually to be carried out.

For judging the acceptability of potentially risky projects, there is also a need beyond above considerations, for some commonly agreed-on process on implementation, openness to fresh scrutiny if required, and openness to modification in the project profile based on scrutiny analysis. Engineers must keep in mind the following ethical question: under what conditions someone in society is entitled to impose a risk on someone else, on behalf of a supposed benefit to yet others? Here we must not restrict our thoughts to average risks and benefits, but we should also consider those worst-case scenarios of persons exposed to maximum risks while they reap only Minimum Benefits. Are their rights violated? Are they provided safer alternatives?

16.3.3 Personal and Public Risks

Exposure to personal risk is recognized as a normal aspect of everyday life. We accept a certain level of risk in our lives as necessary to achieve certain benefits. With most of these risks we feel we have some sort of control over the situation. For example, driving an automobile is a risk most people take daily. The controlling factor appears to be perception of their individual ability to manage the risk-creating situation. Analyzing the risk of a situation is, however, very dependent on the individual doing the analysis.

When individuals are exposed to involuntary risk (a risk over which they have no control), they make risk aversion their primary goal. Under these circumstances individuals require the probability of risk to be as much as one thousand times smaller than for the same situation under their perceived control.

Thus, difficulty in assessing personal risks is magnified when we consider involuntary risks. These types of situations arise in many cases like proposal for building a dam, a refinery, a chemical plant, a train track, a power plants, nuclear power plant, etc. where the residents being displaced try to oppose the construction even when they are offered adequate compensation.

Risks and benefits to the public at large are more easily determined because individual differences tend to even out as larger numbers of people are considered. Also, assessment studies relating to technological safety can be conducted more readily in the detached manner of a macroscopic view, as statistical parameters take on greater significance.

The conclusions of risk assessment and cost benefit analysis are quite often disputed by special interest groups. Sometimes risk benefit reports become political and legal issue. However, engineers are not involved in such matters except in the capacity of rendering expert advice or opinion. The engineer's responsibility becomes to be very objective in his judgment and do not misuse or abuse the power and faith of the public on profession.

16.4 Examples of Major Disasters to showcase importance of Risk and Safety concern to Engineers

The concept of control of failures is central to engineering designs, because first and foremost objective of engineering design is avoidance of injurious and accidentsprone failures. Thus, the colossal disasters that do occur are ultimately due to failures of design, but the lessons learned from those disasters can do more to advance engineering knowledge than all the successful machines and structures in the world. Indeed, probability of failures rises in designs in the wake of prolonged success, which encourages designs of safety with lower margins and saving the time and cost. Failures in turn lead to greater safety margins and hence new periods of success. Role of engineering and engineers is to understand how failures can happen and how they can contribute more to advance the technology.

16.4.1 Accidents in Escalator

Escalators are inherently nerve wracking. As an escalator transports a passenger from one floor to the next at about one to two feet per minute, there are many things that can go wrong and prevent the passenger from landing safely on the next floor. Although there are many more elevators than escalators operating in the United States, the injuries involving escalators happen fifteen times more frequently than injuries involving elevators.

Many different types of accidents can happen on escalators that cannot happen on elevators. Escalators do not enclose their travelers while in motion and escalator design includes many different entrapments. The injuries frequently obtained on an escalator include falling accidents, accidents involving shoes or clothing getting caught between the stationary skirt on either side of the moving steps, body parts or clothing getting caught in the comb plate at the stationary platform at the end of the escalator, injuries obtained due to clothing or body parts becoming entrapped in the moving handrail and injuries obtained from missing or broken steps in the escalator.

16.4.2 Chernobyl Nuclear Plant accident (Ukraine-1986)

The Chernobyl disaster was a catastrophic nuclear accident that occurred on April 26, 1986 at the Chernobyl nuclear power plant in Ukraine. An explosion and fire released large quantities of radioactive particles into the atmosphere which spread over much of the western USSR and Europe.

The Chernobyl disaster was the worst nuclear power plant accident in history in terms of cost and casualties. The battle to contain the contamination and avert a greater catastrophe ultimately involved over 500,000 workers and cost an estimated 18 billion rubles. During the accident itself 31 people died and long-term effects such as cancers are still being investigated.

The inquiry team effectively placed the blame on the power plant operators. In their view, the catastrophic accident was caused by gross violations of operating rules and regulations. The probable causes of disaster were the operator's errors due to their lack of knowledge of nuclear reactor physics and engineering along with the lack of experience and training. It is alleged that at the time of the accident the reactor was being operated with many key safety systems turned off, most notably the emergency core cooling system (ECCS), local automatic control system (LAR) and AZ (emergency power reduction system). Personnel had an insufficiently detailed understanding of technical procedures involved with the nuclear reactor and knowingly ignored regulations to speed test completion.

16.4.3 Fukushima Nuclear Disaster (Japan-March 11, 2011)

Following a major earth quake and a 15meter high Tsunami wave of seawater quickly flooded the low-lying rooms in which the emergency generators were housed. The flooded diesel generators failed soon afterwards, resulting in a loss of power to the critical coolant water pumps. Consequently, the failure of power supply and cooling of three Fukushima Daiichi reactors caused a nuclear accident on March 11, 2011. All three cores largely melted in the first three days.

The accident was rated 7(i.e. highest point) on the international nuclear and radiological event scale (INES) due to high radioactive releases over days 4 to 6. Four reactors were written off due to damage in the accident. Apart from cooling, the basic ongoing task was to prevent release of radioactive materials, particularly in contaminated water leaked from the three units. This task became newsworthy in August 2011.

There have been no deaths or cases of radiation sickness from the nuclear accident but over 100,000 people had to be evacuated from their homes to ensure this. Official figures show that there have been well over 1,000 deaths from maintaining the evacuation in contrast to little risk from radiation.

The Fukushima nuclear disaster showed us once again that nuclear reactors are fundamentally dangerous. Not only they do cause significant damage to the environment, but they influenced the health of populations and to national economies, the heavy financial cost of a meltdown is inevitably borne by the public, not by the companies that designed, built and operated the plants. None of the world's 436 nuclear reactors are

Chapter 16: Risk Benefit Analysis and Accidents

immune to human errors, natural disasters or any of the many other serious incidents that could cause a disaster. Millions of people who live near nuclear reactors are at risk.

The lives of hundreds of thousands of people were affected by the Fukushima nuclear disaster, especially the 160,000 who fled their homes because of radioactive contamination.

16.5   Provision for Safe Exits

There will always be failures or disasters as engineers and designers push the boundaries by building taller buildings, longer bridges or by reaching further into space. Each time there is a failure or disaster, changes are made and regulations introduced only to be outstripped by further developments.

It is almost impossible to build a completely safe product or one that will never fail. The best one can do is to assure that when a product fails: a) it will fail safely, b) the product can be abandoned safely, and c) the user can safely escape the product.

Let us refer to these three conditions as *Safe Exit*. It is not obvious who should take the responsibility for providing safe exit. But apart from questions of who will build, install, maintain and pay for a safe exit system; there remains the crucial question of who will recognize the need for a safe exit.

Providing for a *safe exit* is an integral part of the social experimental procedure, in other words, of sound engineering. The experiment is to be carried out without causing bodily or financial harm. If safety is threatened, the experiment must be terminated. The full responsibility cannot fall on the shoulders of a lone engineer but one can expect the engineer to issue warnings when a safe exit does not exist or the experiment must be terminated. The only way one can justify the continuation of an experiment without safe exit is for all participants (including the subjects of the experiment) to have given valid consent for its continuation.

16.5.1   Examples of Safe Exit provisions

Here are some examples of what this might involve. Ships need lifeboats with enough spaces for all passengers and crew members. Buildings need usable fire escapes. The operation of nuclear power plants calls for realistic ways to evacuate nearby communities. The foregoing are examples of need of safe exits for people. Provisions are also needed for safe disposal of dangerous products and materials. Altogether too many truck accidents and train derailments have exposed communities to toxic gases and too many dumps have let toxic wastes get to the groundwater table or into the hands of children. Finally, avoiding system failure might require redundant or alternative means of continuing a process when the original process fails. Examples would be *Backup Systems* for computer-based data banks, air traffic control systems, automated medical treatment systems, or sources of water for firefighting.

Apart from a safety conscious design there must be thorough testing of any potentially dangerous product before it is delivered for use. It is of course necessary that its users have in place procedures for regular maintenance and safety checks. Beyond such measures there should also be in place a) avenues for employees to freely report hazardous conditions regarding the design or the operation of the product without having to resort to whistle-blowing; and b) emergency procedures based on *Human-Factors-Engineering* that considers how people react and interact under conditions of stress.

16.6 Examples of improved Safety in products of daily use

Now-a-day products and articles of human consumption are not only designed with utmost safety and care but also from ergonomics considerations also. Ergonomics demands improved designs of everyday products to make them safer and more efficient. Designs should be user friendly. Designs must also consider anatomy, physiology and psychology to make working and life more comfortable. Ergonomics deals with anything involving people.

Here are few samples to show that safety need not rest on elaborate contingency features. Our life encounters many situations every day, which are safeguarded by proper designs and safety measures. For example,

- **Personal safety during travelling**: To guard against any accident there are provision of seat belts in cars, aero planes and any other fast-moving vehicle for personal safety. Designs of seats are also crash resistant. Air travelling passengers are explained with the use and purpose of safety articles before flight takes off.
- **Child safety in Cars**: In cars there are many provisions like separate car seats for small children which can be fastened on back seats with proper latches. Child has his own separate seat belts to ensure child lock to the seat.
- **Protection from impact of collisions in cars:** Nowadays car designs have provision of air bags. Electrical wiring is such that it will not cause fire in case of an accident.
- **Magnetic door latch**: Introduced on refrigerators to prevent death by asphyxiation of children accidentally trapped in them. The catch in use today permits the door to be opened from the inside

without major effort. It also happens to be cheaper than the older types of latches.
- **The dead-man handle for train drivers**: The dead-man handle used by the engineer (engine driver) to control a train's speed. The train is powered only as long as some pressure is exerted on the handle. If the driver becomes incapacitated and lets it go of the handle, the train stops automatically.

16.7 Summary

Risk-Costs-Benefit analysis: *Risk-benefit* analysis is the comparison of the risk of a situation to its related benefits. People accept a certain level of risk in their lives to achieve certain benefits. Normally risks and benefits are assigned certain rupee or dollar amount to select the most favorable ratio between risks and benefits. Thus, a risk–benefit ratio is the ratio of the risk of an action to its potential benefits.

Now-a-day new ventures or products have technology component also. Technology evaluation is one of the most significant methodologies in innovation and technology adaptation or transfer; utilized in screening new ideas, assessing innovative or not innovative products and technologies. *Cost-benefits* analysis aims to facilitate decision makers choose between alternative solutions, in a way that the chosen alternative is the most cost-effective, within the context of budgetary and political considerations. For risk benefit analysis one should also evaluate the potential risks, fixed costs, operational costs and benefits of the project.

Many large projects, especially public works are justified on the basis of a risk-benefit analysis. People are willing to take on certain levels of risk as long as the project (activity, product, or system) promises sufficient benefit or gain also. For example, an inoculation program may produce some deaths but it is worth the risk if many more lives are saved by suppressing an imminent epidemic.

Risks may be converted into dollar value by multiplying the magnitude of the potential loss by the probability of its occurrence. Further if the benefits are about to be realized in the near future but the risks are far off, we need to convert risks and benefits amounts to common time frame of present values. In large projects difficulty is encountered in decision making process if the benefits accrue to one party and the risks are incurred by another party.

Personal and Public Risks Perception: People voluntarily accept a certain level of risk to achieve certain benefits as they feel about having some sort of control over the situation. When individuals are exposed to involuntary risk (a risk over which they have no control), they make *risk aversion* as their primary goal and demand. Further, they require the probability of risk to be as much as one thousand times smaller than for the same situation which is under their perceived control. Thus, difficulty in assessing personal risks is magnified when we consider involuntary risks. These types of situations arise in many cases like proposal for building a Dam, a refinery, a chemical plant, a train track, a power plants, nuclear power plant, etc. where the residents being displaced try to oppose the construction even when they are offered adequate compensation.

Engineering designs have their first and foremost objective of prevention of failure. Even though the colossal disasters that do occur are ultimately failures of design, but the lessons learned from those disasters, for example, accidents in escalators, accident of Chernobyl (Ukraine 1986) and Fukushima nuclear disaster (Japan, March 2011), do contribute more to advancing engineering knowledge than all the successful machines and structures in the world.

Provision for Safe-Exits: Providing for a Safe-Exit is an integral part of the engineering design procedure, and of sound engineering practice. However, there will always be failures or disasters as engineers and designers push the boundaries of projects and technology, by building taller buildings, longer bridges or by reaching farther into space. It is almost impossible to build a completely safe product or one that will never fail. The best one can do is to assure that when a product fails, it will fail safely and the product can be abandoned safely, and the user can safely escape. For example, safe exit provisions in the operation of nuclear power plants are realistic ways to evacuate people in the plant and nearby communities. Provisions are also needed for safe disposal of dangerous products and materials. Finally avoiding system failure might require redundant or alternative means of continuing a process when the original process fails.

Nowadays products and articles of human consumption are not only designed with utmost safety care but also from ergonomics considerations also. Ergonomics demands improved designs of everyday products to make them safer and more efficient. Designs should be user friendly. Designs must also consider anatomy, physiology and psychology to make working and life more comfortable.

Review questions

1. What is the purpose of risk benefit analysis? How it differs from cost benefit analysis?
2. How future risks can be classified and assessed in big projects. In products having multiplicity of objectives in design, how risk benefit analysis is evaluated?

3. Through an example illustrate personal risk vs. public risks. Why risks and benefits to the public at large are more easily determined, than to personal risks.
4. Giving an example explain what do you understand by safe exit? What are conditions of safe exit provision?
5. Giving some examples, explain how improved safety is built in products of daily use.

Section 5: Corporate Culture, Professionalism, Professional Conflicts, Responsibilities and Rights

17 Corporate Work Culture, Profession, Loyalty and Collegiality

Learning objectives

In this chapter you will learn about

- Conflicting demands and dilemmas of engineers on teamwork in industry
- Defining features of a job, occupation, profession and an Organization
- Collegiality, main features and techniques for achieving collegiality
- Virtue of trustworthiness and loyalty, obligations to loyalty and misguided loyalty

17.1 Need for Culture of Teamwork among Different Departments in Industry

Normally engineers face conflicting demands and dilemmas in their job and responsibilities. On the one hand, engineer's problems are centered on a conflict between professional independence *viz-a-viz* bureaucratic loyalties; on the other hand, conflict also arises about the role of the engineer which sometimes is a patchwork of compromises between professional ideals and business demands. Let us learn from the following example about need of proper work culture in the company and interfacing between management and product/project teams.

17.1.1 Example of execution of a Defense Supply Order

Ministry of Defense placed an order for supply of microwave signal generators on a public-sector company. Engineers did a good technical design and produced three samples of signal generators. The lot passed through internal quality control of the company, complying to all the specifications (technical as well as environmental tests) specified in the contract document with the defense. As per the contract a sample signal generator was submitted to defense inspectors for their evaluation and approval for bulk production clearance. However, in evaluation of the sample signal generator by defense inspectors, it failed to meet technical specifications under environmental test condition of temperature and humidity cycle.

17.1.2 Failure of Design Samples

On investigation, it was noticed that during humidity cycle of environment test, there was lot of rusting of nut and bolts; as well as failure of humidity sealing of frequency generating unit, resulting drift in frequency under high temperature and humid conditions. Ripple content in power supply unit was higher than specifications. On review of internal test plan and procedures adopted, it was found that concerned engineers noticed frequency drift, but kept on fine tuning time-to-time to record it within the limit of permitted deviation. In environment test some other short cuts were applied to reduce the stress on the generator. Hardware of nuts and bolts got rusted because of poor quality of stainless steel hardware. Technicians (not engineers) have not properly sealed and tightened frequency generation unit, which resulted in water accumulation inside the unit (due to breathing effect) during humid environment testing, which resulted drift in frequency. Further, all components used in the system were not of military grade. PCBs were not lacquered to protect from humidity, etc. In some total, the generator was perfectly working in normal room temperature but showed drift in performance during temperature and humidity cycle tests because of poor workmanship, manipulations of test parameters during environment testing and use of commercial grade components and not military grade components.

17.1.3 Design Failure Analysis

In the internal inquiry conducted by the company following facts came out:
1. Since lot size was small, production team decided to use, as far as possible, components available in the stocks within the departmental stores, which were not military grade components.
2. Purchase department also bungled in procurement of remaining components disregarding military grade requirement and procured nuts and bolts of inferior quality of steel as quantity of requirement was very small.
3. Technicians were not told about good sealing requirement of frequency generator unit. Although all the concerned departments were very enthusiastic to deliver/clear the items from their respective workstations at the earliest with expectation of

appreciation from the management but missing focused attention on test plans and assembly procedure.

Investigations also revealed following deficiencies/ lacunae in the whole process of sample production

1. Defense requirement was not adequately translated by design teams in terms of internal design parameters and process document of specifications at component level, subsystem level and assembly level.
2. Quality control department did not participate in design review meetings thinking their job is in the end to check the final product.
3. Purchase department focused on cheap and quick procurement of components.
4. Intermediate check points during assembly were not identified.
5. Internal quality control focused more on technical performance, and test of temperature and humidity cycle was performed for one cycle rather than 3 cycles as required under standard procedures.
6. From management side, there was pressure to get defense approval as fast as possible so that production of signal generators can be completed within stipulated delivery schedule.

However, failure in defense tests delayed the whole program causing losses to management as well as embarrassment with Ministry of Defense.

17.1.4 Deficiencies of Organizational Work Culture

Operationally it was failure of engineers and managers of various departments in following aspects: a) Lack of professional approach in their job performance. An engineer or manager should not dilute his professional responsibility towards management and client. Quality, accuracy, precision and perfection must be clearly visible in their operations; b) Lack of teamwork for the whole project. Each department worked independently within their role and responsibility (as perceived by them). There was lack of holistic approach for success of samples production and approval; and c) Lack of project approach where specifications, process, required documentation and associated time frames could have been chalked out for each phase (milestones) of development and production process of the samples. Frequent review meetings with all concerned departments were a must for smooth sailing of the whole project.

Management could not take any action on engineers and managers because failure of sample reflected on poor internal work culture for professional grade products in contrast to commercial grade products. There was lack of critical analysis of design parameters and understanding of the customer requirement. Even though all the engineers and managers were loyal towards management in doing their jobs expeditiously with commitment, but they were working as individual and not as a team. Their concern for management was high and concern about the client was at lower pedestal. Possibly they are driven by desires to look good to management by quickly passing over the job from their section to next stage- thus trying to become an efficient performer.

In the above example management identified failure of engineers and managers to deliver the goods, due to prevailing internal work culture. The message of this example is to emphasize about the moral obligation of any corporate body to evolve internal work culture which is in tune with their chosen market segment. This requires fine-tuned working culture and internal climate for efficient operations of the whole organization. Management should be explicitly concerned about, not only of internal working, but also about their clients, suppliers and outside support system. This raises question about what are defining feature of corporate culture, so that the organization could be efficient and effective in its operations. These features are mentioned below.

17.2 Defining Features of an Organization

An organization should have:
1. **Clearly defined responsibilities**: For all the stakeholders of the company like employees, customers, distributors, etc., responsibilities should be defined for each job or functions. Ensure that corporate code of ethics is widely propagated and understood throughout the spectrum of management, administration, managers and employees alike.
2. **Corporate code of ethics:** Ensure that corporate code of ethics is in tune with professional code of ethics for the particular industry along with statutory guidelines. The code of ethics is widely published. Ethical responsibilities are defined for all departments and layers of management and made part of job description.
3. **Adherence to code of ethics by Top management**: Management must demonstrate explicit adherence to code of ethics, and provide backup support to the professionals who stick to the code in word and spirit. Announcements are made time to time to remind employees about the importance management places on professional conduct as per code of ethics. Brochures of code of ethics are provided to employees and are widely displayed at various points within the campus.
4. **Mechanism for Conflict Resolution:** There are procedures for conflict resolution. Preferably, an executive is designated with whom employees can have confidential discussions about moral concerns. Equally important is educating managers about conflict

resolution. There are also ties of loyalty and collegiality that help to minimize conflicts in the first place.

17.3 Profession *vs.* Job and Occupation

Many people use profession as synonym for job or occupation. For them to be a professional of some field of activity means to earn his living through it. In this sense a player, a stage artist, a musician, comedian, etc. are professionals. But there is substantial difference in content, extent and depth of knowledge and specialization required in the profession. Technically profession is defined with certain features which excludes above listed or similar fields of activities from being called a profession. Let us understand the meaning of these terms.

17.3.1 Job

A job is generally characterized by duties, purpose, responsibilities, scope and working conditions. Job description usually forms the basis of job. Jobs are very precise in work content and from the activity point of view. Aspects specific to a job, such as knowledge and skills, mental and physical demands and working conditions that can be recognized, defined, and assessed precisely.

17.3.2 Occupation

Division of labor and therefore differentiation of population based on occupations is found in all societies. However, the bases of differentiation are markedly different between societies.

In pre-industrial societies division of labor was based on age, sex and caste. In industrial societies, along with these criterions, new criterion such as formal education and training, specialization, etc. are added which makes the bases of division of labor more complex.

In Industrial-urban societies by definition all occupations are open to everybody provided the aspirant acquires the requisite prescribed qualifications

Occupations can be categorized on the basis of level of skills (unskilled, skilled and professional), type of activity (physical or intellectual), and type of working environment (factory, office and farm) or prerequisites of entry (training, experience and certification). Occupation is an activity in which a person is engaged. It may be remunerative or a free service. But normally we call occupation as a person's usual or principal work or business, especially as a means of earning a living. Some occupations require special training and a formal qualification to practice his principal area of activity or business of life. An occupation is not as precise as job and not as wide and extensive as a profession.

17.4 Defining Profession

In general sense people call professional to those persons also, who are engaged in certain activities as profession like playing cricket, wrestling, boxing, conducting cultural or religious programs, etc. which provides earning to the players or programmers just like jobs and occupations. However, in the general sense, extent of expertise of these professionals is limited to one who merely earns his living through an established nature of activity. In the same sense people also sometimes refer to a driver, a barber, a sharp shooter, a smuggler, a politician, etc. as professional.

But word profession is used in other sense also, where to qualify in the profession one requires extensive training before becoming a professional. This definition excludes above referred professions under general sense of the term. According to this sense of the word the occupations that clearly are professions include engineering, medicine, law, veterinary medicine, architecture, accounting (at least certified public accountancy), etc. Let us explain defining features of *profession* and afterword justify status of examine characteristics of engineering as profession.

17.4.1 Defining Features of Profession

Profession term can be applied to certain fields of specialization which meet following criteria.
- **Extensive Training**: Entrance into a profession typically requires an extensive period of training. Training typically required of professionals focuses more on intellectual content than practical skills. This theoretical base is obtained through formal education, usually in an academic institution.
- **Vital Knowledge and Skills**: Professional's knowledge and skills are vital to the well-being of the larger society. A society that has a sophisticated scientific and technological base is especially dependent on its professional elite. We rely on the knowledge possessed by scientists and engineers for many of the technological advances on which our material civilization and national defense rests.
- **Control of Services**: Professions usually have a monopoly on or at least considerable control over the provision of professional services in their area. This control is achieved in two ways. First, the profession convinces the community that only those who have graduated from a professional school should be allowed to hold the professional title. The profession usually also gains considerable control over professional schools by establishing accreditation standards that regulate the quality, curriculum content and number of such schools. Second, a profession often attempts to persuade

the community that there should be a licensing system for those who want to enter the profession. Those who practice without a license are subject to legal penalties.
- **Autonomy in the Workplace**: Professionals often have an unusual degree of autonomy in the workplace. This is especially true of professionals in private practice, but even professionals who work in large organizations may exercise a large degree of individual judgment and creativity carrying out their professional responsibilities. This is one of the most satisfying aspects of professional work. The justification for this unusual degree of autonomy is that only the professional has sufficient knowledge to determine the appropriate professional services in a given situation.
- **Claim to Ethical Regulation**: Professionals claim to be regulated by ethical standards, many of which are embodied in a code of ethics. The enormous degree of control that professional possess over their services are vital to the well-being of the rest of the community. Professional codes are ordinarily promulgated by professional societies which punish members who violate their codes but their powers are limited to expelling errant members. State boards have much stronger legal powers including the ability to withdraw professional licenses and even institute criminal proceedings.

Thus, summarily a profession is a vocation founded upon specialized educational training, the purpose of which is to provide intellectual and conceptual services in the interest of the client and the public with a direct and definite compensation to the practicing professional.

17.4.2 Engineering Qualifying as Profession

Looking at the sociological or economic analysis of professions, engineering seems to qualify only as a borderline profession or quasi-professional status. Engineers have extensive training and possess knowledge and skills that are vital to the public. However, engineers do not have anything like complete control of engineering services because a license is not required to practice many types of engineering. Since engineers do not have to have a license to practice, their practices are not regulated by ethical standards of any professional society. Only licensed engineers (e.g. Institution of Engineers of India or National Society of Professional Engineers of USA) are governed by a compulsory code of ethics. Finally, engineers who work in large organizations and are subject to the authority of managers and employers may have limited autonomy. However, nowadays even doctors and lawyers often work in large organizations as salaried employees. Given that engineers are highly trained and perform services that are vital to the public that some engineers are registered and thus work under a legally enforced ethical code. Autonomy of salaried professionals in the workplace is declining for all professionals.

From the defining feature of social practice by professionals, status of engineering as profession is questionable. But, taking a clue from engineering codes, one might define the goal of engineering as holding paramount the health, safety and welfare of the public. Thus, engineering has a goal of producing technology for the welfare of society. These considerations allow engineering full professional status, as engineering is a group activity, which openly professes special knowledge, skill and judgment. In application of technologies, engineers have special obligations, to protect the health and safety of the public.

17.5 Collegiality

For an engineer to be effective in profession requires the virtues of collegiality, loyalty to employers and organizations respect for authority and contribution to an ethical climate within the organization.

Collegiality is one of the *teamwork virtues* which are especially important in enabling professionals to work successfully with other people. Other virtues include cooperativeness, loyalty and respect for legitimate authority. It is part of professional ethics with emphasis on relationship with peers, both coworkers and members of same profession. Further, just like team spirit of sportsmen collegiality includes cooperative relationship with people of even other profession, as many situations in professional life include cooperative efforts from other professionals also. It also involves respect for the rights of engineers and others who work together to achieve common goals (Elden, 2016).

Ihara suggests that "...*collegiality is a kind of connectedness grounded in respect for professional expertise and in a commitment to the goals and values of the profession and collegiality includes a disposition to support and cooperate with one's colleagues*" (Bagad, 2007, pp. 4.18). For example, when a new machine is designed, it is not work of one engineer. Instead, it is the team of engineers who worked together and invest their time and talent creatively with colleagues as part of a design group. During design and manufacturing, clash of ideas and personality do occur when work schedules and processes, reliability, safety and quality consideration including commitment of delivery schedule, etc. are discussed and negotiated. But any conflict or personality clash is minimized by a commitment to teamwork, collegiality and shared identification with the group's project.

Collegiality in engineering codes of ethics is reflected by citing *acts of don't categories* which are negative and contrary to the spirit of collegiality, hence against professional ethics. For example, the NSPE code states that engineers shall not attempt to injure, maliciously or falsely, directly or indirectly, the professional reputation, prospects, practice or employment of other engineers. Engineers who believe others are guilty of unethical or illegal practice shall present such information to the proper authority for action. These negative aspects of engineering codes of ethics can be fruitfully used to identify techniques required for achieving collegiality.

17.5.1 Main features of Collegiality

- Respect for peers and colleagues, valuing their professional expertise and their devotion to the social goods promoted by the profession. It is reciprocal and not emotional like friendship. This includes affirmation of worth of other engineers producing safe and useful products and services.
- Commitment and devotion to the moral ideals inherent in one's profession. Even in a competitive environment, engineers must feel like competing team in sports, maintaining professional values above winning or losing the game.
- Connectedness as a member of a team with common goal or awareness of participating in cooperative projects based on shared commitments and mutual support. Collegiality is a virtue defining the teamwork essential for pursuing shared goals.

17.5.2 Techniques for achieving Collegiality

Techniques for achieving collegiality to a large extent depend on the particular profession, its core values and code of conduct established by the professional body guiding and controlling the profession. For example, techniques of collegiality among accountants, lawyers, doctors, business people, etc. will be different from each other in content and context. We limit here discussion on techniques applicable to engineering profession only.

- **Develop Collegiality as Personal Character**: Collegiality is a valuable trait of character which should be encouraged among all professionals.
- **Adoption of Social Perspective**: Professionals should realize that by having concern for society, collegiality becomes instrumental and good means to promote their own professional aims.
- **Develop commitment for sharing at peer level:** By shared commitment with others collegiality supports personal efforts to act responsibly and harmoniously with colleagues. This also motivates to live up to professional standards.

- **Associate with professional community**: Collegiality is intrinsically associated with work of professional community- as composed of many individuals jointly engaged in public good and service. Existence of a professional community depends on shared awareness of mutual commitment to professional ideals.
- **Develop Team Spirit rather than Competitive Spirit within the team**: Industrial projects and products are result of teamwork where collegiality among team members is important for success. In projects, competitive spirits breed secretiveness and isolation among team members which is against spirit of collegiality and becomes counterproductive for the project.
- **Avoid unjust efforts to defame colleagues**: This does not mean not condoning unethical practices and be reluctant to criticize peers. We are required to promote moral aims of the profession because collegiality requires making a positive balance in favor of professional codes.
- **Be an active member of Professional Bodies**: to promote professionalism and social relevance of the profession.
- **Develop your own network of professional contacts:** as lot of important information flows within professional groups which is useful for career effectiveness and advancement.
- **Development leadership qualities:** Your visibility within your group and team enables you to bring required change in aims, goals and vision of the team.
- **Practice cooperation**: Promoting professional aims attending conferences that help you to grow and sharing information obtained.

17.6 Engineer's Trustworthiness

For professionals, virtue of being Trustworthy has already discussed under Section 7.3.2 in Chapter 7. Here we discuss some more points of trustworthiness for engineers. An engineer must possess a virtue of taking responsibility of its actions. Trustworthiness is a fundamental virtue for relationship between engineers and their employers and clients. These relationships are based on trust that engineers will perform activities to the best of their abilities. Trustworthiness involves more specific virtues such as:

- **Honesty in actions**: For example, not involving in corrupt practices such as stealing, engaging in bribery, kickbacks, espionage, etc.
- **Honesty in communication**: For example, no falsification of facts, revealing only pertinent information, not deceiving, etc.
- **Competence:** Being well prepared for the Job.

- **Diligence:** Constant and earnest effort to accomplish what is undertaken.
- **Discretion**: Sensitivity for confidential information and privacy concern of the employer or the client.
- **Loyalty:** Acting faithfully on behalf of employer's interest as well as client's interest.

17.7 Loyalty

Loyalty is the quality of being loyal. In loyalty one will have a strong feeling of support or allegiance. Loyalty is faithfulness or a devotion to a person, group, country, or cause.

At the beginning of their career engineers are part of national youth force. In general youth have the nature of strong loyalty and devotion to the goals and personalities with which they associate emotionally and mentally. Youths can be easily mobilized for a cause by a person in whom they have trust and for a cause to which they owe loyalty and therefore can be important force to change.

Many times, youths face conflicts between their duties to different social institutions such as family, occupations, state, etc. Identification with a particular group or association is necessary but obsessive loyalty to a section leads to intolerance. In absence of a general standard, narrow loyalties clash with each other.

Loyalty to one's peers and superiors is the primary virtue for engineers and managers. The successful manager is the team player, the person who can accept a challenge and get the job done in a way that reflects favorably upon him and others. An engineer is required to have loyalty towards employer, profession, customers and team members. Harmonious teamwork, strict discipline and total involvement are the mainsprings of his career growth and achievements.

Actually, engineers have a dual loyalty: loyalty to the organization and loyalty to their profession. Their professional loyalties go beyond their immediate employer.

17.7.1 Two senses of Loyalty

For an engineer loyalty to an employer encompasses two dimensions:
1. **Agency-loyalty:** It is acting to fulfill one's contractual duties to an employer. These duties are specified in terms of the particular tasks for which one is paid, as well as the more general activities of cooperating with colleagues and following legitimate authority within the corporation. As its name implies, agency-loyalty is entirely a matter of *actions* such as doing one's job.

2. **Attitude-loyalty:** By contrast it has as much to do with attitudes, emotions and a sense of personal identity as it does with actions. It implies seeking to meet one's moral duties to a group or organization willingly with personal attachment and affirmation along with a reasonable degree of trust. People who do their work grudgingly or spitefully are not loyal in this sense, even though they may adequately perform all their work responsibilities and hence manifest agency-loyalty.

17.7.2 Obligations to Loyalty

When codes of ethics assert that engineers ought to be loyal (or faithful) to employers, then what agency-loyalty or attitude-loyalty meant? Within proper limits agency-loyalty is a contractual obligation. It is the sum total of obligations to the employers. It comprises of the sum total of obligations to employers or to serve the corporation in return for the contractual benefits from the corporation. But it is not the sole or paramount obligation of engineers. According to the code of ethics of national society of professional engineers (NSPE) and many other codes, the overriding obligation of engineers remains to hold paramount the safety, health and welfare of the public. What about attitude-loyalty: Is it obligatory? It is obligatory if it meets two goals:1) Pleasure of affirming with the group. Recognition from the group, that one's contributions are valuables, and sense of worth and accomplishment in pursuing the goals; and2) Employees treated fairly, each receiving his share of benefit or burden.

If these are met than organization can expect *attitude-loyalty*. Attitude-loyalty is a virtue. If the employer thinks that the employees are only producers of profits only, then he/she can expect Agency loyalty only. If the employer thinks that they are partner in the progress than you can have attitude-loyalty. For some critics, attitude-loyalty is often a virtue but not strictly an obligation.

Loyalty (both agency and attitude) is important to the company and to the employee for many reasons such as productivity, moral, maintaining confidentiality, promoting teamwork, exploiting investment in training and stability in workforce.

17.7.3 Misguided Loyalty

In the case of signal generators discussed above, it appears that all concerned in the process of development of sample were having eagerness to do their job as quickly as possible. They were confident that their sample will pass the qualifying test, because in the past they were very successfully competing and delivering goods to civilian (non-defense) market. Their loyalty to organization was beyond doubt. However, during execution of defense contract, their loyalty was misguided in serving the company's best interest by manipulating the test procedure and parameters during internal quality verification tests. It is also possible that some of them following orders from higher up to adjust the test schedule for acceptable results.

The case mentioned above raises a more pertinent question about relationship between a responsible engineer and his obligations to employer and customer (general public at large). Being a loyal employee is good but not at the cost of professional integrity. Issues of this relationship call for clarity and understanding the meaning of occupation, job and profession which are quite complex and overlapping in contexts with each other. Professionalism must convey to employed engineers that they have obligations to both employers and the public; and these two obligations are not contradictory to each other.

17.8 Summary

Sometimes engineers face conflicting demands and dilemmas in their job and responsibilities. Primarily engineer's problems are centered on a conflict between professional independence and bureaucratic loyalty within the organization. Role of the engineer also includes a patchwork of compromises between professional ideals and business demands. Engineers have major roles within the industry to organize the operational activities involved in production process like analyzing the customer requirement, initiating design process, component selection and purchase, setting up workstations involved in testing, quality control etc. At organization level the primary requirement is an integrated internal work culture and professional approach by engineers and managers. It is moral obligation to any corporate body to be productive to the society

Defining features of an organization: An organization should have clearly defined responsibilities towards all the stakeholders like employees, customers, distributors, etc. Corporate code of ethics is being widely propagated and understood throughout the spectrum of management, administration, engineers, managers and employees alike. Corporate code of ethics is in tune with professional code of ethics for the particular industry along with statutory guidelines. Top management should demonstrate explicit adherence to code of ethics and provide backup support to the professionals who stick to the code in word and spirit. Further, there should be established procedures for conflict resolution.

Profession: Word *Profession* is used where to qualify in the profession one requires extensive training before becoming a professional. Term *Profession* carries an impression of certain fields of specialization which require extensive training, vital knowledge and skills, control of professional services in their area, autonomy to a large extent for individual judgment and creativity in the workplace to carrying out professional responsibilities, subject to ethical regulation which are embodied in a code of ethics. Engineering is qualifying to the professional status as it is a group activity, which openly professes special knowledge, skill and judgment.

Collegiality: For an engineer to be effective in profession requires the virtues of collegiality, loyalty to employers and organizations, respect for authority and contribution to an ethical climate within the organization. Collegiality is a virtue defining the teamwork essential for pursuing shared goals. Other virtues include cooperativeness, loyalty and respect for legitimate authority. It is part of professional ethics with emphasis on relationship with peers, both coworkers and members of same profession. Techniques for achieving collegiality will to a large extent depend on the particular profession, its core values and code of conduct established by the professional body guiding and controlling the profession.

Trustworthiness and Loyalty: An engineer must possess a virtue of taking responsibility of its actions. *Trustworthiness* is a fundamental virtue for relationship between engineers and their employers and clients. These relationships are based on trust that engineers will perform activities to the best of their abilities. Trustworthiness involves more specific virtues such as honesty in actions, honesty in communication, competence, diligence, discretion and loyalty.

Loyalty is the quality of being loyal. In loyalty one will have a strong feeling of support or allegiance. Loyalty is faithfulness or a devotion to a person, country, group or cause. Loyalty to one's peers and superiors is the primary virtue for managers. An engineer is required to have loyalty towards employer, profession, customers and team members. Actually, engineers have a dual loyalty: towards the organization and to their profession. For an engineer loyalty to an employer encompasses two dimensions: 1) *Agency-loyalty* is acting to fulfill one's contractual duties to an employer. These duties are specified in terms of the particular tasks for which one is paid; and 2) *Attitude-loyalty*, by contrast has as much to do with attitudes, emotions and a sense of personal identity as it does with actions. It implies seeking to meet one's moral duties to a group or organization willingly, with personal attachment and affirmation and with a reasonable degree of trust. Codes of ethics assert that engineers ought to be loyal (or faithful) to employers. Within proper limits, *agency-loyalty* is a contractual obligation. It is sum total of obligations to the employers.

Review questions

1. In industry production activity is an interconnected teamwork of various workstations and departments for execution of time bound project. What type of dilemmas engineers face in teamwork operations?

2. Explain defining features of an organization.
3. Distinguish defining features of profession from features of job and occupation.
4. All professions have to qualify certain criteria for being treated as profession. Why engineering seems to qualify only as a borderline profession.
5. What virtue an engineer should possess to be effective in profession. explain "virtue of collegiality" is one of the "teamwork virtues"
6. Describe main features of collegiality? What are techniques used for achieving collegiality?
7. Engineer's trustworthiness is a fundamental virtue for relationship between engineers and their employers and clients; justify.
8. Explain virtue of loyalty. Why loyalty is an important virtue for engineers?
9. What are two senses of loyalty? What is obligation to loyalty for an engineer?
10. How loyalty could be misguided; explain?

18 Professional Rights, Responsibilities and Other Qualities of Professionalism

Learning objectives

In this chapter you will learn about

- Professionalism, Professional Loyalty and career as employee
- Engineers and workers' rights in workplace
- Employment related contractual terms defining rights and obligations of an engineer
- Professional Responsibilities and authority
- Professional duty and obligation for confidentiality and secrecy of proprietary information

18.1 Professionalism

In the previous chapter meaning of profession and its characteristic features are discussed in detail. In common man language, an individual in any profession is a professional and the professional activities of such an individual can be addressed as *professionalism*. A profession involves number of individuals in the same occupation voluntarily organized to earn a living by openly serving a moral ideal in a morally permissible way.

This definition highlights several features of profession which are important in the concept of professionalism.

1. A profession is always composed of a number of individuals.
2. A profession involves an element of public concern. One must openly *profess* to be an engineer, a physician or attorney, such as the dictionary meaning of the term *profession* suggest.
3. A profession is a way of living of people by which they earn their livelihood and enjoy professional status.
4. A profession is something that people enter into voluntarily and can leave voluntarily.
5. Much like advocates of the social practice approach, a profession must serve some goal, although this goal may not be unique to a given profession.

6. Professionals must pursue a morally praiseworthy goal by morally permissible means.
7. Ethical standards in a profession should obligate professionals to act in some way that goes beyond what law, market, morality and public opinion would otherwise require.

18.2 Professional Responsibilities

Professional responsibility of engineers with respect to the *codes of practice* is already discussed in Chapter 12. A great deal of *engineering ethics* concerns itself with the duties and professional responsibilities which engineers owe to clients, colleagues, employers and society. They are required to discharge their responsibilities according to the standards laid down in professional codes of ethics (in various versions). It is reasonable too, from the wider perspective of the public interest. Professional authority, if abused, can adversely affect the interests of society and this may undermine public confidence in a profession and its practitioners. Professional responsibilities for engineers are elaborated in 7.8 IEEE Code of Ethics (See Appendix-F for details).

18.2.1 Responsibilities of Professional Engineers are broadly

- **Loyalty:** To employer, client, public at large and professional codes of conduct as discussed in above paragraphs. Further, there is a *moral obligation* not to act loyally in situations where doing so violates important professional duties.
- **Confidentiality:** Maintenance of confidentiality to the information received from various sources (in content and context); just like doctors maintain confidentiality of patient's information; and not to divulge to unconnected persons and agencies unless required by law or in fulfillment of professional duties.
- **Respect for Authority**: Respect for authority is important in meeting organizational goals. Authority is required to make decisions in situations where allowing everyone to exercise unrestrained individual discretion would create chaos. Organizationally, drawing up clear lines of hierarchy of authority provides a means for identifying areas of personal responsibility and accountability.
- **Professional Behavior**: In application of his professional knowledge, only for good purpose and to resolve issues amicably, avoids conflicts of interest and occupational crimes.
  Topics of conflicts of interest and occupational crimes are discussed in detail in subsequent chapters

18.3 Professionalism *vs.* Loyalty

Loyalty issue for engineers has been discussed in chapter 17. Summarily loyalty virtue demands the following:

- If there is conflict between professional responsibility and loyalty to the company, then professional responsibility to public comes first.
- It is not loyalty to immediate current superiors.
- An engineer has obligation to both public and the employer. But the interest of public comes first.

18.4 Engineers career as Employees

An engineer is an engineer by profession, even though his work may be in any field, technical or non-technical. By nature of work he/she may be doing research, design, be a manager, an executive, a bureaucrat or an administrator. He/ She may go through some of similar stages of positions in due course of his career. His complexion of duties and responsibilities keep on changing with task, status and targets. A common growth pattern is that initially he/she starts career as technical person and in due course of time slowly shifts (or shifted) towards managerial role and finally ends as an administrator. However, with all these movements, he/she continues to be an employee and a professional even though nature of relationship with bosses and management keeps on changing in width and depth with regard to his commitment, his contractual relationship, etc. His *professional rights and responsibilities* more or less remain the same (in accordance to professional code of ethics) at various roles played by him during his career growth.

Many employers are most concerned with economic achievements and growth of their companies. For the employer working hours, remunerations, working conditions, resource constraints, delays in supply chain beyond control of individual engineer are primary and personal commitments of the employee about his family, society, etc. are secondary. Even working hours on paper is limited by statutory regulations like 48 hours per week; employers feel that their employees are 24 hours' servant. This approach from employers and management raises the basic question about employees (particularly engineers and professionals) rights and responsibilities for decent working environment with clear cut policies of employment conditions. This is discussed in following sections.

18.4.1 Employees' Rights at Workplace

Government recognizes that safety and health of employees has a positive impact on productivity, economic and social development. Prevention is an integral part of economic activities. Accordingly, it works for ensuring better working conditions for employees at work places (offices, factories, in the fields and in hazardous operations). These conditions normally relate to better safety, health and environment at workplaces, and for which suitable legislative measures are adopted-thereby improving the quality of work and working life of work force. To enforce legislative measures adopted in this regard, government envisages total commitment and demonstration to that effect by all concerned stakeholders and social partners.

18.5 Engineers Rights as Employee

As humans, engineers have fundamental rights to live and freely pursue their legitimate professional interests; for example, *rights* of not to be are unfairly discriminated against in employment on the basis of sex, race, age, etc. *Employee Rights* are any rights such as moral or legal that involves the status of being an employee. They overlap with some *Professional Rights* which are discussed below and also include some of the *Institutional Rights* created by organizational policies or employment agreements.

As employees, engineers have special rights, including the right to receive one's salary in return for performing one's duties and the right to engage in any other activity like any hobby, social or religious and non-political activities of one's choice; without reprisal or coercion from employers.

18.5.1 Definitions of terms used in connection to employment

Rights: *Employees Rights* are that belongs to him by law, nature or tradition.
Responsibilities are employee's *Obligation* to perform certain tasks and duties
Statutory Rights: Rights conferred to employees based on specific laws and statutes passed by federal, state or local governments. These are basically intended to provide the employees with *equal employment opportunity, rights for collective bargaining and rights to demand workplace safety.*
Contractual Rights: Engineers/employees also have certain *contractual rights*. These are rights available to employees based on a specific contract between employer and employee. These are categorized as:
- **Employment Contract:** An agreement that formally outlines the details of employment. These conditions of employment are mentioned in their appointment letters.
- **Implied Contract:** Notion that a contract exists between employer and employee based on implied promises of employer like

allotment of company shares or other benefits based on good performance. They also include adherence to company's policies, code of ethics etc. as conditions implied in the employment.
- **Non-Compete Agreements:** Prohibit individuals, who quit the company, from competing with employer in the same line of business for some period of time.
    a. Employment contract clauses may include it or it may be implied
    b. Non-piracy agreements
    c. Non-solicitation of current employees
    d. Intellectual property and trade secrets

18.5.2 Rights affecting the employment relationship

Employment-at-will (EAW)
Employer: Employers have the right to hire, fire, demote, or promote as they choose, unless there is a law or contract to the contrary.
Employees: Employees have the right to quit and get another job under the same constraints.
Employment-At-Will restrictions: Employers are restricted by law on following ways to discharge an employee unless the cause is *just* and *due process* of law has been followed.
- **Wrongful discharge:** That is termination of an individual's employment for improper or illegal reasons.
- **Constructive discharge**: An employer deliberately makes working conditions intolerable in an attempt to get (to force) an employee to resign or quit.

Meaning of *just cause* implies that there is reasonable justification for taking an employment related action. It can stand scrutiny by a third party and is not in violation of contract and arbitrary in nature. Further, there is perceptual fairness in process used to make decision and quantum of the action taken.

Meaning of *due process* is that the individual is provided the opportunity to explain and defend their actions against charges or indiscipline issue.
- **Distributive Justice**: Perceived fairness in the distribution of outcomes.
- **Procedural Justice**: Perceived fairness of the process used to make decision about employees.

18.6 Engineer Rights as a Professional

As professionals, engineers have special rights that arise from their professional role and the obligations it involves. Three professional rights have special importance: 1) the basic right of professional conscience, 2) the right of conscientious refusal, and 3) the right of professional recognition.

1. **Right of professional conscience**
   - The right of professional conscience is the moral right to exercise professional judgment in pursuing professional responsibilities. Pursuing those responsibilities involves exercising both technical judgment and reasoned moral convictions. This right has limits and of course they must be balanced against responsibilities to employers and colleagues.
   - Engineering is inherently a risk activity with lot of experimental content and processes in new product design or jobs of project nature. Sometimes this also calls for morally complex decisions. It requires autonomous moral judgment to find reasonable course of action as the correct course of action are not always obvious.
   - The basic professional right is the *Moral Authority* to act without interference from others and engineers have this right as well as obligation to exercise the right of *Professional Conscience* in the course of meeting their *Professional Obligations*. The justification of each duty ultimately yields a justification of the right of conscience with respect to that duty.

2. **Right of conscientious refusal**
   - The right of conscientious refusal is the right to refuse to engage in unethical behavior and to refuse to do so solely because he/she views it as unethical.
   - Engineers and other professionals have a *Moral Right* to refuse to participate in activities that are illegal and clearly unethical (for example, forging documents, altering test results, lying, giving or taking bribery, or padding payrolls). And coercing employees into acting by means of threats (to their jobs) plainly constitutes a violation of this their right.
   - Just as physicians and nurses have a right not to participate in abortions, engineers should be recognized as having a limited right to turn down assignments that violate their personal consciences in matters of great importance, such as threats to human life.

3. **Professional right of recognition**
   - Engineers have a right of *Professional Recognition* for their work and accomplishments. Part of this involves fair monetary remuneration, and part non-monetary forms of recognition.
   - Fair remuneration is essential because without fair remuneration, engineers cannot concentrate their energies on carrying out the duties of their jobs and on maintaining up-to-date skills through formal and informal continuing education.

- Further, the right to professional recognition is not precise to pinpoint what a reasonable salary should be or what should be a fair remuneration for Patent discoveries. Such detailed matters must be worked out cooperatively between employers and employees, for they depend on both the resources of a company and the bargaining position of engineers. Professional societies can be of help by providing general guidelines.

18.7 Complexion of Authority Structure

When we sign on with a company, we are in some sense signing on to their *Institutional Duties*, but only as long as these duties are morally permissible. Sometimes, professional face dilemma on one's moral rights and duties versus institutional rights and duties. Professionals have an obligation to accept their employers *Institutional Authority* but it should not be accepted blindly as they have *professional moral autonomy* to make independent moral judgments. He/ She must remember higher obligation to protect public interests.

Employees respect authority, and obey the directives issued by the employer within the areas of activity covered by the employer's institutional authority. Here employees are assuming that the directives are legal and do not violate norms of moral decency.

1. **Institutional Authority:** The relevant kind of authority has been called executive authority also. Corporate or institutional authority, given to a professional may be defined as the institutional right given to him to exercise power based on resources of the organization. It gives the professional a right to get the things done for the benefit of the organization.
2. **Institutional Duties:** They deal with duties of professional activities or functions. For example, Project engineer's duty is to complete the task within the time, for which they have to be given required authority to fulfill their responsibility. Authority can be delegated but not accountability.
3. **Institutional vs. Expert Authority:** *Expert authority* is gained due to possession of expert knowledge, skill, and competence to perform some task or give advice. Sometimes engineers may have *expert authority* (like consultants) and not *institutional authority*.

18.7.1 Area of Engineers and Managers Authority

In connection to organizational role, authority of engineers and managers has been already discussed in chapter 10. Within the general framework of authority, however, there are wide variations in how engineers and managers relate to each other. At one extreme there is the rigid, top-down control. On the other extreme there is something more like how professors and administrators interact within universities.

In addition to having different roles and authority, managers and engineers typically have different attitudes and approaches. Managers tend to be more distanced from the technical details of jobs. They focus more on jobs in their entirety from wider perspectives and they are more focused on people than things.

18.8 Confidentiality and Secrecy

Integrity and confidentiality have been already discussed in detail in Chapter 3. Issue of confidentiality has also been mentioned in many topics discussed earlier. Confidentiality is the duty of every professional to keep secret of all information deemed and desirable to keep secret. Basically, it is any information that the employer or client would like to keep secret, to compete effectively against business rivals. This could be any data concerning the company's business, design secrets, technical processes or trade secrets that are not available to public knowledge. Although this criterion is somewhat vague, it is the employer or client who is the main source of the decision as to what information is to be treated as confidential.

Confidentiality and secrecy are related terms. Whatever information is secret that becomes confidential. Within any organization there are multiple layers or centers of decision taking, records keeping and its access for various types of information like top management strategy or decision, financial decisions, market negotiation, trade agreements, designs, Patents, etc. Therefore, it makes sense to ask, secrecy of information with whom or with respect to whom?

Confidentiality and secrecy are of prime importance in the issues of industrial products, processes and Patents. It is also crucial in business strategies, marketing and financial information. Similarly, in intelligence, defense and military operations of any government, confidentiality and secrecy play vital role. Engineers and professionals are employed in all these sectors of governance and economic activity and play vital role in maintenance of confidentiality and secrecy. Within governmental agencies and private companies, engineers and other employees are usually expected to withhold information labeled confidential from unauthorized people both inside and outside the organization.

Secrecy sometimes breeds corruption; it becomes a cover for misdeeds, inefficiencies in operations and wrong decisions. Under secrecy safety issues are compromised for workstations having hazardous environment. Confidentiality and secrecy pose ethical problems for engineers in various ways.

As an example of importance of confidentiality and secrecy, consider the role of a number of best known intelligence agencies of India like the research and analysis wing (RAW), India's external intelligence agency and the intelligence bureau (IB), the domestic intelligence agency, central bureau of investigation (CBI), central vigilance commission (CVC), etc. which act as eye and ear of government of India. In these government organizations highly, elaborate systems for classifying information have been developed that identify which individuals and groups may have access to what information.

18.8.1 Defining Confidential and Proprietary Information

There are several related terms in use indicating a degree of confidentiality. Confidential information is information which an agency, employer, or client judge should be keeping secret to serve the organization's or client's interest. Proprietary information and trade secrets are information protected by law. These are explained below:

- Proprietary information is information that a company owns or is the proprietor of. The term is used in legal sense, just as *property* and *ownership* are defined by law. Normally it refers to new knowledge generated within the organization which can be legally protected from use by other. The term is carefully defined by property law. A term roughly synonym for *proprietary information* is *trade secrets*.

In international contracts all parties and companies are required to keep proprietary information of third parties (or each other's proprietary information) confidential, to which they have gained access in accordance with the terms of its disclosure and in strict compliance with all applicable laws and regulations. A wide variety of corporate codes of conduct now exist in this regard. The organization for economic co-operation and development (OECD) has published guidelines for multinational enterprises. Many non-governmental organizations have also publicized sets of global principles dealing with confidentiality.

- Trade secret: Trade secret is the information which can be virtually any type of information that has not become public, which an employer has taken steps to keep secret and which is thereby given limited legal protection in common law that forbids employees from divulging it.
- Patents legally protect specific products from being manufactured and sold by competitors without the express permission of the Patent holder.
- Privileged information literally means "available only on the basis of special privilege," such as the privilege accorded to an employee working on a special assignment or project.

18.8.2 Professional responsibility for maintaining confidentiality while changing jobs

The obligation to protect confidential information of earlier employer does not cease when employees change jobs. If he/she does not maintain confidentiality then it would be impossible to protect such information and it will do great harm to all employers. Then employees can quickly divulge the information to their new employers or perhaps sell it for a price to competitors of their former employers. This practice will be against professional ethics and code of conduct. Thus, the relationship of trust between employer and employee in regard to confidentiality continues beyond the formal period of employment. Unless the employer gives consent, former employees are barred indefinitely from revealing trade secrets. This provides a clear illustration of the way in which the professional integrity of engineers involves much more than mere loyalty to one's present employer.

In practice, it becomes difficult for employers to enforce the confidentiality restrictions on employees leaving the job, as much of the confidential information like design and process etc. are to a large extent part of employee's experience. Rather the employees grab new jobs because of their experience with current employer. Many engineers value professional advancement more than long-term ties with any one company and so they change jobs frequently. Engineers in research and development are likely to have high rates of turnover. They are also the people most likely to be exposed to important new trade secrets. Moreover, when they transfer into new companies they often do the same kind of work as before; precisely the type of situation in which trade secrets of their old companies may have relevance, a fact that could have strongly contributed to them having readily found new employment. However, in spite of consideration of personal growth by engineers, it is their professional moral and ethical duty to maintain confidentiality of information in their possession. Confidentiality obligation also forbids engineers from revealing any trade secrets to their new employer. Professionalism demands that engineer should refrain from explicitly revealing information on processes, formulas, material specifications, etc.

18.8.3 Obligation to Confidentiality vis-à-vis Personal Interest of employees and employers Rights

No doubt that legitimate *personal interest* and *rights* of engineers and other employees have to be recognized but at the same time *rights of employers* also have to be recognized. Thus, there is a need to strike a balance between these two demands of interest and rights. Engineering code of conduct to some extent tries to balance the interest of both parties as well as the interest of general public through professional ethics. Other instrument of balance could be employment contracts that place special restrictions on future employment. This method is employed by many governments also, to restrict any employment by senior executives after retirement, for certain years or certain type of jobs which may cause misuse of confidential information.

Normally employment contracts are hardly agreements between equals and they threaten the right of individuals to pursue their careers freely. For this reason, the courts have tended not to recognize such contracts as binding, although they do uphold part of contractual agreements forbidding the disclosure of trade secrets. Other tactics and provisions, aside from employment contract, have been attempted by various companies to guard their interest of organization. One is to place tighter controls on the internal flow of information by restricting access to trade secrets except where absolutely essential.

One potential solution for employers is to infuse a sense of professional responsibility among their staff. Engineers can then develop a real sensitivity to the moral conflicts, where they may be exposed to while making certain job changes. They develop a greater appreciation of why trade secrets are important in a competitive system and take the necessary steps to protect them.

18.8.4 Confidentiality and Secrecy for both Employees and the Employer

The primary justification of obligation to confidentiality is to respect the autonomy (freedom, self-determination) of individuals and corporations, and recognition to their legitimate control over some private information concerning them. Without such control, they cannot protect their privacy, self-interest and business interest. Employers should have some control over the private information about their companies. All the major ethical theories recognize the importance of autonomy, whether it is understood in terms of *rights to autonomy, duties to respect autonomy, the utility (as in utilitarian ethics) of protecting autonomy, or the virtue of respect* for others.

From social considerations, once obligation of maintaining confidentiality is established, trust and trustworthiness among professionals and clients will grow. Thus, when clients go to lawyer or tax consultant, they expect them to maintain confidentiality, and the professionals in turn assure that the confidentiality of client's information will be maintained. Similarly, the employees, who are empowered to sign the contracts on behalf of the employer, are required not to divulge certain sensitive information considered confidential by the employer.

Confidentiality of patient's information is assured and practiced by doctors which makes patient to feel completely free to reveal the most personal information about themselves to physicians and that helps the physician to arrive at correct diagnosis. Similarly, when companies can maintain some degree of confidentiality about their products, the economic benefits of competitiveness within a free market can be harnessed. Developing new technology or products requires investment of large resources. The motivation to make those investments will not be there if employer cannot keep the information secret and confidential and reap the benefit of investment.

18.8.5 Misuse of Confidentiality clauses

Confidentiality has its limits, particularly when it is invoked to hide misdeeds. Investigations into a wide variety of white-collar crimes covered up by managements in industry or public agencies have been thwarted by invoking confidentiality or false claims of secrecy based on national interest.

18.9 Conflicts due to Indirect Interests in other companies

Conflicts of interest arises when employee is having an interest in a competitor's or a subcontractor's business, not as any direct benefit like part time job, consultant, etc., but having relationship with them in other forms. For example, having substantial shareholdings, in the competitor's or the subcontractor's companies, can be appoint of conflict of interest by virtue of partial ownership in those companies. Another example of conflict of interest could be if one's spouse, son or close relative works in the competitors or subcontractor's company. Conflict of interest arises if one's job involves granting contracts to that subcontractor. Like this there are plenty of situations where conflict of interest can arise. A professional must be careful, while perusing his self-interest, such that employer or public trust on his professional decisions and acts does not fall short of trust reposed on him.

18.9.1 Moral Obligation to avoid Conflicts of Interest

When there is clash of conflict of interest between employer and the employee, and it is reasonable or cannot be avoided, still then employees are having moral obligation to inform the employers and obtain their approval. Conflicts of interest are generally prohibited because: a) the professional obligation to employers is very important, and it supersedes any appeal to self-interest over the commitment towards the job; and b) the professional obligation to employers is threatened by self-interest, and it warrants strong safeguards, to ensure that the obligations are fulfilled faithfully by employees.

18.9.2 Solving Conflict of Interest problem

1. The first step towards solving conflict problem is appreciation of rights and aspirations of employees as well as rights and expectations of employers. Both have to understand each other and cooperate in development of mutual trust and dependence.
2. Employment contracts with employees should be more objectively prepared with minimum gray area on responsibilities, so that employee understands his boundaries well before joining. Contract clauses should not be exploitative in nature. The contract should have a positive note to indicate possibility of growth and reward to employee. Dos and Don'ts must be very practicable.
3. The issues of confidentiality, special restrictions on future employment, conditions at workplace, transferability within the campus or to other campus, etc. must be negotiated and built into the contract explicitly.
4. An understanding (if required built into the contract) between employer and employee must be arrived at, for restrictions of the geographical location or restriction, on the nature of business of the future employers, for specified length of time after leaving the present employer.
5. Even though the contracts are hardly agreements between equals, but they should be designed without threatening the right of individuals to pursue their careers with minimum restrictions. Preferably it should offer positive benefits in lieu of the restrictions imposed on future employment.
6. Since everything cannot be covered in the contract, prospective employee must be exposed to relevant portions of company policies and cultures, to understand the environment in which he/she has to contribute and flourish.
7. One potential solution is that the employers should build a sense of professional responsibility among their staff. Then employees can become sensitized to the moral conflicts they may face while making certain job changes. Further they develop better appreciation about the restrictions on trade secrets in a competitive system, and they can act to protect them, treating it as their moral duty.

18.10 Summary

An individual in any profession is a professional and the professional activities of such an individual can be addressed as professionalism. If there is conflict between professional responsibility and loyalty to the company, then professional responsibility to public comes first. It is not loyalty to immediate current superiors. An engineer has obligation to both public and the employer. But the interest of public comes first.

A profession is an occupation, voluntarily organized to earn a living and openly serving some praiseworthy goal or element of public concern. Ethical standards in a profession should obligate professionals to act in some way that goes beyond what law, market, morality, or the public opinion would otherwise require.

Engineer's Rights in career as Employees: An engineer may work in any engineering field. His nature of work he/she may be technical like doing research, design etc., or non-technical administrative job like working as a manager, an executive, a bureaucrat or an administrator etc. His professional rights and responsibilities more or less remain same whether job isnon-technical or technical i.e. in accordance to the professional code of ethics, at various levels and roles played by him during his career.

Employee rights are any rights, moral or legal, that involve the status of being an employee. They overlap with some professional rights and also include institutional rights created by organizational policies or employment agreements. Employee's rights belong to him by law, nature or tradition. Statutory rights to employees are based on specific laws and statutes passed by federal, state or local governments. These are basically to provide employees an equal employment opportunity; right of collective bargaining and workplace safety. Engineers/employees also have certain contractual rights. These are the rights available to employees based on a specific contract between employer and employee. Engineers have fundamental rights not to be unfairly discriminated against on the basis of sex, race, or age. As professionals, engineers have special rights that arise from their professional role and the obligations it involves. Three professional rights have special importance: *1) the basic right of professional conscience; 2) the right of conscientious refusal; and (3) the right of professional recognition.*

Engineer's Professional Responsibilities: A great deal of *engineering ethics* concerns itself with the duties and professional responsibilities which engineers owe to clients, colleagues, employers, and society. They are required to discharge their responsibilities according to the standards laid down in professional codes of ethics (in various versions). Responsibilities of professional engineers broadly includes loyalty to employer, client, public at large and professional codes of conduct; confidentiality i.e. maintenance of confidentiality of information received from various sources (in content and context); respect for authority for meeting organizational goals; professional behavior in application of his knowledge only for good purpose and resolve conflicts of interest amicably and avoid occupational crimes.

When an engineer signs on with a company, he/she is signing on to their institutional duties. Employees respect authority of the employer within the areas of the employer's institutional authority. Sometimes professionals face dilemma on one's moral rights and duties *vs.* institutional rights and duties. Professionals have an obligation to accept their employer's institutional authority but they have *professional moral autonomy* which makes them independent towards moral judgments.

Responsibility of Confidentiality and Secrecy: Confidentiality is the duty of every professional to keep secret all information deemed and desirable to keep secret. This could be any data concerning the company's business, design secrets, technical processes or trade secrets that are not already in public knowledge. Within any organization there are multiple layers or centers of decision making, records keeping and its access for various types of information like top management strategy or decisions, financial decisions, market negotiation, trade agreements, designs, Patents, etc. It makes sense professionally to ensure secrecy of information and know to share with whom or protect from whom. Further, the obligation to protect confidential information of earlier employer does not cease when employees change jobs. Thus, the relationship of trust between employer and employee in regard to confidentiality continues beyond the formal period of employment.

The primary justification of obligation to confidentiality is to respect the autonomy (freedom, self-determination) of individuals and corporations, and recognition to their legitimate control over some private information concerning them. Sometimes confidentiality clauses are misused to hide misdeeds, for example wide variety of white-collar crimes.

Conflicts of Interests: Conflicts of interest arises when employee is having an interest in a competitor's or a subcontractor's business not as any direct benefit like part time job, consultant, etc. but having relationship with them in other forms. For example, conflict of interest could arise if one's spouse, son or close relative works for his company's subcontractor or if one's job involves granting contracts to that subcontractor. When conflicts of interest are unavoidable or reasonable, employees are obligated to inform their employers and obtain approval.

Review questions

1. What do you understand by professionalism? Explain defining features that are important in the concept of professionalism.
2. Explain career roles and growth avenues available to engineering professionals while working as employee.

3. What are rights of an engineer as employee? What are types of rights an engineer enjoys in connection to employment? What rights have potential of adversely affecting the employment relationship?
4. What are broad rights and responsibilities of engineers as professional?
5. What is nature of authority vested with engineers in their professional role?
6. Explain engineer's duty towards confidentiality and secrecy as professional. how confidential and proprietary information has been defined?
7. While changing jobs from one organization to another, what is engineer's professional responsibility for maintaining confidentiality on information of previous organization?
8. Discuss about obligation to confidentiality by an employee on the ground of personal interest vis-à-vis employers right.
9. What is the primary justification of obligation to confidentiality between employee and employer?
10. Few employees have indirect interests in other companies which gives rise to conflict of interest. How the problem of this conflict of Interest should be solved?

19 Ethical Operational Issues Encountered in Business and Engineering Profession

Learning objectives

In this chapter you will learn about

- Self-Realization, motives of proficiency, compensation, and moral for taking up job
- Business relationship and dealings based on prevailing cultural customs of gift giving
- Ethical dilemmas in business, global ethical framework for ethical corporations
- Global issues of corruption, bribery, kickbacks and gifts giving
- Occupational crime, industrial espionage, price manipulations

19.1 Self-Realization Ethics

Self-Realization ethics is already discussed in chapter5. All ethical theories provide considerable scope for *Self-Interest*, i.e. pursuing what is required for betterment of oneself within the scope of moral and ethical values. Self-interest got greater prominence in self-realization ethics. Self-realization ethics along with self-interest also acknowledges personal commitments for individual development, while pursuing objective of S*elf-Fulfillment*. Based on the concept of the *Self*, there are two versions of self-realization ethics:1) one version is community-oriented, where the *Self* is understood in terms of caring relationships within the communities; and 2) the second version is ethical egoism, where the *self* is central to the individual personality in a highly individualistic sense.

In the community-oriented version of self-realization ethics, the focus is on each individual to pursue self-realization, but to give more importance to the caring relationships with their communities while pursuing of self-realization objective. It argues in favor of communities in which we participate and live, because being social person our identities are linked to the society.

In professional life personal commitments of one's choice of career and choice of jobs are relevant in many ways, which motivates professionalism in them. Professions offer meaningful opportunities for the work, which is the main reason of attraction to talented individuals to take up the professional career.

Basic motives of professional career are proficiency, compensation, and moral considerations, which also serve his *self-realization-need*.

- **Proficiency Motives**: Proficiency motives and their associated values in professional career call for excellence in meeting the professional standards along with related aesthetic values of beauty. Intelligent students are attracted to engineering profession in part because of these opportunities and challenge the profession offers to them.
- **Compensation Motives**: Compensation motives is also an important factor to attract students to engineering profession as it offers social rewards such as income, power, recognition and job or career stability. To a large extent self-interest of students is also responsible to motivate them for the professional life.
- **Moral Motives**: Moral motives include desires to serve the society, contribute to the well-being of others, to meet one's own responsibilities, etc. Such motives of moral caring and respect affirms the natural tendency to accept that other people have inherent moral worth.

19.2 Ethical Corporations

From its inception of engineering profession, Ethical considerations have been embedded in corporations. As engineering aims at production of economical and safe products for the ever-increasing market size; and the complexity of large projects that usually requires many individuals work together; there arises the need for ethical values in corporate life. Formation of corporation placed some responsibilities on corporate world, like introduction of procedures and controls for smooth running of corporate activity, which sometimes give rise to ethical dilemmas for employees. Engineers face problem centered on a conflict between professional independence and administrative bureaucratic loyalty. The role of the engineers requires judicious compromises between professional ideals and business demands.

Corporate influence is not a unique situation to engineering profession. Today, all types of professionals are involved in some way or the other with corporate world. There are multiple functional areas like engineering, medicine, law, administration, finance, journalism, science, etc. where professionals are employed. Not only engineers within the corporation but corporations themselves face ethical dilemmas prevailing in business environment. Most corporations at least strive to be morally responsible as far as possible. There is need for professional ethics and business ethics to be rationalized and harmonized to reduce conflicts among themselves.

19.3   Attempts to evolve a Global Ethical Framework

In global business context, advanced countries particularly USA has been expanding its economic sphere of influence and control over under developed countries. The expansion has been through multinational corporations (MNCs), who had developed advanced technologies and automated production process in all fields of human requirements. In a global environment, with the emergence of multinational corporations there is increasing economic globalization, which necessitates greater concern about the implementation and practice of ethical considerations in global businesses.

Within the United States, interest in global business ethic for multinational firms started in the late 1960's. An important issue of global business ethics has been formulating an acceptable code of conduct for global business. Efforts of US government have been to evolve ethical code of conduct for business through legal means and passage suitable of legislation accordingly. Discussion at great length took place on societal concerns on a variety of issues, thrown up by changing nature of business operations such as environmentalism, equal rights in the workplace, and ethical complexities caused by changes in technology.

With passage of laws, individual behaviors and corporate practices have changed but the complete code of socially acceptable business ethics is far from complete. The problem of defining a code becomes more complex and acute when considered on a global basis.

United States congress passed legislation in 1977, with title *Foreign Corrupt Practices Act* (FCPA), as an attempt to establish *a global ethical framework* for business. The main components of the legislation passed were:
- Making it a crime for American corporations to offer or provide payments to officials of foreign governments for the purpose of obtaining or retaining business.
- Individual employees of a firm could not be prosecuted for violating the FCPA unless the firm itself was found to have violated the law, thus removing the potential for firms to create scapegoats.
- Requiring additional record keeping for firms to make bribery more difficult to conceal.
- Forbidding corporations to indemnify fines imposed on directors, officers, employees or agents.

- Permitting so called *grease* payments to clerical workers in foreign governments.

19.4 Corruption and acceptance of Gifts

Many times, conflicts of interest violate trust and undermining specific obligations. There is a trust relationship between employed professionals with their employers and clients. Allowing any side interests of employees to prevail on their responsibilities towards the organization, distorts one's judgment and violates that trust relationship. Many conflicts of interest are objectionable in business affairs because they pose risks to free and fair competition. In particular, bribery and large gifts are objectionable because they lead to awarding contracts for reasons other than the best work for the best price.

Gift giving is a common practice in international and domestic business. It is one of the techniques of promoting one's products and services by developing smooth relationships with the clients. Executives dealing with international clients sometimes face a tricky complex situation in business towards gift giving, because wherever gift giving is not treated as a good gesture, it may also lead to problems ranging from minor embarrassment to even failure in securing business, if the concept is not properly understood.

Ethical relativism may be used to understand the issue of gift giving (and receiving) in different cultures. In some cultures, business gifts are expected and highly appreciated whereas in some others, it is equated to an attempt of bribing for favorable decisions. In highly developed societies and cultures gift giving is viewed as an important social obligation and a meaningful activity. In most low context cultures, it is an optional activity. In fact, in some cultures and countries people feel uneasy in accepting gifts because they do not like to be obligated by receiving gifts.

19.4.1 Varieties of corruption in Global Business

According to a study more than a trillion dollars a year is paid in bribery. These payments are a problem not just because they end up in the pockets of greedy officials or because they are a drain on the project budgets, but because they set in motion a chain of events, such as, the selection of unqualified contractors, the gross inflation of prices, the delivery of substandard goods or of nothing at all that defeat development and add to unproductive debt. In fact, corruption and its offspring are now widely acknowledged to be the single greatest impediment to development (EY Report, 2012).

Let us see how corruption works and how money is stolen from the projects. Government and project officials can divert funds from projects by:

- Demanding bribes and kickbacks from contractors in exchange for contract awards and other favors. This is the most common method of siphoning funds because it is easy to accomplish, hard to detect and very lucrative: the standard 10% kickback demand on a routine $50 million road rehabilitation project, for example, would yield the dishonest officials $5 million. This is from just one project and many officials supervise many projects.
- Secretly owning front companies that do business with the project. The profit margins are usually higher than kickbacks, especially if the secret owners raise prices and cut back on quality, as is often the case. Corrupt officials also can profit by leasing or selling property to the projects and by using project employees and assets in their front businesses, of course without paying for either.
- Converting project funds and assets to the official's own personal use. These transactions are usually small compared to those described above, and include:
  - Embezzling cash from project accounts
  - Diverting vehicles and computers to personal use
  - Using project funds to pay for vacations, buy cars or build houses, or
  - Selling goods intended for the project such as medicines, food or construction materials, etc. for personal profit (perhaps through their front companies) and so on.

Contractors can also steal from projects funds and recover the cost of their bribes by: overcharging for goods and services supplied for the project; billing extra charges by showing supply of goods or services that are never delivered; and by substituting less expensive, lower quality materials than required as per the contract, or billing lesser-paid employees at higher rates on consulting contracts, etc.

19.5 Impact of Gifts and Bribery on Business

Because of the great variety of possible outside interests, conflicts of interest can arise in business in innumerable obvious as well as subtle ways. It should be noted that even the appearance of conflicts of interest, especially in the nature of seeking a personal profit, at the expense of the employer, is considered unethical because this can harm an organization as much as any actual bias that might result from such practices. Few of the more common form of unethical personal interest are taking or giving bribes, gifts and kickbacks. Let us understand what they mean in personal and corporate life.

- **Bribe:** A bribe is a substantial amount of money or goods offered unethically to corrupt officials which is beyond the stated business contract or with the aim of winning the contract or keeping the contract alive in spite of some irregularities and objections and where the advantage is illegal or otherwise unethical. Typically, but not always, bribes are made in secret. IEEE code of ethics clearly directs its members to reject bribery in all its forms.
- **Gifts:** Gifts are not bribes as long as they are small gratuities offered in the normal conduct of business. A gratuity is an amount of money usually tendered to certain service sector employees for a service performed. In industry gratuities are paid to employees for their services to the company. Often, companies give gifts to selected employees of government agencies or partners in trade. Many such gifts are unobjectionable, though some of them are intended as bribery and still others create conflicts of interest and strictly speaking that do not involve bribery.

19.5.1 Difference between Gift and Bribe

In theory distinctions between gift and bribe may seem clear but in practice they become blurry. Bribes are illegal or immoral as they involve substantial amount of money or assets, which is enough to bring unfairness in impartial decision making in competitive situations. On the other hand, gifts as gratuities are of smaller amounts. Some gratuities play a legitimate role in the normal conduct of business, whereas others can bias judgment like a bribe does. That is why some companies often develop elaborate guidelines for their employees with regard to not to accept gifts from business contactors.

The question arises here about the gifts in routine business contexts? In normal market promotion exercise, it is common practice to offer occasional luncheon paid for by vendors giving sales presentations, or a gift is given in friendship rather than for influence. Codes of ethics sometimes take a hard line in forbidding all such gratuities, but many employers set forth more flexible policies. Company policies generally ban any gratuities that have more than nominal value or exceed widely from normal business practice.

19.5.2 Bribe given as Kickbacks

Kickbacks are prearranged payments made by contractors to companies or their representatives in lieu of award of contract. Thus, it is a payment made to someone who has facilitated a transaction or appointment, especially illicitly. A kickback is one form of bribery in which something valuable is exchanged for a favorable decision.

19.5.3 How Kickbacks work?

A kickback can take many forms, all of which are illegal. For example, it could be a portion of contract money paid by building contractor to a government official for award of the contract or a biomedical company offering training, travel or other benefits to doctors who recommend their product to patients or a financial institution that provides cash or bonuses to mortgage brokers who convince borrowers to select their services over another provider.

Companies should restrain from giving any direct or indirect favors or making payments as facilitation fees, gifts and special payments to family or friends of business-deal-officials. Such actions may be perceived as kickback and subject to penalties/punishment.

19.6 Status of Anti-Graft Laws

There are a number of specific laws prohibiting kickbacks. For example, a payment to a US government official may trigger a fine of three times to the value of the kickback and a prison sentence of up to 15 years. Bank kickbacks are prohibited under the Bank Bribery Amendments Act of 1985, which, in addition to the monetary fine, can also imprison offenders for up to 30 years. The Anti-Kickback Act of 1986 specifically prohibits government contractors from kickback schemes and subject's violators to both civil and criminal charges.

As on Nov 2016, government of India proposed amendment to the Prevention of Corruption Act 1988, making it mandatory for investigating agencies like CBI to take prior approval from the government before initiating investigations against public servants. For private sector a parliamentary committee has recommended criminalization of bribery by bringing corporate and their executives under the ambit of a proposed anti-corruption law. It has recommended a maximum jail term of seven years along with a fine and has also sought punishment for bribe givers.

19.7 Action for prevention of Fraud and Corruption Problem

Action to prevention of menace of bribery and corruption require concerted efforts at employee's level, organization level, industry level and national level. These are discussed below:

19.7.1 Actions at Employees level

Employees have right of conscientious refusal to any compulsive situation requiring bribery and corrupt practice in business and contracts. The right of conscientious refusal is the right to refuse to engage in unethical behavior because one views it as unethical. All employees have a moral right to refuse their participation in activities that are illegal and clearly unethical. For example, forging documents, altering test results, lying, giving or taking bribes or padding payrolls, etc. Forcing employees to act unethically by means of threats (to their jobs) plainly constitutes a violation of this right of theirs.

19.7.2 Actions at Organizational level

Companies while appointing their business partners, like advisors, majority-owned joint venture entities, subcontractors and suppliers should make them aware of the integrity policies of the company, and direct them to refrain from offering, promising or providing (directly or indirectly) any undue advantage to employees in contravention to stated company policies. Here advisors imply to include agents, consultants or intermediaries who assist in promoting, developing, expanding or maintaining a company's interests in business (e.g. sales, marketing and offsets).

Normally companies have written down policies and procedures governing the appointment, management role and payment of advisors. Companies shall make advisors aware of the integrity policies of the company, which shall be consistent with the global principles companies. They are required engaging services of capable personnel trained in anti-corruption, and compliance issues for the vetting of advisor's appointments and operations. Advisor's remuneration shall be based on legitimate services effectively rendered.

Basic countermeasures, which can be employed by an organization/employer, that are required to be implemented to promote the culture against bribe giving include:
- Develop corporate ethics programs for employees and train them at regular interval.
- Adopt strict policies for controlling gifts, entertainment and travel expenses; such requests must be carefully scrutinized at appropriate level.
- Thorough inquiry must be conducted prior to appointment of prospective agents, consultants and subcontractors.
- Build system of close scrutiny and approval by higher-level for appointments of local agent, consulting or supply contracts to be signed in the field.
- Include appropriate business integrity and broad audit clauses in all contracts and agreements.
- Ensure thorough inspection of all goods and works received from suppliers.
- Report suspected corruption, bid rigging or fraud to the organization which is financing the project.

19.7.3 Actions required in execution of International Contracts

Countermeasures that can be employed by host government agencies and lenders include (Kramer, 2012):
- Establish independent fraud and corruption investigation units within the organization or preferably take services of an external professional agency.
- Install and publicize confidential hotlines and other confidential reporting systems.
- Establish contractor compliance and voluntary disclosure schemes and ask contractors and subcontractors to disclose all fees and commissions received or given.
- Publicize through appropriate channels, contracting and payment information, audit and investigation results.
- Use independent inspectors to closely test and inspect goods, services and works received.
- Annual financial disclosure must be compulsory for all projects and government officials involved in procurement or other high-risk corruption areas, such as award of licenses, permits or inspections.
- Include anti-corruption warranties, business integrity and audit clauses in all contracts and large purchase orders.
- Audit clause for inspection rights should include financial records and also certain evidence of bribery, and be effective for at least five years after the contract closes.

19.7.4 Global Principles for Zero Tolerance Corruption

Companies will comply fully with all anti bribery laws applicable to the conduct of their business, such as the U.S. foreign corrupt practices act (FCPA) and those laws enacted pursuant to international conventions (including but not limited to the 1997 OECD convention and the united nations convention against corruption UNCAC 2003). Companies will not offer, promise, or provide any undue pecuniary or other advantage (e.g. payments, gifts, hospitality, as well as political contributions or charitable donations) to public officials, political parties or political candidates or to any private party in order to obtain or retain business or gain any other improper advantage in the conduct of their business.

19.8 Collective Bargaining

In the past, engineering societies have generally not supported the idea of engineer's participation in unions and collective bargaining in engineering.

They interpreted participation in unions as unprofessional and disloyal to employers. Critics argue that such blanket prohibitions reflect the excessive degree of control over engineers and engineering is dominated in favor of interest of corporations alone.

Collective bargaining is a process of negotiation between employers and a group of employees aimed for arriving at an agreement to regulate working conditions of the employees. A collective bargaining agreement (CBA) is usually negotiated *collectively* between management (on behalf of the company) and trades unions (on behalf of employees). This agreement regulates the terms and conditions and duties of employees in their workplace, as well as the duties of the employer. These agreements negotiate usually wage scales, working hours, training, health and safety, overtime, grievance mechanisms, etc.

The union may negotiate with a single employer who is representing a company's shareholders or may negotiate with a group of business managements to arrive at an industry wide agreement. A collective agreement functions as a *union labor contract* between an employer, which could be government also and one or more unions.

19.9 Occupational Crime

Occupational crime is a crime committed in the course of performing a legitimate occupation. Thefts of company property, vandalism, the misuse of information and many other activities come under the rubric of occupational crime. The occupational crime is also one of the principal forms of white collar crimes and has been quite familiar to general public.

White collar crimes also called socio-economic crimes are more or less non-emotional. These crimes are often committed by *respectable people*. These crimes are not easily detected because the people responsible for the crime are part of a wide, invisible social network. For example, financial frauds, misuse of power and authority, falsification of records, corporate evasion of taxes, consumer exploitation by traders, etc. do not come to public knowledge easily. These crimes are committed by government officers or business executives who are otherwise respectable members of society. General public seems to be more articulate for the *crimes of the street* by individuals like juvenile delinquency, robbery, theft, rape, etc. rather than the *crime of the office* by educated and respected people

For white collar crimes of petty type, social attitude of general public is lenient. Due to this crime of the milkmen, the street vendor, the grocery shopkeeper and many others who indulge in adulteration, use of false weights and measures, etc. go unpunished or receive comparatively light sentences by courts.

The most significant element in the commission of white collar crimes is *GREED*. Root cause of educated and professionals being weak in moral and ethical values, is education system which has neglected component of character building in curriculum under the guise of secular education. The weakening of religious and ethical values is to a large extent responsible for greed and corruption. The secular value systems such as capitalism and socialism have not been able to prevent white collar crimes.

19.10 Industrial Espionage

There are many varieties of espionage activities. Espionage for the purpose of national security is a vast area and not within the scope of our discussion. Industrial espionage, economic espionage or corporate espionage is a form of espionage conducted for commercial purposes. Economic espionage is conducted by governments through different channels and is international in scope, while industrial or corporate espionage is more often national and occurs between companies or corporations.

Industrial espionage is spying for the purpose of discovering the secrets of a rival manufacturer or other industrial company. Industrial espionage covers covert activities such as the theft of trade secrets, blackmail, technological surveillance, etc. Industrial espionage is most commonly used in industries which are high on technology front like defense sector, computer and auto sectors in which a significant amount of money is spent on research and development (R&D). Industrial espionage includes the theft of trade secrets confidential or valuable information of competitor by removal, copying or recording using electronic media like Internet and computers.

19.10.1 Forms of Economic and Industrial Espionage

Economic or industrial espionage takes place in two main forms. The purpose of espionage is to gather confidential and secret information about an organization. It may include the acquisition of intellectual property, like information on industrial process, ideas, techniques, formulas, etc. Or it could include proprietary business-related operational information, such as the customer data bank, pricing, sales, marketing, tenders related information, research and development, policies, prospective bids, planning or marketing strategies, etc. It may include other activities also such as theft of trade secrets, blackmail and technological surveillance.

Economic and industrial espionage is most commonly associated with technology-heavy industries such as Internet based computers, their software and hardware, biotechnology, aerospace, telecommunications, transportation and engine technology, automobiles, machine tools, energy, etc. Silicon Valley is known to be one of the world's most targeted areas for espionage, though any industry with information of use to competitors may be a target.

Through physical contact or via the Internet, computers have facilitated ease of access, and the process of collecting large amounts of information from various sources. The rising use of the Internet has also extended opportunities for industrial espionage with the aim of sabotage. One of the means of conducting industrial espionage is by exploiting vulnerabilities in computer software. Malware and spyware are popular tools for industrial espionage in transmitting digital copies of trade secrets, customer plans, future plans and contacts.

19.11 Price Fixing

Consumers have the right to expect benefits of the best goods and services at the lowest prices, obtained through free and open competitive bidding process in the marketplace. The competitive process works only when competitors set prices honestly and independently. When competitors start colluding on prices and inflate them collectively, the customer is cheated. Price fixing, bid rigging and other forms of collusion are illegal and are subject to criminal prosecution in India by competition commission of India (CCI) and in USA by the antitrust division of the United States department of justice.

Many national and International agencies are working jointly to continue their effort, to protect and promote free and open competition in the marketplaces, at the respective areas of operations and control.

19.11.1 Methods of price manipulations

Cartel is a formal or an informal agreement between the sellers to raise or fix prices with utter disregard to the market forces and competition prevalent in the market. Cartelization of sellers (producers or suppliers of products or services) is one of the most popular methods of price fixation in marketplace which defeats spirit of competition. It is aimed at restricting inter firm competition. Bid rigging is another form of cartelization which is the simplest form of price fixing in which an agreement is made by potential competitors to decide who the winning bidder would be. This collusion is similar to cartel with respect to the economic repercussions in the market, except that the former does not require a formal agreement.

19.11.2 US Federal Antitrust Enforcement

Enacted in 1890, the Sherman Act is among the USA's most important and enduring pieces of economic legislation. This act prohibits any agreement among competitors to fix prices, rig bids or engage in other anti-competitive activity. Criminal prosecution of Sherman Act violations is the responsibility of the Antitrust Division of the United States Department of Justice.

In addition to receiving a criminal sentence, a corporation or individual convicted of a Sherman Act violation may be ordered to make restitution to the victims for all overcharges. Victims of bid-rigging and price-fixing conspiracies also may seek civil recovery of up to three times the amount of damages suffered.

19.12   Endangering Lives

Industrial business entities, companies and corporations produce and supply goods and all the necessities and comforts of modern life to the society. For activity of production and supply of goods and services to the public, these organizations are supported by the collective capital of many shareholders and laws giving them protection and favoring their existence as business entities. These business corporations produce vehicle of large variety for transportation; process the food of different varieties that we consume every day; construct the office buildings in which we work and residential apartments where we live; and make a lot of goods we use every day. The manufacturing process provides employment but also profoundly effects our environment. The corporations are thus an essential part of supporting modern life.

Any form of pollution that can be traced to an immediate source to industrial practices is harmful to life. Most of the pollution on the earth can be traced back to industries or industrial products and processes of some kind or the other. In fact, the issue of industrial pollution has become of grave concern to agencies trying to fight for control against environmental degradation. Those countries who are trying for sudden and rapid growth of such industries are finding it to be a more serious problem of how to keep pollution level under control immediately without sacrificing the growth targets.

The corporations have dramatically improved the standard of living in many countries. This progress has not been without social costs in terms of pollution of the environmental degradation. Some corporate activity endangers life itself. For example, unsafe cars, drugs, and food additives endanger the health of consumers. Similarly, hazardous working conditions in some industries and exposure to toxic chemicals used in the manufacturing process put industrial worker's life and health at grave risks. Air and water pollution and the dumping of toxic chemicals in rivers or underground threaten pollution of even drinking water and poses great risk to public health.

19.12.1 Socially harmful corporate activity

As noted above, while industries and corporations are primarily responsible for modernization and the technological advancement of society, their activities have also imposed serious social costs in terms of pollution and environmental degradation. In recent decades, these costs in the form of deleterious effects on the public health, safety and welfare have become increasingly apparent. Corporate life-endangering activity can be divided into three categories:

1. **Occupational Harm:** A survey of the most notable recent occurrences in each of the areas illustrates that millions of Americans are exposed to health and safety risks while they work. Before the advent of the Occupational Health and Safety Act, thousands of people used to die annually from occupational diseases.
2. **Dangers to Consumers**: Some corporate products and activities are not safe and pose a danger to consumers. One study estimate that millions of Americans are injured each year in the home as a result of accidents involving unsafe consumer products- sometimes resulting into numbers of deaths and still larger number getting permanently disabling injuries.
3. **Deterioration of the environment affecting the general public**: In addition to conduct which endangers the life and health of employees and consumers, corporate activity also imperils the general populace by damaging the environment. Toxic chemicals in particular pose a grave health risk.

These examples of occupational, consumer and environmental harm illustrate the need to prevent socially harmful conduct of industries and corporations.

19.13 Summary

Self-Realization Ethics: Each of the ethical theory leaves considerable room for *self-interest* and gives greater prominence to personal commitments that individuals develop in pursuing *self-fulfillment*. There are two versions of *self-realization* ethics. One is *community-oriented* version, where the self to be realized in terms of caring relationships with communities. It emphasizes that we are social beings whose identities and meaning are linked to the communities in which we participate. The second version is *ethical-egoism*, where the self is conceived in a highly individualistic manner. Personal commitments are relevant in many ways to professional life, including one's choice of career and choice of jobs. Basic motives of professionals for taking up any work/project are proficiency, compensation and moral.

Humanism and socially conscious professionals try to orient application of technology to enrich sacred aspects of life and humanity. They work for making human life more interconnected through global communication, as well as attuned to nature. For many engineers, moral motivation and commitments are interwoven with spiritual and religious ones. They include factors like cultural appropriateness, openness, stewardship (frugality in the use of natural resources and energy), harmony (effectiveness of products together with promoting social unity), justice, caring for colleagues and trustworthiness.

Ethical focus of Corporations: Most of the engineering has been embedded into corporations. Today all professions are interwoven with corporations, including engineering, medicine, law, journalism, and science. Most corporations at least strive to be morally responsible. With the emergence of MNCs and increasing economic globalization, there is greater concern about the ethics of businesses with focus on societal concerns on a variety of issues, such as environmentalism, equal rights in the workplace and increasing ethical complexities caused by changes in technology.

Culture of Gift giving in Business: Gift giving is an integral part of both international and domestic business. It is a means of promoting one's products and services by strengthening the relationships with clients. *Ethical-Relativism* may be used to understand the issue of gift giving (and receiving) in different cultures. In some cultures, business gifts are expected and highly appreciated and, in some others, it may not be the case. High context cultures reportedly tend to view gift giving as an important social obligation and a meaningful activity. In most low context cultures, it is an optional activity.

Evil of Bribery, Gifts and Kickbacks in Business: In corporate world, common form of unethical personal interest is taking or giving bribes, gifts and kickbacks. Employed professionals are in trust relationships with their employers and clients. Allowing nurturing of any other side interest to influence in their decision making and responsibilities, distorts one's judgment and violates that trust. In particular, bribes and large gifts are objectionable because they lead to awarding contracts for reasons other than the best work for the best price. These payments are a problem because they set in motion a chain of events: the selection of unqualified contractors, the gross inflation of prices and the delivery of substandard goods.

A *Bribe* is a substantial amount of money or goods offered beyond a stated business contract with the aim of winning an illegal or otherwise unethical advantage in gaining or keeping the contract. Whereas, *Gifts* are not *bribes* as long as they are small gratuities offered in the normal conduct of business. Prearranged payments made by contractors to companies or their representatives in exchange for contracts actually granted are called *Kickbacks*. A kickback is a method of bribery in which something of value is exchanged for a favorable decision.

Collective Bargaining: Itis a process of negotiation between employers and a group of employees to regulate working conditions. A collective bargaining agreement (CBA) is a special type of commercial agreement between management and trades unions. The collective agreement regulates the terms and conditions of employees in their workplace, their duties and the duties of the employer. These agreement and negotiations usually set out wage scales, working hours, training, health and safety, overtime, grievance mechanisms and rights to participate in workplace or company affairs.

Occupational crime: It is a crime that is committed while performing a legitimate occupation. Thefts of company property, vandalism, the misuse of information and many other activities come under the rubric of *occupational-crime*. This is one of the principal forms of *white-collar-crimes* and is often committed by respectable people and is not easily detected because the people responsible for the crime are part of a wide, invisible social network.

Industrial espionage: Industrial espionage, economic espionage or corporate espionage is a form of espionage conducted for commercial purposes. Industrial or corporate espionage occurs between companies or corporations. Industrial espionage describes covert activities, such as the theft of trade secrets, bribery, blackmail and technological surveillance. Industrial espionage is most commonly associated with technology-heavy industries like the computer and auto sectors, etc. Information can make the difference between success and failure. Computers have facilitated the process of collecting information, due to the ease of access to large amounts of information through physical contact or via the Internet.

Competitive Bidding *vs.* Price Fixing: Public and private organizations often rely on a competitive bidding process to achieve the best goods and services at the lowest prices. When competitors collude, prices are inflated and the customer is cheated. Then price fixing is carried out through the cartelization of sellers (producers or suppliers of products or services). It is aimed at restricting inter firm competition. Bid rigging is a specific and simplest form of price fixing, in which an agreement is entered into by the potential competitors to decide who the winning bidder would be. Price fixing, bid rigging and other forms of collusion are illegal and are subject to criminal prosecution.

Some Industrial Activities Endangering Lives: Industrial business entities, companies and corporations produce and supply goods and all the necessities and comforts of modern life to the society. However, this progress has not been without social costs. Some corporate activity endangers life itself. These costs are in the form of deleterious effects on the public health, safety and welfare. Corporate life-endangering activity

Chapter 19: Ethical Operational Issues Encountered in Engineers Profession 351

can be divided into three categories: 1) Occupational harm 2) Dangers to consumers and 3) Deterioration of the environment affecting the general public. Hazardous working conditions and toxic chemicals used in industry pose life and health risks to industrial workers.

Review questions

1. What are the motives behind *self-realization ethics*? What are sources of these motives?
2. What are the features of an ethical corporation? Describe how a global ethical framework for ethics of businesses in a global environment can be evolved?
3. Explain how corruption works and how money is stolen from the projects. How Government and project officials can divert funds from projects?
4. Comment on practice of gift giving and how can you differentiate it from bribery?
5. What is status of legal provision to check graft in the private sector in India? What steps do you suggest for solving fraud and corruption problem?
6. Explain global principles for *zero tolerance corruption*. What actions are required in execution of International contracts to check corruption?
7. What is the purpose of collective bargaining between employees and employers? What it tries to achieve, prevent or safeguard?
8. What types of activities are counted as occupational crime? What are white collar crimes and who performs it? Give examples of *crimes in office* and *crimes on the street*.
9. What are the types of espionage activities faced by industry? Describe briefly each of them.
10. Competitive market assures best prices to consumers. What methods are used by producers and suppliers for Price Manipulations to exploit the ultimate users? What are legal measures to protect consumers' interest?
11. Describe Socially Harmful Corporate Activities which endanger Lives?

20 Whistleblowing

Learning objectives

In this chapter you will learn about

- Historical background of whistleblowing
- Function of whistleblowing, when to blow whistle and who are protected by Law?
- *Whistleblowing Protection Act, 2011* of India and public interest whistleblowing
- Types of whistle blowing and steps for preventing whistleblowing

20.1 Introduction

The term whistleblowing probably is called so because of analogy with the whistles blown by referee or umpire in games to draws public attention to a foul in the game. The term whistleblowing is of relatively recent use in public and corporate affairs in India, although the phenomenon itself is not new.

Whistleblowers are the individuals who expose wrongdoing of public concern. For example, wrongdoing or negligence in industry with regard to quality and safety issue on products and services, health hazards, environmental and pollution issue, financial irregularities/ mismanagement, corruption and fraud in organizations; or wrongdoing in government departments, bureaucracy, public services etc. could become the matter of whistleblowing. Whistleblowing could be by filing a written complaint with higher authorities; or raising the issue through any other agency (internal or external); or with the government authorities that initiates action for an investigation in to the organizations alleged behavior.

For an Engineer, it is important to note that not all whistleblowing involves going outside the organization. However, an individual need not be a member of an organization in order to publicly blow the whistle on it. Journalists, politicians and consumer groups may come to know about corruptions in an organization, even though they do not work for it, but can blow the whistle on them by publishing articles or informing regulatory agencies.

20.2 What is Whistleblowing?

US civic activist Ralph Nader coined the phrase in the early 1970s to avoid the negative connotations found in other words such as *informers*. Whistleblowing is defined by some authors as follows

1. A whistleblower as an employee who believes or perceives certain organizational practices to be illegal or unethical, seeks to stop those practices by informing top management for initiating remedial measures or failing that by notifying authorities outside the organization.
2. Whistleblower could also be a former employee of the organization to disclose what he/she believes to be wrongdoing in or by that organization.
3. Whistleblowing occurs when an employee informs the public of inappropriate activities or practices going on inside the organization.
4. Whistleblowing is the release of information by a member or former member of an organization, with authentic evidence of illegal and/or immoral conduct in the organization that is not in the public interest.

20.3 Historical background of whistleblowing

Attitudes toward whistleblowing have considerably evolved during the last 60 years in corporate world. There was time when loyalty to the company was the ruling norm and whistleblowing was virtually unheard in corporate world. But in the present time, public is more aware of its rights and responsibilities of corporate world, and public outrage about corporate misconduct has created a favorable climate for whistleblowing.

Prior to the 1960s, corporations had substantial autonomy on its policies for employee and could fire an employee at will, sometimes without assigning any reason. Employees were expected to be loyal to their organizations at all costs. In this background, only exceptions were unionized employees who had better legal protection and who could only be fired for *just cause*. The courts upheld employee's constitutional right to fearlessly criticize company policies. In some of the private industries there were few channels of communication built into the corporate system for airing grievances. Some progressive companies like IBM have an effective open-door policy from its earliest days which allowed employees to raise any issue. In majority of organizations there was lack of protection for whistleblowers and problems raised by them were often concealed rather than solved.

In the late 1970s in the wake of the civil rights movement, USA enacted federal and state laws to protect employees in private industry, including anti-discrimination legislation to regulate hiring and firing policies. Many of these laws had provisions forbidding an employer to retaliate against whistleblowers for reporting any violations or wrong practice to public authorities. Complaints about reprisals could be filed with agencies such as the Equal Employment Opportunity Commission and the Occupational Safety and Health Administration (OSHA).

The code of ethics for United States government service says that employees should put loyalty to the highest moral principles and to country above loyalty to persons, party or government department and they should expose corruption wherever discovered.

20.4 Whistleblowers Protection Act 2011 of India

This is an act of the parliament which provides a mechanism to investigate alleged corruption and misuse of power by public servants. The acts also protect anyone who exposes alleged wrongdoing in the government bodies, projects and offices. The wrongdoing might take the form of fraud, corruption or mismanagement. The act will also ensure punishment for false or frivolous complaints.

The Act was approved as part of a drive to eliminate corruption in the country's bureaucracy. It will deal with complaints relating to disclosure on any allegation of corruption or willful misuse of power or willful misuse of discretion against any public servant. The act allows an inquiry into such disclosure to provide adequate safeguards against victimization of the person making such complaint.

The act protects whistleblowers, i.e. persons making a public interest disclosure related to an act of corruption, misuse of power, or criminal offense by a public servant. Any public servant or any other person including a non-governmental organization may make such a disclosure. Every complaint has to include the identity of the complainant. The act prescribes penalties for knowingly making false complaints.

The proposed law has neither provision to encourage whistleblowing (i.e. giving financial incentives) nor deals with corporate whistleblowers; it does not extend its jurisdiction to the private sector. The directorate of income tax intelligence and criminal investigation is one of the only agencies empowered for whistleblower protection.

The bill aims to balance the need to protect honest officials from harassment with protecting persons making a public-interest disclosure. It outlines sanctions for false complaints. However, it does not provide a penalty for attacking a complainant. Obligations to an organization are significant but they are not automatically cancelled or outweighed by the obligation to the public in all situations.

20.5 Types of Whistleblowing

Whistleblowing empowers workers to raise their voice for principles and ethics and blow whistle on unethical practices, wherever they happen to be that can cause harmful consequences for consumers, citizens and colleagues. Broad categorization and types of whistleblowing is mentioned below.

- **Internal:** *Internal whistleblower* is an employee who reports the wrongdoings to the officials at higher position in the organization; for example, a designated officer, workers or bosses in the same organization. Normally such internal whistle blowing is considered disloyal, improper conduct, indiscipline, insubordination, disobedience, etc.
- **External**: Where the wrongdoings or wrong practices are reported to the agencies outside the organization, like media, public interest groups or enforcement agencies. It is called *external whistleblowing*.
- **Alumni:** When the whistleblowing is done by the former employee of the organization it is called *alumni whistleblowing*.
- **Open:** When the identity of the whistleblower is revealed, it is called *open whistleblowing*.
- **Personal:** Where the wrongdoings of an organization are against one person only, disclosing such wrongdoings it is called *personal whistleblowing*.
- **Impersonal:** When the wrongdoing is to harm others in general, it is called *impersonal whistleblowing*.
- **Government:** When a disclosure is made about wrongdoings or unethical practices adopted by the officials of the Government.
- **Corporate:** When a disclosure is made about the wrongdoings in a business corporation, it is called *corporate whistleblowing*.

In USA the type of whistleblowing is categorized differently. It is more focused on fraud against the government which can occur in any industry, corporation, organization or government. Fortunately, individuals from many different backgrounds can blow the whistle to help and bring an end to the destructive practices. There are many different types of whistleblowers and laws that specifically protect them include:

- Corporate Whistleblowers
- Defense Contractor Whistleblowers
- Faulty Products Whistleblowers
- FCPA Whistleblowers
- FDA Whistleblowers
- Government Whistleblowers
- Healthcare Fraud Whistleblowers

- IRS Whistleblowers
- Medicare Fraud Whistleblowers
- Nursing Home Whistleblowers
- OSHA Whistleblowers
- SEC Whistleblowers

20.6 When whistleblowing should be attempted?

20.6.1 Internal whistleblowing

Any internal whistleblower should attempt to blow whistle only after making sure of following checks.
- That he/she has good intention in the interest of organization and interest of public at large.
- He/ She must be clear about his motive. It should not be a response to some anger, retaliation, revenge or publicity.
- He/ She must have correct and accurate information about organization wrongdoings. It should not be in the nature of hearsay or rumor.
- He/ She must possess some evidence which is reliable and can be produced before competent inquiring authority or agency. Circumstantial evidence is not clinching evidence.
- Make sure that Xeroxed copies of proof are not doctored by someone having ulterior motives. Make sure that someone is not using you as pawn for his purpose.
- Make sure that there is no political angle in your whistle. You are not working on somebody's behalf. You should understand that some enemies of business encourage an employee to be disloyal to the enterprise and disloyalty is bad in itself. They want to create and spread suspicion and disharmony and pry into the proprietary interest of business.
- Make sure that you are not dealing with confidential and secret matters/documents of the company. Because you may be charged with stealing or doing espionage unless you are directly involved in the matter.
- You must make use organization's internal channels of communication to blow an internal whistle. You must know how and who should be told or who can take corrective actions. Be careful in putting allegation on any individual by name. In organizations focus has to be on organizational working and not individuals working.

20.6.2 External whistle blowing

Engineer's attempt of whistle blowing is justified in going outside their organizations when safety is involved and they are morally permitted and have *moral obligation* also. To check *moral permissibility* for engineers to engage in external whistle blowing concerning safety, three conditions must be satisfied.
1. If the harm that will be caused by the product to the public is considerably serious.
2. If they make their concern known to their superiors and there is no appropriate remedial action.
3. If getting no satisfaction from their immediate superiors and they exhausted all the channels available within the organization, including going up to the board of directors.

To check *moral obligation,* one should make sure that he/she has documented evidence which would convince any reasonable, impartial observer that his view of situation is correct and the organizational practice or policy is wrong.

20.7 Public Interest whistleblowing

Workers can blow whistle on confirmation of wrongdoing at work and making a disclosure in the public interest. A worker can report about the practices or things that aren't right or proper, if anything is illegal or if anyone at work is neglecting their duties or issues mentioned below:
- Someone's health and safety are in danger and corrective action must be initiated by authorities
- There is damage taking place to the environment which is not being cared or attended
- Something amounting to a criminal offence
- The company isn't obeying the law like not having the right insurance
- Company engaging in covering up the wrongdoing and not taking corrective action

A whistleblower can't be dismissed because of whistleblowing and they are protected by law.

20.8 Legal protection to whistleblowing activity

The following people are protected by law if they are victimized for their act of whistleblowing: employees, agency workers, people that are under training with an employer, but not employed and self-employed workers, if supervised or working off-site. However, workers aren't protected by law from dismissal a) if they break the law when they report something, e.g. if they signed the official secrets act; and b) if they found out about the wrongdoing when someone wanted legal advice (*legal professional privilege*), e.g. if they're a solicitor.

20.9 Preventing whistleblowing

Whistleblowing should be taken as positive feedback on efficiency, productivity and quality and consumer interest of any business or service activity. This approach will definitely reduce cases of whistleblowing. Positive feedback reduces number of operational mismatches and bottlenecks of the system. Preventing whistleblowing requires internal channels to release pressure in the system, thus preventing it to become a whistle later on. It requires a multipronged cultural and operational approach. Some of the salient points of these approaches are given below.

- **Create a culture where leadership is respected and staff is treated fairly**: Employees and executives have equal stake in creating and maintaining an environment where honesty and integrity are valued. A lot depends on both of them that how they approach or develop interrelationship with each other and the methods they use to solicit, close and grow their positive involvement in the growth of business which will benefit both. Internal whistle blowing can be very valuable for an organization; reports of misconduct, given early and taken seriously, can avert disaster.
- **Create an environment of positivity towards whistle blowing**: In many organization whistleblowers revealed in interviews that they did whistleblowing because they felt support by managers and coworkers, and they believed that management will do something positive and they were able to report anonymously. Most of the internal whistle blowers prefer to handle issues within the organization before venturing outside and most will go to their direct supervisor first.
- **Protect your whistleblowers**: According to a study from the ethics resource center 22% of internal whistleblowers reported retaliation from within their organizations for their action. Retaliation deters future whistleblowers; therefore, organizations need to evolve a system that a genuine whistle blower is protected and retaliators are punished. For example, some organizations ensure that those who report wrongdoing, their careers are not derailed.
- **Develop and maintain robust ethics and compliance programs**: To address the retaliation problem, one way appears to have a corporate wise strong ethics and compliance programs. The ethics studies found that retaliation was associated with decrease in

employee's concern for internal operations and their engagement with it; their increased desire level to leave the organization and increased intentions to carry issues outside of the organization. Research suggests that it's usually very difficult to report wrongdoing in organizations and among the main reasons was found that people fear of retaliation for reporting and the belief that in spite of reporting on wrongdoing nothing will be done. This decrease in employee's internal engagement which has to be prevented through policy changes towards whistleblowing.

By fostering a culture of self-regulation and accountability, management can ensure that the interest of staff and the business operations are protected. Whistleblowing is a valuable tool in any organization's corporate governance strategy. It empowers employees to act on incidences of misconduct; and help maintain a safe workplace, while protecting profits and reputation of the organization.

20.10 Summary

The term whistleblower probably arises by analogy with the referee or umpire who draws public attention to a foul in a game by blowing the whistle. Whistleblowers are individuals who expose wrongdoing of public concern. For example, quality and safety issue on products and services, health hazards, environmental and pollution issue, financial irregularities/ mismanagement, corruption and fraud in organizations or wrongdoing in public services, government departments, bureaucracy etc. are areas of whistleblower. An individual, journalists, politicians and consumer groups may come to know about corruptions in an organization, even though they do not work for it but, can blow the whistle on them.

Whistleblowers Protection Act, 2011 of India: This is an act of the parliament which provides a mechanism to investigate alleged corruption and misuse of power by public servants and also protect anyone who exposes alleged wrongdoing in government bodiesand projects.Theactprotects whistleblowers making a public interest disclosure related to an act of corruption, misuse of power or criminal offense by a public servant. Every complaint has to include the identity of the complainant. The act does not deal with corporate whistleblowers. It does not extend its jurisdiction to the private sector.

Types of whistleblowing: There are many types of whistleblowing like internal (by an employee), external (by the people outside the organization like media, public interest groups or enforcement agencies), alumni (by former employee), open (when the identity of the whistleblower is revealed), Personal (where harm is to one person only), Impersonal (when the wrongdoing is to harm others), etc.

Internal whistleblowing: Any internal whistle blowing should attempt to blow whistle only with good intention in the interest of organization and interest of public at large. It should not be a response to some anger, retaliation, revenge or publicity. His information must be correct and accurate. He/ She must possess some evidence which is reliable. Make sure that there is no political angle in your whistle. Make sure that you are not dealing with confidential and secret matters/documents of the company.

External whistleblowing: Engineers whistleblowing outside their organizations is justified only when safety is involved and they have *moral obligation* also. To check *moral permissibility* for external whistle blowing, following conditions must be satisfied *viz. if* the harm that will be done by the product to the public is serious and considerable.

Public interest whistle blowing: Workers can blow whistle on suspecting wrongdoing at work and making a disclosure in the public interest. A worker can report things that aren't right, illegal, a criminal offence, if someone's health and safety is in danger, there is damage to the environment or company isn't obeying the law, any covering up of wrongdoing, etc. A whistleblower can't be dismissed because of whistleblowing. They are protected by law.

Preventing whistleblowing: It should be taken as positive feedback on efficiency, productivity and quality and consumer interest of any business or service activity. This approach will definitely reduce cases of whistleblowing. Positive feedback reduces number of operational mismatches and bottlenecks of the system. Preventing whistleblowing requires internal channels to release pressure in the system, thus preventing it to become a whistle later on. It requires a multipronged cultural and operational approach.

Review questions

1. What is whistleblowing? Give historical background of whistleblowing.
2. Explain main features of Whistleblowers Protection Act, 2011 of India.
3. What are types of whistleblowing?
4. Explain that in what circumstances whistleblowing should it be attempted? What is Internal or external whistleblowing?
5. Who can do *public interest whistleblowing* and who are protected by law for an act of whistleblowing?
6. What are actions recommended to prevent whistleblowing?

Section 6: Globalization of Technology, Engineering and, Consequential Ethical Issues

21 Globalization, Cross-Cultural Operations and Research

Learning objectives

In this chapter you will learn about

- Development of *global industrial culture*, cross-cultural issues of globalization
- Issues of transfer and implementation of technology to host countries
- Ethical problems, military operations, programs and weapon development
- Dual use technologies, engineer's role in development of dual use products
- Environmental problems due to modern industrial and military developments
- Types and objectives of research, universal nature of research ethics

21.1 Science promoting Global Culture

A world in spite of overdose of cultural conflicts is also driven to become a single global entity. Globalization does not imply that cultural diversity has to disappear. The real impediment for process of globalization lies in *cultural intolerance*.

The science brings forth another global culture due to fundamental nature of scientific knowledge that does not depend on ethnic, political or religious background. Science is also process of liberation from the chain of collective myths and prejudices. Engineering and technology are having global reach and applications. They do not have limitation of territory, culture, values, etc.

When we analyze applications of human values and ethics for engineers; their understanding of prevailing local moral, ethical, social values, work practices, and behavior patterns becomes important; because in global business these factors demand different type of response on work culture, and operating ethical considerations. Global business demands its own particular work environment and work culture from operation, process, efficiency and quality point of view. There are many corporations, multinational companies, organizations, international bodies and associations etc., which have global presence with their own prescribed code of conduct, standards, norms and service rules etc. In modern times, the presence of international organizations such as the UNO, UNESCO and ILO etc. attest to international interdependence.

An engineer, for being successful and effective, has to understand global requirements of engineering practice; and develop global outlook in his operations and engineering decisions etc.

21.1.1 Role of MNCs in Cross-Cultural Environment

The word *globalization* refers both to the international context of engineering and to the increasingly wide social dimension of engineer's work. Global issues concern with ethical and operational issues of Multinational Corporations (MNCs) and business entities. The impact of operations of these MNCs on the environmental changes, hygienic consideration, agricultural and food industry, transportation and communication, power and energy generation etc. have given rise to many safety and ethical concerns at global level. There is need to have *global code of conduct on computer ethics* for safety, security and confidentiality of information/data; supervisory control on development of defense related weapons of mass destruction, etc.; with emphasis on maintaining harmony and ecological balance of nature. We shall discuss below some of these issues.

Multinational implies that the company is doing business operations in many countries. For example, Union Carbide in 1984 operated in 38 countries. Purpose of spreading the operations and outsourcing to other countries is optimization of overall cost of raw material, labor, services as well as business friendly culture and legal system. For example, the benefits to US companies of doing business in less-developed countries are inexpensive labor, availability of abundant natural resources, favorable tax arrangements and fresh market for products. In the process developing countries are benefited in terms of new jobs with better perks and remuneration packages, technology upgrade, opportunity to modernize the society with social benefits like impact on work culture and better quality of life style. But at the same time question arises about what should be responsibilities of these corporations in foreign countries in case of disasters or environment pollutions arising due to their faulty operations. The case of Bhopal gas tragedy will amply highlight the point of responsibilities of MNCs in such cases.

The question arises to define the role and the responsibilities of engineering corporations and their engineers towards host country while doing business?

21.1.2 Issues related to Technology Transfer to host countries

MNCs have responsibility to select appropriate technology based on need, working culture, status of supporting infrastructure in the host country. Technology includes hardware (raw material, machines and infrastructure) software, logistics and technical skills (technical, organizational and managerial skills and work culture, procedures). It is a process of transplanting technology to a new location and ensuring its implementation and successful absorption. It also requires building totally new business infrastructure there. Transfer of technology may involve multiple agencies like governments, suppliers, contractures, technical operational and training staffs, consulting firms, multinational corporations, etc.

Selection of location and appropriate technology must be scrutinized from the point of view of long term impact on overall development of the region, as many technologies bring with them harmful side-effects; like environment pollution, mass migration from rural areas to cities (place of work) causing overcrowding of cities, increasing property cost, crime and disease.

21.2 Defense Operations and Weapon Development

The first ethical concern with any new defense program and military weapon system is whether its development, deployment or use would violate any existing international law. Emerging technologies can also raise much larger worries about impact on environment, given their evolutionary nature.

Defense and weapon development have mainly driven development of many technologies which later on were made available to civilian sector as spin off technologies, with suitable adaptation and modifications. These programs were carried out in many branches of engineering like ground segment military preparations, space segment programs, nuclear energy programs, bio-engineering, chemical engineering, etc. In short much of the world's technological activity has military focus or application.

Some of defense technologies pose moral problems of the nature that their magnitude makes national economies and stability of under developed countries shattered thus affecting well-being of their whole population. Developed countries on the other hand thrive on international trade of military hardware and software.

There are several reasons for an engineer to do his or her best on a military job. High among them are patriotism and prudential interest.

21.2.1 Ethical problems of Defense Industry and Military Operations

Across the globe many nations provide special privileges and status to their defense industries without paying sufficient attention to the problems which accompany large military buildups in all countries across the globe. Further, unethical business practices occur in all massive projects. There is always urgency of completing a weapon system before it becomes obsolete in the market, due to competitions on similar systems of rival parties. This pressure of time and secrecy, which surrounds such projects, makes proper oversight particularly difficult.

COSTs overrun are due to delay in development, corruptions in contracts, and obsolescence of technology which sometimes cripples the progress. Secrecy sometimes breeds corruption, becomes a cover for misdeeds, inefficiencies in operations and, wrong decisions. Under secrecy, safety issues are compromised for workstations having radiation hazards like in nuclear plants, aerospace industry, naval bases, etc. Military stores and supplies including food supplies chain (for field staff at remote areas) are prone for pilferage, transit damages, misappropriations and corruption.

Secrecy consideration invites new ethical problems for engineers in various ways. For example, question arises that should the deficiencies discovered in systems of military significance be reported or made available to the government or should they be withheld from the larger scientific and public community?

21.2.2 Globally, Defense Budgets are big compulsive burden on economy

Military in any nation provides protection to its citizens from any external aggression or internal disturbances, whether man made or natural. Defense expenditure does not contribute to general well-being (food, clothes and shelter) of the population at large. However, it is a compulsive burden on economy to protect the sovereignty of the nation.

This raises an important question that how long and how much a nation can divert scarce resources (funds, materials, talent, etc.) into an economically non-contributing sector without overburdening the economy. Every dollar or rupee spent on defense produces fewer jobs than an equal expenditure in civilian sector on essential services and infrastructures such as education, roads, etc. In the present era, a nation is considered strong when its economy is strong. This may require blending of defense industry infrastructure; training of engineers and managers to make them capable of designs, manufacturing and sales techniques; that in peace time can produce reasonably priced, competitive civilian goods on an open market with a chance of success. A changeover to peace time utility of defense resources requires careful planning so that effectiveness of defense does not suffer major dislocations. This issue has been addressed next under *dual-use-policy,* adopted by advanced countries to exploit military technologies available with them for utilization in commercial market, thus gaining economic advantage.

Many academicians have discussed about the definition of *dual-use technology policies* and how much it should be influenced by the social, economic and political factors which determines the *dual-use-relationships.* It is broadly agreed that a dual-use technology policy should mainly address the social network; within which each technology is developed in order to define a positive *dual-use-relationship.* Such technological know-how should be made available for multiple purposes, including both military and commercial ones.

21.2.3 Technology Spin-Offs and diffusion of Dual-Use Technologies

Dual use technology refers to the fields of research and development that have application to both defense and civilian sector (i.e. commercial area of general public). Some technologies are important for both sectors (i.e. military and civilian commercial customers). For example, imaging-sensing technology has broad application in surveillance systems, video cameras and robot vision systems that find both military and commercial uses. Similarly, global positioning systems used for navigation, aircraft engines and most medical and safety equipment are dual use products. In fact, basic technologies are sector neutral and at the generic level, most of today's important technologies can be considered of dual use nature. Dual use products are items used by both military and commercial customers.

21.2.4 Scientists and engineers role in the development of dual-use products and applications

Modern technologies and related equipment have dual use applications both for civilian and military purposes. For human and environmental safety there are national and international conventions, treaties and professional code of ethics. It is the responsibility of organizations to acquaint scientist and engineers employed for research and development purpose with relevant guidelines and work ethics in their jobs. Scientists and engineers should take wider care of ethical responsibilities in design of such equipment and systems as well as their applications and technologies in compliance with the international conventions and treaties relevant to their work.

21.2.5 Environmental problems due to modern industrial and military developments

1. **Biological and Chemical Weapons:** The researchers, engineers, managers and other agencies, share ethical and social responsibility, while funding, conducting, administering and regulating activities of biomedical sciences. Their ethical responsibility is to ensure use of modern knowledge on micro-organisms, toxins or other biological agents for the advancement of human welfare and not any application against any human being. Government of India is taking all necessary steps against bioterrorism activities. Various legislations have been enacted to protect the environment of pollutants and any other subversive activity because of the biological agents. However, to ensure bio-safety and bio-security, awareness programs with active participation of the researchers in the implementation arms of legislations would need to be further strengthened.

2. **Attempt to reduce Electronic Waste:** There are over 20-50 million tons of e-waste generated worldwide each year, consisting of cell phones, computers, music devices and also other electronic devices like microwaves and refrigerators, etc. In west some of this waste languishes in landfills stateside, over 60% of this waste is shipped to places like China and Africa, where it is dealt with in facilities that lack the money, machinery and ability to properly dispose them off. As a result, these items leak toxic chemicals including chemicals like mercury, lead and cadmium into the environment and bodies to which they are exposed. This toxic dump thrown overseas, leaches toxic chemicals into the ground, air and water; and contributing to a global epidemic of improperly disposed electronic waste. Scientists and engineers can pay attention to this environmental problem by using bio-friendly and degradable materials in their designs.

3. **Problem of Nuclear Waste:** Industrial products and processes are in general responsible for generation of wastes which are unavoidable, unrecyclable and hazardous. Such wastes require careful management to ensure adequate protection of humans and the environment. The timescales over which such protection is required can extend for nuclear waste well beyond the lifespan of current or forthcoming generations. Hence there is an ethical point to care about future generations and their consumption, growth and survival requires proper control to reap the benefit from the earth's resources by present generation. Such a concern for the protection of human health and the environment in a developing world has been illustrated by the concept of *sustainable development* put

forward by the World Commission on Environment and Development. This concept is principally an ethical, implying as satisfying the needs of the present, without compromising the ability of future generations to meet their own needs.

21.2.6 Examples of Military Technologies Transferred to Civilian Sector

US Department of Defense (DoD) has often initiated many technologies that have advanced civil societies development. Some of them like antibiotics, jet travel, the Internet, GPS, etc. have been mainstay of the civilian sector and the societies globally.

Some of the major military technologies transferred to civilian sectors are listed below:
1. Internet (supporting global communication network)
2. Satellite communications (supporting communication, remote sensing and satellite imaging/ mapping)
3. Super computers (providing data processing facility to large organizations/ governments and now supporting cloud computing applications)
4. Radar technology (used in weather forecasting)
5. Nuclear technology (power generation)
6. Global position system (GPS): (determining location on the globe, navigation, Google maps)
7. Antibiotics (medical drugs)
8. Jet travel (air industry)

21.3 Research and Development

Research is undertaken within most professions. It is a way of examining and improving your process. More than a set of skills, it is a way of thinking and examining critically the various technical aspects or process of any professional work. It is a habit of probing, questioning and a systematic examination of the observations with the aim to establish more accurate assessment to make appropriate changes for more effective professional service.

21.3.1 Definition of Research

Research is a structured enquiry that utilizes acceptable scientific methodology to solve problems and create new knowledge or technology. Scientific methods consist of systematic observation, classification and interpretation of data.

When a research study is to be undertaken to find answers to a question it implies that the process:
- Is being undertaken within a framework of a set of philosophies (approaches). Philosophies means approaches e.g. qualitative, quantitative and within the concerned academic discipline in which one is trained.
- Applies procedures, methods and techniques which have been tested for their validity and reliability. Validity means that correct procedures have been applied to find answers to a question and reliability refers to the quality of a measurement procedure that provides repeatability and accuracy.
- Adopted is designed to be unbiased and objective. Unbiased and objective means that each step is taken in an unbiased manner and drawn each conclusion to the best of ability and without introducing any vested interest. Bias is a deliberate attempt to either conceal or highlight something.

Adherence to the three criteria mentioned above enables the process to be called research. However, the degree to which these criteria are expected to be fulfilled varies from discipline to discipline and so the meaning of research differs from one academic discipline to another.

21.3.2 Characteristics of Research

Research is a process of collecting, analyzing and interpreting information to answer question. But to qualify as research the process must have certain characteristics: it must, as far as possible, be controlled, rigorous, systematic, valid and verifiable, empirical and critical.
- **Controlled:** In real life there are many factors that affect an outcome. The concept of control implies that, in exploring causality in relation to two variables (factors), it requires to set up study in a way that minimizes the effects of other factors affecting the relationship. This can be achieved to a large extent in the physical sciences where most of the research is done in a laboratory. However, in the social sciences (hospitality, tourism, etc.) it is extremely difficult as research is carried out on issues related to human beings living in society, where such controls are not possible.
- **Rigorous:** One must be scrupulous in ensuring that the procedures followed to find answers to questions are relevant, appropriate and justified.
- **Systematic:** This implies that the procedure adopted to undertake an investigation should follow certain logical sequence. The different steps cannot be taken in a haphazard way.

- **Valid and Verifiable:** This concept implies that conclusions of research findings are correct and can be verified by others also.
- **Empirical:** In case of social and life sciences this means that any conclusion drawn are based upon hard evidence gathered from information collected from real life experiences or observations.
- **Critical:** Critical scrutiny of the procedures used and the methods employed are crucial to a research enquiry. The process of investigation must be foolproof and free from drawbacks. The process adopted and the procedures used must be able to withstand critical scrutiny.

For a process to be called research, it is imperative that it has the above characteristics.

21.3.3 Nature of Research

Research can be classified from three perspectives: 1) application of research study, 2) objectives in undertaking the research, and 3) inquiry mode employed. From application point of view there are two broad categories of research.

1. **Pure Research:** Pure research involves developing, testing theories and hypotheses that are intellectually challenging to the researcher but may or may not have practical application at the present time or in the future. The knowledge produced through pure research is sought in order to add to the existing body of research methods.
2. **Applied Research:** Applied research is done to solve specific, practical questions; for policy formulation, administration and understanding of a phenomenon. It can be exploratory, but is usually descriptive. It is almost always done on the basis of basic research. Applied research can be carried out by academic or industrial institutions. Often, an academic institution such as a university will have a specific applied research program funded by an industrial partner interested in that program.

21.3.4 Types of Research

From the viewpoint of objectives, a research can be classified as
- **Descriptive Research** attempts to describe systematically a situation, problem, phenomenon, service or program, or provides information about, say, living condition of a community, or describes attitudes towards an issue.
- **Correlational Research** attempts to discover or establish the existence of a relationship/interdependence between two or more aspects of a situation.

- **Explanatory Research** attempts to clarify why and how there is a relationship between two or more aspects of a situation or phenomenon.
- **Exploratory Research** is undertaken to explore an area where little is known or to investigate the possibilities of undertaking a particular research study (feasibility study / pilot study).

It may be noted that most of the studies are a combination of the first three categories.

Inquiry Mode: From the process adopted to find answer to research questions the following two approaches are used:
1. **Structured approach:** The structured approach to inquiry is usually classified as quantitative research.
2. **Unstructured approach:** The unstructured approach to inquiry is usually classified as qualitative research.

Steps in Research Process:
1. Formulating the research problem
2. Extensive literature review
3. Developing the objectives
4. Preparing the research design including sample design
5. Collecting the data
6. Analysis of data
7. Generalization and interpretation
8. Preparation of the report or presentation of results-formal write ups of conclusions reached.

21.3.5 Ethics and Research

It is necessary that fundamental ethical principles be included from the beginning in the design and implementation of research wherever participation of human beings is involved as participants. Ethical values of truth, honesty, transparency, sincerity, discipline, etc. to be practiced along with the code of ethics of particular profession in which research is being carried out. How ethical issues can affect the research study and how those problems can be overcome, should be thoroughly examined at the problem formulating stage.

Universal nature of Research Ethics: Ethical research principles are considered universal, transcending geographic, cultural, economic, legal and political boundaries. These principles are universal but the availability of the resources needed to maintain these principles are not universally made available. Similarly, the procedures used for the ethical vigilance of research studies may not be optimal.

Human participation in research projects has contributed to better quality of life through the development of diagnostic tools and successful treatments.

International character of Research Ethics in the field of social life sciences: Today a great amount of attention is directed at research that involves human participants. International research ethics ensure that research conducted at the local level follows international expectations and standards.

Human research ethics rest on 3 basic principles that are considered the foundation of all regulations or guidelines governing research ethics. These principles are 1) respect for persons; 2) beneficence; and 3) justice. These principles are considered universal, transcending geographic, cultural, economic, legal and political boundaries. Researchers, institutions, and human society, are obligated to assure that these principles are followed whenever research on humans is conducted.

21.3.6 Guidelines and Codes for Ethical problems in Research

Many guidelines, codes and regulations have been created in recent decades to guide the conduct of research involving human participants. These guidelines were created in response to keep under control ethical lapses to guide the ever-changing world of research, and provide answers to new problems and challenges created by the ever-changing research environment. Each reflects the principles of respect for persons, beneficence and justice.

Some of these codes are briefly described below:

Nuremberg Code: At the end of World War-II, the International Military Tribunal prosecuted Nazi war criminals, including Nazi doctors who performed experiments on concentration-camp prisoners. The tribunal's decision includes what is now called the Nuremberg Code, a 10-point statement outlining permissible medical experimentation on human participants.

The code clarified many of the basic principles governing the ethical conduct of research. The first provision of the code requires that "the voluntary informed consent of the human subject is absolutely essential". Other provisions require the minimization of risk and harm; a favorable risk/benefit ratio; qualified researchers using appropriate research designs; and freedom for the participant to withdraw at any time.

The Declaration of Helsinki: Recognizing the shortcomings of the Nuremberg Code, the World Medical Association created the Declaration of Helsinki in 1964. Considered by many to be the first world standard for biomedical research. This document provides extra protection for persons with diminished autonomy and urges caution on the part of the physician researcher who enrolls his own patients.

At the heart of the declaration is the principle that the well-being of the participant should take precedence over the interests of science and society.

It also recommends written consent forms like the Nuremberg code, and requires that risks be reduced to a minimum.

Belmont Report: In 1974 the National Commission for the Protection of Human Subjects of Biomedical and Behavioral Research was established. In 1978, the commission submitted its report titled, *The Belmont Report: Ethical Principles and Guidelines for the Protection of Human Subjects of Research*. The report sets forth the fundamental ethical principles underlying the acceptable conduct of research involving human participants. These principles respect for persons, beneficence and justice are accepted as the 3 fundamental principles for the ethical conduct of research involving human participants.

The U.S. Code of Federal Regulations (also called *The Common Rule*) recommends:
- Prior approval by ethics committee
- Written informed consent and documentation
- Equitable recruitment of research participants
- Special protection for vulnerable groups
- Continuing review of approved research

This code applies to all research sponsored by the U.S. government. In 1991 the federal policy (referred to as *The Common Rule*) was adopted by 16 federal agencies that conduct, support or otherwise regulate research, on human participant in the United States. As is implied by its title, The Common Rule is designed to standardize the human participant protection system in all relevant U.S. federal agencies and departments.

Clinical Research in India: The past few years have seen of a tremendous rise in the number of clinical trials conducted in India. This has been attributed to the huge patient population, genetic diversity and rich technical pool in the country. However, the economical upsurge in the clinical trial industry has also caused concerns pertaining to the efficiency of the regulatory agencies and ethics committees (EC). The EC plays an important role in the regulation of clinical research at the local level. The ethics committees in India need to work in close association with forums such as the forum for ethics review committees (FERC) in India and FERCs in Asia Pacific in an effort towards empowering themselves.

21.4 Summary

The science promotes global culture. Fundamental nature of scientific knowledge is that it does not depend on ethnic, political or religious background. Engineering and technology are having global reach and applications. They do not have limitation of territory, culture, values, etc. An engineer, for being successful and effective has to understand global requirements of engineering practices and develop global outlook in his operations and engineering decisions. In global business, understanding of local moral, ethical, social values, work practices and behavior pattern, is important as these factors demand different type of response on prevailing work culture and ethics.

Global Issues: Multinational implies that the company is doing business operations in many countries. MNCs have responsibility to select appropriate technology based on need, working culture, status of supporting infrastructure in the Host country etc. Technology includes hardware (machines and installations) software, logistics and techniques (technical, organizational, and managerial skills and procedures). It is a process of transplanting technology to a new location and ensuring its implementation and successful absorption. Global issues of business concern with ethical and operational issues of MNCs and business entities. Global issues of technology are concerned with the impact on the environmental changes, hygienic consideration for agricultural and food industry, safety of transportation and communication infrastructures, safe power and energy generation, computer ethics for safety, security and confidentiality, development of defense related weapons of mass destruction, etc. with emphasis on maintaining harmony and ecological balance of nature.

Ethical Issues of Defense Development Programs: The first ethical concern with any new military weapon system is whether its development or use would violate existing international laws. Emerging technologies can also raise much larger worries because of their revolutionary nature. Defense and weapon development programs have mainly contributed development of many technologies which later were made available to civilian sector as spin off with suitable adaptation and modifications. Some of defense technologies pose moral problems of the nature that their magnitude has potential to shatter the national economies and stability of under developed countries- thus affecting well-being of their whole population. Developed countries on the other hand thrive on international trade of military hardware and software.

Further, ethical problems associated with defense and military operations are unethical business practices that occur in all massive projects. Secrecy sometimes breeds corruption, becomes a cover for misdeeds, inefficiencies in operations and wrong decisions. Under secrecy safety issues are compromised for workstations having radiation hazards like in nuclear plants, aerospace industry, naval bases, etc. Defense is a compulsive burden on economy to protect the sovereignty of the nation.

Environmental Problems caused by Industrial activity: Industrial processes and activities are in general also responsible for production of wastes, which are unavoidable, unrecyclable and hazardous. Safe disposal of nuclear waste is serious problem. Million tons of e-waste is generated worldwide each year. Such wastes require careful management to ensure adequate protection of humans and the environment. Scientists and engineers can pay attention to this environmental problem by using bio friendly and degradable materials in their designs. Similarly, the researchers, managers and the agencies involved in funding, conducting, administering and regulating biological and chemical weapons development should share ethical and social responsibility to ensure use of modern knowledge on micro-organisms, toxins or other biological agents for the advancement of human welfare.

Dual-Use Technologies: *Dual-Use* technology refers to fields of research and development that have application to both defense and civilian sector. US Department of Defense (DoD) has often served as a launching pad for many Dual-Use technologies that have advanced civil society development. Some of the major military technologies transferred to civilian sector are Internet: (supporting global communication network); satellite communications: (supporting communication, remote sensing and satellite imaging/ mapping); super computers: (providing data processing facility to large organizations/ governments, now supporting cloud computing applications),radar technology (used in weather forecasting); nuclear technology: (power generation); global position system (GPS): (determining location on the globe. navigation, Google maps); antibiotics: (medical drugs); jet travel (air industry), etc.

Ethics in Research and development: Research is undertaken within most professions. Research is a process of collecting, analyzing and interpreting information to answer questions. But to qualify as research the process must have certain characteristics: it must be controlled, rigorous, systematic, valid and verifiable, empirical and critical. Types of Research can be classified as pure research and applied research

It is essential that fundamental ethical principles be included in the design and implementation of research involving human participants. Ethical values of truth, honesty, transparency, sincerity, discipline, etc. to be practiced along with the code of ethics of particular profession in which research is being carried out. How ethical issues can affect the research study and how ethical problems can be overcome should be thoroughly examined at the problem formulating stage. Today a great amount of attention is directed at research that involves human participants. International research ethics ensure that research conducted at the local level follows International Expectations and Standards. Human research ethics rest on three basic principles of respect for persons, beneficence and justice. These are considered to be the foundation of all regulations or guidelines governing research ethics.

Review questions

1. What types of cross-cultural issues come up in the process of globalization?
2. What should be considerations on selection and implementation of technology transfer to host countries?
3. How technology in civilian sector is benefited by defense and weapon development programs?
4. What types of ethical problems germinate due to secrecy around operations of Defense industries and Military Operations.?
5. What do you understand by "Dual Use" Technologies? Give example of two technologies which were developed for certain sector but later on migrated to other sector with different application.
6. Explain in brief the environmental problems developing due to modern Industrial and Military developments.
7. What are features and characteristics of an activity to qualify as research?
8. What are types of perspectives on which Research can be classified? What is objective of research?
9. Describe briefly code and regulations proposed to guide the conduct of research involving human participants

22 Environmental Ethics

Learning objectives

In this chapter you will learn about

- Moral basis of environmental ethics and human values
- Principles of justice-sustainability, sufficiency-compassion, solidarity- participation
- Modes of ethical reasoning, impact on environmental and related human problems
- Environmental ethics, holism concept in ecology, impact on global climate
- Engineers concern on environmental ethics and engineering codes to reflect it

Environmental ethics deals with the relationship of dependence of human beings natural environment of the earth. Environmental ethics have application in many fields like pollution, resource degradation, the threat of extinction, global climate disruption, etc. which largely affects human society in different ways. Therefore, it is important for every engineer, every organization and every industry to understand the moral significance of nature, the ethical dimension of sustainability and environmental ethics. This way engineers and technocrats can contribute through their jobs to develop technology which can help in control of bad impact on environment. At present, we are consuming resources at a faster rate than they are naturally replenished and it causes degrading our planet's ability to provide the services we humans need for survival.

22.1 Environmental Ethics and Human Values

Environmental ethics is the discipline that studies the moral and ethical relationship of dependence of human beings to the environment. It focuses on the question of moral obligation men have to the preservation and care of the earth resources, environment and ecology. As human being we share a common environment and a common ecosphere.

Attention to ethical issues concerning the environment became prominent as a result of increased awareness about the rapidly growing world population and its impact on the environment as well as the environmental consequences of growing use of pesticides technology, and industry to satisfy increasing demand to sustain the world population.

Environmental ethics defines men's moral and ethical obligations toward the environment. Environmental ethics along with human values also raised few challenging questions about the interaction of man with the environment. Domain of environmental ethics range from water and air pollution, the depletion of natural resources, loss of biodiversity, destruction of ecosystems and global climate change, etc. to mention a few. There are different trends, voices, and diverse opinions on the level of environmental degradation, optimum level for sustenance, mechanism and solution to control damage within the field of environmental ethics (Singh et al. 2010).

22.2 Moral basis of Environmental Ethics

Moral reasoning adds a powerful direction and purpose to scientific knowledge about the natural resources of the earth. Scientific knowledge in general is neutral and does not provide reasons for environmental protection. Science and economics provide data, information and knowledge about Environment. Environmental ethics humanizes scientific understanding of nature by bringing human values and moral principles into focus, thus improving decision making on scientific lines. Thinking ethically about the environment becomes one of the responsibilities for engineers, technocrats and professionals to contribute in creating awareness and sensitivity about environmental problems and finding their solutions.

In the general sense, environmental ethics suggests us to consider three key propositions, 1) the earth and its creatures have their own moral status and are worthy of our ethical concern; 2) the earth and its creatures have their own intrinsic value merely because they exist; and they have moral value irrespective of the fact that some of them meet human needs; and 3) Ecosystem should be considered as a whole by human beings that include other forms of life and the environment.

There are three main pair of principles of moral reasoning and they include justice and sustainability; sufficiency and compassion; and finally, solidarity and participation. These principles point towards environmental concerns for the well-being of the natural world and our human duties to it. We can evaluate our actions by applying these ethical principles as our standards or benchmarks. They can also be treated as signposts to orient our thinking and actions and understand the difference between right and wrong, especially in situations of multiple problems and where the interests of more than one party are involved.

Ethical principles are not as hard and fast as scientific principles are and they are less likely to give us one correct answer, but can be used to evaluate conflicting claims, a decision-making process, or the outcome of a decision.

22.3 Justice and Sustainability

The principle of justice stipulates that equals should be treated equally unless there is sufficient reason to distinguish and treat them unequally. From point of ethics it can be called environmental justice. Environmental justice is concerned with the inequitable access to environmental resources (clean food, air and water) and the injustice of greater pollution around lower-income communities and not wealthy suburbs. The principle can be also extended to animals as living creature and their welfare also, thus treating equality of humans and animals as living creatures. It requires far more humane treatment of animals also.

Sustainability extends justice into the future. It requires balancing act of consumption of earth resources such that meeting the needs of the present generation should be on the condition without compromising the projected requirement of future generation to meet their own needs. Today the world's consumption or degradation of many earth resources (such as fossil fuel energy, topsoil and water) is at much faster pace than they can be replenished in natural way, which implies that they will not be available to the future generations. Thus, environmental ethics is concerned about fundamental fairness between generations and stretches it to include those yet to be born, as an ethical issue.

22.4 Sufficiency and Compassion

The principle of sufficiency demands that all forms of life are entitled to enough goods to live on and flourish. The principle implies that no one should waste or hoard resources, i.e. to ensure that everyone has access to the goods that they need to live a life of dignity. The ethical norm of sufficiency means that we consider the needs of others for what is important, or worthy of our concern. When we are asserting the moral principle of sufficiency, we consider the needs of others, such as poor people in our society or poor countries in the world and it underlies the practice of empathy.

Compassion extends the notion of sufficiency to the earth. According to environmental ethics animals, plants and the elements (such as water, soil or air) are morally significant. Humans have responsibility to act judiciously so that their needs of survival and growth are also met. Our moral concern begins with assertion that any wild animal also is worthy of living and thereby begins the process of learning about the interdependence of all creatures on the habitat and food resources provided by other creatures in an ecosystem. Ultimately the future of humans is tied to the well-being of all other creatures.

22.5 Solidarity and Participation

The principle of solidarity calls for consideration of how we relate to each other in community. It assumes that we recognize that we are a part of one family i.e. human family consisting of chain of relationships such as our biological family, our local community, or our national community, which then calls for inclusion of full range of relationships with others (countries). In a global economy, we participate in international economic community where goods and services are provided for us by those on the other side of the world and vice-versa. Solidarity requires us to consider this kind of extended community and to act in such a way that reflects concern for the well-being of others who are all the natural stakeholders.

Participation is making the idea of solidarity practically realizable proposition. The demand of solidarity leads to the principle of participation which requires that those affected by an environmental decision should also contribute in shaping the decisions. But in practice often those most affected are unaware of the environmental decisions or the long-term effects on their health and the well-being of their environment.

22.6 Modes of Ethical reasoning about the Environment

There are three modes of moral reasoning known as commands, consequences and character. Whenever we look into an ethical problem, we usually precede giving reason along one or more of these lines. And this is as much the case in environmental ethics as in any other kind of ethics.

- **Commands:** We can use the notion of *commands* for referring to those things that we ought to do, no matter what the consequences are. This type of reasoning is also adopted for other ethical categories such as commandments, laws, rights and justice. In environmental ethics, the classic command is *do no harm*, just like in all ethics; and therefore, our first general duty toward the environment is to do no harm to it. We are reasoning in a command mode when, we say that animals have rights too and therefore justice requires that we do not harm them. This is often the ethical conviction behind those who do not eat meat.
- **Consequences:** The ethical notion of consequences is most often associated with the theory of utilitarianism. According to this ethical reasoning, commands are not sufficient to decide and tell what should be done in a typical ethical situation or dilemma. Instead, we have to think about the consequences of our actions. Thus, our criteria of determining the correct ethical action could be to choose the one that will maximize the balance of good consequences and minimize the bad consequences. Working to

protect the full diversity of life on earth is an example of ethical action with a positive consequence.
- **Character:** In the face of a situation of environmental ethics, our character means any particular action that may affect the environment. It also means the kind of person I am in my actions when dealing with environmental issues. Am I becoming more just, humble and generous towards maintaining good balance in environment? This mode of ethical reasoning calls for careful and honest self-reflection. It can also be a kind of reasoning used very well by a group.

22.7 Impact of Environmental degradation creating Human Problems

Science, technology and engineering have made tremendous contribution to society by generation of wealth and comfort to human life. However along with tremendous benefits to society application of the scientific methods also have negative impacts on the earth. For example, the automobiles have brought us comfort of transportation at the cost of loss of fertile farmland to make roads. Similarly, fossil fuels of oil and gas, being extensively used by industry, contribute to the emission of carbon dioxide from its burning and in turn polluting badly to our atmosphere and climate. Nuclear technologies promoted health through radiation treatments of cancer. But the same nuclear energy if used in war could cause unimaginable harm to humanity and bring about indescribably horrific suffering for generations. Nuclear energy produces no greenhouse gasses, which is good but disposal of nuclear waste products is a great problem, which are radioactive (acutely dangerous) for 10,000 years or more. The wealthy nations of the world benefited from technology and became great economic powers. At the same times these technologies required raw material and other goods which were extracted from poorer countries and frustrating their economic growth. The scientific method attempts to be free of bias, but the technological products of science have tremendous implications for social and environmental ethics.
- **Contributions of Ecology:** Science has many branches of scientific disciplines. It is not a single, homogenous entity. Physics, chemistry and biology all follow proper scientific methods. The discipline of ecology under biological sciences plays strong role in understanding relationship between humanity with the natural world. Ecology is the study of living organisms in the nature and the interactions among organisms and their environment. Whereas biology studies living organisms in laboratories under a conditioned environment different from the actual environment in which organisms naturally lives. Ecologists study over some

length of time about the dynamics of relationships between populations, groups of organisms and food, and energy flows on the one hand, and exposure to various stresses such as pollutants, etc. on the other hand. They often research the impact of human behavior on natural communities.

- **The Ecosystem:** The science of ecology has brought the concept of ecosystem. An ecosystem consists of an association of organisms, their physical environment and their interconnection by the circulation of energy and nutrients. An ecosystem may be any size, from a drop of water to entire planet. All creatures live within some kind of ecosystem and relate or influence each other and their environment by their behavior. The idea of an ecosystem is critical to understanding the patterns of life on earth and points to the inescapable inter-relatedness of all life.

22.8 The special relationship of Ecology and Environmental Ethics

Ecology plays an important role in environmental ethics. The principle of coexistence, and interdependence of the earth and its creatures, is having intrinsic value which is particularly strong in ecology. According to Ecological point of view "*...a thing is right when it tends to preserve the integrity, stability, and beauty of the biotic community. It is wrong when it tends otherwise*" Leopold (2014, pp.109). This is very clear and ethically explicit statement about the importance of an ecosystem. Ecology articulates a vision for how humans should live in relationship to the earth as they are a part of the earth.

- **Concept of Holism in Ecology:** The concept of the ecosystem has contributed to the idea of holism. The ethical implication of holism is that entire ecosystem is considered to have moral significance, meaning that we must consider not merely individual members but the entire set of relationships and attributes of whole ecosystem. Environmental ethics works to suggest how we should live in order to conserve the ecological processes upon which all life depends.
- **Impact on Global Climate:** The disruption of our global climate by human beings and their activities poses a grave threat to the human family and its environment. The environmental issue of disruption of global climate requires seriousness of unprecedented scale. It is anticipated that the impacts of climate disruption will be much stronger for human society over the coming decades.

International efforts are being seriously pursued among nations on the scale of technological, economic and social transformation required to reverse the trend of carbon dioxide pollution. Confronting climate

disruption requires confronting the un-sustainable western lifestyle. Professionals find themselves confronted by an array of ethical issues, problems and dilemmas that have to do with environmental responsibilities. Below is a non-exhaustive list of issues in environmental ethics:
1. Animal Rights
2. Biocentrism
3. Conservation
4. Ecology
5. Moral Standing
6. Environmental Justice
7. The Value of Nature
8. Economics and the Environment
9. Obligations to Future Generations
10. Sustainable Development and Ethics

22.9 Engineers responsibility towards Environmental Ethics

Engineers have a complex relationship to the environment. On the one hand, they have helped humanity with better life but on the other hand technology they deal with also produced some of the environmental problems that plague human society. Chemical Projects designed by engineers produce toxic chemicals that pollute the land, air and rivers. Engineers also design projects that sometimes flood farmlands, drain wetlands and destroy the forests. On the other hand, with conscious efforts to guard against the deleterious impact on the environment and ecosystem, engineers can design projects, products and processes that reduce or eliminate threats to environmental integrity. Thus, engineers need to be aware of their role as agents of change and as experiment reengaged in application of technology for benefit of the society.

22.10 Concern about Environment included in Engineering Codes

Many engineering codes make no reference to the environment at all, but increasingly they are adopting some environmental provisions. The codes of the American Society of Civil Engineers (ASCE), the Institute of Electrical and Electronics Engineers (IEEE), the American Society of Mechanical Engineers (ASME), the American Institute of Chemical Engineers and the Association for Computing Machinery have environmental provisions in their codes. The latest addition to the list is the National Society of Professional Engineers (NSPE). The ASCE code, however, still has the most extensive references to the environment. The code requires engineers to "...*strive to comply with the principles of sustainable development*" (Harris et al. 2013, pp.193).

22.11 Summary

Environmental Ethics and Human Values: Environmental ethics is the discipline that considers the moral and ethical relationship of human beings to the environment. It focuses on the question of moral obligation men have to the preservation and care of the earth resources, environment and ecology. Environmental ethics have application in many fields like pollution, resource degradation, the threat of extinction and global climate disruption. Emergence of ethical issues concerning the environment was the result of increased awareness of the environmental consequences that came with the growing use of pesticides, technology and industry. Therefore, for every engineer it is important to understand the moral significance of nature, the ethical dimension of sustainability and environmental virtue ethics. As human beings we share a common environment and a common ecosphere.

Moral basis of Environmental Ethics: Environmental ethics humanizes scientific understanding of nature by bringing human values and moral principles into focus, thus improving decision making on scientific lines. There are three main pairs of principles of moral reasoning: justice and sustainability; sufficiency and compassion; and solidarity and participation. These principles point towards environmental concerns for the well-being of the natural world and our human duties to it.

Justice and Sustainability: The principle of justice stipulates that equals should be treated equally. From the point of ethics, it can be called *environmental justice*. Environmental justice is concerned with the equitable access to environmental resources (clean food, air and water) to all. Sustainability can be defined as meeting the needs of the present generation without compromising the ability of future generation to meet their own needs.

Sufficiency and Compassion: The principle of *sufficiency* demands that all forms of life are entitled to enough goods to live on and flourish. *Compassion* extends the notion of sufficiency to the earth. Environmental ethics asserts that other animals, plants and the elements (such as water, soil or air) are morally significant and that humans have responsibilities to act so that their needs are met.

Solidarity and Participation: In a globalizing economy, we participate in a vast, international economic community in which goods and services required by us are produced by those on the other side of the world. *Solidarity* requires us to consider this kind of extended community, so we should care for the well-being of others also as they are all the natural stakeholders. *Participation* extends the idea of solidarity to make it practical.

Modes of Ethical Reasoning about the Environment: There are three modes of moral reasoning known as *commands, consequences and* *character*. We can use the notion of *commands* for referring to those things that we ought to do, no matter what the consequences. Environmental ethics *commands* that our first general duty toward the environment is to do no harm. The ethical notion of *consequences* is most often associated with the theory of utilitarianism as commands are not sufficient to tell what should be done. Instead, we need to think about the consequences of our actions. Working to protect the full diversity of life on earth is an example of ethical action with a positive consequence. In environmental ethics, *character* means our particular actions that may affect the environment. It also means the kind of person I am in my actions in relation to the environment.

Issue of Environmental Degradation: Science, technology and engineering have made tremendous contribution to society by generation of wealth and comfort to human life. However, applications of the science and engineering also have negative impacts on the earth. For example, loss of fertile farmland for expansion of civic amenities and infrastructure; depletion of natural reserve of fossil fuels of oil and gas due to extensive consumption by industry, contribution to the emission of carbon dioxide from its burning, which in turn is disrupting our atmosphere and climate. The disruption of our global climate by human beings and their activities poses a grave threat to the human family and its environment. The scientific method attempts to be free of bias, but the technological products of science have tremendous implications for social and environmental ethics.

Ecosystem and Field of Ecology: The discipline of *Ecology* under biological sciences plays strong role in understanding the relationship between humanity with the natural world. Ecology is the study of living organisms in the nature and the interactions among organisms and their environment. The science of ecology has contributed to the concept of *ecosystem*. An ecosystem is an association of organisms and their physical environment, interconnected by the circulation of energy and nutrients. The concept of the ecosystem has contributed to the idea of holism. The ethical implication of holism is that entire systems have moral significance, meaning that we have duties to consider not merely individual members but the entire set of relationships and attributes of whole ecosystems.

Engineer's Role and Responsibility towards Environmental Ethics: Engineers have a complex relationship to the environment. On the one hand, they have helped humanity with better life but their technology also produced some of the environmental problems that plague human society. Projects designed by engineers produce toxic chemicals that pollute the land, air and rivers. Engineers also design projects that flood farmlands, drain wetlands and destroy the forests. On the other hand, engineers can design projects, products and processes that reduce or eliminate these threats to environmental integrity. Thus, engineers need to be aware of their role as agents of change, as experimenters. Some engineering codes refer to the environment. The ASCE code has the most extensive references to the environment.

Review questions

1. Explain nature and scope of environmental ethics and relationship with human values.
2. What type of moral reasoning is applied to build a case for environmental ethics?
3. What are the basic considerations of moral principles of justice and sustainability; sufficiency and compassion; solidarity and participation?
4. Explain in detail modes of moral reasoning known as commands, consequences and character.
5. What type of human problems are results of impact of environmental degradation.
6. How do you relate environment to ecology? What is the scope of ecological studies and how human beings are affected by ecological changes?
7. What is special relationship between ecology and environmental ethics? Explain concept of holism in ecology.
8. In what way engineers share responsibility towards environmental Ethics. Explain specific clauses in Code of professional ethics mandating professional to take responsibility towards environmental protection.

23 Ethical Issues on Computer, Internet and Data Processing

Learning objectives

In this chapter you will learn about

- Global networking, Internet ethics, global laws on Internet and cyberspace
- Internet and high computing power provide higher operational power
- Privacy and computer ethics and the ten commandments of computer ethics
- Computers as the instrument of unethical behavior and objects of unethical acts
- Issues of computer crime, computer security, autonomous computers and Internet

23.1 Global Networking and issues of Internet Ethics

In most countries of the world, the *information revolution has* brought revolutionary changes in the field of communication, commerce, medicine, security, transportation, entertainment, and so on. Computer is virtually at the center of all these developments. Their computing power, speed of information processing, applications are growing at a fast pace. These applications are strongly impacting on the life style, moral values and ethics of different individuals, organizations, and societies. Information revolution and Internet provide global connectivity and access to information. The world has become truly a global village from the information delivery, access and storage point of view.

The influence of information and communication technology (ICT) has been good and bad for the family life, community life, human relationships, education, careers, freedom and democracy. Communication heavily depends upon computer technology and has grown dramatically through widespread use of the cell phones, Internet, computer networks, electronic exchanges, data centers/storage, global positioning systems, etc.

Computing has become so integrated with all functions in the society that computer ethics has expanded dramatically to issues involving most of the activities within the society including education, law, business, government and the military. Ethical considerations of ICT broadly referred as *computer ethics* and also sometimes called *cyber ethics* and *Internet ethics*. Hence, ICT is a branch of applied ethics which studies and analyzes social and ethical impacts of ICT.

Global networks like the Internet and especially the World-Wide-Web (WWW)are connecting people all over the globe. The computer revolution has also created the problem of global ethics. Extensive efforts are being made globally to develop mutually agreed standards of conduct to defend human values from misuse of ICT. It is worth noticing that issue of computer ethics is not limited to a particular geographic region or constrained by a specific religion or culture. Let us just consider few of the global issues.

23.2 Need for Global Laws on Internet and Cyberspace

As the Internet web technology provides worldwide connectivity, the issue of rights and responsibilities of individuals on the Internet becomes complex. Different countries have different set of their own laws and customs; therefore, have different level of concerns about the Web. Any country will have great difficulty in enforcing its concerns with type of information coming and going beyond its borders. For example, consider the scope of freedom of speech in different countries. If computer users in India and United States wish to protect their freedom of speech on the Internet, then laws of which country should apply? Nearly two hundred countries are already interconnected by the Internet, so the constitutional guarantee of freedom of speech in India and United States are just *local laws* for the Internet, which does not apply to the rest of the world. Similarly, the difficulty due to the usage of Internet arises to ensure protection to Intellectual Property Rights, invasions of privacy and many other activities and privileges which are to be governed by law. But how is it possible when so many countries are involved in this process?

23.2.1 Global Cyber-Business

The computer technology is very close to provide foolproof electronic privacy and security on the Internet, where one can safely conduct international business transactions. Right now, this technology is mature enough and boosting rapid expansion of *global cyber-business*. Nations with adequate technological infrastructure are enjoying rapid economic growth, while the rest of the world is lagging behind. The ethical question arises about accepted business practices in one part of the world which are perceived as *cheating* or *fraud* in other parts of the world?

23.2.2 Global Online information via Internet

Internet can provide inexpensive access to the global information over net to rich and poor alike and there is possibility that nearly everyone on earth can have access to daily news from a free press; to texts, documents and art works from great libraries and museums of the world. This raises ethical issue due to different political, religious and social practices of peoples everywhere. This sudden and instant online *global information* will also impact upon political dictatorships, isolated communities, coherent cultures, religious practices, etc.

23.2.3 Disbursal of information among rich and poor

There are many areas of global operations where ICT is making positive as well as negative impact, thus raising issue of ethics globally. For example, the gap of infrastructure and support system to public between rich and poor nations is large and even gap of income level between rich and poor citizens in industrialized countries is also already wide. When educational opportunities, business and employment opportunities, medical services and many other necessities of life shift more into cyberspace, these gaps between the rich and the poor will become even worse which is an ethical issue.

23.3 Impact of Computing Power and Internet on Power Structure among people and organizations

Computers provide power to individuals to perform multiple tasks more easily, faster and accurately which could never be possible to do without them. Thus, those who have access to computers are in powerful position to perform complex tasks almost instantly. Internet power sometimes changes power balance through making strong even stronger. By Internet large corporations can outsource jobs to cheaper labor markets and improve profitability. Defense establishments and military operations enhance their capabilities by switching over to computerized communication and weapon systems. As a consequence, this creates large disparity between haves and have-not to the advantage of those who have higher access to computing power.

Computers are capable of processing and handling large amount of data with multiple variables. Performances of top-notch super computers demonstrated both the rapid increase in top performance and the widespread growth of supercomputing technology worldwide. This high level of computing power enabled governments and large organization to create centralized control of operations and managing high volume of data involving large number of variables and at astonishing fast speeds. This promoted centralized bureaucracies with central control mechanism in governments. Socially conscious people opposed centralization of power with the fear that the concentration of computers power into few centralized agencies or persons may lead to totalitarianism. Thus, this became an ethical issue. This ethical question of the centralization of power coincides with the ethical concern that technology contributes to feeling of alienation. Alienation has to do with the loss of control in the world in which one lives.

With gradual introduction of PCs of different architectures and applications having higher processing power and speeds, computer technology reached to common man and computer power shifted in favor of general public. With development of Internet, remote access and remote processing including time sharing of resources of larger computer system by multiple users became possible. These changes brought public awareness on usefulness of computers in their daily life as well as economic, quick and reliable public services. Thus, the fear of large centralized computer system waned out in due course of time. Along with development of powerful PCs and other gadgets like laptops, tablets, smart phonesetc. Internet has greatly helped to correct the imbalance of power and even shift power toward the individual.

But the Internet's ability to shift power to the individual also has negative contribution to allow one person to send spam e-mails to millions of people and to spread viruses and worms. All antisocial elements and terrorists use Internet for operation of their network.

Therefore, along with computer technology a whole new field of ethical dilemmas came to surface. From computer crime to privacy to the power of computer professionals, computer technology raised the questions on the modus operandi of Internet and how-to safe guards the transactions from unethical activities and unauthorized intrusions into data banks.

23.4 Computers and Invasion of Privacy

The computer's most basic function is its capacity to store, organize and exchange data/records. The issue of privacy arises on this function of computers. A great deal of the privacy concern is due to computers capability to gather large amount of personal and private information. For example, personal information such as medical documents, criminal records, credit histories, etc. are easily retrievable from hospital records and can be transmitted to others electronically. Accordingly, private information of individuals is vulnerable to the improper disclosure with the possibility of the introduction of unknown errors into their records. If someone hacks into the computer system, all this private information about individuals is accessible to him and in this way the crimes of identity theft can occur.

The threat to privacy is increasing partly because computing technology enables information gathering to take place in very subtle and undetectable ways. Internet stores, tracks transactions of individuals and places cookies on their personal computers inconspicuously. Further, computerized cameras in public places, in private establishments, personal cell phones, etc. are capable of recording images and activities without notice.

Computers in association with global-positioning satellites track routinely geographical locations of vehicles. Spyware installed on computers surreptitiously keeps surveying the computing activities of unsuspecting users. Personal information of any individual can be collected from many sources and can be correlated, assembled in databases and mined, merged and matched, to construct profiles and history of their lives. Many fears, that computers are creating a semi-transparent channel of personal information, which is accessible to criminal minded people like hackers, etc. without any control and restrictions, creating a society, where levels of privacy of people are dramatically reduced and too many details of individual lives are known to others.

It is to be understood that Computer technology has both good and bad consequences of computerized records. A good consequence is that an organization through use of computer can access the relevant information from database to improve decision making process. Therefore, this makes organizations more efficient with some economic advantages. This economic advantage in turn could result in better service conditions or savings. For example, by studying medical data, consumer data, or insurance data, very valuable information can emerge from the statistical facts which are sometimes benefiting the society at large. However, the concerns about individual privacy prevent the dissemination of such databases.

Bad part of computers processing capability is that there is no way to make sure that the organizations are exercising power to access the information in fair manner and purpose. Thus, a fair balance is desirable between the need for information on the part of an organization and the interests of the individual. For example, Internet banking has been widely adopted in many countries including India, but in some countries, there are large numbers of customers unwilling to the use online banking services due to the fear of misuse of account numbers and passwords. They have lack of confidence on efficacy of Internet, maintenance of privacy, safety and security in online banking operation. There are fears of theft of identity because of frequent news of various frauds and hacking on Internet.

23.5 Field of Computer Ethics

Computer technology is developing very fast in complexity, applications and their penetration in all spheres of public life. It is difficult to assess the impact of computers on human values and ethics, though some bad effects already started surfacing up, for example access and use of this technology by anti-social elements and terrorist organizations.

Some of the issues of concern in computer ethics are (1) computer crime (2) changed power relationship due to additional processing power acquired through computers (3) protection and safety of computer property, records and software (4) privacy of the company, workers and customers (5) responsibility for computer failure, etc.

The term *computer ethics* is applied to analysis of ethical issues arising in applications that involve computers and computer networks. The ethical issues are analyzed based on ethical theories like utilitarianism, Kantianism, or virtue ethics. Computer ethics is a branch of engineering ethics for the team of engineers engaged in design, manufacture and application of computers for specific purpose. Therefore, it is more important for the team of professionals like web designers, programmers, system analysts, operators, etc. to take care of ethical concerns as they work as a team for successful development of computer technology (Martin and Schinzinger, 2010). Computer professionals must conform to codes of ethics and standards of good practice, which are already framed for their profession. However, responsibility of application is shared by team of engineers who use the computers.

Computer ethics can be studied from the point of view of ethical issues arising from three broad aspects of using computers like 1) computers as the instrument of unethical behavior; 2) computer as the objects of unethical acts; and 3) networks of autonomous computers and Internet. Modern computing technology involves application of hardware, software and networks for its operations. It is highly flexible in dynamic restructuring to be best suited to particular application and so becomes highly powerful taskmaster. Computers can be programmed and trained to perform a wide range of functions.

23.6 The Ten Commandments of Computer Ethics

The ten commandments of computer ethics written by the computer ethics institute to computer professionals are given as follows (Fitzpatrick and Bronstein, 2006, pp.116)

1. Thou shalt not use a computer to harm other people.
2. Thou shalt not interfere with other people's computer work.
3. Thou shalt not snoop around in other people's computer files.
4. Thou shalt not use a computer to steal.
5. Thou shalt not use a computer to bear false witness.
6. Thou shalt not copy or use proprietary software for which you have not paid.
7. Thou shalt not use other people's computer resources without authorization or proper compensation.
8. Thou shalt not appropriate other people's intellectual output.
9. Thou shalt think about the social consequences of the program you are writing or the system you are designing.
10. Thou shalt always use a computer in ways that ensure consideration and respect for your fellow humans.

Meaning and implications of these Ten Commandments is explained below (Fitzpatrick and Bronstein, 2006):

- **Commandment 1** simply says that "*...do not use the computer in ways that may harm other people*". Here harm is used in broader sense and includes any attempt to corrupt or steal other user's data, file or record, personal information, any manipulation like destroying the files, attempt to copy or unauthorized access to other user's data. Computer ethics does not permit practices like hacking, spamming, phishing or cyber bullying, etc.
- **Commandment 2** simply says that "*... do not use computer technology to cause interference in other users' work*". The commandment prohibits use of computer software which disturbs or disrupts work of other users. Action of sending viruses and malicious software can corrupt normal functioning of computer in many ways like overloading memory, making computer slow, cause a computer function wrongly or even stopping the computer are unethical.
- **Commandment 3** simply says that "*...do not spy on another person's computer data*". This means acts of reading other's emails or files, getting data from another person's private files amounts to invasion of privacy of others hence unethical. However, these are not unethical for the authorized purpose of spying and collection of intelligence for crime detection, etc.

- **Commandment 4** simply says that "*...do not use computer technology to steal information*". This implies that stealing sensitive information or leaking confidential information is like robbery and hence unethical. It is unethical to acquire from respective databases, personal information of employees, patient history from a hospital or any information which is confidential. Similarly, to collect information about the account or account holder, illegal electronic transfer of funds, etc. are unethical.
- **Commandment 5** simply says that "*...do not contribute to the spread of misinformation using computer technology*". Spreading of misinformation using Internet to make it viral is unethical. Thus, spreading of false news, emails or rumors through social networking sites is unethical.
- **Commandment 6** simply says that "*...refrain from copying software or buying pirated copies. Pay for software unless it is free*". Software is Copyrighted like any other artistic or literary work. A piece of code is the original work of the individual and it is Copyrighted in his name. If a developer is writing software for the organization, the organization holds the Copyright for it. Obtaining illegal copies of Copyrighted software is unethical.
- **Commandment 7** simply says that "*...do not use someone else's computer resources unless authorized to*". Specific users are provided individual passwords to access the multi-user systems. Act of breaking into some other user's password and intruding into his private space to hack passwords for gaining unauthorized access to a password-protected computer system or attempt to access to another user's computer without his permission is unethical.
- **Commandment 8** simply says that "*...it is wrong to claim ownership on a work which is the output of someone else's intellect*". This means that claiming ownership on a work which is not yours is ethically wrong and applies to programs developed by a software developer for himself or his organization equally well. Copying them and propagating them in one's own name is unethical. This applies to any creative work, program or design.
- **Commandment 9** simply says that "*...before developing software, think about the social impact it can have*". The commandment says that if you are a software engineer, you must consider the social consequences of your program and its application in the broader perspective of technology because your Software on release, reaches millions. For example, a computer game for kids should not have content that can convey negative values to them. Similarly, writing malicious software is ethically wrong.

- **Commandment 10** simply says that "*...while using computers for communication, be respectful and courteous with the fellow members*". The basic behavioral etiquette of everyday life must be observed in computer communication also. In Internet communication one should treat others with respect, should not intrude others' private space or use abusive language, make false statements or pass irresponsible remarks about others.

23.7 Computers as the Instrument of Unethical Behavior

The main concern of computer ethics has been to protect and advance human values such as quality of life, health, security, happiness, freedom, knowledge, resources, power and opportunity. Often it has been guiding theme for major computer-ethics conferences, focusing upon security, property, privacy, knowledge, freedom and opportunities.

Computer is very indispensable instrument in today's world to bring improvement in the quality of human life. However unethical computer usages in some situations have negatively affected social life. Computers as instruments can also play a central role in unethical or illegal conduct/operation. For example, they can be used to mimic voice of somebody else than the original speaker in a phone conversation. This way a criminal can carry out his criminal activities with the help of computer under disguised voice of another person. As an example, in India an ex-army captain and intelligence officer called over phone to the chief cashier of a bank mimicking voice of Prime Minister and instructing him to withdraw 6 million rupees to be handed over to a contact person for a secret mission. The chief cashier did not cross-check before following voice instruction over phone. The cashier got a shock of his life when he had gone to PM office to get a receipt for the sum withdrawn for the mission, where he learnt about the impersonation of the PM's voice.

Some of the common unethical usages of computer as instrument are listed here includes: cybercrime, theft, gambling, spamming, extortion, violation of privacy, computer as object of unethical acts, hacking into computer systems, unauthorized access to information and databases; modification of original information amounting to corrupting it; and destruction of information. Unethical behaviors could be due to different reasons such as economic, social, moral or personal reasons. Therefore, unethical behavior should be investigated in terms of factors such as society, personality, culture, gender, computer skills and self-efficacy.

23.7.1 Why people resort to use computers as instrument of unethical behavior?

In the light of known personality traits, individuals' aggressive behaviors could show up towards others and the society as unethical computer usage. Individuals utilize computer technologies by means of software and Internet activities such as searching, having fun, gaming, chatting, communicating, shopping, etc. Unethical behavior of computer usage includes improper usage of intellectual property, creating bad social impact, tampering with safety and quality matters, diluting net integrity and information integrity. Unethical computer use behavior (UECUB) could be due to aggressive behaviors directed to satisfy individuals' personal needs or to harm someone else. A link between personality and computer use has been established and *personality trait of individuals* is found as a relevant factor in determining behaviors on the Internet.

Student's community normally uses computers very frequently. Their use of computers is mostly for preparing assignments, searching information, connecting with friends or others. However, some students display unethical and undesirable behaviors on computer usage. These unethical behaviors need to be studied especially on student's community as they are an emerging adult preparing for a professional life.

23.8 Computer Crime

Computer crime is intellectual and white-collar crime. Those who indulge in committing such crimes are intelligent enough to access the computer in the first place and then manipulate the computer system. For example, stealing funds via computer is a computer crime. Often the worst that can happen to such a thief is that if caught he/she is required to return the stolen money.

Quite often such a person is fired if he/she is an employee but may be quickly hired by other companies because of his/her special skills. Thus, there is practically no deterrence to committing computer theft. Most often legal actions are not taken against the perpetrator.

Another example of computer crime is unauthorized entry into a computer system and attempt to steal a company's trade secrets and data. Such a crime could be easily committed by an employee, with the purpose of selling such secrets to a competitor or stealing by an outside agency with the intention to steal such secrets to promote his/her own business interest. Such crime involves both an invasion on property and privacy and it compromises the computer system itself.

This type of crime raises ethical question on practice of hacking. Hacking is defined as "...*any computer-related activity which is not sanctioned or approved of by an employer or owner of a system or Network*" (Himma, 2007, pp.7). Ethical dilemma of such an activity is that who actually owns information and who should have access to that information.

23.9 Computer Security

Computer security from computer *viruses* and international spying by *hackers* is an issue in the field of *computer ethics*. This is not a problem of physical security of the hardware (protecting it from theft, fire, flood, etc.) but rather *logical security*, which deals with five aspects:
1. Privacy and confidentiality
2. Integrity –ensuring that data and programs are not modified without proper authority
3. Unhindered service without any impairment
4. Consistency – ensuring that the data and behavior will not change with time.
5. Controlling access to resources

Computer security is significantly challenged by malicious kinds of software, or *programmed threats*. These include *viruses* which are inserted into other computer programs and cannot run on their own. *Worms* can move from machine to machine across networks. *Trojan horses* appear to be one sort of program, which actually do the damage behind the scenes. *Logic bombs* check for particular conditions and execute when those conditions arise. Bacteria or rabbits multiply rapidly and fill up the computer's memory.

23.10 Computer as the Object of Unethical Acts

Computer as the object of unethical act points finger towards people who design and operate the computer or those who know about computers and have access to them. Many people who design and operate computing systems call themselves as computing professionals. Similarly, people with little training, irrespective of their educational background, can be hired by some companies to do computing and are called computing professional. Unethical acts of these professionals need to be regulated.

The question arises about the professional standards and ethical standards, which should guide and regulate the behavior of computing professionals and to that they should adhere. Even though several codes of ethics have been prescribed on duties and responsibilities of computer professionals, they have been difficult to implement for at least two reasons. First, unlike medicine and law, in the computer field there is no system of any professional qualifying examinations and licensing. Second, the nature of computing itself makes the assessment of responsibility difficult. Therefore, enforcement of any code of ethics for computer professionals is practically difficult.

Further, computer programs are often enormously complex, written by dozens of people, and incomprehensible to any one person. Moreover, such large computer programs are brittle, meaning that a tiny, obscure error can shatter the performance of the entire system under certain conditions. To what extent should computing professionals be regarded as liable when it is difficult to predict such errors that lead to major failures or even catastrophic results?

23.11 Computer Codes of Ethics

Professional organizations in the USA, like the Association for Computing Machinery (ACM) and the Institute of Electrical and Electronic Engineers (IEEE), have established *Codes of Ethics* (See Appendix-F and H), curriculum guidelines and accreditation requirements, to help computer professionals to understand and manage their ethical responsibilities. For example, in 1991 a joint curriculum task force of the ACM and IEEE adopted a set of guidelines (Curriculum 1991) for college programs in computer science. The guidelines say that a significant component of computer ethics (in the broad sense) should be included in undergraduate education in computer science (Turner, 1991).

In addition, both the ACM and IEEE have adopted codes of ethics for their members. The ACM Code (2014), for example, includes terms like *general moral imperatives*, such as *avoid harm to others* and *be honest and trustworthy*. The Code also included more specific professional responsibilities like *acquire and maintain professional competence* and *know and respect existing laws pertaining to professional work*. The IEEE Code of Ethics (1990) includes such principles as *avoid real or perceived conflicts of interest whenever possible"* and *"be honest and realistic in stating claims or estimates based on available data.*

The Accreditation Board for Engineering Technologies (ABET) has long required an ethics component in the computer engineering curriculum and in 1991 the Computer Sciences Accreditation Commission/Computer Sciences Accreditation Board (CSAC/CSAB) also adopted the requirement that a significant component of computer ethics be included in any computer sciences degree granting program that is nationally accredited (Conry, 1992).

It is clear that professional organizations in computer science recognize and insist upon standards of professional responsibility for their members.

23.11 Autonomous Computers and Internet

- **Autonomous System:** An autonomous system (AS) is a network of computers that is administered by a single set of management rules and controlled by one person or group or organization. Autonomous systems normally use only one routing protocol, although use of multiple protocols can be supported by the network. Railway reservation system, police network, banks network of communication systems, ATMs communication system etc. are examples of Autonomous Computers systems.

    The core of the Internet is made up of many autonomous systems, whereas an AS itself is a heterogeneous network typically governed by a large enterprise. Concept of autonomous systems was introduced to regulate organizations such as Internet Service Providers (ISPs), large organizations spread over many locations and government bodies, etc. These systems are made up of many sub-networks of different sizes but are operated under the umbrella of a single entity for easy management. Each sub-network is assigned a globally unique 16-digit identification number (known as the AS number or ASN) by the Internet Assigned Numbers Authority (IANA). Large enterprises tend to have large network infrastructures with many smaller networks, dispersed geographically but interconnected using a similar operating environment.

- **Autonomic Computing:** Autonomic computing refers to the self-managing characteristics of distributed computing resources, adapting to unpredictable changes while hiding intrinsic complexity to operators and users. Started by IBM in 2001, this initiative ultimately aims to develop computer systems capable of self-management to overcome the rapidly growing complexity of computing systems management and to reduce the barrier that complexity poses to further growth.

    The system makes decisions on its own, using high-level policies; it will constantly check and optimize its status and automatically adapt itself to changing conditions. An autonomic computing framework is composed of autonomic components (AC) interacting with each other. An AC can be modeled in terms of two main control loops (local and global) with sensors (for self-monitoring), effectors (for self-adjustment), knowledge and planner/adapter for exploiting policies based on self- and environment awareness

- **Internet and its Operations:** The Internet has revolutionized the computer and communications world and has global communication presence. Internet provides an instant world-wide broadcasting capability, a network for information dissemination without limitations of any boundary and a medium for collaboration and interaction between individuals via mobile phones or their computers without regard for geographic location. Key to the rapid growth of the Internet has been the free and open access to the basic system configuration documents, especially the specifications of the protocols. The Internet is as much a collection of communities, as a collection of technologies.

The government, industries and academia have been partners in evolving and deploying this exciting new technology. It is complex and involves many aspects such as technological, organizational and community. Its influence reaches not only to the technical fields of computer communications but throughout society as we move toward increasing use of online tools to accomplish electronic commerce, information acquisition and community operations.

Technically it is an open-architecture network, where the individual networks may be separately designed and developed and each may have its own unique interface which it may offer to users and/or other networks including Internet Service Providers (ISP). Each network can be designed in accordance with the specific environment and user requirements of that network. There are generally no constraints on the types of network that can be included or on their geographic scope.

23.12 Summary

Global Internetworking: The *Internet* has revolutionized the computer and communications world like nothing before. The Internet has an instant world-wide broadcasting capability, a mechanism for information dissemination and a medium for collaboration and interaction between individuals and their computers without regard for geographic location. Key to the rapid growth of the Internet has been the free and open access to the basic *Technical Documents,* especially the *Specifications of the Protocols.*

The *information revolution* has brought revolutionary changes in the field of communication, commerce, medicine, security, transportation, entertainment, and so on. These applications are strongly impacting on the life style, moral values and ethics of different societies, organizations and individuals. The influence of ICT has been both good and bad for the community life, family life, human relationships, education, careers, freedom and democracy. Today computer ethics has become burning issue for most of the activities within society including education, law, business, government and the military.

Limitation of National Laws for Internet: Due to global connectivity by Internet operations, the issue of rights and responsibilities of individuals on the Internet becomes complex. Different countries have different laws and customs and therefore have different concerns about the web. Any country will have great difficulty enforcing its concerns with information coming and going beyond its borders. For example, to protect freedom of speech on the Internet, laws of which country should apply? Nearly two hundred countries are already interconnected by the Internet, so the constitutional guarantee of freedom of speech in India and United States are just *local laws* for the Internet. Similarly, in the use of Internet, difficulty arises to ensure protection to *Intellectual Property Rights*, invasions of privacy and many other activities and privileges which are to be governed by law when so many countries are involved.

Ethical view on Internet: International business transactions can be safely conducted on Internet. The ethical question arises about accepted business practices in one part of the world, being perceived as *cheating* or *fraud* in other parts of the world. Nearly everyone on earth can have access to daily news from a free press, media, books, documents from great libraries, etc. This can raise ethical issue due to different political, religious and social practices of people everywhere. Similarly, *online global education* will impact upon political dictatorships, isolated communities, coherent cultures, religious practices, etc. Further, in developed nations educational opportunities, business and employment opportunities, medical services and many other necessities of life are adapting more and more ICT and cyberspace, causing gaps between the rich and the poor to become worse.

Ethical Issues of Higher-level of Centralized Computing Power: Those who have access to computers have access to power. Computing power sometimes changes power balance through making strong even stronger. By using Internet large corporations can outsource jobs to cheaper labor markets. Defense establishments and militaries enhance their capabilities with computerized communication and weapon systems. Higher computing power promoted centralized bureaucracies with central control mechanism in governments. Socially conscious people opposed centralization of power with the fear that the concentration of computers power into few centralized agencies or persons may lead to totalitarianism. Thus, this became an ethical issue. It is difficult to envisage the impact of computers on human values and ethics, though some bad effects already started surfacing up, for example access and use of this technology by anti-social elements and terrorist's organization.

Further, new field of ethical dilemmas came to surface, in the form of computer crimes, threat to privacy, power of computer professionals etc.

The question here arises on the modus operandi of Internet and how it safe guards the transactions from unethical activities and unauthorized intrusions into data banks.

Computer Ethics: The main concern of computer ethics has been to protect and advance human values such as life, health, security, happiness, freedom, knowledge, resources, power and opportunity. The term *computer ethics* is applied to analysis the ethical cases that involve computers and computer networks. Some of the issues of concern in computer ethics are 1) computer crimes 2) changed power relationship due to additional processing power acquired through computers 3) protection and safety of computer property, records and software 4) privacy of the company, workers and customers 5) responsibility for computer failure, etc. Computer security from computer *viruses* and international spying by *hackers* is also an issue in the field of computer ethics.

Computer ethics is a branch of engineering ethics for the team of engineers engaged in design, manufacture and deployment of computers for specific application. Computer professionals must conform to codes of ethics (like The Ten Commandments of Computer Ethics) and standards of good practice, which are already framed for their profession.

Computer Crime: It is an intellectual and white-collar crime. Those who indulge in committing such crimes are intelligent enough to access the computer in the first place and there after manipulate the computer system. For example, stealing funds *via* computer is a computer crime. Another example of computer crime is unauthorized entry into computer system. By such unauthorized entry, the perpetrator can steal a company's trade secrets and data. Such a crime could be committed by an employee. Such crime involves invasion of property and privacy; and also compromises the computer system itself. Ethical dilemma of such an activity is that who actually owns information and who should have access to that information.

Autonomous System: It is a network of computers, that is administered by a single set of management rules that are controlled by one person, group or organization. Autonomous systems often use only one routing protocol, although multiple protocols can be used. The core of the Internet is made up of many *autonomous systems*.

Railway reservation system, police network, banks network of communication systems, ATMs, communication system, etc. are examples of autonomous computers systems. These systems are made up of many different networks but are operated under the umbrella of a single entity for easy management. *Autonomic computing* refers to the self-managing characteristics of distributed computing resources, adapting to unpredictable changes while hiding intrinsic complexity to operators and users.

Review questions

1. Explain how Internet brings up ethical issues on global networking?
2. When cyber laws are already implemented in many countries, what is the need of global laws on Internet and cyberspace?
3. What are the major fields of international transactions facilitated by global Internet working between nations?
4. Explain how acquiring higher computing powerand Internet accessibility have facilitated change in power structure and power balance between large organizations and MNCs?
5. The issue of privacy focuses on the computer's most basic functions is "its capacities to store, process, organize, and exchange records". How this function of computers causes invasion of privacy?
6. Computer technology and applications have penetrated in all spheres of public life. What is the impact of computers penetration on human values and ethics i.e. concern of computer ethics?
7. Explain the *Ten Commandments of Computer Ethics* mandated for computer professionals.
8. How computers as instruments can also play role in unethical or illegal conduct/operation? Give examples of unethical uses of computers.
9. What type of activities or applications of computers can be called as Computer Crime?
10. Computer security is rather *logical security*, where security issues are divided into five aspects. What are these 5 aspects of studies on computer security; explain?
11. What is the function of computer code of ethics? Give salient features of these coded.
12. What do you understand by Autonomous system? Give examples of Autonomous Computer systems.

24 Intellectual Property Rights

Learning objectives

In this chapter you will learn about

- *Intellectual property* and scope of *intellectual property law*
- *Trademarks*, kind of signs that can be used as trademarks, and functions of trademarks
- *Copyrights* and related economic and moral rights, transfer of economic rights
- *Patents* and protection of inventions, *trade secrets*, forms of intellectual property
- Unfair competition, protection of trade-secrets, *industrial-designs* and *layout-designs*

24.1 What is Intellectual Property?

Every layman is aware of term *property* or personal property like owning a house, a car, an oven, lot of furniture, etc. But term *intellectual property* may not be clear precisely to even educated persons. Actually, there are three types of properties that an individual or organizations/ companies possess. Land and buildings are called real estate properties, whereas specific items like mobiles phones, cameras, cars, jewelry, dining sets, sofa and furniture, etc. are called *personal properties*. Intellectual property refers to the products of human creativity including literature, books, advertising slogans, songs, musical creations, scientific and engineering, innovations, etc.

In all countries, laws exist to protect personal and real estate properties of individuals and companies. In the same fashion laws have been framed nationally and internationally to protect intellectual property (IP) of individuals and corporate world throughout the globe. These are called *Intellectual Property Rights* (IPR). Many of the rights of ownership common to real and personal property are also common to *intellectual property*. Rationale behind protecting intellectual property of individual and company is: a) principle of natural justice; b) creator has a right to economic reward; and c) creator has a right to control the use of his creation.

Evolution of society, economy and technology necessitated a transparent system. Brands are intellectual property and in today's highly competitive business world, brands play very crucial role. Protection of IPR is vitally important for pharmaceuticals, biotechnology and other such industries as these industries make huge risky investments in innovation and discovery, hence they have right to harness benefits of their research outcomes. Whenever a new product or service or an idea is realized, it has potential of accruing profit, benefit or fame; there is every possibility that someone else may imitate it. The possibility of imitation depends on the fact whether IPR exists or not. There is little purpose served in holding IPR unless they can be enforced against people who infringe or intend to infringe the same.

Following categories of items and activities are treated as intellectual property: literary, artistic and scientific works, performances of artists, phonograms, and broadcasts, inventions in all fields of human endeavor, scientific discoveries, industrial designs, trademarks, service marks and commercial names, industrial property/ Patents, Copyright, geographical indications, layout designs/topographies integrated circuits and protection of new plant varieties.

24.2 Scope of Intellectual Property Law

IPR is provided by law. Reprotection provides exclusive rights to a person or to a company to use its own plans, ideas or other intangible assets without any fear of competition, at least for a specific period of time. Provision of intellectual property encourages innovation without the fear of any competitor stealing the idea and/ or taking the credit for it. IPR protects innovator's right on their creation from infringement, or the unauthorized use and misuse of their creations.

The concept of intellectual property in India and the world over is taken to be sacrosanct. Intellectual property is treated as an impregnable property, which has made Patents, trademarks, Copyright, designs and confidential information (trade-secrets), technical know-Howmet. as intangible property/asset. IP rights are valuable assets, which need to be scrupulously guarded against from being infringed or misused.

IPRs are of great importance for modern industry and commerce. In many cases, they cast a very important role on the well-being of economy and sometimes on the very existence of a business entity. The value of intellectual property cannot be defined in monetary terms; it is an intangible asset of any innovator or corporate entity. IPR defines variety of legal rights for protecting products of intellectual efforts of creativity. These rights may be enforced by a court via a lawsuit. Basically, IPRs give protection to intellectual property owner against those persons who want to reap the fruits of his ideas or work.

24.3 India's Intellectual Property Regime

1. India is fully committed to protecting intellectual property. India has a complete eco-system supporting a well-settled, stable and robust *intellectual property regime*. Its three main pillars are a) comprehensive laws, b) detailed rules to back them up, and c) strong enforcement mechanisms including system for dispute resolution. In India, the IP framework is rooted in law.
2. The full complement of laws on Patents, designs, trademarks and geographical indications is in place and follows the *Trade Related Intellectual Property Rights*(TRIPS) of WTO. The main acts of parliament that address the IP regime in India include:
   - The Patents Act, 1970 (amended in 1999, 2002 and 2005);
   - The Designs Act, 2000;
   - The Trademarks Act, 1999; and
   - The Geographical Indications of Goods (Registration & Protection) Act, 1999;

   These are administered through the office of the Controller General of Patents, Designs and Trademarks (CGPDTM).
3. Other IP issues are also governed by law:
   - Copyright is protected through the Copyright Act, 1957 as amended in 1999.
   - Layout of transistors and other circuitry elements is protected through the Semiconductor Integrated Circuits Layout Design Act, 2000.
   - New varieties of Plants are protected through the Protection of Plant Varieties and Farmers' Rights Act, 2001.
4. In India Patents act specifically is one of the most comprehensive acts and it is rigorously enforced. The award of Patents is a transparent legal process with decisions and processes subject to legal scrutiny.

The act does not discriminate between Indian nationals and others. According to the Indian Patents Act, residents of India cannot apply for Patents outside India without prior written permission from the Controller (unless an application for a Patent for the same invention has been made in India, not less than six weeks before the application outside India).

24.4 Trademarks

A trademark is a sign which is used to identify certain goods and services as those produced or provided by a specific individual or enterprise. In all cases, the trademark must be distinctive: it must be capable of distinguishing the goods or services with which it is used. Trademark helps to distinguish those goods and services from similar ones provided by another agency. For example, DELL is a trademark that identifies goods (computers and computer related objects); CITY BANK is a trademark that relates to services (banking and financial services).

What kind of signs can be used as Trademarks?

Trademarks may consist of a word (e.g., BISLERI, CATERPILLAR, TATA,) or a combination of words (Coca-Cola), letters and abbreviations (e.g. BAJAJ, TELCO, VOLVO, AOL, BMW and IBM), and names (e.g. Ford, Dior). They may consist of drawings (like the *logo* of the Shell oil company or the *Penguin* drawing for Penguin books).

Certification marks are the marks used to distinguish goods or services that comply with a set of standards and have been certified as such (e.g. AGMARK is a certification mark employed on agricultural products in India, ISI mark for industrial product, FPO mark is a mandatory mark for all processed fruit products in India).

What function does a Trademark perform?

Trademarks may perform different functions and they include the following:

- Trademarks help consumers to identify and distinguish among products or services of different companies.
- Trademarks enable companies to differentiate their products from similar products of other companies.
- Trademarks encourage companies to invest in maintaining or improving quality of their products.
- Trademarks are a marketing tool and the basis for building a brand image and reputation.
- Trademarks are a crucial component of intangible assets of business.
- Trademarks May be useful for obtaining finance.
- Trademarks may be licensed and provide a direct source of revenue through royalties.

24.5 Copyrights and related rights

Under Copyright laws exclusive rights are granted to authors, artists, composers and publishers to produce and distribute their expressive and original work. Copyright protection may be available only to expressive pieces, or writings and the writing need not be words on paper. In Copyright law, it could be a painting, sculpture, or other work of art etc. The writing element merely requires that a work of art, before receiving Copyright protection must be reduced to some tangible form. This may be on paper, on film, on audiotape, or on any other tangible medium that can be reproduced (i.e. copied).

Works covered by Copyright include but are not limited to literary works such as novels, poems and plays; reference works such as encyclopedias and dictionaries; databases; newspaper articles; films and TV programs; musical compositions; choreography; artistic works such as paintings, drawings, photographs and sculptures; architectures; advertisements, maps and technical drawings; etc. Copyright also protects computer programs.

Copyright does not however extend to ideas, but only to the *expression of thoughts*. For example, the idea of taking a picture of a sun rise or a landscape on full moon night is not protected by Copyright. Anyone may take such a picture. But a particular picture of a sunrise or landscape on full moon night taken by a photographer may be protected by Copyright. In such a case, if someone else makes copies of the photograph and starts selling them without the consent of the photographer, that person would be violating the photographer's rights.

24.5.1 Type of rights under Copyrights

There are two types of rights under Copyright: *economic rights allow* the owner to get financial reward from the use and exploitation of his Copyright work; and *moral rights highlight* the personal link existing between the author and his Copyright work.

Economic Rights: Under economic rights, the creators of a work can use their work as they see fit. They can also authorize or prohibit the following acts in relation to a work:

- Reproduction in various forms, for example in a printed publication or by recording the work in cassettes, compact disks or videodiscs or by storing it in computer memories.
- Distribution, for example through sale to the public of copies of the work.
- Public performance, for example by performing music during a concert or a play on stage.
- Broadcasting and communication to the public by radio or TV, cable or satellite.
- Translation into other languages.
- Adaptation, for example by converting a novel or a play into a screenplay for a film.
- Recent international developments also allow for works to be protected in the context of the Internet. The WIPO Copyright Treaty (WCT) concluded in 1996 addresses the challenges posed by today's digital technology, thus ensuring that Copyright owners will be adequately and effectively protected when their works are disseminated through new technology and communication systems such as the Internet.

Moral Rights: Under moral rights, the author may claim
- The right to have authorship recognized on the work. That is basically the right of the creator to have his or her name mentioned as the author, in particular when the work is used.
- The right to integrity of the work that is the right to object to the work being modified, or being used in contexts that may cause harm to the reputation or honor of the author.

24.5.2 Transfer of economic rights

Many creative works protected by Copyright require financial investment and professional skills for their production and further dissemination and mass distribution. Activities such as book publishing, sound recording or film producing are usually undertaken by specialized business organizations or companies and not directly by the authors. Usually, authors and creators transfer their rights to these companies by way of contractual agreements in return for compensation. The compensation may take different forms, such as lump sum payments or royalties based on a percentage of revenues generated by the work.

24.5.3 Extent of use of someone else's work without permission

The most important exception to the exclusive rights of the Copyright holder is the *fair use* doctrine. This doctrine allows the general public to use Copyrighted material without permission in certain situations. To varying extents, these situations include some educational activities, some literary and social criticism, some parody and news reporting, or making quotations in a way compatible with fair practices, or by way of illustration for teaching. Such cases of free use may vary from country to country and it is advisable to revert to the national law of that country, in order to verify whether advantage can be taken of such a possibility.

24.6 Patents

A patent is an exclusive right granted in respect of an *invention*, which may be a product or a process that provides a new and inventive way of doing something or offers a new and inventive technical solution to a problem. Examples of Patents range from electric lighting (Patents held by Edison and Swan) and plastic (Patents held by Baekeland), to ballpoint pens (Patents held by Biro), microprocessors (Patents held by Intel), telephones (Patents held by Bell) and CDs (Patents held by Russell).

Patent laws encourage private investment in new technologies by granting to innovator the right to forbid all others to produce and distribute technological information that is new, useful and non-obvious. The statutory requirements for Patent protection are more stringent than those for Copyright protection. Furthermore, because Patent protection for commercial products or processes can give a tremendous market advantage to businesses, those seeking Patents often find opposition to their applications.

What kinds of Inventions are protected?
An Invention must, in general, fulfill the following conditions to be protected by a Patent:
- It must be new or novel, that is, it must show some new characteristic which is not known in the body of existing knowledge (called *prior art*) in its technical field. The novelty requirement focuses on events that occur prior to the Invention. Under Section 102 of the Patent Act, an Invention is not novel if it is publicly used, sold, or Patented by another inventor within 12 months of the Patent application.
- It must be non-obvious or involve an inventive step, that is, it could not be deduced by a person with average knowledge in the technical field.
- It must be useful or capable of industrial application.
- Finally, the Invention must be part of the so-called *Patentable subject matter* under the applicable law. In many countries scientific theories, mathematical methods, plant or animal varieties, discoveries of natural substances, commercial methods, or methods for medical treatment (as opposed to medical products) are not considered to be Patentable subject matter.

24.7 Trade Secrets and other forms of intellectual property

Trade Secrets: The body of IP law also includes laws relating to Trade Secrets, unfair competition and the right of publicity. Some Inventions, data, information cannot be protected by any of the available means of IPRs. Such information is held confidential as a Trade *Secret. Trade* Secrets do not receive Patent protection because they are not inventive.

A Trade Secret is commonly defined as any confidential business information which provides an enterprise a competitive edge. It basically means any kind of confidential information or know-how which is not in public domain and has a commercial advantage. Trade Secret laws protect any information like technical or non-technical data, formula, pattern, device, compilation, drawing, program, technique, process etc. that provides a business advantage over competitors who do not use or know of it. Trade Secret laws are included in intellectual property laws because, like other intellectual property laws, they prevent the unauthorized use of certain intangible subject matters. Trade Secret can be an Invention, idea, survey method, manufacturing process, experiment results, chemical formula, recipe, financial strategy, client database, etc.

When Trade Secrets are preferred?
- When Invention is not Patentable
- Patent protection is limited to 20 years, whereas Tread Secret can be kept beyond that period
- When cost of Patent Protection is prohibitive

How to guard Trade Secret?
- Restricting number of people having access to secret information
- Signing confidentiality agreements with business partners and employees
- Using protective techniques like digital data security tools and restricting entry into area where Trade Secret is worked or held
- National legislations provide protection in form of injunction and damages if secret information is illegally acquired or used

24.7.1 Unfair Competition

The unauthorized use of Trade Secret information by persons other than the holder is regarded as an unfair practice and a violation of the Trade Secret. Depending on the legal system, the protection of Trade Secrets forms part of the general concept of protection against unfair competition or is based on specific provisions or case law on the protection of confidential information.

24.7.2 Protection of Trade Secrets

Contrary to Patents, Trade Secrets are protected without registration, i.e. Trade Secrets are protected without any procedural formalities. A Trade Secret can be protected for an unlimited period of time. However, there are some conditions for the information to be considered as a Trade Secret. These conditions vary from country to country; some general standards exist which are referred to in Article 39 of the agreement on Trade-Related Aspects of Intellectual Property Rights (TRIPS Agreement):
- The information must be secret (i.e. it is not generally known among or readily accessible to circles that normally deal with the kind of information in question)
- It must have commercial value because it is a secret
- It must have been subject to reasonable steps to keep it secret by the rightful holder of the information (e.g., through confidentiality agreements)

24.8 Industrial Designs

Designs are also an important component of Intellectual Property Rights, which are worthy of protection. Design indicates any aspect of the features of shape, configuration, pattern or ornament applied to any article by any industrial process, whether external or internal of the whole or part of an article. A new or novel design can be registered as per the provisions of the Designs Act and such registration gives the proprietor a Copyright in the design for five years, which can be renewed for two further terms of five years each.

The purpose of the Act is to preserve for the owner of the design, the commercial value resulting from customers preferring the appearance of articles, which have new and innovative designs, reproduced upon articles on a mass scale, application being done by the industrial process or mechanical and chemical means. The design rights may be infringed by unauthorized reproduction of the design for commercial purposes. To be protected under most national laws, an industrial design must appeal to the eye. This means that an industrial design is primarily of an aesthetic nature and does not protect any technical features of the article to which it is applied.

The owner of a protected industrial design is granted the right to prevent unauthorized copying or imitation of the design by others. This includes the right of making, offering, importing, exporting or selling any product in which the design is incorporated or to which it is applied. He/She may also license or authorize others to use the design on mutually agreed terms. The owner may also sell the right to the industrial design to someone else.

Layout-designs (topographies) of Integrated Circuits

A lay out design is a dimensionally precise design and accurate pictorial view of actual layout of transistors and other circuit elements, including lead wires connecting elements and expressed in any manner in a semiconductor Integrated Circuit (IC).

Layout design (topography) of IC is a relatively new area in IP, which has appeared with computer technology and has acquired importance as the technology makes rapid advances. The design of circuitry on the chip requires great investment of knowledge, skills and capital and it needs to be protected as IP.

The *right* in topography aims to prevent copying of the layout design but reverse engineering to come up with improved design is regarded as fair. It may also be noted that, while for claiming a Patent, an Invention is required to meet the criteria both of novelty and non-obviousness, a layout design is only required to be original. Protection of layout design confers no monopoly right. Independent development of a design, identical with a protected design is permitted. The protection of layout designs is provided in the TRIPS Agreement.

24.9 Summary

Intellectual Property Rights: Every layman is aware of term *property* or personal property. Intellectual Property refers to the products of human creativity including literature, books, advertising slogans, songs, musical creations, scientific and engineering, innovations, etc. Laws have been framed nationally and internationally to protect *intellectual property* (IP) of individuals and corporate world throughout the globe. These are called Intellectual Property Rights (IPR). These rights may be enforced by a court *via* a lawsuit. Protection under IPR is available to a person or to a company to have exclusive rights to use its own plans, ideas or other intangible assets without the worry of competition. In today's highly competitive business world, *Brands* play very crucial role and protection of IPR is vitally important for pharmaceuticals, biotechnology and other such industries that commit risky investments in innovation and discovery. Basically, an IPR gives a remedy to its owner against those persons who want to reap the fruits of his ideas or work. Rationale of protecting IP of individual and company is based on principle of natural justice, i.e. creator has a right to economic reward and creator has a right to control the use of his creation. These rights also include Copyrights, Patents, trademarks, design and Trade Secrets.

Trademarks: A *trademark* is a sign that is used to identify certain goods and services as those produced or provided by a specific person or enterprise. In all cases, the trademark must be distinctive: it must be capable of distinguishing the goods or services with which it is used. For example, DELL is a trademark that identifies goods (computers and computer related objects). CITY BANK is a trademark that relates to services (banking and financial services).

Trademarks may consist of a word (e.g., BISLERI, CATERPILLAR, and TATA) or a combination of words (Coca-Cola), letters and abbreviations (e.g. BAJAJ, TELCO, VOLVO, AOL, BMW and IBM) and names (e.g. Fordor Dior). They may consist of drawings (like the logo of the Shell oil company or the penguin drawing for Penguin books).

Certification marks are marks used to distinguish goods or services that comply with a set of standards and have been certified as such (e.g. AGMARK is a certification mark employed on agricultural products in India, ISI mark for industrial product, FPO mark is a mandatory mark for all processed fruit products in India).

Copyrights and related rights: Copyright laws grant to authors, artists, composers and publishers the exclusive right to produce and distribute expressive and original work. Only expressive pieces, or writings, may receive Copyright protection. Writing need not be words on paper. In Copyright law, it could be a painting, sculpture or other work of art. The writing element merely requires that a work of art, before receiving

Copyright protection must be reduced to some tangible form. Copyright also protects computer programs.

There are two types of rights under Copyright: *economic rights* allow the owner to derive financial reward from the use and exploitation of the work; and *moral rights* highlight the personal link existing between the author and the work.

Patents: A Patent is an exclusive right granted in respect of an Invention, which may be a product or a process that provides a new and inventive way of doing something or offers a new and inventive technical solution to a problem. Examples of Patents range from electric lighting (Patents held by Edison and Swan) and plastic (Patents held by Baekeland), to ballpoint pens (Patents held by Biro), microprocessors (Patents held by Intel), telephones (Patents held by Bell) and CDs (Patents held by Russell). Patent laws encourage private investment in new technologies by granting to inventor the right to forbid all others to produce and distribute his patented product or process. Patent protection for commercial products or processes gives tremendous market advantage to businesses.

Trade Secrets: Some Inventions, data, information cannot be protected by any of the available means of IPRs. Such information is held confidential as a Trade Secret. A Trade Secret is commonly defined in broad terms as any confidential business information which provides an enterprise a competitive edge. It basically means any kind of information or know-how which is not publicly known and has a commercial advantage. Trade Secret laws protect any technical or non-technical data, formula, pattern, device, compilation, drawing, program, technique, process, etc. of information that provides a business advantage over competitors who do not use or know of it. Trade Secrets do not receive Patent protection because they are not inventive. Trade Secret laws are included in intellectual property laws because, like other intellectual property laws they prevent the unauthorized use of certain intangible subject matter. Trade Secret can be an Invention, idea, survey method, manufacturing process, experiment results, chemical formula, recipe, financial strategy, client database, etc.

Industrial designs and layout-designs (topographies): Designs are also an important component of Intellectual Property Rights, which are worthy of protection. *Design* indicates any aspect of the features of shape, configuration, pattern or ornament applied to any article by any industrial process, whether external or internal of the whole or part of an article.

A lay out design is a dimensionally precise design and accurate pictorial view of actual layout of transistors and other circuit elements, including lead wires connecting such elements and expressed in any manner in a semiconductor ICs. Layout design (topography) of ICs is a relatively new area in IP, which has appeared with computer technology and has acquired importance as the technology makes rapid advances. The design of circuitry on the chip requires great investment of knowledge, skills and capital and it needs to be protected as an IP.

Review questions

1. What is intellectual property and why there should be rights for such property; explain?
2. What categories of items and activities are treated as intellectual property?
3. Explain scope of intellectual property law. What is status of Intellectual Property Regime in India?
4. Why trademarks are treated as an industrial property? What kind of signs can be used as trademarks and what function does a trademark perform?
5. Whose work or creation can be granted Copyrights and related rights? Explain, by giving examples, which type of work can be Copyrighted?
6. What types of rights are provided/ available under Copyrights? Explain these rights in detail. Are these rights transferable?
7. What type of Inventions, products or processes can be provided Patent rights?
8. Intellectual property law also includes laws relating to Trade Secrets, unfair competition, and the right of publicity. Explain each of these bank or business or organization-based information.
9. Explain what types of industrial designs and layout-designs qualify for industrial property rights?

25 Bibliography

[1] ACM, Computing Machinery. "ACM code of ethics and professional conduct." [Online] available at URL: <http://www.acm.org/about-acm/acm-code-of-ethics-and-professional-conduct>, accessed [May 10, 2014]

[2] Agosta, L. (2011). Empathy and sympathy in ethics. [Online] available at URL: <http://www.iep.utm.edu/emp-symp/>, accessed [September 19, 2013].

[3] AICTE-ETHICS (2014). Ethics. [Online] available at URL: <http://www.aicte-india.org/sethic.php>, accessed [July 31, 2013].

[4] AICTE-MORAL EDUCATION (2014). Moral Education. [Online] available at URL: <http://www.aicte-india.org/fsmoraledu.php>, accessed [July 31, 2013].

[5] Alavudeen, A., KalilRahman, R. and Jayakumaran, M. (2008) *Professional Ethics and Human values*. 1st Ed. Lakshmi publication, New Delhi-India.

[6] Ansari, M.H. (2010). Dr.V.N. TewariMemorial Lecture at Panjab University Chandigarh, [online] available at URL: <http://www.pib.nic.in/newsite/erelcontent.aspx?relid=60185>.

[7] Bagad, V.S. (2007). *Professional Ethics and human Values*. 1st Ed., Technical Publications.

[8] Bagad, V. S. and Dhotre, I. A. (2007). *Professional Ethics and Human Values*. 1st Ed. Technical Publications. Pune-India.

[9] Barkely GGSC (2016). Empathy. [Online] available on URL: <http://greatergood.berkeley.edu/topic/empathy/definition>, accessed [September 19, 2013]

[10] Basis, S. (2009) *In Praise of Science: Curiosity, Understanding and Progress*. MIT Press, Cambridge-Massachusetts.

[11] Boylan, M. (Ed.). (2013). *Business ethics*. John Wiley & Sons.

[12] Chaudhury, N. and Kumar, N.K. (2006). "Ethical Guidelines for Biomedical Research on Human Participants". Indian Council of Medical Research (ICMR), New Delhi.

[13] Chernoff, M. (2007). What is Adulthood? 20 Defining Characteristics of a True Adult. [Online] available at URL: <http://www.marcandangel.com/2007/08/17/>, accessed [March 19, 2015]

[14] Conrad, E., Misenar, S., and Feldman, J. (2012). *CISSP study guide*. Newnes.
[15] Conry, S. (1992). Interview on Computer Science Accreditation. *T. Bynum and J. Fodor (creators), Computer Ethics in the Computer Science Curriculum*.
[16] Elden, W.L. (2016). Ethical Rights and Responsibilities of Practicing Engineers. [Online]available at URL: <https://www.nspe.org/resources/ethics/ethics-resources/other-resources/ethical-rights-responsibilities-practicing>, accessed [January 21, 2016]
[17] EY Report (2012). Bribery and Corruption: Group Reality in India – A Survey by EY's Fraud Investigation & Dispute Services Practice. Ernst & Young LLP Ltd. Kolkata-India.
[18] Fernando. A.C. (2011). *Business Environment*. Pearson, Delhi.
[19] Fitzpatrick, K., and Bronstein, C. (Eds.). (2006). *Ethics in public relations: Responsible advocacy*. Sage.
[20] Florman, S.C. (2002). Engineering ethics: the conversation without end. BRIDGE Washington, 32(3), 19-23.
[21] Gaur, R.R., Sangal, R. and Bagaria, G.P. (2009). *A foundation course in Human Values and Professional Ethics*. 1st Ed. EXCEL Books, New Delhi-India.
[22] Goodman, G.T. and Rowe, W. D. (1979). *Energy Risk Management*. Science, Academic Press.
[23] Gotterbarn, D., Miller, K., Rogerson, S., Barber, S., Barnes, P., Burnstein, I., Davis, M., El-Kadi, A., Fairweather, N.B., Fulghum, M. and Jayaram, N., (2001). Software engineering code of ethics and professional practice. *Science and Engineering Ethics*, 7(2), pp.231-238.
[24] Govindarajan, M., Natarajan, S. and SenthilKumar, V.S. (2004). *Engineering Ethics: Includes Human Values*. PHI Learning.
[25] Gordon, J.S. (2012). Modern Morality and Ancient Ethics. [Online] available on URL: <http://www.iep.utm.edu/anci-mod/ >, available [February 25, 2013]
[26] Gosh, P.K. (2012). Proceedings: The Power of the Interfaith Movement: World Congress of Religions 2012. [Online] available at URL: <http://www.worldcongressofreligions2012.org/proceedings/>, accessed [May 12, 2015].
[27] Goyal, A and Goyal, M. (2010) *Business Environment*. V.K. Enterprises. New Delhi, India.
[28] Halsmer, D. (2010). AC 2010-1984: Exploring Connections between Engineering and Human Spirituality.

[29] HarrisJr., C.E., Pritchard, M.S., Rabins, M.J., James, R., and Englehardt, E. (2013). *Engineering ethics: Concepts and cases.* Cengage Learning.

[30] Himma, K.E. (2007). *Internet security: Hacking, counter hacking, and society.* Jones & Bartlett Learning.

[31] Johnston, D. W., ThomasAhluwalia, N., and Gwyn, M.B. (2007). Improving the professional engineering licensure process for construction engineers. *Journal of Construction Engineering and Management, 133*(9), 669-677.

[32] Khosla, V. R. and Bhagat, K. (2009). *Human Values and Professional Ethics.* 1st Ed. Technical Publications, Pune.

[33] Kolb, J. and Ross, S.S. (1980) *Product Safety and Liability: A Desk Reference.* New York: McGraw-Hill.

[34] Kramer, W.M. (2012). Summary of Fraud and Corruption cases in International Development Projects. [Online] available at URL: <http://iacrc.org/fraud-and-corruption/summary-of-fraud-and-corruption-cases-in-international-development-projects/>, accessed [May 12, 2014]

[35] Leopold, A. (2014). The land ethic. In *The Ecological Design and Planning Reader* (pp. 108-121). Island Press/ Center for Resource Economics.

[36] Martin, M.W. and Schinzinger, R. (2010). *Introduction to Engineering Ethics.* 2ndEd.McGraw-HillHiger Education.

[37] Mendelson, M.I. (2013). *Learning Bio-micro-nanotechnology.* CRC Press.

[38] MindTool Editorial (2017). Building Self-Confidence: Preparing Yourself for Success. [Online] available at URL: <https://www.mindtools.com/selfconf.html >, accessed [January 26, 2015]

[39] Oommen, T.K. and Venugopal, C.N. (1993). *Sociology for Law Students.* Eastern Book Company.

[40] Raelin, J.A. (1986). *The clash of cultures: Managers and professionals.* Harvard Business Press.

[41] Raggad, B.G. (2010). *Information security management: Concepts and practice.* CRC Press.

[42] Ramdass, B. (2010). *Now Be Here.* The Crown Publishing Group, New York-USA.

[43] Sander-Staudt, M. (2011). Care ethics. [Online] available on URL: <http://www.iep.utm.edu/care-eth/#H2>, accessed [September 18, 2013].

[44] Schinzinger, R. and Martin, M.W. (2000). *Engineering as Social Experimentation.* Introduction to Engineering Ethics. Boston: McGraw-Hill.

[45] Schwing, R.C. and Albers, W.A., (2013). *Societal risk assessment: How safe is safe enough?*. Springer.
[46] Singh. P., Panwar, D. and Chaudhary. R. (2010). *Human Values & Professional Ethics*. 1st Ed. Krishna Prakashan Media (P) Ltd. Meerut, India.
[47] Sirvastava, S. (2009). *Human Values and Professional Ethics*.Kataria& Sons.
[48] Sunstein, C.R. (1997). A Note on Voluntary Versus Involuntary Risks. *Duke Envtl. L. &Pol'y F.*, *8*, 173.
[49] Suresh. J. and Raghavan. B.S. (2012). *Human Values and Professional Ethics – Values and Ethics of Profession*. 4th Ed. S. Chand & Company Ltd. New Delhi, India.
[50] Thompson, N.H. (1998). *Religious Pluralism and Religious Education*. Religious Education Press. Birmingham-Alabama.
[51] Tiberius, V. (2015). Well-being, virtue and personal projects: A normative framework for virtue ethics and public policy. *Unpublished MS., Department of Philosophy, Minneapolis: University of Minnesota.*
[52] Turner, A.J. (1991). "Summary of the ACM/IEEE-CS Joint Curriculum Task Force Report: Computing Curricula, 1991". *Communications of the ACM,* Vol. 34, No.6., 69-84.
[53] Watch, W. (2011). Aviation database reveals frequent safety problems at airports. [Online] available at URL: <http://wisconsinwatch.org/2011/02/aviation-database-reveals-frequent-safety-problems-at-airports/>, accessed [March 12, 2014]
[54] Williamson, T. (2013). 10 Ways to Stop Stressing and Star Living Peacefully. [Online] available on URL: <http://www.mindbodygreen.com/0-11192/10-ways-to-stop-stressing-start-living-peacefully.html>, accessed [June 14, 2014]
[55] Wright, D., and De Hert, P. (2012). Introduction to privacy impact assessment. In *Privacy Impact Assessment* (pp. 3-32). Springer Netherlands.

26 Appendix

Appendix-A: The salient features of Sociological Models of study of Society

A.1: Salient features of Society have been highlighted by its proponents as Positivism by Durkheim, Humanism by Weber and Materialism by Karl Marx. The salient features of these models of society are given below.

A.1.1: Positivism

Theory of positivism is based on natural science concept where conclusions are drawn empirically from observations and experiences. The Positivist believes that all knowledge is acquired through sense experience, and experience, perception and observations are the only source of any knowledge.

Further, *Social Facts* are different from *Biological* and *Psychological Facts*. Social Facts are collective in nature, whereas psychological facts are individualistic. However, to identify Social facts is difficult because combination and interaction of individuals who constitute a society and their association produces a new type of facts, the social facts, with features and characteristics which are not found in individuals.

Social Facts are external to individuals, exert coercive power over them. Social facts are independent of the individual will, they constrain individuals and it is impossible to be free them from social facts. Individuals are usually inclined to adhere to rules of society out of habit or custom. Many of social values are internalized by individuals because of mediation through parents and teachers.

Thus, Socialization is a process to produce conformist individuals and man is a mere creature of society.

A.1.2: Humanism

Humanists look at human being as *Free Agent* capable of *Meaningful Acts* and as *Creators* of their *Social World*. Human beings have ability of reflection and capable of attributing meaning to objects and entities which are beyond sensory experiences.

Accordingly, to Weber, *Cultural Sciences* are not like *Natural Sciences* and have some peculiarities due to inter-related features like value-relevance, interpretive understanding and idealization. Weber distinguishes individual social actions, their meanings and causes, from other social entities such as States, Institutions, Classes, and Collective Conscience etc.

Weber also distinguishes between action and behavior. They require proper interpretation for their understanding. This type of understanding is applicable to *Emotional Reactions* such as anger, jealousy, hate, greed, ambition, etc., which are inner states of human being. An understanding of these requires an imaginative understanding of the psyche of others. This approach is more useful to understand human acts and there meaning in daily life. Thus, clearly the focus is on the Human dimension in understanding society.

A.1.3: Materialism

Doctrine of Materialism assumes/stand that universe consists of only of matter. In this way of thinking, thought and consciousness are treated as appearances and not of much value for social well-being. Materialism in theory treats economic life as the sole determinant of social well-being or material life is the essence of society. Materialist philosophy asserts primacy to economic structure (base) in molding the character of the superstructure like Ideology, Values and Institutions.

A.2: Theories of Operational Feature of Society

A.2.1: Theory of Functionalism

The basic tenet of *Functionalism* is that society is an integrated system of interrelated parts and in order to understand any part, it must be seen in relation to society as a whole. This relationship means that any change in any part is bound to have impact on other parts also. Further, according to this theory, functional relationships in society are structured and, are regulated by rules and norms. In order to achieve this societal state, the individuals and the groups in the society should have consensus on common set of values which are translated into concrete set of norms, rules and regulations.

While, some norms are universal in nature, most norms are role-specific, related to the role one plays like father, teacher, professional, politician etc. Thus, according to Functionalism, social structure is the totality of social relationship which is governed by norms. The major component of society, its institutions such as family, the economy, the polity, the religious system etc. are important aspects of *Social Structure.* Any institution within this social structure is a sub-structure made up of interrelated roles. For example, Institution of family is made up of a cluster of roles like father/mother, husband wife, son daughter, brother/sister, mother-in law/ daughter-in-law etc. The relationships between these roles are guided by norms relevant to each of these roles.

The term 'FUNCTION' refers to the contributions an institution makes to the maintenance and survival of the society. Thus, an important function of family is to inculcate norms and values of society into children of the family, as shared norms and values are the basis of order and stability in society. Inadequate socialization leads to questioning and challenging of norms-called social deviance. Conformity to norms is ensured by any institution through reward and punishment mechanism. Reward and punishment mechanism are different in different Institutions. For example, to punish or reward a student, a college, and university, a State or Nation do have different yard sticks to ensure conformity to their norms and values.

How are the functions of different parts of social structure determined? Societies must meet certain basic needs or requirements if they are to survive. These needs are referred as *functional prerequisites*. For example, in order that societies should continue to exist, human reproduction is necessary; it is functional prerequisites. The institution of marriage provides for legitimate reproduction of human being. Once children are borne, socialization is a functional prerequisite so that they learn the norms and values of the society. The institution of family undertakes this task. Similarly, survival of children depends on availability of food. Thus, production of food is a functional prerequisite and this task is undertaken by economic institutions.

Various institutions should have mutual compatibility. Therefore, a certain degree of coordination of activities between institutions is functional prerequisite. This coordination could be by a State or a Centralized Body.

The basic postulates of Functionalism may be stated as follows:
- Society must be looked at holistically as a system of inter-related parts.
- Parts of a society contribute to the well-being and survival of society.
- Society functions on the basis of value consensus, common norms and shared interests.

These are inculcated into individuals through socialization and training.
- Society tends to seek stability, order and harmony. But tension and disorder may creep in, due to inadequate internalization of values and norms.
- Change in society occurs through the stresses and strains that take place in one or the other part of the society, in the process of societal functioning.

A.2.2: Theory of Karl Marks

Marxian theory simply based on the fact that man cannot live without bread and therefore his prime concern is to gear up for food production and other material objects supporting life and their production process. This necessitates formation of society to build infrastructure for the chain of production activities. Forces of production include technology, raw material and scientific knowledge. According to Marxian theory, history of mankind is history of class struggles built around materialism. In all societies, people are divided into hostile classes by virtue of their position in the production process. This division appeared as masters and slaves, lords and serfs etc. in ancient world. The forces of production and relationship of men with these forces taken together form the economic infrastructure of the society. Over this infrastructure, a superstructure of political, legal, educational and beliefs and values are superimposed.

A.2.3: Theory of Interactionism

- Max Weber, a German sociologist, philosopher and jurist, laid the foundation for *Interactionism* by emphasizing the importance of *Subjective Meaning*, which actors of social action attach to their actions. Interactions assume that every individual is influenced by and in turn influences every other individual with whom he/she comes into contact. Human society is a product of this interaction. Sociologist looking into this element carefully realized that both Functionalism and Marxism dealt with large scale operation of social process and, social life is not looked into from the perspective of social actor.
- Interactionism assumes that human action is meaningful to those who are involved in it. Therefore, understanding meanings and motivation which actors attribute to their activities is important. Meanings are not fixed forever, they vary contextually. Further, meanings are created, modified and changed in and through the process of interaction (For example perceptions of students on ragging, drinking, dancing, dress code etc.). Thus, based on his perception, the way an actor looks at the situation, has important consequences for him and for others.
- The manner in which an actor interprets other's actions is at least partly based on his *definition of himself.* For this reason, the *concept of self* is of great significance in Interactionism. Actors develop a *Self-Concept* about themselves which exerts influence on their actions. Self-Concept develops from an interaction process since it is largely a reflection of the reactions of others towards the individual.

Appendix

- Interaction theorists are concerned with definitions of situations, self as well as the process through which these definitions and *Social Reality* are constructed. To find an answer, one must investigate the *construction of meaning* in the interaction process. This calls for an analysis of a variety of things – appearance, gestures, the interpretation and use of language, the context in which interaction takes place.

Let us consider an example. In India a girl, 'if she wears dresses in quite modern style, using dark goggles, puts on attractive make-up, having bobs cut hair, using high heel foot wear etc.', is taken as a 'mod' girl and some boys assume her to be 'loose' and approachable. Based on this perception of boys, they tend to be friend with such girl and attempt for a date with her. However, this image of girl built by boys may be totally wrong. The boys may discover to their dismay that a particular girl may be very reserved when it comes to hetero-sexual friendship. She may be successfully promoting an image of herself quite contrary to the prevalent stereotype, as a modern young person without any trace of loose morality. Thus, while it is true that definitions and meanings are constructed in interaction situations, the process can also change them.

Appendix-B: Background Information on Evolution of Society and Development of various types of Social Units/ Groupings in India

B.1: Purpose of study of evolution of societies is to understand background of evaluation of social system and values among human beings.

Social evolution can explain some of the major differences between societies. Each society inherits some of its cultural traditions and values and, adds some new elements based on contemporary needs.

Evolution of societies starts from *Horticultural Societies* which are built upon the foundation of a gardening economy. Slowly gardening economy expanded into elementary agriculture and rearing of milk cattle etc. Such societies are called *Pastoral Societies*. Pastoral tribes have been found in many parts of the world, often within the agricultural societies.

B.1.1: Agrarian Society

These societies are characterized by their settled agriculture. They have their dependence on water resources. For example, in Asia, Africa and Europe, the major rivers provided the means of cultivation and developed into a more complex economy.

In agrarian societies the dynastic rule was predominant. Further, these agrarian societies have complex religious practices and doctrines, traditions, a high level of art and craft, an emphasis on traditional values on the way of life, and concern with social solidarity rather than social progress.

B.1.2: Industrial Society

When man started harnessing inanimate energy, the transition took place from agriculture to Industrial Production. High level technology, mass communication systems and means-end relationship characterize the contemporary world. Industrialization produced vast quantities of consumer goods which have reached the common man. The societies of West Europe, East Europe, Soviet Russia and the USA are now heavily industrialized. India is also in the path of Industrialization and counted as a developed Nation.

Industrial societies are characterized by the democratic or socialist pattern of polity, in which masses participate through their legislators etc. The industrial culture is pre-eminently urban, fast changing, and quite often takes on transnational characteristic. Due to rapid developments in science and technology, people of the world communicate with each other, frequently and efficiently.

The decline of religion in industrial societies has resulted in a secular view of life. The urban Industrial centers have witnessed vast improvements in the quality of life, in terms of civic facilities and comfort. At the same time, urban congestion, crime and civilian unrest have also increased.

B.2: Society *vs.* Nation-State and its value orientation

As societies become more complex in the social organization, a more distinct political structure emerges and the evolution of more complex forms, political institutionalization takes place. Nation-state of India, Egypt, Babylonia, Greece and Rome left their imprint on human history as distinct political entities.

The Nation-State (ancient or modern) is one in which a variety of ethnic, territorial and linguistic groups are politically and jurisdictionally united under a common national culture. In this integrative process religion, ideology, military and civilian bureaucracies provide decisive institutional supporting structure. But depending on social pressures or forces, a nation-state may be predominantly religious (ancient Egypt), militaristic (ancient Rome) or secular (Soviet Russia). Nation –state is not coterminous with society. A nation-state may disappear but society continues.

After the breakup of colonial rule, a number of countries in Asia have become independent Nation-States. Sociologically viewed, State is just one of the many associations of the society. Society is more pervasive and more basic than a State. State and society are independent but society is the ultimate arbiter of people's destiny.

B.2.1: Community

The term community can be defined as a body of men inhabiting usually the same locality and having identity of character, some joint ownership of property, some degree of political organization (e.g. among the tribes), and a sense of fellowship. In some communities, there may be uniformity with regard to religious beliefs and similarity of ethnic background. In community, there exists a considerable degree of interpersonal acquaintance and distinctive cohesiveness. However, the community has a more limited self-sufficiency than society. In an ethnic sense, communities emerge through the biological basis of reproduction and social basis of kinship, clan, etc.

B.3: Classification of groups

A group is different from society. Groups are collections of human beings existing within society, whereas society is a system of social relationship. Membership is normally voluntary in a group, whereas in case of society it is compulsory. A group is formed to realize certain goals while community is a natural entity. A community has a locality but a group may be formed without such a precondition.

B.3.1: Institution

The term *Institution* has been defined and used in a variety of ways. Firstly, an institution is defined as a *Complex* of norms regulating social activities. Secondly, it has been regarded as a unit of social organization. In this sense institutions are groups in which social interaction between the members is regulated by customs, laws, etc. Examples are family, marriage, sect, cult, political party, industrial organization, trade union, government offices, schools and colleges, voluntary cultural associations etc.

Between one type of institution (for example, family) and another (for example school), there is a reciprocal or interdependent relationship. Indeed, in a day-to-day life it is often difficult to separate institutions from associations or organizations.

B.3.2: Associations *vs.* Institutions

In popular usage, the term *Associations* and *Institutions* are often used interchangeably. However, it is necessary to make a distinction between the two. The college, for instance, is an association but modes of training, education etc., are institutions. Similarly, church is an association but its sacraments, mode of worship and rituals are all institutions. The individuals belong to association but not institutions. Association and institutions often intermesh with one another. Family is both an association and an institution.

Voluntary associations like clubs or welfare agencies are an important phenomenon in modern complex societies. They come into existence when people come together voluntarily to pursue cultural or social interests. Voluntary associations are based on a common identity of ends and a consensus to conform to a code of conduct.

B.3.3: Formal Organizations and Bureaucracy

The term refers to the social unit which makes optimum use of men and materials to attain its goal. It often goes under the name *Bureaucracy*. It has entered into all aspects of modern life. The military, police, administration, medical care, education are all organized. *Organizations* are based upon rational-legal principles.

The following principles govern the formal Organization in an ideal typical sense:(1) The Organizations are based on rules and procedures; (2) there is division of labor which ensures the distribution of work and authority to several people; (3) there is a hierarchy of statuses in which some are in a superior position and some others are in a subordinate position; (4) the duties of the employees are discharged objectively without fear or favor; (5)The Organization aims at an efficient use of its resources (men and material) to attain its goals; and (6) the Organization endures even if particular holders of authority or power leave it.

B.4: Understanding functioning and value assessment of society

The question to be addressed is how to '*construct social reality*' and how to arrive at an understanding of society. Sociologist calls it *Science of Society* and wants to study through the methods of natural science. However, it is realized that in case of *Field Sciences* like sociology, Humanism and Materialism etc., to generate data directly from the fellow human being is particularly complex.

The main problem is of objectivity. Many sociologists feel that pursuit of objectivity is a mere illusion as no human being is capable of detaching himself from his past experiences, that is, his investigation is bound to be colored by them. However, Robert Bierstadt, an American Sociologist, defines objectivity as, *"Objectivity* means that conclusions arrived at as the result of inquiry and investigation are independent of the race, color, creed, occupation, nationality, religion, moral preferences, and political dispositions of the investigator. If his investigation is truly objective, it is independent of any subjective elements, any personal desire, that he/she may have". But in practice the investigator sociologist, as other human being, is incapable of shedding his ideological predispositions, taken-for-granted assumptions, prejudices and commitments.

Appendix-C: Major Religions of India

C.1: Hinduism

Hinduism is the third largest religion in the world, and the predominant religion of India. It is neither necessary nor possible to attempt an elaborate analysis of Hinduism which is so rich in terms of its value streams and accepted practice or customs. It doesn't have a single founder nor a single holy book but a number of sacred texts, namely the Vedas, Upanishads, Puranas, the Bhagavad-Gita and the epic poems of the Mahabharata and the Ramayana, which provide spiritual and practical guidance.

Hinduism regards worldly pursuits such as Kama (Sensual pleasure) or Artha (pursuits of wealth) lower in hierarchy in goals of life compared with moksha i.e. spiritual liberation. In this scheme of thinking history is not important, because it is swallowed up in the vastness of cosmic process. Hindus believe in reincarnation and this attitude fosters tolerance of fellow human being and reverence to nature.

In Hinduism, ultimate reality or supreme spirit is nameless, formless, without quality. Reality is one. But multiple paths to attain the goal are permitted. This in turn meant multiplicity of Gods, life system, worship patterns etc. all of which can coexist. This philosophy of coexistence is very well demonstrated in India where the protestant Hindu religion such as Jainism and Buddhism and alien faiths such as Judaism, Zoroastrianism, pre-colonial Christianity, and pre-military Islam all coexisted harmoniously in India.

Hinduism is marked by absence of ecclesiastical organization, congregational worship, professional clergy, all of which inhibit (a) organized political action and (b) initiation and institutionalization of internal reforms. The institutional (like church) vacuum is often filled by caste system regulating social life to the finest detail, leading to societal totalitarianism. The social regulation of individual and collective life through caste system is buttressed through ideological justification provided by the Hindu theory of origin of Man and law of Karma and Reincarnation. Hinduism is not against preaching of other religions but it disapproves of conversion.

C.2: Islam

Islam is perceived as a product of political conquest. Middle East Muslims came conquers, settled down, got attuned to native ways and ruled India for seven centuries. In due course of time the British rule and emergence of Indian Nation rendered the Muslims a minority community status. India, is home of the third largest Muslim population in the world.

The source of Muslim law is the sacred texts, and its official legal interpreters, the Ulemas, have religious sanctions behind them. This inextricable intertwining between the secular and the religious in the Muslim thought and actions inevitably puts a high premium on religious sanctions and becomes a constant source of tension in *Secular* state such as India. As a religious community, their life style and values system towards other communities, the Muslims could not develop their community into economically prosperous group.

C.3: Jainism

Jainism emerged around 6th century BC as protest against orthodox Brahmanism. Jainism is the most ascetically demanding of all Indian religions. Jainism denied the authority of Vedas and revolted against Vedic sacrifice. Value orientation of Jainism was to the cause of common people, asserting common spiritual right of all men, acknowledging compassion and love for all life and preaching in the language of common people. It advocates Ahimsa in any form and doing harm to any living thing. Jainism was founded by Vardhman, called Mahavira, a contemporary to Buddha. Both renounced all worldly possession to live life of ascetics at about the same time. Jainism does not have one main God but has several lesser deities for different aspect of life. Three guiding principles or value emphasis by Jainism are right belief, right knowledge and right conduct. All devotees are expected by 5 MAHAVRATAS (five great vows): nonviolence, non- attachment to possessions, not lying, not stealing and sexual restraint. Jains are strict vegetarian.

In spite of its relatively small size, the Jain community, whose members are mostly from the mercantile class, has had a strong influence on Indian life. Jains are economically prosperous community. Most of them live in urban settlement and dispersed throughout the country.

Although Jainism emerged as a protest against Brahmanical supremacy and caste system, in course of time it also got trapped in it. There are two main sects in Jainism namely Digambar and Svetambara. While Digambar sect has accommodated a few low caste groups, Svetambara are all of clean caste origin. Generally speaking Svetambara's have close social interaction with Hindus of upper caste origin in terms of intermarriage etc., and have accommodated Hindu rituals, worship forms and priests.

C.4: Buddhism

Buddhism, which originated 2500 years ago, was born in India at a time when the idea of reincarnation-the constant cycle of birth, death and rebirth- was growing among Hindus. Buddhism focuses on personal spiritual development and strives for an insight into the truth of life. Its founder is Siddhartha Gautama, who advocated purity and goodness as a way to escape the cycle of reincarnation. Buddha taught the Wheel of Dharma which includes the Four Noble Truths and the Noble Eightfold Path. The Four Noble Truths are: Suffering is the condition of all existence; suffering is due to desire, craving and selfishness; suffering can be overcome and the way to overcome it is by following the Eightfold Path, which leads to right viewpoint, values, speech, actions, livelihood, efforts, mindfulness and meditation. Buddha preached middle path approach, which is the practice of moderation as opposed to the extremes of self-indulgence and self-mortification. Mauryan Emperor Ashoka (272BC-231BC) converted to Buddhism and tried to bring about a moral and spiritual revival in his kingdom. He is also credited with helping spread Buddhism beyond India; however, by the 4th and 5th century, Buddhism was in decline in India while gaining popularity in Central Asia and China.

Although Buddhism is contemporary religion to Jainism, its life history and social identity is substantially different. Today Buddhism is practically an expatriate religion from India. There are several Buddhist majority nation-states in Asia. In India majority of Buddhists are converts from Hinduism. The staggering increase of Buddhists was due to initiative of
Dr. B. R. Ambedkar through organizing conversion ceremonies. Conversion as an escape from caste oppression was also responsible for growth of ISLAM and Christianity in India

Buddhism accepts the essential teachings of the Upanishads but denounced Vedic sacrifice. Like Jainism, value orientation of Buddhism was also to the cause of common people, asserting common spiritual right of all men, acknowledging compassion and love for all life and preaching in the language of common people. It advocates Ahimsa in any form and not doing harm to any living thing.

C.5: Sikhism

Sikhism is fifth religion in India, borne in Punjab in 16th century. It was founded by Guru Nanak who propagated a transcendent, formless divinity that exists everywhere. Sikhism is a monotheistic religion and stresses carrying out good deeds, living honestly and caring for others, rather than rituals and rites. Sikhism shares the concept of Karma and rebirth with other religions such as Hinduism, Buddhism and Jainism. A Sikh serves God by serving other people every day, a concept known as *Seva*. By devoting their lives to service, they get rid of their own ego and pride.

Guru Nanak taught unity and reform to his followers. He fought against the dominance of Brahmin priests and their legalistic controls. Similarly, he/she also fought against Islamic orthodoxy. Thus, on the one hand Nanak rejected both Hinduism and Islam and on the other hand, he/she tended to fuse them together. With Guru Nanak's this attitude towards Hindus and Muslims led some people to depict him as a reconciler of two religions.

Guru Govind Singh, the 10th and last guru, decreed that after his death, the spiritual guide of the Sikhs would be the teachings contained in 'Guru Granth Sahib'. The spiritual Book has the status of Guru and is venerated as the living presence of the gurus. He also established the Khalsa Panth and entrusted the task of regulating the Sikh conduct to Panch Pyarasas (the five beloved). From then onward, the Khalsa brotherhood, popularly known as Keshdhari (bearded one) came to be identified as the orthodox Sikhs, while the others, the Shahajdharis (shaven one) came to be perceived as deviants.

In the Sikhs perception religion and politics are inextricably intertwined and they believe the Khalsa has right to rule over Sikhs. This feeling is at variance with the secular ethos of Indian constitution. Although started as protest against Hindu caste system, the Sikhs themselves have been entrapped into their own caste system, rendering Sikh social structure less distinct from that of the Hindu Social structure.

C.6: Christianity

Christianity came to Kerala state in India long back, with arrival of St Thomas, an apostle of Jesus Christ. St Thomas converted the local people to the Christian way of life. Then racially distinct European Christians came as colonizers, ruled over India and left. However, Christianity was firmly established in India by 15th century through arrival of missionaries from Portugal, Spain, Italy, Germany and France, who started converting the local people to Christianity. The mass conversion movements to Christianity took place in 19th and 20th century, coincident with the national liberation movement. New converts were pro- British posture with colonial masters.

Christians in India are predominantly rural, economically poor and engaged in low prestige occupations.

"Core" message of Christianity is a message of love and redemption, salvation and hope. A Christian is a follower of Christ. This means believing in Jesus, entrusting whole life to him, and following him in every area of life. "The essence of Christianity is not an idea, not a system of thought, not a plan of action. The essence of Christianity is a Person: Jesus Christ Himself. The Christian message is called the "gospel" of Jesus Christ. "Gospel" literally means "good news."

Appendix-D: Social Process of Cultural Interactions

D.1: There are many ways of propagation of *Cultural Values* through Interaction between Individuals and groups. Cultural values are classified as Traits, Complexes, and Patterns. The Cultural traits consisting of beliefs and practices etc. tend to travel from one society to another, and undergo modifications in another culture. There exist Sub-cultures within a cultural entity which interacts through, Ethnocentrism, Diffusion and process of Acculturation. Assimilation, Integration, Cooperation and Conflict are some of the social processes of cultural interaction through which cultural equilibrium is maintained in the society. These points are explained below.

It is necessary to distinguish between *Society* and *Culture*, although these two terms have many elements in common. Society consists of groups of people who interact within a normative order. Culture refers to the manifold ways in which societies differ from each other, in regard to the personal, social or symbolic behavior of their individuals. For example, family is universal, but the behavior of its members varies according to cultural patterns.

According to E.B.Taylor culture is that complex whole which includes knowledge, belief, art, morals custom and any other capabilities and habits acquired by man as a member of society. Scope of culture includes mental as well as material achievements. Only human beings are capable of a complex culture, which they can inherit and transmit to others. Culture includes several processes such as *diffusion, assimilation*, etc., which arise from interactions among people in an intra-cultural or a trans- cultural situation. Processes, therefore, denote the dynamic interchange of cultural elements between two groups, or between two societies.

D.2: Social processes

Social change implies a direction, which is variously expressed as *'social evolution'*, *'social development'*, *'social progress'*, etc. Cooperation, Competition, Conflict, Accommodation, Assimilation etc. are the constituent elements of social process.

D.2.1: Traits, complexes and patterns

The smallest unit of culture is defined as *cultural traits*. The Cultural traits consisting of beliefs, techniques etc., which tend to travel from one society to another, but undergo modifications in another culture.

Cultural traits seldom exist in isolation. Instead they exist in relation to other traits with which they form what are called *cultural complexes*. When the traits become too large it comes to be called *cultural pattern*.

D.2.2: Universal, Alternatives and Specialty Traits

Cultural traits may be classified into one of these categories. The *universal* refers to those traits that apply to all the members of the society, with no one excluded. *Cultural Alternatives* are traits that offer choices, all of which are socially acceptable e.g. different modes of dress. The term

Cultural Specialty refers to the trait applicable to a section of individuals, for example doctors, lawyers, teachers, etc.

D.2.3: Sub-Culture

When a group isolates itself from a larger society and maintains physical and social distance, it is called a sub-culture. Its members interact with each other on a face-to-face level, and function as a cohesive group. The sub-culture may include deviant groups such as criminal gangs, or occupational groups such as miners, truck drivers, building workers etc. All sub-cultures have private social norms, and are distinct from each other. Often hostile relationship exists between a society and its subculture.

D.2.4: Ethnocentrism

This term denotes the view that one's own culture is better than of others. In human history, *ethnocentrism* has played havoc on civilization. The superior attitude of colonials towards the natives, the Nazi notion of Nordic racial superiority etc. are examples.

Within a given country also, ethnic tensions arise owing to the differences between two groups. In India, the antipathy that exists between different regions is to an extent based on ethnocentric attitudes. However, ethnocentrism as a national trait is not devoid of positive aspects. The many achievements in sports, arts, adventure, technical proficiency, etc., are often inspired by the feeling that the individuals must strive to enhance the glory of their country.

D.2.5: Diffusion

When two people come into contact with one another or live in physical proximity, words, gestures, customs, beliefs, tools, techniques and practices etc., spread from one to other. When people migrate into a new area for settlement, they may carry cultural traits with them and communicate the same to the inhabitants of that area. Such transmission of culture is called *Diffusion*.

D.2.6: Acculturation

While diffusion refers to achieved cultural transmission with time and historical process, *acculturation* refers to the cultural contact process that is in contemporary times. After the Industrial revolution in Europe, the establishment of colonies by Europeans in Asia, South America and Africa set in motion the process of acculturation. Ideas, beliefs, scientific techniques, pattern of administration, judicial procedures of Europe reached the farthest centers of these countries.

The spread of western culture in the colonies, while it brought about several far-reaching changes for the good of the native people, also led to chaos in some societies, wherein the natives were up rooted from their tradition.

D.3: Types of Acculturation

D.3.1: Assimilation: This refers to the process whereby group differences gradually disappear. Assimilation is not necessarily limited to the incorporation of one social group with all its ideals and cultures into another group.

Assimilation is delayed or altogether held up if racial prejudices etc., intervene between two cultures. For example, the white settlers in South Africa have kept distance with native South African. It may be mentioned that at present distinctiveness in culture is sought to be retained. In the many Nation-states of Asia, Africa etc., the different ethnic groups aim at a separate identity for themselves.

D.3.2: Integration

Integration is a process of becoming whole. Integration refers to the social process where the diversities of culture are reconciled to a macro-structure of values, beliefs, etc. Yet, this process does not destroy diversity. Integration is inclusive of both order and change. Even while the parts are in the process of becoming the whole, there is a changeover to a new social pattern.

D.4: Types of social interactions

D.4.1: Cooperation: Cooperation refers to the process whereby individuals or groups work together to attain common goals. It is a universal process. Individuals and groups can cooperate in spite of antagonism. Cooperation is a normative process; whereby human behavior is governed by rules and procedures. Cooperation exists in nature also, among plants and animals.

In informal modes of cooperation, as when few friends come together to achieve something, the norms are implicit rather than explicit. In large, complex societies, cooperative work is often undertaken on voluntary basis. Socialist philosophy is based on cooperative thinking. Today, international cooperation is witnessed in the work done by the UNO, UNESCO, UNICEF, etc.

D.4.2: Competition: Competition is also a universally known form of social interaction. It arises because people compete for scarce resources, positions, etc. Competition can be either personal or impersonal. It is personal when the competitors are face to face and in limited numbers, as in family where siblings compete for mother's affection. It is impersonal when groups or organizations compete with each other. Thus, political parties, service organizations, etc., compete amongst themselves to prove that they are better, more serviceable and superior to the others. In human evaluation, cooperation has played a notable part, but men have thrived on the cooperative element. Competition inspires men to become more efficient, more dynamic in their endeavors.

D.4.3: Conflict

Conflict is an extreme form of behavior. In conflict, there are no rules of the game which found in cooperation or competition; each party seeks to win at any cost.

Appendix-E: *code of ethics* and *code of conducts* from professional bodies like IETE, institution of engineers (India), Indian society for technical education (ISTE) and university grants commission (UGC) from India IETE

E.1: IETE

The Institution of Electronics and Telecommunication Engineers (IETE) is India's leading recognized professional society devoted to the advancement of Science and Technology of Electronics, Telecommunication & IT. Code of Ethics of IETE is furnished below.

****

THE INSTITUTION OF ELECTRONICS AND TELECOMMUNICATION ENGINEERS (IETE)
(http://www.iete.org/Byelaws.pdf)

PROFESSIONAL ETHICS
(Pursuant to Byelaw 6 Form-A)

PREAMBLE

To uphold the concept of Professional conduct amongst its Corporate Members, the Governing Council of the Institution felt the need to evolve a Code of Ethics for Corporate Members.

A Corporate Member should develop spirit-de-corps among the fraternity and uphold the principles of honesty, integrity, justice and courtesy to guide him in the practice of his responsibilities and duties to the public and the profession.

He/She should scrupulously guard his professional and personal reputation and avoid association with persons and organizations of questionable character and uphold the dignity and honor of the Institution.

THE CODE

1. A Corporate Member will, at all times, Endeavour to protect the engineering profession from misrepresentation and misunderstanding.
2. A Corporate Member will interact with others in his profession by free exchange of information and experience. He/She will contribute to the growth of the Institution to maximum effectiveness to the best of his ability.

3. A Corporate Member will not offer his professional services by advertisement or through and commercial advertising media, or solicit engineering work, trading, teaching either directly or through agencies/organizations in any manner derogatory to the dignity of the profession and the Institution.
4. A Corporate Member will not directly or indirectly injure the professional reputation; work or practice of another Corporate Member.
5. A Corporate Member will not divulge confidential findings or actions of the Governing Council or Committees of which he/she is a member, without obtaining official clearance.
6. A Corporate Member will not take credit for an activity, professional work, engineering proposal when engaged in a team and give due recognition to those where due.
7. A Corporate Member will express an opinion only when it is founded on facts and honest conviction before a forum, court, commission or at an inquiry.
8. A Corporate Member will exercise due restraint in criticizing the work or professional conduct of another Corporate Member which would impinge or hurt his character and reputation.
9. A Corporate Member will not try to supplant another Corporate Member in a particular employment, office or contract.
10. A Corporate Member will be upright in all his dealings with person(s), organizations, in business, Contractors, agencies. He/She should not take actions that lead to groupism, political connotation or unethical conduct in the discharge of these official powers.
11. A Corporate Member will not misrepresent his qualifications to gain undue advantage in his profession.
12. A Corporate Member will act with fairness and justice in any office, employment or contract.
13. A Corporate Member will not associate in engineering work which does not conform to ethical practices.
14. A Corporate Members will not compete unfairly with another Corporate Member by means, which in the opinion of others, are based on garnering support for personal gain, enlisting uncalled for sympathy, espousing unjust cases or amounts to use of unconstitutional methods.
15. A Corporate Member will act in professional matters as a faithful agent or trustee.
16. A Corporate Member will not receive remuneration, commission, discount or any indirect profit from any work with which he/she is entrusted, unless specifically so permitted.

Appendix

17. A Corporate Member will not accept financial or other compensation from more than one source for the same service or work connected thereto, unless so authorized.
18. A Corporate Member will immediately inform his organization/Institution of any financial interest in a business, engineering work which may compete with, adversely affect or hamper the growth of the parent body.
19. A Corporate Member will engage or enlist the services of specialists/experts, when in his judgment such services are in the best interest of his employer or to the profession.
20. A Corporate Member will endeavor to develop a team among his colleagues and staff and provide equal opportunity to them for professional development and advancement.
21. A Corporate Member will subscribe to the principle of appropriate norms, appreciation and adequate compensation for those engaged in office, technical and professional employment including those in subordinate positions.
22. A Corporate Member, if he/she considers that another Corporate Member is guilty of unethical, illegal, unfair practice, defalcation will not present such information to the Governing Council of the Institution for necessary action, unless armed with substantial proof.

E.2: Institution of Engineers (India)

The Institution of Engineers (India), is the national organization of engineers in India. It is the world's largest multi-disciplinary engineering professional society in engineering and technology world. Code of Ethics of IEI for corporate members is furnished below.

****

CODE OF ETHICS FOR CORPORATE
MEMBERShttps://www.ieindia.org/readmrCodeofethic.aspx

Effective from March 1, 2004

1.0 Preamble

1.1 The Corporate Members of The Institution of Engineers (India) are committed to promote and practice the profession of engineering for the common good of the community bearing in mind the following concerns:

    1.1.1 Concern for ethical standard;

    1.1.2 Concern for social justice, social order and human rights;

    1.1.3 Concern for protection of the environment;

1.1.4 Concern for sustainable development;
1.1.5 Public safety and tranquility.

2.0 The Tenets of the Code of Ethics

2.1 A Corporate Member shall utilize his knowledge and expertise for the welfare, health and safety of the community without any discrimination for sectional or private interests.

2.2 A Corporate Member shall maintain the honor, integrity and dignity in all his professional actions to be worthy of the trust of the community and the profession.

2.3 A Corporate Member shall act only in the domains of his competence and with diligence, care, sincerity and honesty.

2.4 A Corporate Member shall apply his knowledge and expertise in the interest of his employer or the clients for whom he/she shall work without compromising with other obligations to these Tenets.

2.5 A Corporate Member shall not falsify or misrepresent his own or his associates' qualifications, experience, etc.

2.6 A Corporate Member, wherever necessary and relevant, shall take all reasonable steps to inform himself, his employer or clients, of the environmental, economic, social and other possible consequences, which may arise out of his actions.

2.7 A Corporate Member shall maintain utmost honesty and fairness in making statements or giving witness and shall do so on the basis of adequate knowledge.

2.8 A Corporate Member shall not directly or indirectly injure the professional reputation of another member.

2.9 A Corporate Member shall reject any kind of offer that may involve unfair practice or may cause avoidable damage to the ecosystem.

2.10 A Corporate Member shall be concerned about and shall act in the best of his abilities for maintenance of sustainability of the process of development.

2.11 A Corporate Member shall not act in any manner which may injure the reputation of the Institution or which may cause any damage to the Institution financially or otherwise.

3.0 General Guidance

The Tenets of the Code of Ethics are based on the recognition that –

3.1 A common tie exists among the humanity and that The Institution of Engineers (India) derives its value from the people, so that the actions of its Corporate Members should indicate the member's highest regard for equality of opportunity, social justice and fairness;

3.2 The Corporate Members of the Institution hold a privileged position in the community so as to make it a necessity for their not using the position for personal and sectional interests.

4.0 And, as such, a Corporate Member –

Appendix

4.1 Should keep his employer or client fully informed on all matters in respect of his assignment which are likely to lead to a conflict of interest or when, in his judgement, a project will not be viable on the basis of commercial, technical, environmental or any other risks;
4.2 Should maintain confidentiality of any information with utmost sincerity unless expressly permitted to disclose such information or unless such permission, if withheld, may adversely affect the welfare, health and safety of the community;
4.3 Should neither solicit nor accept financial or other considerations from anyone related to a project or assignment of which he/she is in the charge;
4.4 Should neither pay nor offer direct or indirect inducements to secure work;
4.5 Should compete on the basis of merit alone;
4.6 Should refrain from inducing a client to breach a contract entered into with another duly appointed engineer;
4.7 Should, if asked by the employer or a client, to review the work of another person or organization, discuss the review with the other person or organization to arrive at a balanced opinion;
4.8 Should make statements or give evidence before a tribunal or a court of law in an objective and accurate manner and express any opinion on the basis of adequate knowledge and competence; and
4.9 Should reveal the existence of any interest – pecuniary or otherwise – which may affect the judgment while giving an evidence or making a statement.
5.0 Any decision of the Council as per provisions of the relevant Bye-Laws of the Institution shall be final and binding on all Corporate Members.

E.3: Indian society for technical Education (ISTE)

The Indian Society for Technical Education is a national, professional, non-profit Society registered under the Indian Societies Registration Act of 1860 and works to enlarge its activities to advance the cause of Technology education. Code of Conduct for ISTE members is furnished below.

****

Code of Conduct for ISTE members
(http://www.isteonline.in/topics.aspx?mid=12)

The following Code of Professional Conduct and Ethics shall be applicable to office bearers and members of all categories of the Society:

- Members should at all times preserve the dignity and interest of the profession and of the Society by maintaining a high standard of professional and personal conduct;
- They should work in the best interest of the Society;
- They should neither engage in personal advertisement, nor canvas for an appointment, nor take any action which is detrimental to sister Institutions;
- They should at all times endeavor to establish and maintain the best possible conditions of service for their colleagues and other staff;
- When a Member represents the Society, he/she should as far as possible state the policy of the Society. If he/she has any disagreement with a policy of the Society, he/she may so inform the Society. The Executive Council will then decide the further course of action (including the question of the Society's representation) that is to be taken.
- Where, having regard to this Code of Conduct a Member wishes to make a complaint against another Member of the Society, he/she should do so in writing to the Executive Council. If the Executive Council is of the opinion that prima-facie case of infringement of the Code of Conduct has been established it will appoint a Committee for investigation. On the basis of the report of the Committee, the Executive Council will take a final decision on the matter.

For Engineering Teachers Dealing with Students

- Deal justly and impartially with students regardless of their social, economic, regional and religious background.
- Recognize the differences among students and seek to meet their individual needs.
- Encourage students to work for higher individual goals. Aid students to develop an understanding and appreciation not only of opportunities and benefits but also responsibilities.
- Inculcate in students respect for teachers, love towards fellow students and loyalty to institution and the country.
- Acquaint students with civic responsibilities and environmental protection.
- Never use students to solve his/her personal problems.
- Accept no remuneration for tutoring except in accordance with approved policies of Government / Institutions.

Appendix

Dealing with Society

- Adhere to any reasonable pattern of behavior accepted by the Society for professional persons.
- Respect the community in which employed and be loyal to the institute system and the counter.
- Render possible assistance to the development of the Society and use your knowledge and skill for enhancement of human welfare.

Dealing with Employer

- Strive to fulfill one's obligation to the Institute for maintaining a high level of professional service.
- Maintain the dignity and interest of the profession by maintaining high standard of professional and personal conduct.
- Co-operate in the development and implementation of institutional policies and programs.
- Conduct professional business through proper channel.
- Refrain from discussing confidential and official information with unauthorized persons.
- Accept no compensation from equipment suppliers and other agencies. Never engage in any gainful employment outside the institution where the employment effects adversely the professional status or standing with students, associates and society.

General Behavior

- Seek to make professional growth continuous by such procedures as study, research, and attending conferences, professional meetings and continuing education programs.
- Make the teaching profession so attractive in ideals and practices that sincere and able young men / women want to enter it.
- Be punctual and regular in teaching work, correspondence with others and keeping appointments with other persons.
- Encourage one's fellow teachers to adhere to proper ethical behavior.
- Speak constructively of other teachers but report honestly to responsible persons in matters involving the welfare of students, institution system and the profession.
- Maintain active membership in professional organization and through participation, strive to attain the objectives that justify such organizations.

- Never engage in personal advertisement of canvass for an appointment.
- Never seek self-enhancement through expressing evaluations or comparisons damaging to other professional workers.

E.4: University Grants Commission (UGC)

The University Grants Commission (UGC) of India is a statutory body set up by the Indian Union government under Ministry of Human Resource Development, and is charged with coordination, determination and maintenance of standards of higher education.

****

UGC Regulations

AND MEASURES FOR THE MAINTENANCE OF STANDARDS INHIGHER EDUCATION

No.F. 3-1/2009　　　　　　　　　　　　　　　　　30th June 2010
17.0: Code of Professional Ethics:

I Teachers and their Responsibilities:

Whoever adopts teaching as a profession assumes the obligation to conduct himself/ herself in accordance with the ideal of the profession. A teacher is constantly under the scrutiny of his students and the society at large. Therefore, every teacher should see that there is no incompatibility between his precepts and practice. The national ideals of education which have already set forth and which he/she should seek to inculcate among students must be his/her own ideals. The profession further requires that that the teachers should be calm, patient and communicative by the temperament and amiable in disposition.

Teachers Should

I. Adhere to a responsible pattern of conduct and demeanor expected of them from the community;
II. Manage their private affairs in a manner consistent with the dignity of the profession;
III. Seek to make professional growth continuous through study and research;
IV. Express free and frank opinion by participation at professional meetings, seminars, conferences etc. towards the contribution of knowledge;

V. Maintain active membership of professional organizations and strive to improve

Education and profession through them

VI. Perform their duties in the form of teaching, tutorial, practical, seminar and research work conscientiously and with dedication.
VII. Cooperate and assist in carrying out functions relating to the educational responsibilities of the college and the universities such as: assisting in appraising the Applications for admission, advising and counseling students as well as assisting the Conduct of university and college examinations, including supervision, invigilation and evaluation; and
VIII. Participate in extension, co-curricular and extra-curricular activities including community service.

II Teachers and the Students

Teachers should

i) Respect the dignity of Student in expressing his or her opinion;
ii) Deal justly and impartially with students regardless of their religion, caste, political, economic, social and physical characteristics;
iii) Recognize the difference in aptitude and capabilities among students and strive to meet their individual needs;
iv) Encourage students to improve their attainments, develop their personalities and at the same time contribute to community welfare;
v) Inculcate among students a scientific outlook and respect for physical labor and ideals of democracy, patriotism and peace;
vi) Be affectionate to the students and not behave in a vindictive manner towards any of them for any reason;
vii) Pay attention to only the attainment of the student in the assessment of merit;
viii) Make themselves available to the students even beyond class hours and help and guide students without any remuneration or reward;
ix) Aid students to develop an understanding of our national heritage and national goals; and
x) Refrain from inciting students against other students, colleagues or administration.

III Teachers and Colleagues

Teacher should

i) Treat other members of the profession in the same manner as they themselves wish to be treated;
ii) Speak respectfully of other teachers and render assistance for professional betterment.
iii) Refrain from lodging unsubstantiated allegations against colleagues to higher authorities; and
iv) Refrain from allowing considerations of caste, creed, religion, race or sex in their professional endeavor.

IV Teachers and Authorities

Teacher should

i) Discharge his professional responsibilities according to the existing rules and adhere to procedures and methods consistent with their profession in initiating steps through their own institutional bodies and/or professional organizations for change of any such rule detrimental to the professional interest;
ii) Refrain from taking any other employment and commitment including private tuitions and coaching classes which are likely to interfere with their professional responsibilities;
iii) Cooperate in the formulation of policies of the institution by accepting various offices and discharge responsibilities which such offices may demand;
iv) Co-operate through their organizations in the formulation of policies of the other institutions and accept offices;
v) Cooperate with the authorities for the betterment of the institution keeping in view the interest and in conformity with dignity of the profession;
vi) Should adhere to the conditions of the contract;
vii) Give and expect due notice before a change of position is made; and
viii) Refrain from availing themselves of leave except on unavoidable grounds and as far as practicable with prior intimation, keeping in view their particular responsibility for completion of academic schedule;

Appendix

V. Teachers and Non-Teaching Staff

i) Teachers should treat the non-teaching staff as colleagues and equal partners in a cooperative undertaking, within every educational institution; and
ii) Teachers should help in the function of joint staff-council covering both teachers and the non-teaching staff.

VI. Teachers and Guardians

Teachers should

i) Try to see through teacher's bodies and organizations, that institution maintain contact with the guardians, their students, send reports of their performance to the guardians whenever necessary and meet the guardians in meetings convened for the purpose for mutual exchange of ideas and for the benefit of the institution.

VII. Teachers and Society

Teachers Should

i) Recognize that education is a public service and strive to keep the public informed of the educational programmers which are being provided;
ii) Work to improve the education in the community and strengthen the Community's moral and intellectual life;
iii) Be aware of social problems and take part in such activities as would be conducive to the progress of the society and hence the country as a whole;
iv) Perform duties of citizenship, participate in community activities and shoulder responsibilities of public offices;
v) Refrain from taking part in or subscribing to or assisting in any way activities which tend to promote feeling of hatred or enmity among different communities, religions or linguistic groups but actively work for national integration.

Appendix-F: IEEE Code of Ethics

The IEEE is the world's largest professional association advancing innovation and technological excellence for the benefit of humanity. IEEE is the trusted "voice" for engineering, computing and technology information around the globe. IEEE Code of Ethics and Code of Conduct are furnished below.

****

IEEE Code of Ethics
(http://www.ieee.org/about/corporate/governance/p7-8.html)

The following is from the IEEE Policies, Section 7 - Professional Activities (Part A - IEEE Policies).
1.8 IEEE Code of Ethics

We, the members of the IEEE, in recognition of the importance of our technologies in affecting the quality of life throughout the world, and in accepting a personal obligation to our profession, its members and the communities we serve, do hereby commit ourselves to the highest ethical and professional conduct and agree:

1. To accept responsibility in making decisions consistent with the safety, health, and welfare of the public, and to disclose promptly factors that might endanger the public or the environment;
2. To avoid real or perceived conflicts of interest whenever possible, and to disclose them to affected parties when they do exist;
3. To be honest and realistic in stating claims or estimates based on available data;
4. To reject bribery in all its forms;
5. To improve the understanding of technology; it's appropriate application, and potential consequences;
6. To maintain and improve our technical competence and to undertake technological tasks for others only if qualified by training or experience, or after full disclosure of pertinent limitations;
7. To seek, accept, and offer honest criticism of technical work, to acknowledge and correct errors, and to credit properly the contributions of others;
8. To treat fairly all persons and to not engage in acts of discrimination based on race, religion, gender, disability, age, national origin, sexual orientation, gender identity, or gender expression;

Appendix 453

9. To avoid injuring others, their property, reputation, or employment by false or malicious action;
10. To assist colleagues and co-workers in their professional development and to support them in following this code of ethics.

Changes to the IEEE Code of Ethics will be made only after the following conditions are met:

- Proposed changes shall have been published in THE INSTITUTE at least three (3) months in advance of final consideration by the Board of Directors, with a request for comment, and
- All IEEE Major Boards shall have the opportunity to discuss proposed changes prior to final action by the Board of Directors, and
- An affirmative vote of two-thirds of the votes of the members of the Board of Directors present at the time of the vote, provided a quorum is present, shall be required for changes to be made

IEEE CODE OF CONDUCT
(http://www.ieee.org/about/ieee_code_of_conduct.pdf)

We, the members and employees of IEEE, recognize the importance of our technologies in affecting the quality of life throughout the world and we accept a personal obligation to our professions, the members of IEEE, and other individuals involved in IEEE activities in our fields of interest. By this obligation we commit ourselves to the highest standards of integrity, responsible behavior, and ethical and professional conduct. We agree to be bound by the following rules:

1. **Be respectful of others**
   - We will be respectful of others, including IEEE members and IEEE employees, and will act in a professional manner while participating in IEEE activities.
   - We will be respectful of the privacy of others and the protection of their personal information and data.
2. **Treat people fairly**
   - We will not engage in harassment of any kind, including sexual harassment, or bullying behavior whether in person, via cyber technology or otherwise.
   - We will not discriminate against any person because of characteristics protected by law (e.g., age, ancestry, color, disability or handicap, national origin, race, religion, gender, sexual or affectional orientation, gender identity, gender expression, appearance, matriculation, political affiliation, marital status, veteran status).

3. **Avoid injuring others, their property, reputation or employment**
    - We will avoid injuring others, their property, data, reputation, or employment by false or malicious action.
    - We will not engage in or participate in the spreading of any malicious rumors, defamation or any other verbal or physical abuses, against an IEEE member, employee or other person, whether on the Internet or otherwise.
4. **Refrain from retaliation**
    - We will not retaliate against any IEEE member, employee or other person who reports an act of misconduct, or who reports any violation of the IEEE Code of Ethics or this Code of Conduct.
    - We will not retaliate against any person who makes IEEE aware of the violation of any laws, rules or regulations in connection with IEEE activities.
5. **Comply with applicable laws in all countries where IEEE does business and with the IEEE policies and procedures**
    - We will comply with all applicable laws, rules and regulations governing IEEE's business conduct worldwide and all relevant procedures established by IEEE whenever and wherever we are acting on behalf of IEEE, or participating in IEEE activities, including but not limited to the following:
        a. Rejecting bribery in all forms.
        b. Avoiding real or perceived conflicts of interest whenever possible, and disclosing them to affected parties when they do exist.
        c. Protecting confidential information belonging to IEEE and personal information belonging to IEEE members, employees and other persons.
        d. Not agreeing with competing persons to fix prices or reduce price competition through allocation of customers or markets, manipulate bids in any competitive bidding process, or engage in other acts that result in restraining trade.
        e. Not misusing or infringing the intellectual property of others.

Appendix-G: NSPE Code of Ethics for Engineers

(http://www.nspe.org/resources/ethics/code-ethics)

Preamble

Engineering is an important and learned profession. As members of this profession, engineers are expected to exhibit the highest standards of honesty and integrity. Engineering has a direct and vital impact on the quality of life for all people. Accordingly, the services provided by engineers require honesty, impartiality, fairness, and equity, and must be dedicated to the protection of the public health, safety, and welfare. Engineers must perform under a standard of professional behavior that requires adherence to the highest principles of ethical conduct.

I. Fundamental Canons

Engineers, in the fulfillment of their professional duties, shall:
1. Hold paramount the safety, health, and welfare of the public.
2. Perform services only in areas of their competence.
3. Issue public statements only in an objective and truthful manner.
4. Act for each employer or client as faithful agents or trustees.
5. Avoid deceptive acts.
6. Conduct themselves honorably, responsibly, ethically, and lawfully so as to enhance the honor, reputation, and usefulness of the profession.

II. Rules of Practice

1. Engineers shall hold paramount the safety, health, and welfare of the public.
    a. If engineers' judgment is overruled under circumstances that endanger life or property, they shall notify their employer or client and such other authority as may be appropriate.
    b. Engineers shall approve only those engineering documents that are in conformity with applicable standards.
    c. Engineers shall not reveal facts, data, or information without the prior consent of the client or employer except as authorized or required by law or this Code.
    d. Engineers shall not permit the use of their name or associate in business ventures with any person or firm that they believe is engaged in fraudulent or dishonest enterprise.
    e. Engineers shall not aid or abet the unlawful practice of engineering by a person or firm.
    f. Engineers having knowledge of any alleged violation of this Code shall report thereon to appropriate professional bodies and, when relevant, also to public authorities, and

cooperate with the proper authorities in furnishing such information or assistance as may be required.
2. Engineers shall perform services only in the areas of their competence.

Engineers shall undertake assignments only when qualified by education or experience in the specific technical fields involved.

    a. Engineers shall not affix their signatures to any plans or documents dealing with subject matter in which they lack competence, nor to any plan or document not prepared under their direction and control.

    b. Engineers may accept assignments and assume responsibility for coordination of an entire project and sign and seal the engineering documents for the entire project, provided that each technical segment is signed and sealed only by the qualified engineers who prepared the segment.

3. Engineers shall issue public statements only in an objective and truthful manner.

Engineers shall be objective and truthful in professional reports, statements, or testimony. They shall include all relevant and pertinent information in such reports, statements, or testimony, which should bear the date indicating when it was current.

    a. Engineers may express publicly technical opinions that are founded upon knowledge of the facts and competence in the subject matter.

    b. Engineers shall issue no statements, criticisms, or arguments on technical matters that are inspired or paid for by interested parties, unless they have prefaced their comments by explicitly identifying the interested parties on whose behalf they are speaking, and by revealing the existence of any interest the engineers may have in the matters.

4. Engineers shall act for each employer or client as faithful agents or trustees.

Engineers shall disclose all known or potential conflicts of interest that could influence or appear to influence their judgment or the quality of their services.

    a. Engineers shall not accept compensation, financial or otherwise, from more than one party for services on the same project, or for services pertaining to the same project, unless the circumstances are fully disclosed and agreed to by all interested parties.

    b. Engineers shall not solicit or accept financial or other valuable consideration, directly or indirectly, from outside agents in connection with the work for which they are responsible.

    c. Engineers in public service as members, advisors, or employees of a governmental or quasi-governmental body or department shall not participate in decisions with respect to services solicited or provided by them or their organizations in private or public engineering practice.

    d. Engineers shall not solicit or accept a contract from a governmental body on which a principal or officer of their organization serves as a member.

5. Engineers shall avoid deceptive acts.

Engineers shall not falsify their qualifications or permit misrepresentation of their or their associates' qualifications. They shall not misrepresent or exaggerate their responsibility in or for the subject matter of prior assignments. Brochures or other presentations incident to the solicitation of employment shall not misrepresent pertinent facts concerning employers, employees, associates, joint ventures, or past accomplishments.

    a. Engineers shall not offer, give, solicit, or receive, either directly or indirectly, any contribution to influence the award of a contract by public authority, or which may be reasonably construed by the public as having the effect or intent of influencing the awarding of a contract. They shall not offer any gift or other valuable consideration in order to secure work. They shall not pay a commission, percentage, or brokerage fee in order to secure work, except to a bona fide employee or bona fide established commercial or marketing agencies retained by them.

III. Professional Obligations

1. Engineers shall be guided in all their relations by the highest standards of honesty and integrity.
    a. Engineers shall acknowledge their errors and shall not distort or alter the facts.
    b. Engineers shall advise their clients or employers when they believe a project will not be successful.
    c. Engineers shall not accept outside employment to the detriment of their regular work or interest. Before accepting any outside engineering employment, they will notify their employers.
    d. Engineers shall not attempt to attract an engineer from another employer by false or misleading pretenses.
    e. Engineers shall not promote their own interest at the expense of the dignity and integrity of the profession.

2. Engineers shall at all times strive to serve the public interest.

Engineers are encouraged to participate in civic affairs; career guidance for youths; and work for the advancement of the safety, health, and well-being of their community.

   a. Engineers shall not complete, sign, or seal plans and/or specifications that are not in conformity with applicable engineering standards. If the client or employer insists on such unprofessional conduct, they shall notify the proper authorities and withdraw from further service on the project.
   b. Engineers are encouraged to extend public knowledge and appreciation of engineering and its achievements.
   c. Engineers are encouraged to adhere to the principles of sustainable development1 in order to protect the environment for future generations.

3. Engineers shall avoid all conduct or practice that deceives the public.

Engineers shall avoid the use of statements containing a material misrepresentation of fact or omitting a material fact.

   a. Consistent with the foregoing, engineers may advertise for recruitment of personnel.
   b. Consistent with the foregoing, engineers may prepare articles for the lay or technical press, but such articles shall not imply credit to the author for work performed by others.

4. Engineers shall not disclose, without consent, confidential information concerning the business affairs or technical processes of any present or former client or employer, or public body on which they serve.

Engineers shall not, without the consent of all interested parties, promote or arrange for new employment or practice in connection with a specific project for which the engineer has gained particular and specialized knowledge.

   a. Engineers shall not, without the consent of all interested parties, participate in or represent an adversary interest in connection with a specific project or proceeding in which the engineer has gained particular specialized knowledge on behalf of a former client or employer.

5. Engineers shall not be influenced in their professional duties by conflicting interests.

Appendix 459

Engineers shall not accept financial or other considerations, including free engineering designs, from material or equipment suppliers for specifying their product.

   a. Engineers shall not accept commissions or allowances, directly or indirectly, from contractors or other parties dealing with clients or employers of the engineer in connection with work for which the engineer is responsible.

6. Engineers shall not attempt to obtain employment or advancement or professional engagements by untruthfully criticizing other engineers, or by other improper or questionable methods.

Engineers shall not request, propose, or accept a commission on a contingent basis under circumstances in which their judgment may be compromised.

   a. Engineers in salaried positions shall accept part-time engineering work only to the extent consistent with policies of the employer and in accordance with ethical considerations.
   b. Engineers shall not, without consent, use equipment, supplies, laboratory, or office facilities of an employer to carry on outside private practice.

7. Engineers shall not attempt to injure, maliciously or falsely, directly or indirectly, the professional reputation, prospects, practice, or employment of other engineers. Engineers who believe others are guilty of unethical or illegal practice shall present such information to the proper authority for action.

Engineers in private practice shall not review the work of another engineer for the same client, except with the knowledge of such engineer, or unless the connection of such engineer with the work has been terminated.

   a. Engineers in governmental, industrial, or educational employ are entitled to review and evaluate the work of other engineers when so required by their employment duties.
   b. Engineers in sales or industrial employ are entitled to make engineering comparisons of represented products with products of other suppliers.

8. Engineers shall accept personal responsibility for their professional activities, provided, however, engineers may seek indemnification for services arising out of their practice for other than gross negligence, where the engineer's interests cannot otherwise be protected.

Engineers shall conform with state registration laws in the practice of engineering.

    a. Engineers shall not use association with a non-engineer, a corporation, or partnership as a "cloak" for unethical acts.

9. Engineers shall give credit for engineering work to those to whom credit is due, and will recognize the proprietary interests of others.

Engineers shall, whenever possible, name the person or persons who may be individually responsible for designs, Inventions, writings, or other accomplishments.

    a. Engineers using designs supplied by a client recognize that the designs remain the property of the client and may not be duplicated by the engineer for others without express permission.

    b. Engineers, before undertaking work for others in connection with which the engineer may make improvements, plans, designs, Inventions, or other records that may justify Copyrights or Patents, should enter into a positive agreement regarding ownership.

    c. Engineers' designs, data, records, and notes referring exclusively to an employer's work are the employer's property. The employer should indemnify the engineer for use of the information for any purpose other than the original purpose.

    d. Engineers shall continue their professional development throughout their careers and should keep current in their specialty fields by engaging in professional practice, participating in continuing education courses, reading in the technical literature, and attending professional meetings and seminars.

Footnote 1 "Sustainable development" is the challenge of meeting human needs for natural resources, industrial products, energy, food, transportation, shelter, and effective waste management while conserving and protecting environmental quality and the natural resource base essential for future development.

Appendix-H: ACM Code of Ethics
(Source-http://www.acm.org/about/code-of-ethics)

Summary

Preamble

Commitment to ethical professional conduct is expected of every member (voting members, associate members, and student members) of the Association for Computing Machinery (ACM).

This Code, consisting of 24 imperatives formulated as statements of personal responsibility, identifies the elements of such a commitment. It contains many, but not all, issues professionals are likely to face. Section 1 outlines fundamental ethical considerations. Statements in Section 3 pertain more specifically to individuals who have a leadership role, whether in the workplace or in a volunteer capacity such as with organizations like ACM. Principles involving compliance with this Code are given in Section 4. The Code shall be supplemented by a set of Guidelines, which provide explanation to assist members in dealing with the various issues contained in the Code. It is expected that the Guidelines will be changed more frequently than the Code.

The Code and its supplemented Guidelines are intended to serve as a basis for ethical decision making in the conduct of professional work. Secondarily, they may serve as a basis for judging the merit of a formal complaint pertaining to violation of professional ethical standards.

Contents & Guidelines
1. General Moral Imperatives.
2. More Specific Professional Responsibilities.
3. Organizational Leadership Imperatives.
4. Compliance with the Code.
5. Acknowledgments.

1. General Moral Imperatives

As an ACM member I will....

1.1 Contribute to society and human well-being.

This principle concerning the quality of life of all people affirms an obligation to protect fundamental human rights and to respect the diversity of all cultures.----- When designing or implementing systems, computing professionals must attempt to ensure that the products of their efforts will be used in socially responsible ways, will meet social needs, and will avoid harmful effects to health and welfare.-----In addition to a safe social environment, human well-being includes a safe natural environment.----

1.2 Avoid harm to others.

"Harm" means injury or negative consequences, such as undesirable loss of information, loss of property, property damage, or unwanted environmental impacts. This principle prohibits use of computing technology in ways that result in harm to the general public, employees, employers. Harmful actions include intentional destruction or modification of files and programs leading to serious loss of resources or unnecessary expenditure of human resources such as the time and effort required to purge systems of "computer viruses. --------One way to avoid unintentional harm is to carefully consider potential impacts on all those affected by decisions made during design and implementation.

In the work environment the computing professional has the additional obligation to report any signs of system dangers that might result in serious personal or social damage. ------

1.3 Be honest and trustworthy.

Honesty is an essential component of trust. Without trust an organization cannot function effectively. The honest computing professional will not make deliberately false or deceptive claims about a system or system design, but will instead provide full disclosure of all pertinent system limitations and problems.

A computer professional has a duty to be honest about his or her own qualifications, and about any circumstances that might lead to conflicts of interest.

1.4 Be fair and take action not to discriminate.

The values of equality, tolerance, respect for others, and the principles of equal justice govern this imperative. Discrimination on the basis of race, sex, religion, age, disability, national origin, or other such factors is an explicit violation of ACM policy and will not be tolerated.

1.5 Honor property rights including Copyrights and Patent.

Violation of Copyrights, Patents, Trade Secrets and the terms of license agreements is prohibited by law in most circumstances. Even when software is not so protected, such violations are contrary to professional behavior. -----

1.6 Give proper credit for intellectual property.

Computing professionals are obligated to protect the integrity of intellectual property. Specifically, one must not take credit for other's ideas or work, even in cases where the work has not been explicitly protected by Copyright, Patent, etc.

1.7 Respect the privacy of others.

Computing and communication technology enable the collection and exchange of personal information on a scale unprecedented in the history of civilization. Thus, there is increased potential for violating the privacy of individuals and groups. It is the responsibility of professionals to maintain the privacy and integrity of data describing individuals.

User data observed during the normal duties of system operation and maintenance must be treated with strictest confidentiality, except in cases where it is evidence for the violation of law, organizational regulations, or

Appendix

this Code. In these cases, the nature or contents of that information must be disclosed only to proper authorities.

1.8 Honor confidentiality.

The principle of honesty extends to issues of confidentiality of information whenever one has made an explicit promise to honor confidentiality or, implicitly, when private information not directly related to the performance of one's duties becomes available. The ethical concern is to respect all obligations of confidentiality to employers, clients, and users unless discharged from such obligations by requirements of the law or other principles of this Code.

2. More Specific Professional Responsibilities

As an ACM computing professional, I will ....

2.1 Strive to achieve the highest quality, effectiveness and dignity in both the process and products of professional work.

Excellence is perhaps the most important obligation of a professional. The computing professional must strive to achieve quality and to be cognizant of the serious negative consequences that may result from poor quality in a system.

2.2 Acquire and maintain professional competence.

Excellence depends on individuals who take responsibility for acquiring and maintaining professional competence--------.

2.3 Know and respect existing laws pertaining to professional work.

ACM members must obey existing local, state, province, national, and international laws unless there is a compelling ethical basis not to do so. Policies and procedures of the organizations in which one participates must also be obeyed.

2.4 Accept and provide appropriate professional review.

Quality professional work, especially in the computing profession, depends on professional reviewing and critiquing.

2.5 Give comprehensive and thorough evaluations of computer systems and their impacts, including analysis of possible risks.

2.6 Honor contracts, agreements, and assigned responsibilities.

Honoring one's commitments is a matter of integrity and honesty. For the computer professional this includes ensuring that system elements perform as intended. Also, when one contracts for work with another party, one has an obligation to keep that party properly informed about progress toward completing that work. -------

The computing professional's ethical judgment should be the final guide in deciding whether or not to proceed. Regardless of the decision, one must accept the responsibility for the consequences.

2.7 Improve public understanding of computing and its consequences.

Computing professionals have a responsibility to share technical knowledge with the public by encouraging understanding of computing, including the impacts of computer systems and their limitations. This imperative implies an obligation to counter any false views related to computing.

2.8 Access computing and communication resources only when authorized to do so.

Theft or destruction of tangible and electronic property is prohibited by imperative 1.2 - "Avoid harm to others." Trespassing and unauthorized use of a computer or communication system is addressed by this imperative. Trespassing includes accessing communication networks and computer systems, or accounts and/or files associated with those systems, without explicit authorization to do so. Individuals and organizations have the right to restrict access to their systems so long as they do not violate the discrimination principle (see 1.4). No one should enter or use another's computer system, software, or data files without permission. One must always have appropriate approval before using system resources, including communication ports, file space, other system peripherals, and computer time.

3. Organizational Leadership Imperatives

As an ACM member and an organizational leader, I will ....

BACKGROUND NOTE: This section draws extensively from the draft IFIP Code of Ethics, especially its sections on organizational ethics and international concerns. The ethical obligations of organizations tend to be neglected in most codes of professional conduct, perhaps because these codes are written from the perspective of the individual member. This dilemma is addressed by stating these imperatives from the perspective of the organizational leader. In this context "leader" is viewed as any organizational member who has leadership or educational responsibilities. These imperatives generally may apply to organizations as well as their leaders. In this context" organizations" are corporations, government agencies, and other "employers," as well as volunteer professional organizations.

3.1 Articulate social responsibilities of members of an organizational unit and encourage full acceptance of those responsibilities.

Because organizations of all kinds have impacts on the public, they must accept responsibilities to society. Organizational procedures and attitudes oriented toward quality and the welfare of society------

3.2 Manage personnel and resources to design and build information systems that enhance the quality of working life.

Organizational leaders are responsible for ensuring that computer systems enhance, not degrade, the quality of working life. -------Appropriate human-computer ergonomic standards should be considered in system design and in the workplace.

3.3 Acknowledge and support proper and authorized uses of an organization's computing and communication resources.

Appendix

Because computer systems can become tools to harm as well as to benefit an organization, the leadership has the responsibility to clearly define appropriate and inappropriate uses of organizational computing resources.

3.4 Ensure that users and those who will be affected by a system have their needs clearly articulated during the assessment and design of requirements; later the system must be validated to meet requirements.

3.5 Articulate and support policies that protect the dignity of users and others affected by a computing system.

Designing or implementing systems that deliberately or inadvertently demean individuals or groups is ethically unacceptable.

3.6 Create opportunities for members of the organization to learn the principles and limitations of computer systems.

This complements the imperative on public understanding (2.7). Educational opportunities are essential to facilitate optimal participation of all organizational members. In particular, professionals must be made aware of the dangers of building systems around oversimplified models, the improbability of anticipating and designing for every possible operating condition, and other issues related to the complexity of this profession.

4. Compliance with the Code

As an ACM member I will ....

4.1 Uphold and promote the principles of this Code.

The future of the computing profession depends on both technical and ethical excellence. Each member should encourage and support adherence by other members.

4.2 Treat violations of this code as inconsistent with membership in the ACM.

Adherence of professionals to a code of ethics is largely a voluntary matter. However, if a member does not follow this code by engaging in gross misconduct, membership in ACM may be terminated. This Code and the supplemental Guidelines were developed by the Task Force for the Revision of the ACM Code of Ethics and Professional Conduct. This Code and the supplemental Guidelines were adopted by the ACM Council on October 16, 1992.

ACM Code on Software Engineering (Copyright Doc)
(Source http://www.acm.org/about/se-code)
Summary

Software Engineering Code of Ethics and Professional Practice (Version 5.2) as recommended by the ACM/IEEE-CS Joint Task Force on Software Engineering Ethics and Professional Practices and jointly approved by the ACM and the IEEE-CS as the standard for teaching and practicing software engineering. Software Engineering Code of Ethics and Professional Practice (Short Version)

PREAMBLE

The short version of the code summarizes aspirations at a high level of the abstraction; the clauses that are included in the full version give examples and details of how these aspirations change the way we act as software engineering professionals. Without the aspirations, the details can become legalistic and tedious; without the details, the aspirations can become high sounding but empty; together, the aspirations and the details form a cohesive code.

Software engineers shall commit themselves to making the analysis, specification, design, development, testing and maintenance of software a beneficial and respected profession. In accordance with their commitment to the health, safety and welfare of the public, software engineers shall adhere to the following Eight Principles:

1. **PUBLIC** - Software engineers shall act consistently with the public interest.
2. **CLIENT AND EMPLOYER** - Software engineers shall act in a manner that is in the best interests of their client and employer consistent with the public interest.
3. **PRODUCT** - Software engineers shall ensure that their products and related modifications meet the highest professional standards possible.
4. **JUDGMENT** - Software engineers shall maintain integrity and independence in their professional judgment.
5. **MANAGEMENT** - Software engineering managers and leaders shall subscribe to and promote an ethical approach to the management of software development and maintenance.
6. **PROFESSION** - Software engineers shall advance the integrity and reputation of the profession consistent with the public interest.
7. **COLLEAGUES** - Software engineers shall be fair to and supportive of their colleagues.
8. **SELF** - Software engineers shall participate in lifelong learning regarding the practice of their profession and shall promote an ethical approach to the practice of the profession.

Index

A

Accelerated Life Testing (ALT Testing), 282
Accountability, 227
Accreditation Board for Engineering and Technology (ABET), 11
Agency-Loyalty, 314
Agrarian Society, 25
Agreeableness, 217
Alien Religion, 176
Alienation, 394
Alumni Whistleblowing, 356
Ambition, 166
American Society of Mechanical Engineers (ASME), 63
Antisthenes, 93
Aparigraha, 92
Aristippus, 93
Ashrma, 90
Authoritarian, 23
Authority, 131
Autonomy, 132

B

Belief System, 179
Belmont Report, 376
Bid Rigging, 346
Brahamacaryam, 92
Bribe, 340
Buddhism, 90
Business, 167
Business Environment, 180

C

Cardinal Values, 174
Caring, 57
Cartel, 346
Cartelization, 346
Casuist Ethical Theory, 99
Christian Morality, 93
Christianity, 93
Civil Aviation Administration (CAA), 234
Civil Aviation Organization (CAO), 234
Classifications of Risks, 252
Code of Conduct, 1, 62, 235
Code of Conducts, 230, 441
Code of Ethics, 1
Code of Practice, 231, 235
Codes of Ethics, 230
Cognitive, 78
Collective Approach, 79
Collective Bargaining, 344
Colonial Importation, 176
Columbia Spacecraft, 271
Commitment, 19, 56, 67
Common Morality, 40
Community, 26
Compassion, 383
Component Derating, 280
Computer Crime, 400
Concept of Professional Ethics, 121
Concept of Risk, 248
Confidentiality, 326
Conflict, 22
Conscientiousness, 217
Consequences, 180
Contemporary Engineering Practice, 229
Contemporary Morality, 94
Context-Oriented Reasoning, 110
Contractual Rights, 322
Conventional Level, 106, 109
Cooperation, 66
Core Values, 10
Corporate Ethics Codes, 132
Corporate Whistleblowing, 356
Cost Benefits Analysis, 290
Courage, 64

Courtesy, 144
Creative and Hobbyist People, 163
Cultural-Value System, 29
Culture, 173
Custom, 24, 173

D

Deceptive Advertising, 209
Declaration of Helsinki, 375
Democracy, 184
Democritus, 92
Denial Stage, 56
Deontological Ethics, 93, 95
Deontology Theory, 97
Descriptive Ethics, 41
Desire of Acceptance, 147
Deviance, 22
Dhamma, 91
Dharma, 76, 88
Diogenes of Sinope, 93
Divergent, 92
Divergent Patterns, 22
Divine Reason, 93
Doctrine of Karma, 90
Dual-Use-Policy, 369
Dual-Use-Relationships, 369
Duty Ethics, 238

E

Ecology, 386
Economic Espionage, 345
Economic Theory, 164
Educated Mind, 79
Education, 27
Effective Engineering, 200
Ego System, 5
Egoism, 94
Emotional Needs, 141
Empathy, 68
Employment Contracts, 331
Engineer, 230
Engineering Ethics, 116, 119, 130
Engineering Marvels, 192
Engineering Standards, 237
Engineering Venture, 196
Enterprise Risk Management, 266

Environmental Risk Analysis, 261
Environmental-Risk-Analysis, 261
Equalitarian, 23
Error Theory, 42
Ethic of Reciprocity, 161
Ethical Behavior, 179
Ethical Commitment, 121
Ethical Issues, 239
Ethical Personality, 18
Ethical Principles, 69
Ethical Theories, 96, 103
Ethical Values, 122
Ethicism, 132
Ethics, 39, 75, 119, 133, 222, 272
Etiquettes, 24
Evolution of Man, 148
Evolution of Universe, 24
Exploration Stage, 56
External Whistleblowing, 356

F

Fads, 24
Failure Mode and Effects Analysis, 279
Failure Mode and Effects Analysis (FMEA), 280
Fairness and Justice, 144
Family, 182
Fashion, 24
Fault Tree Analysis, 279
Fault Tree Analysis (FTA), 273, 279, 280
Financial Risk, 262
Financial Risks, 265
Finite Element Method (FEM), 280
Five-Factor Model (FFM), 217
Flutter, 232
FMEA, 279
Fundamental Canons, 236
Fundamental Risks, 251

G

Geeta, 89
Gifts, 340
Gilligan Theory, 107
Golden Rule, 161

Grade Point Average (GPA), 4
Greek Philosophy, 92
Groups, 26

H

Harm, 248
Hazard, 264
Health, Safety, and Environment (HSE), 260
Hedonism, 92, 93
Hedonistic, 92
High Reliability Organization (HRO), 266
Higher Education Institutions (HEI), 10
Honesty, 62
Horticultural Societies, 25
Human Behavior, 123
Human Spirituality, 77
Human Value Systems, 10
Human Values, 177, 178

I

ICT, 178
IEEE Code of Ethics, 247
Impersonal Whistleblowing, 356
Indian Socialism, 184
Indian Society for Technical Education (ISTE), 230, 441
Industrial Espionage, 345
Industrial Pollution, 198
Industrial Society, 25
Industries, 211
Inferences, 149
Information Age, 274
Information Anxiety, 179
Information Assurance (IA), 268
Information Security, 268
Information Security Management System (ISMS), 267
Information Security Risk, 262
Inquiry, 101
Institute of Electrical and Electronics Engineers (IEEE), 63
Instrument of Observation, 150
Intended Function, 281

Internal whistleblowing, 356
International Standards Organization (ISO), 240
Interpretation, 149
IT Risk, 267

J

Jainism, 91
Joint Accountability, 228

K

Kant's Deontological Ethics, 96
Kantianism, 95, 118
Kickbacks, 340
King Street Bridge, 232
Known Risks, 252
Kohlberg Theory, 105

L

Leadership, 210
Leading, 210
Legal Environment, 180
Legislative, 29
Liability, 267
Liability Losses, 274

M

Manager's Function, 207
Managing, 210
Mandatory Standards, 240
Marriage, 181
Mass Communication Systems, 29
Materialistic Interpretation of History, 94
Mean Time Between Failure (MTBF), 273
Mean Time To Failure (MTTF), 281
Mean-Time-To-Repair (MTTR), 282
Meditation, 76
Mega Projects, 266
Methodology, 265
Modern Civilization, 3
Modern Education, 30

Modern Education System, 29
Modern Humanism, 3, 176
Modern Virtue Ethics, 96
Modernization, 30
Moral, 40
Moral Autonomy, 121, 131
Moral Autonomy of Engineers, 116
Moral Code, 88
Moral Dilemmas, 105, 117
Moral Education, 41
Moral Obligation, 180
Moral Relativism, 43
Moral Theory, 103
Moral Values, 40
Morality, 61, 90, 119
Mores, 24
Motivational Factors, 145
MTBF, MTTR, 127
Multicultural Society, 39

N

Nation Society of professional Engineers (NSPE), 235
National Assessment and Accreditation Council (NAAC), 10
National Motto, 63
Neuroticism, 218
Niti-Shastra, 88
Non-financial Risks, 251
Normative Ethics, 42, 101
Nurturing, 147

O

O.C.E.A.N, 217
Obedience, 106
Occupational Crime, 344
Occupational Safety and Health Administration (OSHA), 273
Open Whistleblowing, 356
Openness, 217
Opium of People, 78
Organizational Disobedience, 130
Overly Optimistic Attitude, 249
Ownership Attitude, 228

P

Paganism, 93
Panchasila, 90
Particular Risks, 251
Peace of Mind, 51
Peaceful Living, 52
Peer Group, 23
Perceptions, 149
Peril, 261
Personal Commitments, 68
Personal Environment, 180
Personal Morality, 41
Personal Motivation, 55
Personal Properties, 409
Personal Unbalance, 51
Personal Values, 180
Personal Whistleblowing, 356
Personality, 215, 218
Perspective of Engineering, 212
Philosophical Thinking, 88
Physical Needs, 141
Physics of Failure, 280
Piaget Theory, 104
Planning Process, 28
Playing Role, 181
Post-Conventional, 106
Post-conventional Level, 110
Practical Risks, 200
Pre-conventional Level, 109
Primary Function of Engineers, 206
Privileged Information, 327
Probabilistic Risk, 273
Probability Density Function (PDF), 281
Probability of a Negative Event, 264
Product Liability, 275, 276
Product Safety, 274
Product Standards, 240
Productivity, 262
Professional, 130
Professional Behavior, 13
Professional Code of Ethics, 122
Professional Delinquency, 2
Professional Environment, 180
Professional Fitness, 246
Professional Obligations, 236
Profit Margin, 66

Project Management, 266
Proper Engineering Decision (PED), 208
Proper Management Decision (PMD), 208
Proximity Effect, 250
Psychic Energy, 7
Public Morality, 63
Pure Risks, 252
Pursuit of Excellence, 144

Q

Quality, 284
Quality Control, 284
Quantitative Risk, 264

R

Rate of Occurrence, 264
Real Knowledge, 175
Redundancy, 279
Regulatory Standards, 246
Relationship Needs, 141
Reliability, 143, 222, 273, 280
Reliability Centered Maintenance (RCM), 280
Reliability Design, 279
Reliability Engineering, 283
Reliability Hazard Analysis, 280
Reliability Hazards, 283
Reliability Risk Assessments, 280
Religion, 78, 175
Reservoir of Knowledge, 29
Resistance Stage, 56
Respect, 79, 143
Respect for Authority, 206
Responsible People, 227
Responsiveness, 19
Rights Ethical Theory, 99
Rights Theory, 118
Risk, 254, 272
Risk Appetite, 262
Risk Assessment, 259, 264
Risk Assessments, 263
Risk Benefit Analysis, 290
Risk Management, 245, 263
Risk Perception, 255
Risk Prediction, 259
Risk Sources, 263
Risk-Benefit Analysis, 289
Risk-Benefit Ratio, 289
Runway Safety, 234

S

Safety, 272, 273, 277
Safety Engineering, 283
Scientific Education, 2
Scientific Knowledge, 201
Scientific Laws, 196
Scriptures, 176
Secular Education, 345
Secularism, 184
Self, 162
Self-Confidence, 72
Self-Control, 144
Self-Efficacy, 73
Self-Interest, 163
Self-Introspection, 6
Selfish Mentality, 75
Self-Realization Ethics, 162
Sensitivity, 19
Service Oriented People, 163
Sharing Ethics, 58
Situation Ethics, 134
Six-Sigma, 284
Social control, 26
Social Control, 26
Social Evolution, 25
Social Experimentation, 192, 198
Social Factors, 28
Social Impact, 221
Social Norms, 23
Social Stability, 51
Socialistic Pattern of Society, 28
Socialization, 22
Societal Environment, 179
Society, 26
Society Respect, 79
Sociological Values, 178
Software Reliability, 282
Solidarity, 384
Special Rights, 120
Speculative Risks, 252
Spirituality, 74, 75

Standard of Care, 246
Standards, 240
Static Risks, 251
Statistical Confidence, 282
Stress, 282
Stress Testing, 282
Success, 140
Success of Leadership, 211
System Reliability, 282
Systems Engineering, 284

T

TACOMA Narrow Bridge, 231
Teamwork Virtues, 310
Technology Evaluation, 290
Ten Meritorious Deeds - Buddha, 90
The Common Rule, 376
Titanic, 194
Tolerance and Acceptance, 143
Tolerance or Benchmark, 263
Totalitarianism, 405
Trade Secret, 327
Traits, 216
Transmigration of Soul, 90
Triratnas, 91
Trustworthy, 143
Type of Risks, 251

U

Uncertainty, 254, 261
Unhappiness, 160

Unintended Effects, 221
Universalizability, 48
Universalization, 48, 118
University Grant Commission (UGC), 12
Urban Life, 183
Utilitarianism, 94, 118, 384

V

Value Education, 3, 8, 13
Value Judgement, 250
Values, 1, 90
Values and Ethics, 25
Violating, 61
Virtue, 69, 93
Virtue Ethical Theory, 100

W

Wellbeing of Employer, 272
Wellbeing of Engineer, 272
Western Culture, 32
Western Life Styles, 31
Whistleblowing, 239
White Collar Crimes, 344
Work Ethics, 45
Workplace Risk, 260

Y

Yoga, 76

About the Author

Kameshwar Singh Verma was Professor of Satellite and Wireless Communication Engineering, and Dean Curriculum Development, in Sreenidhi Institute of Science and Technology (SNIST) - a very reputed and Autonomous Engineering College in Hyderabad, Telangana. He retired in 2013 from SNIST. He has total experience of 42 years of which Academic experience is 12 years.

Mr. Verma has 30 years of experience in Electronic Industry (Wireless and Satellite Communication Systems), spread over wide spectrum of functions like Design and Development, Project management, Marketing and Business Development, Strategic Planning, Team Building etc.

In connection with Technical Collaborations, Know-How Transfers and Trainings for Technology-Absorptions from foreign sources, Mr. Verma has widely travelled abroad and developed familiarity with industrial work cultures of respective countries.

With the excellent blend of theoretical and practical experiences, of Academic field and the Engineering practices in Industry Mr. Verma developed very good familiarity with moral and ethical issues associated with Industrial and economic growth, which motivated him to write this book so that prospective engineers and professional are benefited.

Mr. Verma holds, M.E. Degree (Advanced Electronics) from University of Roorkee (now an IIT) and, M.Sc. Tech. Degree (Electronics & Radio Engineering) from University of Allahabad, UP, India. He is life member of IETE and ISTE India, and Member of IEEE.

About the Book

Purpose of the book is to sensitize professionals on their social responsibility of application of technology, to safe guard short and long-term interest of consumers, public and humanity at large.

The book provides exposure to comprehensive understanding of Human Values and Professional Ethics, thus enabling professionals to sail through conflicts arising due to multitude of perceptions, arguments, and reasoning from people, and agencies involved.

It expounds Professionals to be more caring, balanced, humane, effective and efficient in Jobs, Professional life, Family life, Social environment, and interactions at national and international level.

Broad spectrum of subjects covered in the book understands:

- Self, Identity, Personality and Impact of family on individual Value System.
- Sociological understanding of society, community, culture, religion etc.
- Moral responsibility, Authority, Rights, Autonomy and dilemmas of Engineers and Professionals.
- Professions and Professional Code of Conducts
- Engineers Responsibility for Design, Safety, Risks, and Quality and Reliability
- Moral and Ethical considerations in National and Global Business and Laws of Trade, Patents, Copyrights Etc.
- Global ethical issues arising from industrialization, Science and Technology, Internet, Cyberspace, environment pollution etc.

Each one of the above areas of consideration is loaded with a set of 'Values'. These values are used to evolve model code of conduct as guidance for desirable transactional behavior of individual engineers and professionals.

www.ingramcontent.com/pod-product-compliance
Lightning Source LLC
Chambersburg PA
CBHW070115100426
42744CB00010B/1842